EVERY PERSON IN THE NEW TESTAMENT

EVERY PERSON IN THE NEW TESTAMENT

by

Lynn F. Price

First Printing: November 2002

International Standard Book Number:
0-88290-720-4

Horizon Publishers' Catalog and Order Number:
C2031

Printed and distributed
in the United States of America by

Address:
925 North Main Street
Springville, Utah 84663

Local Phone: (801) 489-4084
Toll Free: 1 (800) SKYBOOK
FAX: (800) 489-1097

E-mail: skybook@cedarfort.com
Internet: http://www.cedarfort.com

Contents

Alphabetized Synopsis of Every Person in the New Testament

People Whose Names Begin With:

References Used and Their Abbreviations as Used in the Text

Bible Dictionary
BD

Book of Mormon
BM

Discourses of the Prophet Joseph Smith, Alma P. Burton, Deseret Book Company, 1965, Salt Lake City, Utah.
DPJS

Doctrine and Covenants
D&C

Doctrinal New Testament Commentary, 3 Vols., Bruce R. McConkie, Bookcraft Inc., Salt Lake City, Utah, 1973.
DNTC

Joseph Smith—History
JSH

Joseph Smith's "New Translation" of the Bible, 1970, Herald Publishing House, Independence, Missouri.
JST

New Testament
NT

Old Testament
OT

The New Encyclopædia Britannica, 30 Vols., William Benton, Publisher, 1943-1973, Helen Hemingway Benton, Publisher, 1973-1974; Chicago/London/Toronto/Geneva/Sydney/Tokyo/Manila/Seoul.
EB

Webster's Third New International Dictionary, Unabridged, 3 Vols., Encyclopædia Britannica, Inc., G. & C. Merriam Co., 1909-1976, Chicago, London, Toronto, Geneva, Sydney, Tokyo, Manila.
WTNID

Foreword

The New Testament is the fourth and final book of scripture of which this writer has compiled a synopsis of people mentioned therein. It, along with the other books—*Every Person in the Book of Mormon; Every Person in the Doctrine and Covenants;* and *Every Person in the Old Testament*—is intended to help people identify and remember more easily just who the people were who played such a significant role in our religious heritage. The intent has also been to determine what the scriptures actually say versus what people attribute to them.

People are listed alphabetically. In most cases, scriptural references appear in the order they appear in the New Testament. However, in the case of Mary and Joseph and Jesus, information from Luke precedes information from Matthew so as to present the story in a more chronological order. The ancestors of Joseph and Old Testament people mentioned in the New Testament are listed alphabetically in Appendix A. Joseph's ancestors are presented in chart form in Appendix B.

Because events are sometimes repeated by the various authors of the New Testament, an effort has been made to group all references involving a particular person and that event. For instance, see **Mary Magdalene.** References for Matt. 27:56, 61; Mark 15:40-41; and Luke 23:47-49, 55-56 are all together because they all say essentially the same thing. However, sometimes one writer adds or omits some detail. Thus, information in parentheses presents what was added by the second, third or fourth reference but was not included in the first reference: i.e., the account in Matt. 27 refers to Mary Magdalene and Mary the mother of James and Joses, and the mother of Zebedee's children. However, Mark 15 says, "Mary Magdalene, and Mary the mother of James the less and of Joses, and Salome;" therefore, (the less, and Salome) is bracketed, indicating the different information provided.

Explanatory information is also given in parentheses and is italicized; i.e., *(The mother of Zebedee's children is not mentioned in Mark, but Salome is named. In Luke, the women are not mentioned by name at all, just as "the women who followed him. . . .")*

If the information enclosed in parentheses is directly from the scriptural reference cited, it will not be italicized. Thus, brackets and parentheses are used in a variety of ways:

- square brackets [ ] are used to present information included in a second or third reference that was not included in the original reference;
- parentheses ( ) and non-italicized text means the information comes directly from the cited scriptures;
- parentheses *( )* and *italicized text* means the information is explanatory or may be from some othere source than the NT scripture cited;
- parentheses are also used to enclose citations and numbers indicating which person someone is, when more than one person has the same name: i.e., MARY (2);
- parentheses are also used to show additional names by which a given person may be referred: i.e., Paul (Saul); and

• the names of people of the Old Testament who are referred to in the New Testament frequently vary from the Old Testament spellings. They are usually listed under the New Testament spelling; thus, Isaiah is presented as Esaias in Appendix A. In many cases, the Old Testament spellling is provided in parentheses. (See Appendix B, The Generations of Joseph.)

Where more than one reference is given, only the verses are cited for the first reference *(i.e., vs. 21-22)*. However, book, chapter and verse are cited for each additional reference; i.e., James (1) has a reference of Matt. 4; Mark 1; and Luke 5. Thus, the reference is written: *(vs. 21-22; Mark 1:19-20; Luke 5:10)*.

As in the Old Testament, many people in the New Testament are referred to by more than one name; i.e., Peter (Simon, Cephas, Simeon) and Paul (Saul). When they are referred to by different names, the name is **bolded** in the reference where it first appears.

The version of the New Testament used for this project was the authorized King James version which includes a Bible Dictionary (BD) and which has explanatory notes and cross references to the Standard Works of The Church of Jesus Christ of Latter-day saints, published by The Church of Jesus Christ of Latter-day Saints in Salt Lake City, Utah, U.S.A. The readers are frequently referred to the *Old Testament* (OT), *Bible Dictionary* (BD), *Joseph Smith's History* (JSH) located after the *Pearl of Great Price* in the combined scriptures or to other scriptural references: *Joseph Smith's "New Translation of the Bible"* (JST); the *Book of Mormon* (BM) or the *Doctrine and Covenants* (D&C). Additional references and their abbreviations as used in the text are: *Discourses of the Prophet Joseph Smith* (DPJS), *The New Encyclopædia Britannica* (EB), *Doctrinal New Testament Commentary* (DNTC), and *Webster's Third New International Dictionary* (WTNID). Information taken from these references is placed in parentheses and/or indented and written in italics, as are other explanatory comments, so as not to confuse the reader as to what is from the New Testament and what is supplemental information.

A special thank you is extended to the many people *(family and friends)* who have encouraged me to complete this project, especially my very patient and supportive husband, Dick, and my sisters—Faye Tholen and Elaine Bettridge—who have rejoiced with me in each successful accomplishment I have made. I have gained a deeper love for the scriptures, an appreciation for their continuity and constancy, and a greater knowledge of how each volume of scripture supports and validates the other books of scripture. Together, they serve as a witness and testimony of our Savior, Jesus Christ.

NAMES THAT BEGIN WITH "A"

ACHAICUS

1 Cor. 16:17-18; Postscript. **ACHAICUS**, Fortunatus and Stephanas visited Paul and brought him information regarding the saints in Corinth for which Paul said he was glad, "for that which was lacking on your part they have supplied. For they have refreshed my spirit and yours." *(The first epistle from Paul in Philippi to the saints in Corinth was carried to them by Stephanas, Fortunatus, Achaicus and Timotheus.)*

ÆNEAS

Acts 9:33-34. **ÆNEAS** was a man who lived in Lydda. He had been sick in bed with the palsy for eight years. Peter told him, "Jesus Christ maketh thee whole: arise, and make thy bed." The man immediately arose and was healed.

AGABUS

Acts 11:28. **AGABUS** was a prophet who went to Antioch from Jerusalem. He prophesied that there would be a great dearth throughout all the world: "which came to pass in the days of Claudius Cæsar."

Acts 21:10-11. Agabus met with Paul and his company in Cæsarea while they abode with Simon the evangelist. He took Paul's girdle and, binding his own hands and feet with it, prophesied, "So shall the Jews at Jerusalem bind the man that owneth this girdle, and shall deliver him into the hands of the Gentiles."

AGRIPPA I (See Herod IV)

AGRIPPA II (See Herod V)

AHAZIAH (See Ozias)

ALEXANDER (1)

Mark 15:21. **ALEXANDER** was a son of Simon of Cyrene. His brother was Rufus.

ALEXANDER (2)

Acts 4:6. **ALEXANDER** was with Annas the high priest, Caiaphas and John and as many of the kindred of the high priest as there were gathered together at Jerusalem to confer about what to do with or to Peter and John for preaching and teaching about Christ. *(According to the BD, nothing else is known about him.)*

ALEXANDER (3)

Acts 19:33-34. **ALEXANDER** was in Ephesus when the multitude caught Gaius and Aristarchus, two of Paul's traveling companions, and rushed them into the theatre. The multitude drew Alexander out from the crowd and the Jews put him forward. He beckoned with his hand so as to make his defense; but the people, when they learned he was a Jew, shouted him down for two hours crying out, "Great is Diana of the Ephesians."

ALEXANDER (4)

1 Tim. 1:6, 19-20. **ALEXANDER** was one of the early apostates of the church. He was among those who "having swerved have turned aside unto vain jangling." Paul identified the apostates: "having put away concerning faith have made shipwreck: of whom is Hymenæus and Alexander;" and said he had delivered them unto Satan, "that they may learn not to blaspheme."

ALEXANDER (5)

2 Tim. 4:14-15. **ALEXANDER** was a coppersmith. He did Paul much evil. Paul warned Timothy to be especially wary of Alexander.

ALEXANDER (6)

(Note: **ALEXANDER**, *son of Herod the Great, his mother Mariamne and his brother Aristobulus, were all slain by his father. Reference is made to them in the BD but not in the NT, itself.)*

ALPHÆUS (1)

Matt. 10:3; Mark 3:1; Luke 6:15; Acts 1:13. **ALPHÆUS** was the father of James, one of Jesus' 12 apostles. *(The BD indicates that some scholars identify him with Cleopas, Luke 24:18, and Cleophas, John 19:25.)*

ALPHÆUS (2)

Mark 2:14. **ALPHÆUS** was the father of Levi (Matthew), a tax collector.

AMPLIAS

Rom. 16:8. **AMPLIAS** was Paul's "beloved in the Lord." Paul sent greetings to him in his epistle to the Romans.

ANANIAS (1)

Acts 5:1-10. **ANANIAS** was the husband of Sapphira. They were followers of Christ following the Lord's death and resurrection at the time that the congregation had all things in common. He and his wife sold a possession but kept part of the profit rather than giving it all to the church. When Peter confronted him, saying, "Thou has not lied unto men, but unto God," Ananias fell down and died. His wife did likewise shortly thereafter. They were carried out and buried together.

ANANIAS (2)

Acts 9:9-17. **ANANIAS** was a disciple of Christ who lived in Damascus. The Lord directed him in a vision to go to the house of Judas and ask for Saul. Saul had seen in a vision a man named Ananias coming in and restoring his sight. Ananias was fearful of Saul because he knew Saul hated the followers of Christ. However, the Lord told him to go to him because Saul was "a chosen vessel unto me, to bear my name before the Gentiles, and kings, and the children of Israel." Ananias did as the Lord commanded.

Acts 22:12-16. Ananias was guided by the Lord to go to Saul and restore his eyesight. He counseled Saul to be baptized and to get about doing the Lord's work. Paul recounted the event to the Jews in Jerusalem as he told them of his conversion.

ANANIAS (3)

Acts 23:2. **ANANIAS** was the high priest in Jerusalem. As Paul was earnestly pleading his case before the council, Ananias commanded those who stood by Paul to smite him across the mouth. Paul called him a "whited wall" for sitting in judgment of him according to the law but commanding him to be smitten contrary to the law.

Acts 24:1-9. Ananias, along with the elders and a man named Tertullus, arrived five days after Paul was taken to Felix, the governor, and testified against Paul. Tertullus, an orator, was their spokesman.

Acts 25:2-7. Ananias and the chief of the Jews informed Festus, who succeeded Felix as procurator of Judæa, about Paul and desired that he have Paul brought to Jerusalem. They planned to lay in wait for him to kill him. However, Festus declined and said he should remain in Cæsarea, and suggested they return to Cæsarea with him and tender their complaint there. Ten days later, Festus returned to Cæsarea and sat on the judgment seat the next day. The Jews who went with him "laid many and grievous complaints against Paul, which they could not prove." *(The BD states that Ananias, an evil man, was eventually murdered by the general populace during a disturbance in Jerusalem.)*

ANDREW

Matt. 4; Mark 1. **ANDREW** was the brother of Simon called Peter. They were fishermen. When Jesus saw them fishing in the Sea of Galilee, he called them to come follow him, saying he would make them fishers of men. The brothers immediately left their nets and followed Jesus *(vs. 18-20; Mark 1:16-18). (Andrew is not mentioned by name in the account retold in Luke 5:1-11.)*

Matt. 10; Luke 9. Jesus called 12 disciples: Simon Peter, Andrew, James, John, Philip, Bartholomew; Thomas, Matthew, James, Lebbæus (Thaddæus), Simon the Canaanite, and Judas Iscariot *(vs. 2-4).* Jesus empowered these apostles and sent them forth to teach, but instructed them that they should not go to the Gentiles nor to the Samaritans. They were to go to the lost sheep of the house of Israel. They were to heal the sick and cast out devils. They were to travel without purse or scrip. They were instructed to leave their peace upon those who received them, but to shake the dust off their feet when leaving the houses of those who reject them *(vs. 5-14; Luke 9:1-5).* They were told they would be persecuted for Christ's sake, but that "he that endureth to the end shall be saved." They are of more value than the sparrows for which the Father provides. The hairs of their heads are even numbered *(vs. 16-32).*

Mark 1:29-31. Andrew was with Jesus, James and John when they went into his and Peter's house and Jesus healed Peter's mother-in-law.

Mark 13. Andrew, Peter, James and John asked Jesus what calamities would precede the Second Coming. Jesus told them there would be false Christs; wars and rumors of wars; nation would rise against nation and kingdom against kingdom; there would be earthquakes and famines and troubles. The prophets would be persecuted for Christ's sake. Brother would betray brother and fathers would betray their sons; children shall rise against their parents. The desolation prophesied by Daniel will come to pass. The sun shall be darkened; the moon will not give its light; and the stars of heaven shall fall. Then the Son of Man will come in the clouds in great power and glory *(vs. 3-27).* Jesus said to watch for the signs, just as we know summer is near when the fig tree puts forth her tender branches, so the signs will signal the Second Coming. Nevertheless, Jesus stressed that no man knows the day, time, nor place. We should be prepared and not caught "sleeping" *(vs. 28-37; also see Matt. 24:32-34; Luke 21:29-36; also see Luke 17:20-37 for a variation on this subject).*

John 1:40-42. Andrew brought his brother Simon Peter to hear Jesus. Jesus changed Peter's name to Cephas. Andrew and Peter were sons of Jona.

John 6:5-7. Andrew told Jesus there was a lad among the multitude who had five barley loaves and two small fishes when Jesus asked Philip where they could buy bread to feed the multitude and Philip responded that two hundred pennyworth of bread would not be enough to feed the crowd.

John 12:22. Andrew and Philip conveyed to Jesus that certain Greeks who had come to the feast of the Passover desired to see him.

Acts 1:13-14. Following Jesus' ascension into heaven, Jesus' disciples, including Andrew, met together in an upper room, along with several women *(including Mary the mother of Jesus)* and his brethren, where they continued in prayer and supplication.

ANDRONICUS

Rom. 16:7. **ANDRONICUS** was one of Paul's kinsmen. He and Junia were fellow prisoners with Paul, and were "of note among the apostles." They, apparently, were followers of Christ prior to Paul's conversion.

ANGEL, AN

Luke 22:43-45. **AN ANGEL** from heaven ministered unto Jesus as he prayed in the garden of Gethsemane and his disciples slept as they waited with him. *(Note: Christ is above the angels. Angels are ministering spirits, sent forth to minister for those who shall be heirs of salvation. Heb. 1:13-14.)*

ANGEL OF GOD, AN (1)

Acts 10:3, 30. **AN ANGEL OF GOD** instructed Cornelius in a vision to send to Joppa for Simon Peter who would tell him what he ought to do. The angel was a man dressed in bright clothing.

Acts 11:13-14. Peter recounted to his fellow apostles and brethren about an angel of God speaking to Cornelius and having him send for Peter to teach him what he should do.

ANGEL OF GOD, AN (2)

Acts 27:23-24, 37. **AN ANGEL OF GOD** comforted Paul as the ship on which he was sailing to Italy encountered a terrible prolonged storm. He told Paul that he would survive *(because he needed to go before Cæsar)* and that all 276 souls on board would be saved with him.

ANGEL OF THE CHURCH AT EPHESUS

Rev. 2:1-7. See entry for **John,** son of Zebedee.

ANGEL OF THE CHURCH OF THE LAODICEANS

Rev. 3:14-22. See entry for **John (1),** son of Zebedee.

ANGEL OF THE CHURCH AT PERGAMOS

Rev. 2:12-17. See entry for **John (1),** son of Zebedee.

ANGEL OF THE CHURCH IN PHILADELPHIA

Rev. 3:7-13. See entry for **John (1),** son of Zebedee.

ANGEL OF THE CHURCH IN SARDIS

Rev. 3:1-6. See entry for **John (1),** son of Zebedee.

ANGEL OF THE CHURCH AT SMYRNA

Rev. 2:8-11. See entry for **John (1),** son of Zebedee.

ANGEL OF THE CHURCH IN THYATIRA

Rev. 2:18-29. See entry for **John (1),** son of Zebedee.

ANGEL OF THE LORD, AN (1)

Matt. 2:19-20. **AN ANGEL OF THE LORD** appeared to Joseph in a dream after Herod died and instructed him to take Mary and Jesus back to Israel because those who sought his life were dead.

ANGEL OF THE LORD, AN (2)

Matt. 28:2-7; Luke 24:1-10. **AN ANGEL OF THE LORD** came in an earthquake and rolled the stone away from the sepulchre wherein Jesus was laid. The keepers of the sepulchre were so frightened they became as dead men. The angel told the two Mary's who had come to the sepulchre not to be afraid, that Jesus was not there: he had risen as he said he would. He instructed them to go tell Jesus' disciples. *(Note: The account in Luke is modified.)*

ANGEL OF THE LORD, AN (3)

Acts 12:7-10. **AN ANGEL OF THE LORD** caused the chains which bound Peter to fall off him, and then he led Peter out of prison while Herod's soldiers slept and the keepers before the door kept the prison.

ANGEL OF THE LORD, THE

Matt. 1:20. **THE ANGEL OF THE LORD** appeared to Joseph *(to whom Mary was espoused)* when Joseph thought to put Mary away "privily" when he discovered she was with child, and told him that he needn't fear to take Mary for his wife: her child was of the Holy Ghost. She would bring forth a son and they were to call him Jesus because he would save the people from their sins.

Matt. 2:13. After the wise men departed after worshipping Jesus, the angel of the Lord appeared to Joseph in a dream and told him to take Mary and the young child and flee into Egypt and to stay there until he brought him other instruction.

ANGEL(S) OF THE LORD

Luke 2:9-14. An **ANGEL OF THE LORD** appeared to shepherds abiding in a field, tending their sheep, and proclaimed the birth of the Savior. Suddenly, a multitude of angels appeared, singing and praising the Lord.

ANNA

Luke 2:36-38. **ANNA** was a prophetess, a widow, and a daughter of Phanuel of the tribe of Aser (Asher). She was widowed after seven years of marriage and was about 84 years old at the time Joseph and Mary brought Jesus to the temple to be blessed. Anna served in the temple and "departed not from the temple, but served God with fastings and prayers night and day." She acknowledged Jesus as the Savior. *(Note: The BD indicates Anna had been a widow for 84 years at the time of the Savior's birth which would suggest she would have been over 100 years old. However, the passage of scripture could also be interpreted to mean that she was an 84 year-old widow who had been married to her husband just seven years before he died.)*

ANNAS

Luke 3:2-3. **ANNAS** and Caiaphas were the high priests when Tiberius Cæsar was in the fifteenth year of his reign, Pontius Pilate was governor of Judæa, Herod was tetrarch of Galilee, and John the Baptist came into the country about Jordan preaching the baptism of repentance for the remission of sins. *(Note: Annas was appointed high priest in A.D. 7 by the Roman legate Quirinius and deposed in A.D. 15 by Valerius Gratus. . . In accordance with Jewish custom he kept the title "high priest" after he was deposed from office." His son-in-law Caiaphas was high priest from A.D. 18 to A.D. 36. See the BD.)*

John 18:13, 24. Annas was the father-in-law of Caiaphas. The band of men and officers from the chief priests and Pharisees who went with Judas to apprehend Jesus, first took Jesus to Annas. Annas then sent Jesus to Caiaphas.

Acts 4:1-22. The priests, captain of the temple and the Sadducees arrested Peter and John as they spoke unto the people about Christ. Peter, filled with the Holy Ghost, spoke boldly, testifying of Christ, saying that it was through Christ's name that a certain impotent man was healed. The next day, the rulers, elders, scribes, Annas the high priest, Caiaphas, John and Alexander, and as many kindred of the high priest as there were, met to confer as to what to do about Peter and John. The healed man was with the apostles so they could not deny he had been healed, and they feared the people. They resolved to threaten them and let them go. They commanded Peter and John not to speak or teach in the name of Jesus. They responded with a question: "Was it better to hearken unto them or unto God?"

ANOTHER DISCIPLE

Matt. 8:21-22. **ANOTHER DISCIPLE** wanted to bury his deceased father before following Jesus, but Jesus told him to follow him and let the dead bury their dead.

ANTIPAS (1) (Antipater)

*(Note: Herod the Tetrarch's real name was Herod ANTIPAS. He is the one who had John the Baptist beheaded. However, he is not referred to as Antipas nor Antipater in the New Testament (except in the BD), but as Herod the Tetrarch. See **Herod the Tetrarch**.)*

ANTIPAS (2)

Rev. 2:13. **ANTIPAS** was a faithful martyr, slain in Pergamos.

APELLES

Rom. 16:10. **APELLES** was one of those who Paul said was "approved in Christ." Paul sent greetings to him in his epistle to the Romans.

APOLLOS

Acts 18:24-28. **APOLLOS**, a Jew born at Alexandria and very eloquent and mighty in the scriptures, went to Ephesus. However, he only knew of the baptism of John. Therefore, Aquila and his wife Priscilla taught him the fuller gospel. When he left for Achaia, they wrote to the disciples there to receive him because he had been a great help to them, "For he mightily convinced the Jews, and that publickly, shewing by the scriptures that Jesus was the Christ."

Acts 19:1. Apollos was at Corinth while Paul traveled on to Ephesus.

1 Cor. 1:12-13. The saints in Corinth were divided, with some claiming to be of Apollos, Paul, Cephas or Christ. In his epistle to them, Paul chastised them for having contentions among them, and reminded them that they were baptized in the name of Christ, not in any other person's name.

1 Cor. 3:5-6, 22-23. Apollos "watered" what Paul "planted," said Paul, and they were ministers of Christ; but God gave the increase. All things are Christ's; and Christ is God's.

1 Cor. 4:6. Apollos and he, said Paul, were examples of why the saints in Corinth should not think of men as being greater than they are, "that no one of you be puffed up for one against another."

1 Cor. 16:12. Apollos, Paul had hoped, could go to the Corinthians; however, Paul indicated in his epistle to the saints that it was not Apollos' will to come at that time but that he would come when it was more convenient.

Titus 3:13. Paul instructed Titus to hasten Apollos and Zenas on their journey diligently so that nothing would be wanting unto them.

APPHIA

Philem. 1:2. **APPHIA** was apparently in Colosse with Philemon and Archippus. Paul and Timothy sent greetings to each of them in Paul's epistle to Philemon.

AQUILA

Acts 18:2, 18, 24-26. **AQUILA** was a Jew born in Pontus. His wife was Priscilla. Because Claudius had commanded all Jews to depart from Rome, they had come from Italy to Corinth. He was a tentmaker. Because Paul was of the same craft, he stayed with them. When Paul sailed to Syria, he took Aquila and Priscilla with him, leaving them in Ephesus. When a certain Jew by the name of Apollos came to Ephesus, preaching diligently but only knowing the baptism of John, Aquila and Priscilla taught him "the way of God more perfectly."

Rom. 16:3-4. Aquila and Priscilla were Paul's helpers in the work. In Paul's epistles to the Romans, he commended Aquila and Priscilla to the Roman saints, and invited them to greet them. He told the saints that Aquila and Priscilla had put their own necks on the line for him. He and all the churches of the Gentiles were grateful to this couple.

1 Cor. 16:19. Aquila and Priscilla sent greetings to the saints in Corinth via Paul's epistle.

2 Tim. 4:19. Paul asked Timothy to salute Aquila and Prisca (Priscilla) for him.

ARCHELAUS (See Herod II)

ARCHIPPUS

Col. 4:17. **ARCHIPPUS** was a Colossian saint who was not being faithful in discharging his responsibilities. In Paul's epistle to the Colossians, he asked them to admonish Archippus to take heed to the ministry which he had received "in the Lord" and that he fulfill it.

Philem. 1:2. Archippus was, apparently, in Colosse with Philemon and Apphia. Paul and Timothy sent greetings to each of them in Paul's epistle to Philemon.

ARETAS

2 Cor. 11:32-33. **ARETAS**, the father-in-law of Herod the tetrarch (Antipas), was king of Damascus when the Jews sought to kill Paul and the governor of Damascus set up a garrison around the city in order to apprehend him. However, Paul escaped by being lowered in a basket through a window near a wall.

ARISTARCHUS

Acts 19:29-41. **ARISTARCHUS** was one of Paul's traveling companions. When Demetrius and his fellow craftsmen rallied the people against Paul, the people caught Aristarchus and Gaius and rushed them into the theatre. After the town clerk talked to the people about using appropriate legal channels, the crowds were dismissed.

Acts 20:4. Aristarchus of the Thessalonians accompanied Paul into Asia, along with Sopater of Berea, Secundus *(also of the Thessalonians),* Gauis of Derbe, Timotheus, and Tychicus and Trophimus of Asia.

Acts 27:2. Aristarchus was among the prisoners placed aboard the ship with Paul which was set to sail for Italy. *(See the entry for **Paul** for a detailed account of the trip.)*

Col. 4:10. Aristarchus was imprisoned in Rome with Paul. He sent his greetings, along with Paul and others, in Paul's epistle to the Colossians.

Philem. 1:24. Aristarchus and other fellow laborers with Paul sent their salutations, along with Paul's, to Philemon.

ARISTOBULUS (1)

(Note: According to the BD, ARISTOBULUS was a son of Herod the Great. Herod killed his wife, whom he loved. Later, he also killed her two sons, Aristobulus and Alexander. There is no reference to them in the NT.)

ARISTOBULUS' (2) HOUSEHOLD

Rom. 16:10. **ARISTOBULUS' HOUSEHOLD** were among the followers of Christ. Paul sent greetings to them in his epistle to the Romans. *(The BD states that this Aristobulus is "probably to be identified with the Aristobulus who was the younger brother of Herod Agrippa I and who lived in Rome and was a friend of the Emperor Claudius.")*

ARTEMAS

Titus 3:12. **ARTEMAS** was, apparently, a convert working in the ministry with Paul. Paul indicated in his epistle to Titus that he was sending Artemas or Tychicus to him, and asked Titus to come to him in Nicopolis as soon as either of them arrived.

ARTEMIS (See Diana)

ASYNCRITUS

Rom. 16:14. **ASYNCRITUS** and several other specific disciples, "and the brethren which are with them," were sent greetings by Paul in his epistle to the Romans.

NAMES THAT BEGIN WITH "B"

BARABBAS

Matt. 27:16-26; Mark 15:6-15; Luke 23:18-25; John 18:40. **BARABBAS** was a notable prisoner, a robber. When Pontius Pilate offered to release a prisoner of the people's choice during the feast of the Passover, the people chose to have Barabbas released instead of Jesus.

BARACHIAS

Matt. 23:35; Luke 11:51. **BARACHIAS** was the father of Zacharias, which Zacharias was slain between the temple and the altar. Jesus chastised the scribes and Pharisees and said the blood of the righteous which had been shed from Abel to Zacharias would be upon them.

BARBAROUS PEOPLE OF MELITA

Acts 28:1-10. The **BARBAROUS PEOPLE OF MELITA** treated Paul and the other shipwrecked passengers very kindly. They built a fire to warm them from the cold wet storm. When a viper bit Paul, they thought Paul must be a murderer and that vengeance was upon him. When he suffered no ill effects from the viper bite, they thought he must be a god. Publius, the chief man of the island, lodged them in his place for three days. His father became ill, and Paul healed him. Then, the islanders brought their other ill and diseased people to Paul to be healed. They honored Paul and his companions and gave them all that was necessary for their journey when they left three months later. *(The BD explains that "barbarian" means foreigner, and is synonymous with stranger, alien, sojourner, and gentile. "In the NT it connotes peoples of the Graeco- Roman culture, and/or those whose language is not familiar to the hearer.")*

BAR-JESUS (Elymas)

Acts 13:6-11. **BAR-JESUS**, a Jew, was a false prophet and sorcerer living in Paphos. He was with Sergius Paulus, a prudent man who was the deputy of the country. Bar-jesus (also called **Elymas**) contended against Barnabas and Saul. Saul rebuked him and called him a "child of the devil, thou enemy of all righteousness." He told him the hand of the Lord would be upon him and he would be blind for a season; and it was so. Bar-jesus had to seek help to get around.

BAR-JONA (i.e., son of Jona. See Peter)

BARNABAS (Joses (3), Surnamed Barnabas)

Acts 4:36-37. **BARNABAS**. **Joses** ["son of consolation"] is another name for Joseph, a Levite of Cyprus. The apostles surnamed him Barnabas. He sold all that he had and brought money and laid it at the feet of the apostles.

Acts 9:27. When Saul joined the disciples in Jerusalem, Barnabas took him to the apostles and told them about the experience Saul had had with the Savior on the road to Damascus, how he then had preached boldly at Damascus in the name of Jesus, and how the people had sought to kill him.

Acts 11:22-26. Barnabas, a good man, full of the Holy Ghost and of faith, was sent to travel as far as Antioch. Many people joined the church. He went to Tarsus seeking Saul and had him go to Antioch with him where they taught for a year. It was here that the disciples were first called Christians. Because of a dearth in the land, which was prophesied by Agabus who went up to Antioch from Jerusalem, the disciples and every man, according to his means, sent relief to the brethren in Jerusalem by the hands of Barnabas and Saul.

Acts 12:25. Barnabas and Saul returned from Jerusalem after their ministry there and took John, whose surname was Mark, with them.

Acts 13. Barnabas and Saul, along with certain other prophets and teachers—Simeon *(called Niger),* Lucius of Cyrene and Manaen—were preaching in Antioch when the Holy Ghost indicated that Barnabas and Saul should leave Antioch. They went to Seleucia and then sailed to Cyprus. They preached in Salamis, along with John who was there. They went through the isle unto Paphos and found Bar-jesus *(also called Elymas),* a sorcerer and false prophet, who was with the deputy of the country, Sergius Paulus. Saul (Paul) rebuked Bar- jesus and said the Lord would cause him to be blind for a season. Sergius Paulus witnessed what happened and believed Barnabas and Paul *(vs. 1-12)*. Barnabas and Paul left Paphos and went to Perga in Pamphylia. John *(i.e., Mark)* returned to Jerusalem. From Perga they went to Antioch where they preached in the synagogue *(vs. 13-14)*. Following a powerful sermon by Paul *(vs. 16-41),* the Jews left; however, the Gentiles asked that the same words be preached again the following Sunday. Barnabas and Paul encouraged those Jews and religious proselytes who followed after them to continue in the grace of God *(vs. 42-43)*. When the Jews saw the multitudes that returned the following Sunday, they were envious and spoke against Barnabas and Paul, who testified that it was necessary that the word first be delivered to them but, since they rejected it, the Lord commanded that the word be given to the Gentiles. Barnabas and Paul were expelled from the land by the people who had been stirred up by the Jews. They shook off the dust of their feet against them as they left *(vs. 44-51)*.

Acts 14. Barnabas and Paul taught together in Iconium. The unbelieving Jews stirred up the people who then sought to stone them, so they fled to Lystra and Derbe *(vs. 1-6)*. In Lystra, they saw a man who had been crippled from birth. Paul healed him; and the people who witnessed it hailed Barnabas and Paul as gods come down from heaven. They called Barnabas, "Jupiter," and Paul, "Mercurius." The apostles quickly denied they were gods, saying, "We also are men of like passions with you . . ." Even so, they could scarcely keep the people from offering sacrifice unto them *(vs. 8-18)*. Certain Jews came from Antioch and Iconium and stirred up the people and stoned Paul. He was presumed to be dead. The disciples stood around him and he rose up the next day and departed with Barnabas to Derbe *(19-20)*. After converting many people in Derbe, they returned to Lystra, Iconium and Antioch. They ordained elders in every church. From Pisidia, they went to Pamphylia. From Perga, they went down to Attalia and then sailed to Antioch, where they stayed a long time with the disciples there *(vs. 21-28)*.

Acts 15. Barnabas and Paul and certain other men were sent to Jerusalem to inquire of the apostles and elders there regarding the matter of circumcision. Disputations had risen after certain men came down from Judæa to Antioch preaching that every man had to be circumcised or he could not be saved. When they got to Jerusalem, some of the converted Pharisees also claimed that it was needful for them all to be circumcised so as to keep the law of Moses *(vs. 1-5).* The apostles discussed the matter and concluded that it was not necessary for the Gentiles who joined the church to be circumcised. The Gentiles were admonished to "abstain from meats offered to idols, and from blood, and from things strangled, and from fornication." And they sent Barnabas, Paul, Judas Barsabas and Silas back to Antioch with letters stating the same *(vs. 6-29).* After delivering the epistle to the multitude in Antioch, Judas decided to return to Jerusalem, but Silas decided to stay in Antioch. Some days later, Barnabas and Paul also decided to leave Antioch and see how the church members were doing in the areas where they had been previously. However, the two disciples disagreed sharply over taking John Mark with them. The disagreement was so sharp that Barnabas and Paul parted ways: Barnabas took John Mark with him; and Paul took Silas with him *(vs. 33-40).*

1 Cor. 9:3-11. Apparently, there were those who questioned Barnabas' and Paul's apostleship or actions because Paul felt a need to respond to those who "do examine me." He indicated that even though he was an apostle, he was still free to eat and drink and enjoy family relationships as were the other apostles *(including Peter, i.e., Cephas)* and the brothers of the Lord. He defended his and Barnabas' right to be temporally fed, writing, "who planteth a vineyard, and eateth not of the fruit thereof? Or who feedeth a flock, and eateth not of the milk of the flock?" Those who spend their time sowing spiritual things are entitled to have their material needs met.

Gal. 2:1, 9, 13. Barnabas went with Paul and Titus to Jerusalem where Paul met with the leaders of the church. James, Cephas (Peter) and John extended the right hand of fellowship to them. Barnabas got taken in by some of the doctrines being "dissembled."

Col. 4:10. Barnabas' sister's son was Marcus (John Mark).

BARSABAS (1) (Joseph called Barsabas, surnamed Justus)

Acts 1:23-26. **BARSABAS** (**Joseph called Barsabas**) was one of the two men considered to fill the vacancy in the Twelve left by Judas' removal from the apostleship. However, Matthias was the man chosen to replace Judas.

BARSABAS (2)

Acts 15:22, 27-33. See **Judas (7)** Surnamed Barsabas.

BARTHOLOMEW (Nathanael (?))

Matt. 10; Mark 3; Luke 9. **BARTHOLOMEW** was one of Jesus' 12 disciples: Simon Peter, Andrew, James, John, Philip, Bartholomew; Thomas, Matthew, James the son of Alphæus, Lebbæus (Thaddæus), Simon the Canaanite, and Judas Iscariot. Jesus empowered these apostles and sent them forth to teach. They were to heal the sick and cast out devils. He instructed them that they should not go to the Gentiles nor to the Samaritans. They were to go to the lost sheep of the house of Israel. They were to travel without purse or scrip. They were instructed to leave their peace upon those who received them, but to shake the dust off their feet when leaving the houses of those who reject them *(vs. 1-14; Mark 3:14-19; Luke 9:1-5). (The disciples are not listed by name in Luke 9:1-5.)* They were told they would be persecuted for Christ's sake, but that "he that endureth to the end shall be saved." They are of more value than the sparrows for which the Father provides. The hairs of their heads are even numbered *(vs. 16-32).*

Luke 6:13-16. Bartholomew is again named among Jesus' 12 disciples. However, the names of the disciples vary from Matthew and Mark above: Simon Peter, Andrew, James and John, Philip and Bartholomew, Matthew and Thomas, James the son of Alphæus, Simon called Zelotes, Judas the brother of James, and Judas Iscariot. *(This listing includes Judas the brother of James whereas the above listings include Lebbæus, i.e., Thaddæus. Apparently, Judas ,the brother of James, Lebbæus and Thaddæus are all one and the same. See* ***Thaddæus.****)*

John 1:43-51. (The BD indicates that Bartholomew and Nathanael are probably one and the same because he is always spoken of in conjunction with the apostles. Matthew, Mark and Luke always link Bartholomew with Philip—never Nathanael. However, John links Nathanael with Philip—never Bartholomew.) When Jesus called Philip to follow him, Philip found **Nathanael** (Bartholomew) and told him they had found Jesus of Nazareth, the son of Joseph, of whom Moses and the prophets had written. Nathanael asked if any good thing could come out of Nazareth. Philip told him to come and see. Jesus recognized Nathanael as one in whom there was no guile. When Nathanael wondered how Jesus knew that, Jesus said he had seen him under the fig tree before Philip called him. Because of Nathanael's belief, Jesus told him he would see heaven open and the angels of God ascending and descending upon the Son of Man.

John 21. Nathanael of Cana, Peter, Thomas, James and John and two other disciples were fishing on the sea of Tiberias when Jesus showed himself to his disciples a third time following his resurrection. Jesus stood on the shore and asked if they had any meat. They did not recognize Jesus, but responded that they had none. He told them to cast their nets on the right side of the ship. They did and their nets were so full they were unable to draw them. John declared to Peter, "It is the Lord." Peter quickly put something on and cast himself into the sea. When the disciples were gathered together on shore, Jesus dined with them on bread and fishes *(vs. 1-14).*

Acts 1:13-14. Following Jesus' ascension into heaven, Jesus' disciples, including Bartholomew, met together in an upper room, along with several women *(including Mary the mother of Jesus)* and his brethren, where they continued in prayer and supplication.

BARTIMÆUS

Mark 10:46. **BARTIMÆUS** was the name of a blind man healed by Jesus. His father was Timæus. *(See* ***Two Blind Men.****)*

BERNICE

Acts 25:13-27. **BERNICE** was the sister of King Agrippa II and Drusilla, wife of Felix. Bernice, Agrippa and Drusilla visited Festus, procurator over Judæa. Festus discussed with them his dilemma regarding Paul: the Jews' complaints didn't amount to anything worthy of death, and Paul had appealed to be heard by Augustus. Agrippa said he wanted to hear Paul himself. Festus agreed that on the morrow they would hear Paul. When Festus, King Agrippa, Bernice, and others present were ready, Festus explained that, because he found nothing worthy of death in Paul, he had determined to send him to Augustus. However, he felt he should send a letter detailing the crimes laid against him and hoped that perhaps they, after hearing Paul, could help him come up with what to include in the letter.

Acts 26:30-31. Bernice, King Agrippa, the governor and those who were with them, drew aside and conferred after Paul's presentation. They concluded that Paul had done nothing worthy of death or of bonds.

BLIND MAN, A

Mark 8:22-25. **A BLIND MAN** was brought to Jesus in Bethsaida. Jesus spit on his eyes and put his hands upon him. The man said, "I see men as trees, walking." Jesus put his hands upon him a second time, and this time the man could see clearly.

NAMES THAT BEGIN WITH "C"

CÆSAR

(Note: The BD indicates there were five Cæsars: (1) Augustus, 31 B.C. *(see* **Cæsar Augustus***); (2) Tiberius,* A.D. *14 (see* **Tiberius Cæsar***); (3) Caligula,* A.D. *37 (see* **Gaius Cæsar***); (4) Claudius,* A.D. *41 (see* **Claudius Cæsar***); (5) Nero,* A.D. *54 (see* **Nero***). (1) Augustus, prior to 27* B.C. *was known as Octavian. His original Latin name was Gaius Octaviaus. His adopted name was Gaius Julius Cæsar Octavianus, and was also known as Cæsar Augustus. He was born Sept. 23, 63* B.C.*, and died Aug. 19,* A.D. *14 (EB, vol. I, p. 650). (2) Tiberius, whose full name was Tiberius Claudius Nero Cæsar Augustus, was born Nov. 16, 42* B.C.*, in Rome and died March 16,* A.D. *37, in Capri (ibid., vol. IX, "Tiberius," p. 994). (3) Caligula's real name was Gaius Cæsar. He was born Aug. 31,* A.D. *12, in Antium, modern Anzio, Italy, and died Jan. 24,* A.D. *41, in Rome. He was emperor from 37 to 41, following Tiberius (ibid., vol II, p. 459). (4) Claudius was originally named Tiberius Claudius Drusus Nero Germanicus. He was born Aug. 1, 10* B.C.*, in Lugdunum, now Lyon, and died Oct. 13,* A.D. *54. He "ascended the throne suddenly in* A.D. *41 when the reigning emperor was murdered and became a firm friend of the army. He was poisoned by his niece Agrippina, whom he had married" (ibid., p. 976). (5) Nero's original name was Lucius Domitius Ahenobarbus. He was born Dec. 15,* A.D. *37, in Rome, and died* A.D. *68, in Rome. He put both his mother (in* A.D. *59) and his wife Octavia (in* A.D. *62) to death. He is "remembered for his unstable character and his cruelty" (ibid., vol. VII, p. 263).*

CÆSAR AUGUSTUS (i.e., Cæsar (1))

Luke 2:1-6. **CÆSAR AUGUSTUS** was the first Roman emperor and began his reign in 31 *B.C.* He issued a degree that all the world should be taxed. This required everyone to return to his own city to be taxed. Joseph and Mary, therefore, traveled to Bethlehem; and, thus, it was there that Jesus was born.

CAIAPHAS

Matt. 26:3, 57-66; Mark 14:53-64; Luke 22:54. **CAIAPHAS**, son-in-law of Annas, was the high priest *(A.D. 18 to A.D. 36)* who plotted with the chief priests, scribes and elders of the people to take Jesus and kill him. After Jesus was betrayed by Judas Iscariot, he was taken before Caiaphas and the others and tried. After the chief priests and elders found false witnesses to testify against Christ, Caiaphas found Jesus guilty of blasphemy and sentenced him to die.

Luke 3:2-3. Caiaphas and Annas *(A.D. 7 to A.D. 14)* were the high priests when Tiberius Cæsar was in the fifteenth year of his reign, Pontius Pilate was governor of Judæa, Herod was tetrarch of Galilee, and John the Baptist came into the country about Jordan preaching the baptism of repentance for the remission of sins.

John 11:49 (47-53). When the chief priests and Pharisees met in council to decide what to do regarding Jesus, fearing that if they left Jesus alone all men would believe on him and then the Romans would come and take away their station and their nation, Caiaphas told them that they knew nothing at all. He told them that it was expedient for them that one man should die for the people so that the whole nation would not perish. He prophesied that Jesus should die for that nation, "and not for that nation only, but that also he should gather together in one the children of God that were scattered abroad." From that day forth, they counseled together on how they might put Jesus to death.

John 18:13-14, 19-24, 28. Caiaphas' father-in-law was Annas. Christ was first delivered to Annas who then sent him bound unto Caiaphas, who had counseled the Jews that it was expedient that one man should die for the people. After Caiaphas questioned Jesus, Jesus was led into the hall of judgment where Pilate questioned him.

Acts 4:1-22. The priests, the captain of the temple and the Sadducees arrested Peter and John as they spoke unto the people about Christ. Peter, filled with the Holy Ghost, spoke boldly, testifying of Christ and that it was through Christ's name that the lame man was healed. The next day, the rulers, elders, scribes, Annas the high priest, Caiaphas, John and Alexander, and as many kindred of the high priest as there were, met to confer as to what to do about Peter and John. The healed man was with the apostles so they could not deny he had been healed, and they feared the people. They resolved to threaten them and let them go. They commanded Peter and John not to speak or teach in the name of Jesus. They responded with a question: "Was it better to hearken unto them or unto God?"

CALIGULA (See Gaius Cæsar; i.e., Cæsar (3))

CANDACE

Acts 8:27. **CANDACE** was queen of Ethiopia. Philip was directed by the Spirit to teach her eunuch the gospel. The eunuch believed and was baptized.

CAPTAIN OF THE GUARD

Acts 27:16. The **CAPTAIN OF THE GUARD** in Rome received from the centurion the prisoners who had traveled with and been shipwrecked with Paul. Paul was allowed to dwell by himself with a soldier that kept him.

CARPUS

2 Tim. 4:13. **CARPUS** had Paul's cloak and books with him in Troas. Paul asked Timothy to bring them to him when he came to see him, especially the parchments.

CENTURION, A (1)

Matt. 8:5-13; Luke 7:2-10. **A CENTURION** asked Jesus to heal his servant. When Jesus said he would go to his house, the centurion declined, saying he was not worthy to have Jesus under his roof, but said if Jesus would just speak the word he knew his servant would be healed. Jesus said he had not found so great faith in Israel. He healed the servant of the centurion that same hour. *(According to the BD, a centurion was an officer of the Roman army, in command of a century, or company of 100 men, forming one-sixtieth part of a Roman legion;*

although, in NT times a century was not always up to its full strength and varied from 50 to 100 men.)

CENTURION, A (2)

Matt. 27:54; Mark 15:39; Luke 23:47. **A CENTURION**, and they that were with him when Jesus was crucified, saw the earthquake and the other signs and proclaimed, "Truly this was the Son of God" ["Certainly this was a righteous man"].

CENTURION, A (3) (Julius)

Acts 27. See **Julius.**

CENTURION, A (4)

Acts 28:16. **A CENTURION** guarding Paul and the other prisoners on the journey to Rome delivered the prisoners to the captain of the guard. However, "Paul was suffered to dwell by himself with a soldier that kept him."

CEPHAS (See Peter called Simon)

CERTAIN BLIND MAN, A

Luke 18:35-43. **A CERTAIN BLIND MAN** near Jericho *(when Christ and his apostles went there prior to Christ's death and resurrection)* petitioned Jesus to heal his eyes. As Jesus healed the blind man, he said, "Receive thy sight: thy faith hath saved thee."

CERTAIN DAMSEL POSSESSED WITH A SPIRIT OF DIVINATION, A (See Damsel Possessed with a Spirit of Divination, A)

CERTAIN DISCIPLES AT EPHESUS

Acts 19:1-6. **CERTAIN DISCIPLES AT EPHESUS** met Paul as he traveled there. These disciples, which numbered about 12, had been baptized with the baptism of John *(the baptism of repentance)* but not with the baptism of Jesus Christ. He baptized them in the name of the Lord Jesus Christ and laid his hands upon them and conferred upon them the gift of the Holy Ghost. Immediately, they spake with tongues and prophesied.

CERTAIN GREEKS (See Greeks)

CERTAIN JEWS

*Acts 14:19-20. See **Jews.***

CERTAIN LAWYER, A

Luke 10:25-37. **A CERTAIN LAWYER** tried to tempt Jesus by asking what he should do to inherit eternal life. Jesus asked him what the law said, and told him to follow the law. The lawyer asked, "And who is my neighbor?" Jesus then taught the parable of the good Samaritan. The man who helped the injured man showed himself to be neighbor unto the man. Jesus told the lawyer to go and do likewise.

CERTAIN MAN, A

Matt. 17:14-16; Mark 9:17-28; Luke 9:38-42. **A CERTAIN MAN** with a "lunatic" son *(a son with a dumb spirit)* requested that Jesus heal him and said the disciples had been unable to cure him. Jesus complied with the man's request.

CERTAIN MAN, AND ANOTHER AND ANOTHER, A

Luke 9:57-62. **A CERTAIN MAN, AND ANOTHER AND ANOTHER** offered to follow Jesus. Jesus told the first that he had no place to even lay his head. The second wanted to bury his father first. Jesus said to let the dead bury the dead. The third wanted to tell his family farewell first. Jesus said that he that puts his hand to the plough and then looks back is not fit for the kingdom of God.

CERTAIN MAN AT LYSTRA, A

Acts 14:8-15. **A CERTAIN MAN AT LYSTRA**, who was crippled from birth, was healed by Paul who perceived that the man had faith to be healed. When Paul told him to stand upon his feet, he leaped up and walked. The people who witnessed the healing then hailed Paul and Barnabas as gods, but the apostles quickly disclaimed such.

CERTAIN MAN BY THE POOL OF BETHESDA, A

John 5. **A CERTAIN MAN BY THE POOL OF BETHESDA** had had an infirmity for 30 years. Many people surrounded the pool waiting for the chance to be healed in the water. On a Sabbath day, Jesus was near the pool of Bethesda and saw the man lying there and knew that he had been there a long time. Jesus had compassion on him and healed him with the instruction to take up his bed and walk *(vs. 2- 9)*. The Jews said it was not lawful for the man to carry his bed on the Sabbath and demanded to know who told him to do it. After seeing Jesus in the temple, the man told the Jews that Jesus had healed him and had told him to take up his bed and walk *(vs. 10-15)*.

CERTAIN MAN LAME FROM BIRTH, A

Acts 3:2-13, 16. **A CERTAIN MAN LAME FROM BIRTH**, who was daily placed at the temple gate that was called "Beautiful," asked alms of Peter and John as they went to the temple to pray. Peter told him they had neither silver nor gold, but would give them what they did have, and then he told him, "In the name of Jesus Christ of Nazareth rise up and walk," and the man was healed. When the people gathered around John and Peter in amazement, Peter admonished them and said the God of Abraham, Isaac and Jacob had glorified his Son by healing the man *(vs. 1-13)*, and that it was through faith in Christ's name that he had been made strong *(v. 16)*.

Acts 4:22. Because the man was over forty years of age, the chief priests and elders who sought ways to stop Peter and John from preaching could not deny that the man had been healed by them.

CERTAIN MEN FROM JUDÆA

Acts 15:1-2. **CERTAIN MEN FROM JUDÆA** went to Antioch and preached that the brethren all needed to be circumcised or they could not be saved. This caused great dissension in the church, so they decided that Barnabas and Paul and some of the other men should take the matter to the apostles and elders in Jerusalem.

CERTAIN NOBLEMAN, A

John 4:46-54. **A CERTAIN NOBLEMAN** had a son who was ill. The nobleman asked Jesus to heal his son. Jesus told him to go his way, that his son liveth. The man believed. As he journeyed home, his servants met him along the way and told him his son was well. The man wanted to know what hour he had begun to get better. They said it was the seventh hour of the previous day. That was the same hour Jesus had told him that his son liveth. This was Jesus' second miracle when he came out of Judæa into Galilee.

CERTAIN OF PETER'S BRETHREN

Acts 10:23, 45. **CERTAIN OF PETER'S BRETHREN** accompanied him to Cæsarea to meet with Cornelius. They were amazed that the Holy Ghost would fall upon Cornelius and his kinsmen and friends as well as upon those of the circumcision.

CERTAIN RULER, A (1)

Matt. 9:18-19, 23-26. See **Jairus.**

CERTAIN RULER, A (2)

Luke 18:18-23. **A CERTAIN RULER** asked Jesus what he had to do to inherit eternal life. Christ explained he had to keep the commandments. The ruler had done that. Christ told him to sell what he had and give to the poor. The man was very sorrowful because he was rich.

CERTAIN RULER'S DAUGHTER, A

Matt. 9:18-19, 23-26. See **Jairus' Daughter.**

CERTAIN SCRIBE, A

Matt. 8:19-20. **A CERTAIN SCRIBE** desired to follow Jesus. Jesus warned him that he had no place to even lay his head.

CERTAIN WOMAN, A (1)

Mark 5:25-34; Luke 8:43-48. **A CERTAIN WOMAN** who had had an issue of blood 12 years touched Jesus' garment as he made his way to the home of Jairus to heal his daughter. This woman was immediately healed. Jesus felt strength leave him as the woman touched him and asked, "Who touched my clothes?" The woman came forward and Jesus told her that her faith had made her whole.

CERTAIN WOMAN, A (2)

Mark 7:25-30. See **Woman of Canaan, A.**

CERTAIN WOMAN, A (3)

Luke 11:27-28. **A CERTAIN WOMAN**, recognizing that Jesus was the Son of God, indicated that Christ's mother was a blessed woman. Christ, however, indicated that giving birth to him was not what makes one blessed, but keeping the word of God.

CERTAIN YOUNG MAN, A

Mark 14:51-52. **A CERTAIN YOUNG MAN** followed Jesus. He wore a linen cloth around his naked body. Young men grabbed the linen cloth off him, and he fled from them naked.

CHIEF CAPTAIN OF THE BAND, HIS SOLDIERS AND THE CENTURIONS

(See Claudius Lysias)

CHIEF OF THE JEWS IN ROME

Acts 28:17-25. The **CHIEF OF THE JEWS IN ROME** were called together by Paul after he had been there three days. He explained why he was there and that he had done no wrong. They said they had not received any letters out of Judæa concerning him, nor had any of the brethren who had come their way said anything negative about him. They appointed a day wherein they could hear him speak. After listening to Paul, some believed, some did not, and they departed.

CHIEF PRIESTS AND SCRIBES

Matt. 2. 4-6. **CHIEF PRIESTS AND SCRIBES** were assembled by Herod after wise men came to Jerusalem seeking the "King of the Jews." Herod demanded to know where Christ should be born. They responded that the prophets had written that he would be born in Bethlehem of Judæa.

Matt. 15:1. Scribes and Pharisees of Jerusalem queried Jesus as to why his disciples transgressed the traditions of their elders by not washing their hands prior to eating bread. *(During the days of the Hebrew monarch, scribe was the title of a court official, i.e., a secretary of state. It was a title given to Ezra and others who were teachers of the law; sometimes they were called lawyers. They were an influential part of the court of the Sanhedrin, and as a rule were Pharisees, although there were also Sadducean scribes. They generally opposed the Lord because of his disregard for the "tradition of the elders." (BD).)*

Matt. 21; Mark 11, 12; Luke 20. The chief priests and elders of the people queried Jesus as to where he got the authority to do what he did. When Jesus asked them whether John's baptism was from heaven or of men, they said they couldn't tell. He then responded that neither would he say where he got his authority *(vs. 23-27; Mark 11:27-33; Luke 20:1-8).* The chief priests and Pharisees recognized that Jesus' parable regarding the wicked husbandmen pertained to them. However, they didn't dare lay hands on him because the people regarded Jesus as a prophet *(vs. 33-46; Mark 12:1-12; Luke 20:9-19).*

Matt. 23. The scribes and Pharisees were condemned and called hypocrites by Jesus. He counseled the people to follow their teachings but not their works because "they say, and do not" *(v. 3)* and appear beautiful and righteous on the outside but inside they are full of iniquity and hypocrisy *(v. 28).* They, along with their forefathers, kill the prophets and will not escape the damnation of hell *(vs. 29-35).* Jesus lamented, "O Jerusalem, Jerusalem, . . . how often would I have gathered thy children together, even as a hen gathereth her chickens under her wings, and ye would not!" *(v. 37).*

Matt. 26; Mark 14; Luke 22. The chief priests, scribes and elders of the people met in the palace of Caiaphas the high priest to conspire on ways to take Jesus and kill him *(vs. 3-4; Mark 14:1; Luke 22:2).* Judas Iscariot, one of Jesus' disciples, went to them and promised to deliver him unto them for thirty pieces of silver *(vs. 14-15; Mark 14:10-11; Luke 22:3-6).* As Jesus and the other disciples were leaving the garden of Gethsemane, a group of people sent from the chief priests and elders of the people, led by Judas, took Jesus after Judas indicated who he was by kissing Jesus on the cheek, a previously arranged sign *(vs. 47-50; Mark 14:43-46; Luke 22:47-48; see John 18 for a modified account).* They took Jesus to Caiaphas, the high priest, where the scribes and elders were assembled. They found false witnesses to testify against him, found him guilty of blasphemy, and said he was guilty of death *(vs. 57, 59-66; Mark 14:55-64).*

Matt. 27; Mark 15; Luke 23; also see entry for John 19. The chief priests and elders conspired to have Jesus put to death and took him to Pontius Pilate, the governor *(vs. 1-2; Mark 15:1; Luke 23:1).* When Judas regretted betraying Jesus, he tried to return the thirty pieces of silver to the chief priests, but they declined to take it. He threw the money down in the temple and went and hung himself. The chief priests took the silver and bought the potter's field wherein strangers could be buried *(vs. 3-7).* The chief priests and elders accused Jesus, but he answered nothing *(v. 12; Mark 15:2-5).* Pilate wanted to release Jesus, but the chief priests and elders persuaded the multitude to request the release of Barabbas and not Jesus *(vs. 13-26; Mark 15:6-15; Luke 23:2-25). (Note: The account in Luke states that the people took Christ to Pilate, who subsequently sent him to Herod. Herod returned him again to Pilate, who wanted to release Jesus, but finally acquiesced to the people's demands.)* After Christ was sentenced to be crucified, the chief priests, scribes and elders mocked him *(vs. 41-43; Mark 15:16-20, 29-32).* After he was placed in the tomb of Joseph of Arimathæa, the chief priests and Pharisees went to Pilate and asked him to make sure the tomb was secure so Jesus' disciples could not steal the body *(vs. 62-66).*

Matt. 28:11-15. Some of the guard ran to the chief priests in the city and reported what had happened after the angel came and rolled the stone away from the sepulchre. The chief priests and elders bribed the soldiers with money to get them to falsely state that Jesus' disciples came by night and stole his body. They promised to protect them if word got to Pontius Pilate.

Mark 2. Certain scribes felt that Jesus blasphemed when he told the man who was sick with palsy, "Son, thy sins be forgiven thee." Jesus rebuked them and asked if it was easier to say, "Thy sins be forgiven thee; or to say, Arise, and take up thy bed, and walk?" In order to teach them that the Son of Man hath power on earth to forgive sins, he had said the former. He then told the man with palsy to take up his bed and go home *(vs. 6-12).* The scribes and Pharisees were appalled that Jesus ate meat with publicans and sinners. He taught them that he didn't come to call the righteous to repentance, but the sinner *(vs. 15-17).* They complained that Jesus' disciples didn't fast but the disciples of John and of the Pharisees did. Jesus taught that while he was with them there was no need to fast. When the "bridegroom" was taken from them, then they would have need to fast *(vs. 18-20).*

Mark. 12:28-34; 38-40; Matt. 22:34-40. A scribe (Pharisee) asked Jesus which was the greatest commandment. Jesus said the first commandment is to love the Lord and the second is like unto it, to love thy neighbor as thyself. To obey these two laws is more important than "all whole burn offerings and sacrifices." *(Note: Matthew includes the statement: "On these two commandments hang all the law and the prophets.")* Jesus cautioned people about hypocritical scribes.

Mark 14. See entry for Matt. 26.

Luke 6:7. The scribes and Pharisees watched Jesus to see if he would heal on the Sabbath day so they could accuse him of breaking the law. Jesus knew their thoughts and taught that it is lawful to do good on the Sabbath.

John 11. After the Pharisees were informed by some of the Jews who had gone to comfort Mary when her brother died that Jesus had raised Lazarus from the dead, the chief priests and Pharisees gathered together a council and plotted how to take Jesus so they could put him to death *(vs. 46-53).* When the Jews' Passover was near, they issued a command that whosoever knew where Jesus was needed to inform them so they could take him *(v. 57).*

John 12:10-11, 42-43. The chief priests wanted to put Lazarus to death because many people believed on Jesus after he raised Lazarus from the dead. Many leaders believed on Jesus but did not admit it because they feared being removed from the synagogue by the Pharisees. They loved the praise of men more than the praise of God.

John 18:3-12, 22. A band of men and officers from the chief priests and Pharisees were led by Judas to the garden where Jesus and his disciples were. Peter smote off the ear of Malchus, one of the servants. The band and the captain and officers of the Jews bound Jesus and took him to Annas, the father-in-law of Caiaphas the high priest. When an officer took offense at Christ's response to Caiaphas' questions, he struck Jesus with his palm.

John 19. The chief priests and officers demanded that Pilate crucify Jesus, and the Jews said their laws required it "because he made himself the Son of God" *(vs. 6-7).* When Pilate asked if they really wanted him to crucify their King, the chief priests said the only king they had was Cæsar *(v. 15).* Pilate wrote a title in three languages—Hebrew, Greek and Latin—and had it placed on the cross on which Jesus was nailed. It read: "JESUS OF NAZARETH THE KING OF THE JEWS." The chief priests asked Pilate to change it and write, "He said, I am King of the Jews." Pilate refused and said, "What I have written, I have written" *(vs. 19-22).*

Acts 4:1-22. The priests, the captain of the temple, and the Sadducees arrested Peter and John as they spoke unto the people about Christ. Peter, filled with the Holy Ghost, spoke boldly, testifying of Christ and that it was through His name that the lame man was healed. The rulers, elders, scribes, Annas the high priest, Caiaphas, John and Alexander, and as many kindred of the high priest as there were, met to confer as to what to do about Peter and John. The healed man was with the apostles so they could not deny he had been healed, and they feared the people. They resolved to threaten them and let them go. They commanded Peter and John not to speak or teach in the name of Jesus. They responded with a question: "Was it better to hearken unto them or unto God?"

Acts 9:1. The high priest was approached by Saul who desired that he give him letters to Damascus to the synagogues so he (Saul) could bind any men or women he found who were followers of Christ and take them back to Jerusalem.

Acts 22:30 (22-30). The chief priests and all their council were commanded by the chief captain to gather as the Jews were making demands regarding Paul, who was a Roman. The chief captain set Paul before the chief priests and council.

Acts 25:2, 15. The chief priests, when Festus was in Jerusalem, informed him of their complaints against Paul and requested he be returned to Jerusalem. *(They planned to lay in wait and kill him as he returned.)* However, Festus declined and said Paul should stay in Cæsarea and they could return there with him and make their complaint before the judgment seat there.

CHILDREN OF THY ELECT SISTER, THE

2 Jn. 1:13. **THE CHILDREN OF THY ELECT SISTER** are not identified. John merely says he and the children of thy elect sister send their greetings to "the Elect Lady and her children" to whom he has addressed this epistle.

CHLOE

1 Cor. 1:11. **CHLOE** was a member of the church in Corinth. Members of her household informed Paul of the division and contentions that were dividing the saints in Corinth.

CHRISTIANS (See Jesus' Disciples)

CHUZA

Luke 8:3. **CHUZA** was Herod's steward and the husband of Joanna.

CLAUDIA

2 Tim. 4:21. **CLAUDIA** joined Paul and all the brethren in sending greetings to Timothy.

CLAUDIUS CÆSAR (i.e., Cæsar (4))

Acts 11:28-30. **CLAUDIUS CÆSAR** was the emperor of Rome A.D. 41-51. *(Note: He was the fourth of five Cæsars. See Cæsar Augustus. Claudius was originally named Tiberius Claudius Drusus Nero Germanicus. He was born Aug. 1, 10 B.C., in Lugdunum, now Lyon, and died Oct. 13, A.D. 54. He "ascended the throne suddenly in A.D. 41 when the reigning emperor was murdered and became a firm friend of the army. He was poisoned by his niece Agrippina, whom he had married" (EB vol. II, p. 976).)* It was during his days that the dearth throughout the world prophesied by Agabus came to pass and the disciples and church members sent relief from Antioch to their brethren in Judæa by the hands of Barnabas and Saul.

Acts 18:2. Because Claudius commanded all Jews to depart from Rome, Aquila and his wife Priscilla went to Athens, where Paul came unto them.

CLAUDIUS LYSIAS (Chief Captain of the Band, His Soldiers and the Centurions)

Acts 21:31-40. **CLAUDIUS LYSIAS [The CHIEF CAPTAIN OF THE BAND], HIS SOLDIERS AND THE CENTURIONS** in Jerusalem responded quickly when they heard there was an uproar over Paul. When they arrived on the scene, the people stopped beating Paul. The chief captain commanded that Paul be chained, and then he demanded to know who he was and what he had done. The people gave conflicting responses. He had the soldiers carry him into the castle. Paul requested permission to speak to the captain, and it was granted. Paul also requested permission to speak to the people, and that, too, was granted.

Acts 22:22-30. Because the people were not persuaded, the chief captain commanded that Paul be brought into the castle and be scourged. However, Paul asked the centurion if it was lawful to scourge a man who was a Roman and who was uncondemned. When the centurion told the chief priest, the chief priest was afraid because he knew he was a Roman and that he had bound him. He had the bands loosed on Paul, called the chief priests and council together, and set Paul down before them.

Acts 23. As Paul was pleading his case, a great dissension ensued and the chief captain, fearing that Paul would be pulled in pieces, commanded the soldiers take him by force from among the people and take him to the castle *(vs. 6-10)*. Forty Jews plotted to kill Paul, and bound themselves to neither eat nor drink until they had accomplished the deed. However, Paul's nephew *(his sister's son)* reported the plan to Paul, and Paul asked a centurion to take the young man to the chief captain because he had something to tell him. After the chief captain learned of the plan, he gave orders to two centurions to prepare 200 soldiers, 70 horsemen, and 200 spear men to go to Cæsarea at the third hour of the night. They were to be given beasts for Paul to ride on, and they were to escort him to Felix the governor *(vs. 12-24)*. The chief captain, **Claudius Lysias**, wrote a letter to Felix. The soldiers took Paul by night to Antipatris and left Paul with the horsemen to journey on to Cæsarea. They delivered both Paul and the chief captain's letter to the governor *(vs. 25-33)*.

Acts 24:22. Until Claudius Lysias could give his input to Felix regarding Paul and the complaints of Ananias and the elders as presented by Tertullus, Felix deferred making any decision.

CLEMENT

Philip. 4:3. **CLEMENT** was a fellow laborer with Paul. Paul urged the Philippian brethren to help the women who had labored with him and Clement and their fellow laborers.

CLEOPAS AND ANOTHER DISCIPLE (See Peter Called Simon: Luke 24:18-34)

COLOSSIANS

Col. 1. **COLOSSIANS** were citizens of Colosse, a town of Phrygia in the valley of the Lycus. Colosse was near the great road that led from Ephesus to the Euphrates. *(When Paul wrote his epistle to the Colossians, he probably had never actually visited Colosse. The first Christian teachers to preach there were Epaphras and possibly Timothy. BD.)* Having heard of the faith of the Colossian saints and their love for all the saints from Epaphras, Paul sent his and Timotheus' greetings to them. From the time Paul and his colleagues had learned of the faithfulness of the Colossian saints, they had prayed for them that they might have knowledge and wisdom, and walk worthily before the Lord receiving glorious power and other blessings *(vs. 1-12)*. Paul acknowledged that Christ is the Son of God, "In whom we have redemption through his blood, even the forgiveness of sins." Christ is in the express image of God and is the firstborn of every creature. By him were all things created *(vs. 13-16)*. Christ is the head of the church. He is the beginning and the firstborn from the dead *(v. 18)*. Before they knew of Christ, they were "alienated and enemies in your mind by wicked works." However, they had been reconciled to God through the death and resurrection of the Savior *(vs. 21-22)*. If the Colossians continued in faith, Paul, "who was made a minister, according to the dispensation of God which is given to me for you," said he rejoiced in his sufferings for them *(vs. 23-25)*.

Col. 2. Paul expressed his anguish for the Colossians and all the other saints he had not had a chance to meet personally and his desire that they come to a full understanding of the mystery of God *(those things that cannot be learned by reason but by revelation)*. The Father and the Son have all wisdom and knowledge *(vs. 1-3)*. Though Paul was not with them in body, he was with them in spirit, and encouraged them to be steadfast in their faith in Christ—to be watchful so that no man could lead them after the traditions of men and after the rudiments of the world with philosophy and vain deceit *(vs. 4-8)*. All the attributes of the Godhead are embodied in Christ *(v. 9)*. Paul again reminded the Colossians that circumcision of the flesh does not lead to salvation, only circumcision of the spirit. He also reminded them that being buried in the waters of baptism and rising from the water was a similitude of Christ's burial and resurrection. Those who are baptized, who are spiritually uncircumcised, gain a forgiveness of their sins. Christ fulfilled the law of Moses, thus blotting out the ordinances and performances which pertained to the carnal law, symbolically nailing the law of Moses to Christ's cross *(vs. 11-14)*. The Colossian saints were reminded that they were not to be judged according to the law of Moses and should not let anyone lead them into thinking they needed to follow it *(vs. 16-17)*.

Col. 3. Paul admonished the Colossians to set their affections on the things of Christ and not on the things of the earth; to avoid the carnal things of this world: fornication, uncleanness, inordinate affection, evil concupiscence, covetousness, anger, wrath, malice, blasphemy, filthy communication, lying. Whereas at one time they walked in sin, they had now put off the "old man" and had put on the "new man" "which is renewed in knowledge after the image of him that created him" *(vs. 1-10)*. With followers of Christ, there are no distinctions between them, "neither Greek nor Jew, circumcision nor uncircumcision, Barbarian, Scythian, bond nor free" *(v. 11)*. Paul exhorted the saints to follow Christ and engage in

Christlike behavior: being merciful, kind, humble, meek, longsuffering, etc., and reminded them that the greatest attribute is charity, the bond of perfectness *(vs. 12-14)*. He said they should do everything they did in the name of Jesus Christ, giving thanks to God the Father through Jesus Christ, suggesting that if they did all that he said, they would have the peace of God in their hearts. They were admonished to let the word of Christ dwell in them and to teach each other with psalms, hymns and singing *(vs. 15-17)*. As with the Ephesian saints, Paul counseled wives to submit unto their husbands; husbands were counseled to love their wives; and children were instructed to obey their parents. Fathers were told not to provoke their children to anger; and servants were told to obey their masters *(vs. 18- 22)*. Nevertheless, whatsoever they did, they were to do it "heartily" unto the Lord and not unto men; thus, the Lord would bless them. Those who do wrong will also reap their reward. God is no respecter of persons *(vs. 23-25)*.

Col. 4. Paul counseled masters to be fair and just with their servants, remembering they, themselves, have a Master in heaven *(v. 1)*. They were admonished to continue in prayer *(praying also for him and his colleagues who were in prison so a door would be opened for them to preach the gospel)*; to walk in wisdom; and to speak with grace, "seasoned by salt, that ye may know how ye ought to answer every man" *(vs. 2-6)*. Paul said he was sending his message to them via Tychicus and Onesimus. He also included greetings from Aristarchus, Marcus, Jesus (Justus), Epaphras, Luke and Demas *(vs. 7-14)*. Paul asked that greetings be sent to the saints in Laodicea and to the saints in the house of Nymphas. He also requested that his epistle be shared with the Laodiceans and that the Colossians read the epistle that had been sent to Laodicea *(v. 16)*. *(Apparently, this epistle has been lost.)* Archippus was counseled to take heed and fulfill his ministry in the Lord *(v. 17)*.

CORINTHIANS

*1 Cor 1. (Note: **CORINTHIANS** were citizens of Corinth. Paul wrote two epistles to the saints in Corinth around* A.D. *55, 57.)* Paul was apparently joined by Sosthenes in sending greetings to the Corinthians *(v. 1)*. There were contentions among the saints—with some claiming to be of Paul, Apollos, Cephas or of Christ—and Paul admonished them to be united and have no divisions among them. He reminded the saints that Christ is not divided and that it was Christ who had been crucified for them, no one else *(vs.10-13)*. Christ did not send Paul to baptize, but to preach; and Paul was glad he had only baptized Crispus, Gaius and the household of Stephanas *(vs.14-17)*. The gospel is not preached with wisdom of words, but by faith in Christ. Thus, wise men after the flesh are not called to preach, but "God hath chosen the weak things of the world to confound the things which are mighty" *(vs.17-27)*.

1 Cor. 2. Paul reminded the saints that he did not come to them preaching with "excellency of speech or of wisdom," but with the testimony of God. God uses the weak to spread his word lest people are converted by the enticing words of man's wisdom: their faith should not be based upon man's wisdom but in the power of God *(vs.1-6)*. God's wisdom is a mystery to those who do not believe and was ordained to be so by God before the world was created. Nevertheless, those mysteries are revealed to his followers by the Spirit. Man knows the things of man by the spirit of man and the things of God by the Spirit of God *(vs. 7-11)*. Paul testified that he speaks the words which the Holy Ghost testifies to be true. The natural man cannot understand the things of the Spirit because they can only be spiritually discerned *(vs. 12-14)*.

1 Cor. 3. The saints in Corinth were as babes and had to be fed with milk before they could be fed with meat as pertaining to things spiritual *(vs. 1-2)*. The saints were carnal because of their envyings and strife. Paul reminded the saints that he and Apollos and other ministers "planted" and "watered," but only God gave the increase *(vs. 3-7)*. Every man shall be rewarded according to his own labor. We must take heed as to how we labor and upon what foundation we build. The only foundation upon which one should build is Jesus Christ *(vs. 8-11)*. Our works shall be tried by fire *(vs.12-15)*. The saints are the temple of God and the Spirit of God dwells in them. "If any man defile the temple of God, him shall God destroy; for the temple of God is holy, which temple ye are" *(vs. 16-17)*. The faithful will inherit all things *(vs. 18-23)*.

1 Cor. 4. Paul stressed to the Corinthians that stewards must be faithful *(v. 2)*. The apostles at that very time were being persecuted but remained faithful *(vs. 9-14)*. Paul sent Timotheus to Corinth to "bring you into remembrance of my ways which be in Christ, as I teach every where in every church" *(vs. 17)*. If the Lord wills, Paul hopes to come to them himself shortly. The kingdom of God is a kingdom of power, not of words *(vs. 18-21)*.

1 Cor. 5:1-13. Paul had been informed that there were those among the saints in Corinth who engaged in fornication, and he rebuked the saints for tolerating it. He likened a little sin to a little leaven: a little leaven affects the whole lump. He instructed them to separate themselves from sinners: not to keep company with fornicators, those who coveted, extorted, worshiped idols, etc.

1 Cor. 6. Paul chastised the saints for suing each other in the civil courts "before the unbelievers" rather than settling their complaints before leaders of the church, and asked if they couldn't find even one wise man among them who could judge between his brethren. He urged them to suffer wrong rather than go to court against a brother *(vs. 1-8)*. The unrighteous will not inherit the kingdom of God *(v. 9)*. Christ was resurrected by the power of God; likewise, we shall be raised up by his power *(v. 14)*. When two people are married, they become one flesh according to the Lord. When one becomes joined with the Lord, they become one spirit *(vs. 15-17)*. Paul taught the saints that their body is the temple of the Holy Ghost, "which is in you, which ye have of God, and ye are not your own. For ye are bought with a price. . ." *(vs. 19-20)*.

1 Cor. 7. Paul responded to questions the saints had written to him regarding marriage among those called on missions. Ideally, he suggested it would be better for them to be single. He recommended the unmarried and widows remain so. However, if they found that difficult, it would be better for them to be married than to risk sinning *(vs. 1-9)*. Likewise, he told those who were married to remain so and to be faithful to their spouses. He advised against divorce, even when the spouse is a non-believer, "For the unbelieving husband is sanctified by the wife, and the unbelieving wife is sanctified by the husband. . ." Nevertheless, if the unbelieving spouse departs, they should let him or her depart. They are not under bondage in such cases *(vs. 10-16)*. They should not seek to be loosed from their wife, but if they are loosed from a wife they should not seek a wife. It is not a sin for a virgin to marry *(vs. 25-28)*. When people are married, their thoughts and efforts are directed toward their spouses; when they are single, their thoughts and efforts are directed toward the Lord *(vs. 2-34)*. Paul applauded self-discipline *(v. 37)*. A woman is bound by the law as long as her husband lives; if he dies, she is free to marry again. Nevertheless, Paul suggested she would be happier if she remained single *(vs. 9-40)*.

1 Cor. 8. When people have knowledge, they become puffed up in themselves, but charity edifies *(v. 1)*. God knows those who love him *(v. 3)*. In spite of people having many gods, Paul testified there is only one God, the Father, "of whom are all things, and we in him; and one Lord Jesus Christ, by whom are all things, and we by him" *(vs. 4-6)*. Not every one has a knowledge of Christ. Paul cautioned the saints to be sure their behavior doesn't lead someone else astray. If they cause a weak brother to perish and "sin so against the brethren, and wound their weak conscience, ye sin against Christ" *(vs. 7-13)*.

1 Cor. 9. Paul testified to the Corinthians that he was, in deed, an apostle, and that their very existence as a congregation was evidence of his apostleship inasmuch as it was through his teaching that they were converted *(vs. 1-2)*. Apparently, there were those who questioned Paul's apostleship or actions because he felt a need to respond to those who "do examine me." He indicated that even though he was an apostle, he was still free to eat and drink and enjoy family relationships as were the other apostles *(including Peter, i.e., Cephas)* and the brothers of the Lord. He defended his and Barnabas' right to be temporally fed, writing, "who planteth a vineyard, and eateth not of the fruit thereof? Or who feedeth a flock, and eateth not of the milk of the flock?" Those who spend their time sowing spiritual things are entitled to have their material needs met *(vs. 3-11)*. Even though those who spend their time ministering to the spiritual needs of others have a right to have their material needs met, Paul indicated that he had "used none of these things" lest "any man should make my glorying void." He had a duty to preach the gospel, and to preach it willingly, in which case he would receive a reward. If he preached it unwillingly, he would be under condemnation—"a dispensation of the gospel is committed unto me." The gospel was to be preached without charge *(vs. 12-18)*. Paul was free from all men yet was a servant to all, and became as all things to all men—that is, he subjected himself to the same circumstances and rules of those he taught—in order to save souls *(vs. 19-22)*. Nevertheless, he kept control of his physical appetites, bringing his body into subjection, not boasting in his own strength "lest that by any means, when I have preached to others, I myself should be a castaway" *(v. 27)*.

1 Cor. 10. Paul reminded the Corinthians that the ancient Israelites had been led by the cloud and had passed through the Red Sea and, as such, were "baptized unto Moses." The spiritual meat, spiritual drink, and spiritual Rock they followed was Jesus Christ *(i.e., the God of ancient Israel) (vs. 1-4)*. Paul stressed that God was not pleased with many of the Israelites and he destroyed them. He pointed out some of the sins in which the Israelites engaged and cautioned the Corinthians to avoid them. The example of the Israelites had been preserved and recorded so later generations would avoid those evils. Temptations are common to man, but God will not suffer anyone to be tempted beyond his capacity to resist and will "make a way to escape, that ye may be able to bear it" *(vs. 5-13)*. Paul urged the people to flee from idolatry. He compared false sacraments to true sacraments. Through the true sacrament of the Savior, we are made one with him and we can, therefore, gain salvation. People cannot worship both the Lord and the devil *(vs. 14-21)*. Not everything is lawful because not all things are expedient nor edify. *(Note: The JST clarifies verse 23 by including the word "not" and is indicated in the footnote to that verse.)* We should not seek our own happiness, but we should seek for other people's good. Everything in the earth belongs to the Lord. Whatever we do, we should do to the glory of God and, like Paul, do it so that others may be saved *(vs. 23-33)*.

1 Cor. 11. Paul stressed the order of leadership within the Lord's plan: i.e., the man is head of the woman; Christ is head of the man; God is head of Christ *(v. 3)*. Nevertheless, the man is not without the woman; neither is the woman without the man in the Lord *(vs. 8-9)*. Paul addressed the issue of certain customs regarding head coverings. When men prayed, they were to have their heads uncovered. When women prayed or prophesied, they were to have their heads covered *(vs. 4-15)*. *(Note: Having her head uncovered was the same as a woman having her head shaved—a sign, according to local custom, that would identify her as an adulteress. According to Bruce R. McConkie, DNTC, vol. 2, p. 361, in the eternal scheme of things, it is immaterial as to whether or not a woman wears a hat when she prays. However, in Paul's day, if a woman prayed bareheaded, it was a sign of irreverence.)* There were divisions and heresies among the saints in Corinth. Paul indicated that heresies provide a means whereby people may be proven—"that they which are approved may be made manifest among you." Paul encouraged them to eat dinner at home and then gather together to partake of the sacrament, because they apparently were gathering for the wrong purposes and were profaning the sacrament. Christ instituted the sacrament: the bread represents his body "which is broken for you." With the cup, Christ admonished his followers to "drink in remembrance" of his blood which was shed for them. Paul cautioned the saints to neither eat nor drink unworthily *(vs. 18-30)*.

1 Cor. 12:1-31. Paul wrote to the Corinthians about spiritual gifts. Only by the power of the Holy Ghost can one know that Jesus is the Lord. No one speaking by the power of the Holy Ghost can deny Jesus is the Lord. There are many different spiritual gifts. Just as the body has different parts *(i.e., hands, feet, eyes, etc.)* with each member of the body contributing to the good of the whole body; likewise, there are different spiritual gifts given to the members of the church so that the entire body of the church can be benefited. Just as one body part cannot reject another *(or dismiss itself as unimportant)* because it plays a different role, those with one gift cannot reject themselves nor those who have different gifts because they think they are useless. All are important to the whole. Paul urged the people to seek after the best gifts.

1 Cor. 13:1-13. Paul taught the importance of charity. While prophecies may fail, tongues may cease, and knowledge may vanish, charity will never fail. If we have not charity, we are nothing. Out of faith, hope and charity, charity is the greatest. *(Note: Moroni, an ancient Book of Mormon prophet, recorded some of the teachings of his father, Mormon, regarding faith, hope and charity, which more fully explains the relationship of these three qualities to each other.)*

And again, my beloved brethren, I would speak unto you concerning hope. How is it that ye can attain unto faith, save ye shall have hope?

And what is it that ye shall hope for? Behold I say unto you that ye shall have hope through the atonement of Christ and the power of his resurrection, to be raised unto life eternal, and this because of your faith in him according to the promise.

Wherefore, if a man have faith he must needs have hope; for without faith there cannot be any hope.

And again, behold I say unto you that he cannot have faith and hope, save he shall be meek, and lowly of heart.

If so, his faith and hope is vain, for none is acceptable before God, save the meek and lowly in heart; and if a man be meek and lowly in heart, and confesses by the power of the Holy Ghost that Jesus is the Christ, he must needs have charity; for if he have not charity he is nothing; wherefore he must needs have charity.

And charity suffereth long, and is kind, and envieth not, and is not puffed up, seeketh not her own, is not easily provoked, thinketh no evil, and rejoiceth not in iniquity but rejoiceth in the truth, beareth all things, believeth all things, hopeth all things, endureth all things.

Wherefore, my beloved brethren, if ye have not charity, ye are nothing, for charity never faileth. Wherefore, cleave unto charity, which is the greatest of all, for all things must fail

But charity is the pure love of Christ, and it endureth forever; and whoso is found possessed of it at the last day, it shall be well with him." (Moro. 7:40-47.)

1 Cor. 14. Paul compared the relative value of the gift of tongues with the gift of prophecy and stressed that the gift of prophecy is the greater gift. Those who speak in unknown tongues edifieth only themselves, unless they have an interpreter *(vs. 4-5).* If people fail to recognize what is being said, they won't understand the message being given *(vs. 6-11).* We should seek gifts that will allow us to edify the church *(v. 12).* The gift of tongues is for a sign to those who do not believe. Prophecy benefits those who believe *(v. 22).* Unless there is an interpreter present, those speaking in an unknown tongue should remain quiet *(vs. 27-28).* All may prophesy so that all may be benefited. God is the author of peace, not confusion *(vs. 31-33).* Paul taught that the women should keep silence in the churches *(14:34-35).* Men should covet to prophesy but should not forbid speaking in tongues *(v. 39).*

1 Cor. 15. Paul testified that Christ died for our sins and was buried and then resurrected on the third day as had been prophesied in the scriptures. After his resurrection, he was seen by many people: Cephas (Peter), the twelve, 500 brethren at one time, James, all of the apostles, and by Paul, himself *(vs. 3-9).* Apparently, there were those among the Corinthians who denied the resurrection of the dead. Paul reasoned with them that if there is no resurrection of the dead, then Christ be not risen. If Christ be not risen, then their preaching and faith were in vain and the apostles were false witnesses. Also, if Christ be not risen, then they were yet in their sins, and all who die simply perish. Our hope in Christ would be in this life only, and we would be most miserable *(vs. 12-19).* He testified that Christ had risen, and that just "as in Adam all men die, even so in Christ shall all be made alive." There will be order in the resurrection: Christ would be the "firstfruits," and then those who will be made Christ's at his coming *(vs. 20-23)*. All things will be subject to Jesus Christ. Death is the final enemy that shall be destroyed *(vs. 24-26)*. The one thing (person) that will not be subject to Jesus Christ is the Father: "For he (the Father) hath put all things under his (Christ's) feet. But when he saith all things are put under him, it is manifest that he is excepted, which did put all things under him. And when all things shall be subdued unto him, then shall the Son also himself be subject unto him that put all things under him, that God may be all in all" *(vs. 27-28)*. Again, Paul testified of the resurrection and that the reason they engaged in baptism for the dead was because people would be resurrected *(v. 29)*. If there were no resurrection, Paul said they might as well just "eat and drink; for tomorrow we die" *(v. 32)*. There are different kinds of flesh: man, beasts, fishes, birds, etc. Likewise, there are different degrees of glory in the resurrection: celestial bodies *(compared to the glory of the sun);* terrestrial bodies *(compared to the glory of the moon);* and telestial bodies *(compared to the glory of the stars) (vs. 39-41). (Note: Verse 40 (JST) identifies the third degree of glory referred to in verse 41 as the telestial degree.)* Our mortal bodies, which will die, will be resurrected as spiritual or immortal bodies that are no longer corruptible. We will not remain "asleep" in the grave, "and the dead shall be raised incorruptible, and we shall be changed." Death will be swallowed up in victory *(over the grave),* which victory comes through Jesus Christ *(vs. 44-58)*.

1 Cor. 16; Postscript. Paul told the saints in Corinth that he would come to see them when he passed through Macedonia, and hoped to maybe even stay with them through the winter. Meanwhile, he planned to tarry in Ephesus until Pentecost. He indicated that Timotheus might come to them, and Paul asked that they treat Timotheus kindly and be helpful to him. He had hoped Apollos could also go to Corinth. However, he indicated that the time was not convenient for Apollos right then, but that he would come when he could *(vs. 5-12)*. He counseled them to stand fast in the faith, to do all things with charity, and to submit to those—such as the house of Stephanas—who ministered in the work. He appreciated the information he had received from Stephanas, Fortunatus and Achaicus, "for that which was lacking on your part they have supplied," and indicated they had lifted his spirit and theirs. He sent greetings from Aquila and Priscilla and the members of the church in Asia, as well as from "all the brethren" *(vs. 13-19)*. Paul wrote this epistle to the Corinthians from Philippi and sent it to them via the hands of Stephanas, Fortunatus, Achaicus and Timotheus *(Postscript)*.

2 Cor. 1. In his second epistle to the Corinthians, Paul told them that God comforts us all in our tribulations. In turn, having been comforted, we are then able to comfort others "by the comfort wherewith we ourselves are comforted of God." Paul and his companions had been afflicted in Asia, but he said those afflictions were "for your consolation and salvation" *(vs. 4-8)*. Their afflictions in Asia were so great that they "despaired even of life." Paul thanked all those who prayed for them *(v. 11)*. The promises of God are positive to those who believe—not negative—and was so taught to them by Paul, Silvanus and Timotheus. God established the saints in Christ and anointed his ministers, sealed the saints and, through the Spirit, gave them assurance in their hearts *(vs. 17-22)*. Paul indicated that the reason he had not yet come to them in Corinth was to spare them from the afflictions he was enduring in Asia. He also asserted that they were not dependent upon him and his companions to keep them strong, but it was their faith, ". . . for by faith ye stand" *(vs. 23-24).*

2 Cor. 2. Paul told the saints in Corinth that he had determined not to come unto them while he was "in heaviness" because if he caused them to feel bad then they couldn't lift him up. He said he had written out of his afflictions and anguish *(i.e., with sharpness)* so they might understand how much he loved them *(vs. 1-4).* He counseled them to love and forgive one another *(vs. 5-11).* When he went to Troas to preach, he was unable to find Titus, so he went on to Macedonia *(vs. 12-13).* God always causes us to triumph in Christ. Through the saints, God spreads the teachings of Christ and "maketh manifest the savour of his knowledge by us in every place" *(v. 14). (Note: Savor (savour) means that quality of a thing that acts on the sense of taste or smell; the power to arouse interest or zest; to be the source of the flavor or scent of something. (BD).)*

2 Cor. 3. Paul wrote that the gospel of Jesus Christ surpassed the law of Moses, "for the letter killeth, but the spirit giveth life" *(v. 6).* "For if that which is done away was glorious, much more that which remaineth is glorious" *(v. 11).* Many people still clung to the law of Moses. When the day comes that they turn their hearts to the Lord, the veil will be removed from their hearts. Liberty is found in following Christ: "Where the Spirit of the Lord is, there is liberty" *(v. 17).* Just as a mirror reflects our image, we should reflect the image of Christ in the way we live and, bit by bit, by the Spirit of the Lord, we will be changed to be more like him" *(v. 18).*

2 Cor. 4. Paul indicates that he and his companions are legal administrators of God and that they have rejected that which is wicked. What they teach is the truth and not some misrepresentation. If the truth of the gospel is hidden, it is only hidden to those who are lost: "In whom the god of this world hath blinded the minds of them which believe not . . ." Christ is the image of God *(vs. 1-4).* God, who commanded that the light be separated from the darkness when the world was created, shines in the hearts of the saints, giving "the light of the knowledge of the glory of God in the face of Jesus Christ" *(v. 6).* In spite of trouble, persecution, being perplexed and cast down, they are not destroyed nor do they despair. These afflictions are for but a moment when compared with the "far more exceeding and eternal weight of glory." Their focus is not on that which is seen *(that which is temporal),* but on the unseen *(that which has eternal glory) (vs. 8-18).*

2 Cor. 5. Paul reminded the Corinthian saints that even though our mortal bodies die and are "dissolved," we will yet be resurrected and dressed in immortal bodies. While we are mortal, we are separated from the Lord and we walk by faith, not sight. We are willing to undergo death *(be separated from our mortal body)* so we can eventually be present with the Lord *(v. 1-8).* Everyone must appear before the judgment seat of Christ and will be judged and rewarded according to what he has done here on earth *(v. 10).* When a person accepts Christ, he becomes a new person: "old things are passed away; behold, all things are become new." The gospel reconciles man to God. The ministry of Paul and the apostles is a ministry of reconciliation. They are ambassadors for Christ *(vs. 17-20).*

2 Cor. 6. Paul admonished the saints to accept the grace of God because "now is the day of salvation." Those who minister in the gospel were counseled to walk uprightly and to bear all things patiently *(vs. 1-10).* He warned them not to be yoked together with unbelievers, "for what fellowship hath righteousness with unrighteousness?" He reminded them that they are the temple of God; and God had promised to dwell in them and be their God. He urged them to separate themselves from the unbelievers *(vs. 14-17).*

2 Cor. 7. Paul encouraged those whom he referred to as "dearly beloved" to cleanse themselves from all filthiness of the flesh and spirit. He rejoiced in the saints in Corinth and reported that he and his companions in Macedonia were experiencing persecution and trouble on every side. They were comforted by the arrival of Titus who brought them a positive report from Corinth. Paul's first epistle had caused the Corinthians distress, but they had "sorrowed to repentance." Such sorrow is godly sorrow: "godly sorrow worketh repentance to salvation not to be repented of: but the sorrow of the world worketh death" *(vs. 4-10).* They had repented of all their past wrongdoings. "In all things ye have approved yourselves to be clear in this matter." Their spirit had refreshed Titus and his inward affection for them had been greatly increased *(vs. 13-15).*

2 Cor. 8. Everything in the world was Christ's, yet he had nothing so far as this mortal life was concerned in order that we might be rich, i.e., receive eternal life *(v. 9).* Before we can do that which the Lord would have us do, we must first have a willing mind. The saints were encouraged to share their abundance with those in need. Those who have more should give more so that "there may be equality." People are not expected to give what they do not have *(vs. 12-15).* Paul commended Titus to them, indicating that Titus had the same love for them as he did. Titus, along with a couple of companions, was being sent back to the Corinthians. If anyone had questions concerning them, Paul assured them that Titus was "my partner and fellow-helper concerning you," and the other brethren "are the messengers of the churches, and the glory of Christ." He encouraged the saints to show their love to them *(vs. 16-24).*

2 Cor. 9. Paul admonished the Corinthians to give generously and cheerfully, saying, "He which soweth sparingly shall reap also sparingly; and he which soweth bountifully shall reap also bountifully. . . God loveth a cheerful giver" *(vs. 6-7).* Their contributions not only supply the wants of the saints, but also bring many blessings *(v. 12).* Paul praised God for his unspeakable gift *(i.e., the gift of the Holy Ghost in this life and eternal life in the next) (v. 15).*

2 Cor. 10. Paul indicated that in the war against sin—in the war to win men's souls to Christ—they don't use the kinds of weapons that mortals use: their weapons against evil come from God. Their weapons are geared to "casting down imaginations, and every high thing that exalteth itself against the knowledge of God, and bringing into captivity every thought to the obedience of Christ" *(vs. 3-5).* Paul and his companions will be the same in person as they appear to be in their writings. People who measure and compare themselves with themselves are not wise. We should measure ourselves against God's measuring rod *(vs. 11-13).* People should glory in the Lord. He who commends himself is not approved: only he whom the Lord commends *(10:17-18).*

2 Cor. 11. Paul expressed his "godly jealousy" over the Corinthians, "for I have espoused you to one husband, that I may present you as a chaste virgin to Christ." He urged them to maintain the simplicity that is in Christ and not be beguiled by

Satan's subtlety as Eve was, and not to be taken in by the false prophets sent forth by Satan *(vs. 2-4)*. He reminded them that he had never been a burden to them: when he was with them and had certain needs, those needs had been supplied by the brethren from Macedonia *(v. 9)*. Paul warned the saints that Satan can transform himself into an angel of light and can also transform his false apostles into appearing to be ministers of righteousness *(vs. 13-15)*. Paul compared himself to those who gloried after the flesh: he too was a Hebrew, an Israelite, of the seed of Abraham, and a minister of Christ. He enumerated the many sufferings he had experienced for preaching Christ and said, "If I must needs glory, I will glory of the things which concern mine infirmities. The God and Father of our Lord Jesus Christ, which is blessed for evermore, knoweth that I lie not" *(vs. 18-31)*. He recalled how, when the governor of Damascus had tried to capture him, he was protected and had escaped when he was lowered in a basket through a window by a wall *(vs. 32-33; See Acts 9:25)*.

2 Cor. 12. Paul testified that when he had been with them the signs of an apostle had been wrought among them *(i.e., visions, revelations, healing the sick, casting out devils, preaching and teaching and suffering in the cause of Christ, etc.)* just as much as they were among other branches of the church, and asked, "For what is it wherein ye were inferior to other churches, except it be that I myself was not burdensome to you?"*(vs. 12-13)*. He promised that when he came to them, he would still not be a burden to them. He didn't seek their possessions, he sought them. Children should not have to provide for their parents: parents should provide for their children. He said he would give both his means and his life for them. However, he observed that the more he did for them and the more he loved them, the less he was loved by them *(vs. 14-15)*. Paul also claimed that he didn't make any gain through the brethren he had sent to them, nor had those ministers made any gain. Their every action was for the edifying of the saints *(v. 19)*.

2 Cor. 13; Postscript. Paul told the saints in Corinth that "in the mouth of two or three witnesses shall every word be established" *(v. 1)* and rebuked them for seeking proof "of Christ speaking in me," *(v. 3)*. He said that when he came the third time, he would not spare them *(v. 2)* but would use sharpness, "according to the power which the Lord hath given me to edification, and not to destruction" *(v. 10)*. He challenged them to examine themselves as to their righteousness *(v. 5)* and encouraged them to be perfect—to be of good comfort, of one mind, and to live in peace *(v. 11)*. The second epistle to the Corinthians was written from Philippi, a city of Macedonia, and sent to them via Titus and Lucas *(Postscript)*.

CORNELIUS

Acts 10. **CORNELIUS** was a centurion, a very devout man who feared God—he and all his household. An angel appeared to him in a vision and told him his prayers and alms were received by God, and he instructed him to send to Joppa for Simon Peter. Simon Peter was lodging with Simon the tanner. He would tell Cornelius what he should do. Cornelius sent two of his household servants and a devout soldier to Joppa to find Peter *(vs. 1-8)*. While they were gone, Cornelius called together his kinsmen and friends. When Peter came, Cornelius fell down at his feet to worship him. Peter had him get up, and said he, too, was also a man. Cornelius told Peter that he had been fasting four days earlier when a man in bright clothing stood before him and told him to send his men to Joppa to get Peter. Now, he and his kinsmen and friends were assembled together to hear "all things that are commanded thee of God" *(vs. 24-33)*. As Peter preached to Cornelius and his people, the Holy Ghost fell on all of them. The followers of Christ who were with Peter *(they of the circumcision)* were astonished as they witnessed that God is no respecter of persons. Peter commanded them to be baptized in the name of the Lord *(vs. 34-48)*.

CORNELIUS' KINSMEN AND FRIENDS

Acts 10:24, 33, 44-48. **CORNELIUS' KINSMEN AND FRIENDS** were assembled with him when Cornelius had Peter teach them those things which God commanded Peter to speak. The Holy Ghost fell upon all those who heard the word. Peter instructed them to be baptized. Then, they all prayed that Peter would tarry longer with them.

CORNELIUS' SERVANTS AND DEVOUT SOLDIER

Acts 10:7, 17, 23. **CORNELIUS' SERVANTS AND DEVOUT SOLDIER** traveled to Joppa in search of Peter. An angel of the Lord had instructed Cornelius to get Peter and said Peter would tell him what he should do. The servants and soldier found Peter at the home of Simon the tanner. They explained their mission to him and had him accompany them back to Cæsarea.

CRESCENS

2 Tim. 4:10. **CRESCENS**, one of Paul's companions, left Paul in Rome and went to Galatia.

CRISPUS

Acts 18:8. **CRISPUS** was the chief ruler of the synagogue in Corinth. He and all his house believed on the Lord and were baptized. Many Corinthians believed and were baptized.

1 Cor. 1:14. Crispus was one of the small number of people baptized by Paul.

CYRENIUS

Luke 2:2. **CYRENIUS** was governor of Syria and was the one who initiated the practice of taxing the people.

NAMES THAT BEGIN WITH "D"

DAMARIS

Acts 17:34. **DAMARIS** was one of the women in Athens who believed Paul when he preached about being the offspring of God, a day of judgment and the resurrection.

DAMSEL, ANOTHER MAID, AND A GROUP THAT STOOD BY, A

Matt. 26:69-73; Mark 14:66-72; Luke 22:54-62. **A DAMSEL, ANOTHER MAID, AND A GROUP THAT STOOD BY** each approached Peter following the trial of Jesus and accused him of being one of Jesus' followers. Each time, Peter denied knowing Jesus. Immediately following his third denial, the cock crowed just as Jesus had said it would. *(Note: The record in Mark states that the cock first crowed after the first denial and crowed again after the third denial.) (See the entry for John 18 for an expanded and modified account.)*

John 18. When the officers took Jesus away to the high priest, Peter and another disciple followed. While the one disciple who knew the high priest followed the group indoors, Peter remained outside. When this disciple came to bring Peter inside, the damsel at the door asked Peter if he was not also one of Jesus' disciples. Peter said he was not. As the servants and officers warmed themselves beside a fire, Peter stood with them *(vs. 15-18).* When these men asked if Peter was not also one of Jesus' disciples, Peter again denied it. One of the servants of the high priest, whose relative had had his ear cut off by Peter, also asked Peter if he had not been in the garden with Jesus. For the third time, Peter denied it. "And immediately the cock crew" *(vs. 25-27).*

DAMSEL POSSESSED WITH A SPIRIT OF DIVINATION, A

Acts 16:16-23. **A DAMSEL POSSESSED WITH A SPIRIT OF DIVINATION** brought her masters much gain by her soothsaying. However, when she followed Paul around for several days, he finally commanded the spirit of divination to come out of her in the name of Jesus Christ. When she could no longer provide her masters with gain, they had Paul and Silas brought before the magistrates. The magistrates beat Paul and Silas and cast them into prison.

DAUGHTER OF A WOMAN FROM CANAAN, THE

Matt. 15:22-28; Mark 7:25-30. **THE DAUGHTER OF A WOMAN FROM CANAAN** had an unclean spirit possessing her. The woman, who was a Greek, a Syrophenician by nation, asked Jesus to cast the devil out of her daughter. Jesus responded that the children of the kingdom should first be cared for: "for it is not meet to take the children's bread, and to cast it unto the dogs" *(i.e., give that which belongs to the children of the kingdom of God to those who are unworthy).* Her response was that the dogs under the table eat of the children's crumbs. Because of her response, Jesus told her to go her way and that the devil was gone from out of her daughter, and it was so.

DAUGHTER OF HERODIAS (Salome (1))

Matt. 14:6-11; Mark 6:22-28. The **DAUGHTER OF HERODIAS** danced before Herod for his birthday and pleased him. In return, Herod promised to give her whatever she wanted. She asked for John the Baptist's head *(as counseled by her mother).* Her request was granted. John was beheaded in prison and his head was given to her in a charger. She, in turn, gave it to her mother. *(Note: The EB, vol. VIII, p. 816, states that according to the Jewish historian Josephus, the daughter of Herodias, unnamed in the NT, was* ***Salome****.)*

DEAD SON OF A WIDOW WOMAN, THE

Luke 7:11-18. **THE DEAD SON OF A WIDOW WOMAN**, her only son, was restored to life by Jesus who had compassion on the mother, saying, "Young man, I say unto thee, Arise." And he did.

DEAF MAN WITH SPEECH IMPEDIMENT, A

Mark 7:32-35. **A DEAF MAN WITH A SPEECH IMPEDIMENT** was brought to Jesus. Jesus healed both his ears and his speech impediment.

DEMAS

Col. 4:14. **DEMAS** was a colleague of Paul's in Rome. He sent his greetings, along with Paul and others, in Paul's epistle to the Colossians.

2 Tim. 4:10. Demas forsook Paul and went to Thessalonica because he "loved this present world" more than the things of Christ.

Philem. 1:24. Demas and other fellow laborers with Paul sent their salutations to Philemon along with Paul.

DEMETRIUS (1)

Acts 19:24-41. **DEMETRIUS** was a silversmith in Ephesus. He rallied a group of craftsmen who made their living making silver shrines unto Diana; and they raised the people up against Paul (saying not only their craft was at stake but also the worship of Diana was at stake). Thus, the people caught Gaius and Aristarchus, Paul's companions who were of Macedonia, and rushed them into the theatre. Paul's other associates discouraged him from entering the theatre. The town clerk calmed the people down and talked to them about the proper legal recourse and said that if Demetrius and the craftsmen with him had a matter against any man, they should use a legal process. He then dismissed the assembly.

DEMETRIUS (2)

3 Jn. 1:12. **DEMETRIUS**, John wrote to Gaius, had a good report of all men and of the truth, which truth John and his colleagues also bore record.

THE DEVIL, Satan, Lucifer, etc.

Matt. 4. **THE DEVIL** is known by many names: **Lucifer, son of the morning** *(Isa. 14:12);* **the tempter** *(Matt. 4:3);* **prince of this world** *(John 12:31);* **ser-**

pent *(2 Cor. 11:3);* **perdition** *(2 Thes. 2:3);* **dragon** *(Rev. 12:7);* **Satan** *(Rev. 12:9).* After Jesus had fasted 40 days and 40 nights in the wilderness, the devil tried to tempt Jesus by challenging him to change stones into bread *(v. 3).* When Jesus was set upon the pinnacle of the temple, the devil tried to tempt him by taunting that if he were the Son of God, he could cast himself down and the angels would bear him up *(v. 6).* When Jesus was taken up into a high mountain, the devil came and showed him all the kingdoms and glory of the world and offered them to Jesus if Jesus would fall down and worship him *(v. 9).* Jesus rebuffed him each time; and, finally, the devil left him *(v. 11).*

Mark. 1:13. Following Jesus' baptism, he was driven by the Spirit into the wilderness where he stayed for forty days to be tempted of Satan.

Luke 22:3-4. Satan entered into Judas Iscariot; and Judas covenanted with the chief priests to betray Jesus.

John 13:2, 27. Satan put it into the heart of Judas Iscariot to betray Jesus.

2 Thes. 2:3, 8-12. In Paul's second epistle to the Thessalonians, he described some of Satan's traits. Before the second coming of Christ, he will be revealed, "that man of sin . . . the son of perdition." Between Christ's first ministry upon the earth and his Second Coming, there will be a great apostasy, a falling away, because of the works of Satan. Paul referred to Satan as, "Wicked;" he has power to imitate the truth with signs and lying wonders. He leads people astray with all deceivableness of unrighteousness. Those who follow Satan will be damned.

1 Jn. 3:8. The devil sinned from the beginning. Those who commit sin are of the devil. Cain was of the devil and killed his brother because his own works were evil and his brother's were righteous.

1 Jn. 5:18. Satan cannot touch those who keep the commandments and are begotten of God.

Jude 1:9. Satan disputed with Michael the archangel over the body of Moses.

Rev. 2:9. In the Lord's revelation to John, he condemned those who claimed to be Jews but were actually of the synagogue of Satan.

Rev. 3:9. The Lord said he would make those who say they are Jews and are not, "but do lie," to be of the synagogue of Satan.

Rev. 12:7-9. Satan and his angels fought against Michael, the archangel, and his angels in a war in heaven. Michael and his angels prevailed against Satan and his angels. Satan was cast out into the earth, and his angels, also.

Rev. 20. John saw that Satan was bound with chains and then cast into the bottomless pit and locked up. A seal was set upon him so that he could not deceive the nations until 1,000 years had passed, after which time he would be loosed again for a season *(vs. 1-3).* After the 1,000 years, Satan will be loosed to deceive the nations which are in the four corners of the earth, Gog and Magog, to gather them together to battle. John saw them compassed about the camp of the saints and the beloved city. God sent fire down from heaven and devoured them. "The devil that deceived them was cast into the lake of fire and brimstone, where the beast and the false prophet are, and shall be tormented day and night for ever and ever" *(vs. 7-10).*

DIANA, Artemis

Acts 19:24-28. **DIANA** was a goddess in Ephesus unto whom a temple had been built. When Paul preached in Ephesus, Demetrius and other silversmiths rallied the people against Paul, stressing that Diana would be despised and her magnificence destroyed. *(The "Ephesians called her **Artemis** and regarded her as the source of the fruitful and nurturing powers of nature. The image in the temple, said to have fallen from heaven, represented her with many breasts. The lower part of the figure was swathed like a mummy" (BD).)*

DIDYMUS (See Thomas)

DIONYSIUS

Acts 17:34. **DIONYSIUS** the Areopagite was one of the men in Athens who believed Paul when he preached about being the offspring of God, a day of judgment and the resurrection.

DIOTREPHES

3 Jn. 1:9-10. **DIOTREPHES** was an apostate member of the church. John, in his epistle to Gaius, indicated that Diotrephes loved to have preeminence among the members and refused to receive the apostles and other brethren, casting out those who would receive them. John said when he arrived he would remember Diotrephes' deeds against the church leaders.

DRAGON, Satan (See Devil)

DRUSILLA

Acts 24:24. **DRUSILLA** was the wife of Felix, the governor. She was a Jewess. She was with Felix when Felix sent for Paul and had him discuss the matter of faith in Christ. *(Drusilla was the third wife of Felix. She had deserted her husband, King Aziz of Emessa, to marry him. She was Herod Agrippa I's youngest daughter, the sister of Bernice, and the granddaughter of Herod the Great. When she was a very young woman, she had heard Paul speak. Drusilla and Felix's son, Agrippa, died in an eruption of Vesuvius (BD).)*

DUMB MAN POSSESSED WITH A DEVIL, A

Matt. 9:32-35. **A DUMB MAN POSSESSED WITH A DEVIL** was brought to Jesus. Jesus cast the devil out.

NAMES THAT BEGIN WITH "E"

ELDERS OF THE CHURCH IN EPHESUS

Acts 20:17-38. The **ELDERS OF THE CHURCH IN EPHESUS** were summoned to Miletus by Paul as Paul prepared to return to Jerusalem for the day of Pentecost. He reviewed his righteous ministry among them and said he would not see them again. He cautioned them to keep a careful watch on the church because there would be "grievous wolves" who would enter into their midst and try to destroy the flock. There would even be those from among their own group who would speak perverse things and seek to draw away disciples to themselves. After Paul finished speaking, they all kneeled together and prayed. They wept and kissed him, and then accompanied him to the ship.

ELECT LADY AND HER CHILDREN, THE

2 Jn. 1:1, 13. **THE ELECT LADY AND HER CHILDREN** to whom John addressed his second epistle are not identified; nor do we have any indication as to who her elect sister and her elect sister's children are. However, John rejoiced in the fact that the children were walking in truth, and he counseled them to continue keeping the commandment to love one another. He also cautioned them against antichrists who would come into their midst and instructed them not to welcome them into their homes.

ELIAS

(Note: According to the BD, the name ***ELIAS*** *is used in several different ways in the scriptures. It may refer to John the Baptist. It is also the Greek form of Elijah (which is the Hebrew form) and may refer to the prophet Elijah. It is also the title given to someone who is a forerunner and to others who have been given specific missions or restorative functions that they are to fulfill, i.e., John the Revelator; Noah, i.e., Gabriel. There was also a man named Elias who lived in the days of Abraham.)*

ELIAS (John the Baptist)

Matt. 11:14. **ELIAS**, as mentioned in this verse, refers to **John the Baptist**, who was a forerunner of Christ, preparing the way for the Savior.

Matt. 17:9-14 (JST); Mark 9:11-13. When Jesus, Peter, James and John came down from the mount of Transfiguration, Jesus spoke of Elias (John the Baptist), the messenger, who would come before him and prepare the way. Earlier, on the mount, they had seen another Elias (the prophet Elijah) along with Moses *(vs. 3-4, 10-11; Mark 9:4-5.)*

Luke 1:17. Zacharias was told that his son John would go before the Lord preaching in the spirit and power of Elias (Elijah), to turn the hearts of the fathers to their children.

John 1:19-28 (JST). Elias in *vs. 21-22* refers to John the Baptist as one who will come before and prepare the way of Christ. Elias in *v. 28* refers to Christ as the prophet whose shoe's latchets John said he was not worthy to unloose. Elias, in *verses 22 and 26* refers to Elijah who will restore all things.

ELIAS (Elijah)

Matt. 16:13-14; 17:3-4, 10-11, 11-14 (JST); Mark 6:15-16; 8:27-28; 9:4-5, 11-13; Luke 1:17; 4:25- 26; 9:7-9, 30, 33; John 1:19-28 (JST); James 5:17-18. **ELIAS**, as mentioned in these verses, refers to the prophet **Elijah**. See his entry under People of the Old Testament referred to in the New Testament in Appendix A.

ELIAS (Jesus Christ)

John 1:19-28 (JST). **ELIAS** in *v. 28* refers to **Christ** as the prophet whose shoe's latchets John said he was not worthy to unloose. Elias in *vs. 21-22* refers to John the Baptist as one who will come before and prepare the way of Christ. Elias in *verses 22 and 26* refers to Elijah who will restore all things.

ELIAS (during Abraham's day)

Rev. 7:2. **ELIAS**, in this verse, refers to the Elias who lived during Abraham's day. See his entry under People of the Old Testament referred to in the New Testament in Appendix A.

ELISABETH

Luke 1: 5-13, 36-44, 57-63. **ELISABETH** was the wife of Zacharias and the mother of John the Baptist. Elisabeth was barren and well stricken in years when the angel Gabriel told Zacharias that she would conceive and bear a son. They were to name him John. Mary was informed by an angel that her cousin Elisabeth was with child. She went to her. When she entered the house of Zacharias and saluted Elisabeth, the baby leaped in Elisabeth's womb and Elisabeth was filled with the Holy Ghost. Elisabeth recognized Mary as the "mother of my Lord." Elisabeth delivered the baby and when he was eight days old they came to circumcise him. They wanted to name him Zacharias after his father. Elisabeth said his name was to be John. They said that was not a family name and asked Zacharias what they should name him. Zacharias confirmed that the baby was to be named John. *("Elisabeth was of the family of Aaron" (BD).)*

EPÆNETUS

Rom. 16:5. **EPÆNETUS** was the first fruits of Achaia unto Christ. Paul asked the saints in Rome to salute Epænetus, his well-beloved.

EPAPHRAS

Col. 1. 7-8. **EPAPHRAS**, a Colossian, was a fellow servant with Paul, and a faithful minister of Christ unto the Colossians. He had conveyed their "love in the Spirit" to Paul. *(Epaphras is an abbreviated form of Epaphroditus. He, and possibly Timotheus, were the first to preach Christianity to the Colossians (BD).)*

Col. 4:12-13. Epaphras was one of the Colossians. He sent his greetings from Rome, along with Paul and others, in Paul's epistle to the Colossians. While in Rome, Paul said Epaphras always prayed for them fervently that they would be faithful. Paul testified of Epaphras' zeal for them and for those in Laodicea and Hierapolis.

Philem. 1:23. Epaphras sent greetings to Philemon along with Paul and several others.

Philip. 2:25-30. Epaphroditus was, in Paul's words, "my brother, and companion in labour, and fellowsoldier" and, bearing gifts from the Philippians, visited Paul in prison in Rome. While there, he became very ill, nigh unto death. The saints in Philippi heard about how ill he was and became very concerned. He was better now, and Paul sent his epistle to the Philippians via Epaphroditus hoping his return to Philippi would alleviate the saints' concerns.

EPHESIANS

Eph. 1. **EPHESIANS** were citizens of Ephesus, the capital of the Roman province of Asia and a great commercial center. It was three miles from the sea and was an important business center. *(See "Ephesus" in the BD.)* Paul wrote to the saints in Ephesus "and to the faithful in Christ." He prayed they would receive peace and grace from God the Father and from Jesus Christ *(vs. 1-3).* He reminded the Ephesians that the followers of Christ were foreordained before coming to this earth, "before the foundations of the world," to receive the gospel. In the dispensation of the fulness of times *(i.e., in the latter days),* all things will be gathered together in one, "all things in Christ, both which are in heaven, and which are on earth" *(vs. 4-12).* The saints are sealed with the Holy Spirit of promise *(v. 13).* Paul rejoiced in the knowledge that the Ephesian saints were faithful in the Lord Jesus Christ and had love for all the saints. He mentioned them in his prayers, praying that they would receive the spirit of wisdom and revelation so they could have knowledge of God *(vs. 15-19).* God the Father raised Christ from the dead and set him at his own right hand and placed him over all things *(vs. 20-23).*

Eph. 2. Paul taught the Ephesians that we are saved by grace through faith, and not of ourselves: it is a gift of God *(vs. 5, 8).* We are the workmanship of God, created in Christ, unto good works. We were foreordained to walk in good works before coming to earth *(v. 10).* Both Jew and Gentile are reconciled unto God and brought together by the blood of Christ. Both have access through one Spirit unto the Father *(vs. 11-18).* The church is built upon the foundation of apostles and prophets. Jesus Christ is the chief cornerstone *(v. 20).*

Eph. 3. Paul pointed out to the Ephesians that in ages past people did not understand as much as they did now regarding the fact that the gospel was to be preached to the Gentiles as well as to the Jews; that the Gentiles were to be "fellow heirs, and of the same body, and partakers of his promise in Christ by the gospel" *(vs. 5-6).* He prayed that they would be able to comprehend and know the magnitude of Christ's love *(vs. 17- 19).*

Eph. 4. Paul admonished the Ephesians to be unified, forbearing one another in love. There is just one Spirit, one Lord, one faith, one baptism, one God and Father over all *(vs. 2-6).* Everyone is given grace through the gift of Christ *(v. 7).* When Christ was resurrected, he freed all men from the grave; i.e., "he led captivity captive" *(v. 8).* Christ ascended above all heavens that he might fulfill all things *(v. 10).* Paul reminded the Ephesians that Christ established his church with specific offices with specific duties; i.e., apostles, prophets, evangelists, pastors and teachers; for the perfecting of the saints, the work of the ministry, and for the edification of the members of the church. This organization would exist until all come to a unity of the faith and a knowledge of the Son of God, "unto a perfect man, unto the measure of the stature of the fulness of Christ" *(vs. 11-13).* Having gained a knowledge of truth, Paul told the Ephesians they would no longer be as little children tossed to and fro by false doctrines or men's craftiness. He encouraged them to walk not as other Gentiles but to put off the former self, the corrupt man, and to be renewed in the spirit "of your mind;" and to put on the new man which was created in righteousness and true holiness *(vs. 14-24).* He counseled them regarding wrath, stealing, corrupt communications; and cautioned them not to grieve the holy Spirit of God whereby they were sealed unto the day of redemption. They were admonished to be kind and forgiving one to another just as "God for Christ's sake hath forgiven you" *(vs. 25-32).*

Eph. 5. Paul counseled the Ephesians to walk in love and to avoid all uncleanness, covetousness, filthiness, foolish talking, etc., for no unclean thing can have an inheritance in the kingdom of Christ and of God *(vs. 1-7).* He reminded them that while in times past they had walked in darkness, now they walked in light. He cautioned them not to have fellowship with the works of darkness and not to become drunk with wine *(vs. 8-18).* He gave them some positive advice: to speak to each other in psalms, hymns and spiritual songs, to always give thanks to God in the name of Jesus Christ, and to submit "yourselves one to another in the fear of God" *(vs. 19-21).* He encouraged wives to submit themselves to their own husbands as unto the Lord. He instructed husbands to love their wives even as Christ loved the church and gave himself for it. Just as we become one with Christ when we become members of his church, a man and his wife also become one flesh. Husbands were told to love their wives even as they loved their own bodies. He again reminded wives to reverence their husbands *(vs. 22-33).*

Eph. 6. Paul admonished children to honor their parents and reminded them that this is the first commandment with a promise: "That it may be well with thee, and thou mayest live long on the earth." Fathers were counseled not to provoke their children to wrath, but to bring them up in the nurture and admonition of the Lord *(vs. 1-4).* Servants were also counseled to be obedient to their masters; and masters were told to treat their servants kindly: the Lord will judge both masters and servants by the same law *(vs. 5-9).* The saints were told to put on the whole armor of God so they could withstand the evil day. They were to put on the breastplate of righteousness; shod their feet with the gospel of peace; take the shield of faith, the helmet of salvation and the sword of the Spirit, i.e., the word of God *(vs. 11-17). (Paul wrote his epistle to the Ephesians from Rome and sent it to them by Tychicus.)*

ERASTUS (1)

Acts 19:22. **ERASTUS** was one of those who ministered unto Paul in Asia. Paul sent him and Timotheus (Timothy) into Macedonia while he, himself, remained in Asia for a season.

2 Tim. 4:20. Erastus, Paul wrote Timothy, abode at Corinth.

ERASTUS (2)

Rom. 16:23. **ERASTUS** was the chamberlain of the city, the public treasurer at Corinth. He was a Christian convert and joined Paul in saluting the saints in Rome. *(Note: It is possible that Erastus (1) and (2) are one and the same.)*

EUBULUS

2 Tim. 4:21. **EUBULUS** joined Paul and all the brethren in sending greetings to Timothy.

EUNICE (See Timotheus', i.e., Timothy's, Mother)

EUNUCH OF ETHIOPIA, A

Acts 8:27-39. **A EUNUCH OF ETHIOPIA**, who had great authority under Candace queen of the Ethiopians and was in charge of all her treasure, had gone to Jerusalem to worship. He was returning to Ethiopia in his chariot reading Esaias (Isaiah) when an angel of the Lord instructed the apostle Philip to join up with him. Philip explained the scriptural passage to the eunuch and preached unto him Christ. The eunuch believed and was baptized. When he came up out of the water, the Spirit of the Lord caught away Philip, and the eunuch saw him no more.

EUODIAS

Philip. 4:2. **EUODIAS** was one of the Philippians Paul beseeched to be of the same mind in the Lord as he.

EUTYCHUS

Acts 20:9-12. **EUTYCHUS** was a young man in Troas, a disciple of Christ, who fell asleep in an upper window while Paul was giving and extensive talk. He fell from the third loft to his death. However, Paul embraced him and he was restored to life.

NAMES THAT BEGIN WITH "F"

FATHER OF PUBLIUS, THE

Acts 27:8. **THE FATHER OF PUBLIUS** *(Publius was the chief man of the island of Melita),* was sick of a fever and of a bloody flux. Paul prayed and laid his hands upon him and he was healed.

FELIX

Acts 23:24-35. **FELIX** was the governor. Claudius Lysias, the chief captain, had his soldiers and spear men escort Paul safely to him when he learned that 40 Jews were plotting to kill Paul and wrote a letter of explanation to Felix. After Felix read the letter, he asked Paul of what province he was. When he learned that he was of Cilicia, he agreed to listen to Paul "when thine accusers are also come." He then had Paul kept in Herod's judgment hall.

Acts 24. Felix heard the complaints of Ananias the high priest, the elders and the Jews against Paul. Their spokesman was an orator by the name of Tertullus. After hearing Paul's accusers, Felix listened to Paul's self-defense. After hearing both sides, he deferred making a judgment until he could hear from Lysias, the chief captain *(vs. 1-22).* He commanded a centurion to keep Paul but to let him have his liberty and to not deny his association with his acquaintances *(v. 23).* He sent for Paul and had him discuss his faith with him and his wife Drusilla, a Jewess. When Paul spoke of righteousness, temperance and judgment to come, Felix trembled and sent Paul away, saying he would call for him again when he had "a convenient season." Because he hoped Paul would give him money so he would give him his freedom, he called for Paul "the oftener." Two years passed, and Felix, willing to please the Jews, left Paul bound when Porcius Festus succeeded him as procurator of Judæa *(vs. 24-27).*

FESTUS (See Porcius Festus)

FORTUNATUS

1 Cor. 16:17-18; Postscript. **FORTUNATUS**, Stephanas and Achaicus visited Paul and brought him information regarding the saints in Corinth for which Paul said he was glad, "for that which was lacking on your part they have supplied. For they have refreshed my spirit and yours." The first epistle from Paul in Philippi to the saints in Corinth was carried to them by Fortunatus, Stephanas, Achaicus and Timotheus.

NAMES THAT BEGIN WITH "G"

GABRIEL

Luke 1. **GABRIEL** [an Angel of the Lord], announced to Zacharias that his elderly wife would conceive and bear a son whom they were to name John. John would be great in the sight of the Lord and was not to drink wine nor strong drink. The child would be filled with the Holy Ghost even from his mother's womb *(vs. 11-15).* The angel said his name was Gabriel. Because Zacharias questioned how he would know that what he was told would really happen, the angel caused him to be dumb "until the day that these things shall be performed" *(vs. 19-20).* When Elisabeth was six months pregnant, Gabriel was sent from God to the virgin Mary to announce that she had found favor with God. The Holy Ghost would come upon her and she would conceive and bear a son whom she should name Jesus. The Holy Ghost would come upon her and the power of the Highest would overshadow her; therefore, the child would be called the Son of God *(vs. 26-35).* The angel also told her that her cousin Elisabeth was with child *(v. 36). (Note: He is identified by modern-day revelation as Noah. See DPJS, p. 38).*

GAIUS (1)

Acts 19:29-41. **GAIUS** was one of Paul's traveling companions. When Demetrius and his fellow craftsmen rallied the people against Paul, the people caught Gaius and Aristarchus and rushed them into the theatre. After the town clerk talked to the people about using appropriate legal channels, the crowds were dismissed. *(Note: The BD indicates there are four different people by the name of Gaius. However, it would appear that all references could refer to the same person.)*

GAIUS (2)

Acts 20:4. **GAIUS** of Derbe accompanied Paul into Asia, along with Sopater of Berea; Aristarchus and Secundus of the Thessalonians; Timotheus; and Tychicus and Trophimus of Asia.

GAIUS (3)

Rom. 16:23. **GAIUS** was Paul's host "and of the whole church." He, along with others, joined Paul in saluting the saints in Rome.

1 Cor. 1:14. Gaius was one of a small number of people baptized by Paul.

GAIUS (4)

3 Jn. 1. "The well-beloved **GAIUS**," was the one to whom John addressed his third epistle. He commended Gaius for walking in the truth and for his charity which was evident in the help he gave to both those in and out of the church *(vs. 1-6).* John referred to Diotrephes, who had apparently apostatized, and counseled Gaius not to follow evil, only that which is good *(vs. 9-11).* He informed Gaius that Demetrius had good report of all men and of the truth, of which John said he and his colleagues also bore record *(v. 12)*. He declined to write more and indicated that he hoped to see Gaius face to face shortly *(vs. 13-14)*.

GAIUS CÆSAR (i.e., Cæsar (3))

(Note: The BD indicates there were five Cæsars: (1) Augustus, 31 B.C. (see ***Cæsar Augustus****); (2) Tiberius, A.D. 14 (see* ***Tiberius Cæsar****); (3)* **CALIGULA**, *A.D. 37 (***GAIUS CÆSAR***); (4) Claudius, A.D. 41 (see* ***Claudius Cæsar****); (5) Nero, A.D. 54 (see* ***Nero****). (3)* ***Caligula's real name was Gaius Cæsar.*** *He was born Aug. 31, A.D. 12, in Antium, modern Anzio, Italy, and died Jan. 24, A.D. 41, in Rome. He was emperor from A.D. 37 to 41, following Tiberius.) (EB, vol II, p. 459.)*

GALATIANS

Gal. 1. **GALATIANS** were citizens of Galatia, a district in the center of Asia Minor. Some scholars believe that Paul's epistle to the Galatians was written to the people of the cities of Antioch, Iconium, Lystra, and Derbe which he visited on his first journey, and which they regard as being part of Galatia. *(See "Galatia" in the BD.)* Paul and the brethren with him sent greetings to the churches in Galatia. Paul testified that he was called to preach, not by man, but by Jesus Christ and God the Father *(vs. 1-2)*. Jesus Christ gave himself to deliver us from our sins *(vs. 4-5)*. Paul chastised those who had strayed from the church and were preaching false doctrine. Those who preach false doctrine are accursed. The gospel taught by Paul was not of men, but was received by revelation from Jesus Christ *(vs. 6-12)*. He reminded the Galatians of his own conversion and of his subsequent preaching in Arabia, Damascus, Jerusalem *(where he abode with Peter for 15 days)*, in the regions of Syria and Cilicia, and in Judæa *(where the people had heard that he who had once persecuted the church was now preaching the faith to those whom he had sought to destroy) (vs. 13-23)*.

Gal. 2. After preaching for 14 years, Paul, Barnabas and Titus went to Jerusalem where Paul met with the other brethren and reported what he was teaching and verified with them that what he was teaching was the same thing they were teaching *(vs. 1-10)*. Paul was not impressed with the status of the brethren who were leading the church in Jerusalem: they added nothing to what he already knew about the gospel. Furthermore, God "accepteth no man's person" *(v. 6)*. Paul's mission was to the Gentiles, the uncircumcised. Peter's mission was to the circumcised, to the Jews *(vs. 7-9)*. Paul withstood Peter regarding the law of Moses. It was fulfilled in Jesus Christ, but many of the Jews continued to perform Mosaic rituals, i.e., circumcision *(vs. 11-14)*. Man is not justified by the law, but by faith in Jesus Christ *(vs. 16-21)*.

Gal. 3. Paul chastised the Galatians for rejecting the teachings of Christ and reverting back to the law of Moses. He admonished them regarding the works of the law versus faith in Jesus Christ. He reminded them that those who ministered among them and worked miracles did so through faith, not through the workings of the law *(vs. 1-5)*. All who believe and accept Christ become the children of Abraham and are heirs to the blessings promised to Abraham through his seed *(vs. 7-9)*. The law is not of faith and justifieth no man; the just shall live by faith *(vs. 11-12)*. Paul explained that the promise to Abraham that "in thy seed shall all nations of the earth be blessed" *(Gen. 22:18)* referred to one seed (not seeds), and that Christ was the seed through whom all nations would be blessed *(v. 16)*. The law of Moses was given as a schoolmaster to bring the children of Israel unto Christ because they had rejected the gospel of Jesus Christ which had been given to Moses. Everyone who accepts Christ and is baptized unto Christ becomes Abraham's seed and heir to the promise given him. All are equal. All are one in Jesus Christ *(vs. 24-29)*.

Gal. 4. As Paul tried to bring the Galatians back to Christ. He reminded them that a child, even though he is an heir, is no different from a servant, while he is under the control of tutors and governors until the time appointed by his father. Likewise, people governed under the law of Moses are in bondage to the elements of the world. People governed under the gospel of Jesus Christ become adopted children of God and are no more servants but sons, "and if a son, then an heir of God through Christ" *(vs. 1-7)*. He questioned why they would want to be under bondage to the weak and beggarly elements of the world by turning away from Christ *(vs. 8-9)*. He reminded them that they had joyously accepted the truth at one time and wondered why they now desired to be under the law of Moses *(vs. 11-21)*. Paul compared Abraham's two sons, Ishmael and Isaac, to the two different covenants: Ishmael, son of Agar (Hagar) to being under bondage, i.e., the law of Moses received on Mount Sinai; and Isaac, born of promise. The bondwoman (Hagar) and her son (Ishmael) were cast out. They were not to be heirs with the son of the freewoman. Paul reminded them that we are children of the freewoman, not the bondwoman *(vs. 22-31)*.

Gal. 5. Paul reminded the Galatians that neither circumcision nor uncircumcision availeth anything, only faith in Jesus Christ, which "worketh love" *(vs. 1-6)*. Paul admonished them to serve one another and to "love thy neighbor as thyself" *(vs. 13-14)*. He counseled them not to be led by the works of the flesh, which works include adultery, fornication, uncleanness, lasciviousness, idolatry, witchcraft, hatred, variance, emulations, wrath, strife, seditions, heresies, envyings, murders, drunkenness, revellings, etc.," but to be led by the fruit of the Spirit, which fruit includes love, joy, peace, longsuffering, gentleness, goodness, faith, meekness, temperance" *(vs. 16-23)*.

Gal. 6. Paul admonished the Galatians to bear one another's burdens *(v. 2)*. Men should evaluate their own works and, if worthy, can then rejoice in their own good works *(v. 4)*. Men are accountable for their own sins *(v. 5)*. The student and the teacher should communicate with each other to their mutual growth and edification *(v. 6)*. God will not be mocked. Whatsoever a man soweth, he will also reap: if a man soweth to his flesh, he shall reap corruption; if to the Spirit, he will reap life everlasting *(vs. 7-8)*. Paul counseled them not to be weary in well doing and to do good unto all men, especially unto those who are of the household of faith *(vs. 9-10)*. *(Paul wrote this epistle to the Galatians from Rome.)*

GALLIO

Acts 18:12-16, 17. **GALLIO** was the deputy of Achaia. The Jews rose against Paul and took him before the judgment seat. Gallio wouldn't intervene and said their complaint against Paul was not an issue that needed to come before him, and he "drave them from the judgment seat." The Greeks beat Sosthenes, the chief ruler of the synagogue, before the judgment seat, but Gallio still refused to intervene in Jewish religious disputes.

GAMALIEL

Acts 5:34-40. **GAMALIEL** was a doctor of the law, a Pharisee, and a member of the council that sat in judgment of the apostles. He admonished the members of the council to be careful in their actions and reminded them that earlier examples involving Theudas and Judas of Galilee showed that time would reveal the truth or the falseness of what was being taught. "For if this counsel or this work be of men, it will come to nought: but if it be of God, ye cannot overthrow it; lest haply ye be found even to fight against God."

Acts 22:3. Gamaliel was Saul's instructor and mentor. Saul was taught "according to the perfect manner of the law of the fathers, and was zealous toward God . . . and I persecuted this way unto the death, binding and delivering into prisons both men and women," Paul explained to the people in Jerusalem as he told of his conversion.

GOVERNOR OF DAMASCUS

2 Cor. 11:32-33. The **GOVERNOR OF DAMASCUS**, under Aretas the king, set up a garrison around the city in order to apprehend Paul. However, Paul escaped by being lowered in a basket through a window near a wall.

GRECIANS/GREEKS

John 12:20. **CERTAIN GREEKS** came to the feast of the Passover and told Philip they desired to see Jesus. *(Note: Greeks are men who are Greek by lineage. **GRECIANS**, i.e., Hellenists, are those who speak Greek because of living among those who are Greek.)*

Acts 6:1. The Grecians murmured against the disciples for spending all their time in ministering the gospel and not attending to their families.

Acts 9:29. The Grecians sought to slay Saul, Barnabus told his fellow disciples as he sought to allay their fears of Saul, but Saul had seen the risen Lord on the road to Damascus and preached boldly in Damascus in the name of Jesus.

Acts 11:20. Upon the persecution of Stephen, Christ's ministers were scattered abroad. Some were of Cyprus and Cyrene and went to Antioch and preached to the Grecians there, where they met with much success. *(Note: In this instance they were Greeks, not Grecians (BD).)*

Acts 14:1. A great multitude of Greeks believed when Paul and Barnabas taught in the synagogue of the Jews in Iconium.

NAMES THAT BEGIN WITH "H"

HEAVENLY FATHER

Matt. 3:17; Mark 1:11. **HEAVENLY FATHER** spoke from heaven when Jesus came up out of the waters of baptism and declared, "This is [Thou art] my beloved Son, in whom I am well pleased." *(Note: Heavenly Father is the supreme Governor of the Universe and the Father of mankind. See God in the BD. He is the literal father of our spirits as well as the father of Jesus Christ, his Only Begotten in the flesh.)*

Matt.6:9, 14-15, 18. Jesus taught his followers to pray to a Father who is in heaven, who is the Father of us all, i.e., "Our Father which art in heaven." If we forgive men their trespasses, Heavenly Father will forgive ours. If we don't forgive others, he won't forgive us either. That which we do unto the Father in secret, our Father will reward openly.

Matt. 11:25-27. Heavenly Father is Lord over heaven and earth. All things are delivered unto Jesus by the Father. The Son reveals the Father.

Matt. 17:5. When Peter, James and John were on the mount of transfiguration with Jesus, Heavenly Father acknowledged that Jesus was his son when he spoke out of a cloud, saying, "This is my beloved Son, in whom I am well pleased; hear ye him."

Luke 3:38. The lineage of God the Father to Jesus Christ through David's son Nathan is given *(vs. 23- 38).*

1 Cor. 15:24-28. The kingdom will be delivered to the Father by the Son at the end after he has subdued all things and "put all enemies under his feet." The Father is excepted when speaking of all things being put under the feet of the Savior, "But when he saith all things are put under him, it is manifest that he is excepted, which did put all things under him. And when all things shall be subdued unto him, then shall the Son also himself be subject unto him that put all things under him, that God may be all in all."

Eph. 1:3, 20. God is the Father of the Lord Jesus Christ. He wrought his power in Jesus Christ. He raised Christ from the dead. *(See Heb. 13:20-21.)*

1 Thes. 3:11. Paul testified to the Thessalonians that God the Father and the Lord Jesus Christ direct his way unto them.

Heb. 13:20-21. Paul refers to God the Father as the God of peace. He brought the Lord Jesus from the dead. His blessings are effected upon people through Jesus Christ. *(See Eph. 1:20.)*

1 Jn. 1:3. The righteous shall have fellowship with the Father and with his Son Jesus Christ.

1 Jn. 2:1. Our advocate with the Father is Jesus Christ.

1 Jn. 4:9-10, 14. "God sent his only Begotten Son into the world, that we might live through him." God so loved us that he sent his Son to atone for our sins—to be the Savior of the world.

1 Jn. 5:16-20. To know God the Father and his Son Jesus Christ is eternal life.

HEBREWS

Heb. 1. **HEBREWS**. *("Hebrew" refers to a member of or a descendant from one of a group of tribes of the northern branch of the Semites that includes the Israelites, Ammonites, Moabites, and Edomites; especially, the Israelites (WTNID).)* Paul addressed this epistle to his Hebrew brethren. He testified that Christ, the Son of God, was appointed heir of all thing and is in the express image of God the Father. After purging our sins, he sat down on the right hand side of the Father. He is greater than the angels. God the Father never referred to the angels as his Son, but of Christ, the Father said, "Thou art my Son, this day have I begotten thee" *(vs. 2-5).* The angels were instructed to worship Christ *(v. 6).* The earth and the heavens are the works of Christ's own hands *(v. 10).* While the earth and the heavens shall eventually perish, Christ is the same and shall not change *(v. 12).* Christ is higher than the angels: none of them was invited to sit on the right hand of the Father. They are ministering spirits sent forth to minister for them who shall be heirs of salvation *(vs. 13- 14).*

Heb. 2. The law of Moses included a strict code of consequences for various actions: "Every transgression and disobedience received a just recompense of reward" *(v. 2).* If our ancient forefathers were condemned for disobeying the law of Moses, which came from angels through Moses, our condemnation will be even greater for disregarding the laws given by Christ, whose truths were evidenced by signs, wonders, miracles, gifts of the Holy Ghost and attested to by those who heard the Lord *(vs. 3-4).* In order for us to escape the consequences of all our sins and be able to escape the finality of death, be resurrected and inherit eternal life, it was necessary that Christ, "by the grace of God should taste death for every man. For it became him, for whom are all things, and by whom are all things, in bringing many sons unto glory, to make the captain of their salvation perfect through sufferings" *(vs. 9-10).* Those who accept Christ and are sanctified are one with Christ, who sanctifieth *(v. 11).* Through his death and resurrection, Christ destroyed Satan's power of death *(v. 14).* Christ understands temptation. He became like his brethren in all things so he could be a merciful and faithful high priest and could make reconciliation for the sins of the people *(vs. 17-18).*

Heb. 3. Paul referred to Christ as the Apostle and High Priest of our profession, and compared Moses and the children of Israel with Christ and his followers. Moses built a house and was faithful over his house as a servant, "as a testimony of those things which were to be spoken after." Christ, who built all things, was faithful as a son over his house, whose house are those who follow Christ. Christ is greater than Moses, just as the builder of a house is greater than the house *(vs. 1-6).* Paul admonished the Hebrews not to harden their hearts as the children of Israel did those forty years they wandered in the desert. They needed to exhort one another daily so they would remain steadfast and not develop an evil heart of disbelief. Those who remain steadfast are made partakers of Christ *(vs. 8-14).* Paul acknowledged that not all of those who left Egypt with Moses provoked the Lord and reaped his anger, but those who did provoke the Lord were not permitted to enter the promised land because of their unbelief *(vs. 16-19).*

Heb. 4. Paul continued to stress the need to remain steadfast lest they be denied the right to enter into the Lord's rest as promised to the faithful. The children of Israel under Moses rejected the gospel when it was offered to them and "the word preached did not profit them, not being mixed with faith in them that heard it" *(vs. 1-2)*. Saints, those who follow Christ, enter into the rest of the Lord *(v. 3)*. Paul admonished the Hebrews to labor so they could enter into the rest of the Lord *(v. 11)*. The word of God is quick and powerful, sharper than a two-edged sword. Nothing is hidden from the Lord *(vs. 12-13)*. They should hold fast to their profession just as Christ, the great high priest, did *(v. 14)*. Christ was tempted "in all points" like we are, yet he was without sin. Therefore, we ought to come boldly unto his throne of grace that we might obtain mercy and find grace to help in time of need *(vs. 15-16)*.

Heb 5. Ministers must be called of God and be ordained as was Aaron. No one is take that honor unto himself. Even Christ, the great high priest, did not place that honor upon himself, but God the Father said to him, "Thou art my Son, today have I begotten thee." The Father also said, "Thou art a priest for ever after the order of Melchisedec" *(vs. 1-6, 10)*. We learn through experience. Even Christ learned obedience by the things he suffered *(v. 8)*. Being perfect, Christ became the author of eternal salvation unto all who obey him *(v. 9)*. Paul chastised the leaders because at a time when they should be teaching the deeper aspects of the gospel *(i.e., the meat of the gospel)* and not just the simple things *(i.e., the milk of the gospel)*, they, themselves, were having to be taught the simple things all over again. They needed to become skillful in the word so they could discern both good and evil *(vs. 11-14)*.

Heb. 6. Paul encouraged the Hebrews to press on unto perfection. The principles of the doctrine include: faith, repentance, baptism, the laying on of hands *(for the gift of the Holy Ghost)*, resurrection of the dead, and the doctrine of eternal judgment *(vs. 1-2)*. Those who in this life gain a true knowledge of the divinity of Christ through revelation from the Holy Ghost, and then reject Christ—and crucify him to themselves, i.e., commit murder by agreeing to the Lord's death all over again—and put him to an open shame, will receive no forgiveness *(vs. 4-6)*. Better things await the faithful. Those who are not slothful, but are faithful and patient, shall inherit the promises *(of eternal life) (vs. 9, 12)*. God made promises to Abraham that were extended to his posterity and all who through faith and obedience become heirs of Abraham *(v. 13)*. The promise God made to Abraham was the hope and promise of eternal life, into which Jesus Christ, the high priest after the order of Melchizedek, has already entered *(vs. 18-20)*.

Heb. 7. Melchizedek was ordained a high priest after the order of the Son of God. He was called king of Salem, King of righteousness, King of peace. Abraham paid tithes—a tenth of all the spoils—to Melchizedek. Melchizedek did not come through the lineage of Levi, who was "yet in the loins of his father" when Abraham met Melchizedek. This was an indication that the Melchizedek priesthood was greater than the Levitical priesthood *(vs. 1-11)*. This was in similitude of Christ, who sprang from the tribe of Juda (Judah) and not of Levi which held the keys of the Levitical priesthood. Christ's priesthood was not after the law of a carnal commandment, after the power of an endless life *(vs. 15-16)*. The law does not bring perfection; the hope of eternal life does *(v. 19)*. Christ has an unchangeable priesthood, therefore he liveth to make intercession for us *(vs. 24-25)*. High priests of the lineage of Levi needed daily to offer up sacrifices, first for themselves and then for others. Christ *(who is higher than the heavens)* did not need to offer daily sacrifices. He did this once—when he offered up himself upon the cross *(vs. 26-28).*

Heb. 8. Paul's exposition on Christ continues. The sum of Paul's teachings is this: we have a high priest, set on the right hand of the throne of God the Father, through whom salvation comes. His tabernacle is true and was not made by man as was the tabernacle built by Moses and the children of Israel. The first covenant included ordained priests who made daily offerings and sacrifices and a tabernacle made by man. These were a shadow, a similitude, of things to come. If Christ were on earth, he would not be a priest. If he had no more to offer than what the law of Moses offered, there would have been no need for him to be on earth because there were already priests on earth who offered gifts according to the law, "wherefore it is of necessity that this man have somewhat also to offer" *(vs. 1-5).* Christ obtained a more excellent ministry and is the mediator of a better covenant, established upon better promises. Paul pointed out that if the first covenant had been faultless, there would be no need for a second covenant. However, he did promise to make a new and different covenant with the house of Israel and the house of Judah, saying, "I will put my laws into their mind, and write them in their hearts: and I will be to them a God, and they shall be to me a people: . . ." They will not have to teach each other to know the Lord because everyone will already know him. The Lord will be merciful and will remember their sins no more. This new and better covenant, God's covenant of salvation, makes the first covenant "old." That which decays and waxes old is ready to vanish away *(vs. 6-13).*

Heb. 9. The law of Moses included ordinances and services that typified and bore record of Christ. The priests performed their services in the first tabernacle *(vs. 1-6).* Only the high priest went into the second tabernacle, the "Holiest of all," and then that was only once a year. In the "Holiest of all" he made sacrifices for himself and for the errors of others. The Holy Ghost signified that these ordinances were a similitude of the eventual coming of the Savior. These earthly laws and ordinances could not make the people perfect. They were imposed upon the people only until the time of reformation *(vs. 7-10).* Christ, being a high priest, provides a more perfect tabernacle, one not made with hands and does not use the blood of goats and calves. His own blood was offered, allowing him entry into the holy place, "having obtained eternal redemption for us" *(vs. 11-12).* If the blood of animals could purify the flesh, how much greater shall the blood of Christ "purge your conscience from dead works to serve the living God?" Christ is the mediator of the new covenant and offers us remission of our sins and salvation through his atoning sacrifice. The atonement is retroactive and applies to those of Moses' day as well as to others *(vs. 13-15).* Paul said, "Almost all things are by the law purged with blood; and without shedding of blood is no remission *(v. 22). (The blood of animals was shed as part of the ordinances of the law of Moses and pointed to the ultimate shedding of blood when Christ shed his blood to atone for the sins of mankind. However, even Christ's blood cannot atone for those who are guilty of the unpardonable sin: who crucify unto themselves again the Son of God.)* Christ has entered, not into the holy places made by man, but into heaven. His offering of blood does not have to be repeated. In his offering, he bore the sins of many. At the Second Coming, Christ will appear unto those who look for him "without sin unto salvation."

Heb. 10. The law of Moses and the covenants associated therewith foreshadowed the coming of Christ. Burnt offerings and sacrifices pointed the people to a time when Christ would make the ultimate sacrifice by offering up his own blood. The blood of animals cannot take away the sins of man nor make people perfect. Christ fulfilled the law of Moses and established a new law, which superseded the old. We are sanctified through the blood of Christ, which he offered once and for all. After making the final blood sacrifice, Christ sat down on the right hand of God *(vs. 1-12).* By one offering, Christ has perfected forever those who are sanctified *(v. 14).* The Holy Ghost will bear witness to the faithful of the truth. By the Holy Ghost, the Lord will "put my laws into their hearts, and in their minds will I write them; And their sins and iniquities will I remember no more" *(vs. 15-17).* Those who receive a remission of their sins may receive salvation by the blood of Christ *(v. 19).* With Christ as the high priest over the house of God, Paul admonished people to become clean by conforming to the Lord's law *(as opposed to the way people were washed and cleansed through the Mosaic law) (vs. 21-22).* Paul counseled the people to hold fast to their profession and stressed that those who sin wilfully after having a knowledge of the truth receive no forgiveness. Christ's atoning sacrifice is null and void in such cases *(vs. 23-26).* Under the Mosaic law, people were condemned by the testimony of two or more witnesses. The punishment of those who trod under their feet the Son of God and his atoning sacrifice will be much greater. Vengeance belongs to the Lord; and he will judge his people *(vs. 28-30).* Paul remind them of earlier times when they had had compassion for him when he was in bondage, when their testimonies had been strong and they were willing to endure great afflictions for Christ's sake. Paul urged them not to lose their testimony, but to have patience. The time would come when Christ would come again. The just shall live by faith. They were not of those who were drawn back into perdition, but were of the believers *(vs. 34-39).*

Heb. 11. Paul taught the Hebrews that "faith is the substance of things hoped for, the evidence of things not seen" *(v. 1).* He then illustrated that teaching by referring to various individuals. Through faith: Abel offered a more acceptable sacrifice unto God than Cain offered *(v. 4);* Enoch was translated *(v. 5);* Noah prepared an ark and saved his house, i.e., family *(v. 7);* Abraham left his home and sojourned in a strange land, in a land of promise and dwelled in tabernacles with Isaac and Jacob *(vs. 8-9);* Abraham offered up Isaac as a sacrifice as commanded by God *(v. 17);* Sara conceived and bore a son long after her child-bearing years had passed *(v. 13);* Isaac blessed Jacob and Esau *(v. 20);* Jacob blessed the sons of Joseph *(Ephraim and Manasseh) (v. 21);* Joseph made mention of the children of Israel's eventual departure from Egypt and gave commandment concerning his bones *(v. 22);* Moses' parents placed him in an ark in the water and saved his life *(v. 23);* Moses renounced being the son of Pharaoh's daughter *(v. 24);* Moses led the children of Israel to safety though the Red Sea *(v. 29);* the walls of Jericho were brought down *(v. 30);* and Rahab's life was spared *(v. 31).* Paul indicated that he didn't have enough time to go into detail about others who had demonstrated great faith: Gedeon (Gideon); Barak; Samson, Jephthae (Jephthah); David and Samuel, who had subdued kingdoms, quenched violence, obtained promises, etc., nor of women who had received their dead raised to life again. They were all faithful even though the realization of the promises given to them by the Lord had not yet come to pass *(vs. 32-39)*. God's plan provides that those who lived and died before *(and those who live and die after us)* can not be made perfect without us *(v. 40)*.

Heb. 12. We have so many things around us that testify of Christ that we should put aside our sins and endure to the end. We have not had to endure what Christ endured *(vs. 1-4)*. The Lord chastens those whom he loves. We reverence our mortal fathers who correct us, "after their own pleasure." We should be happier to be in subjection to our Heavenly Father, the father of our spirits, who corrects us for our own good, "that we might be partakers of his holiness" *(vs. 5-10)*. Chastening from the Lord yields "the peaceable fruit of righteousness" unto those who learn from it *(v. 11)*. Paul counseled them to be of good cheer when chastened and not to let their behavior cause others to not believe *(vs. 12-15)*. He also counseled them not to regard the gospel as of little worth as Esau did when he sold his birthright for a morsel of meat *(v. 16)*. Jesus is the mediator of the new covenant. Paul warned the Hebrews that if the people who rejected Christ when he was on earth do not escape their just reward, how much more shall we not escape our punishment if we turn away from him that speaketh from heaven. He, then, encouraged them to serve God acceptably with reverence and godly fear *(vs. 25-28)*.

Heb. 13. Paul encouraged the Hebrews to show brotherly love, to entertain strangers, to remember those in bonds and those who suffer adversity. Marriage, he said, is honorable in all. However, God will judge whoremongers and adulterers. He, also, encouraged them not to be covetousness, but to be content with what they have: the Lord had promised he would never leave them nor forsake them, so they could boldly say that the Lord is their helper *(vs. 1-6)*. He admonished them to pray for and obey the church leaders who were over them *(vs. 7, 17)*. Christ is the same yesterday, today, and forever *(v. 8)*. He cautioned them not to get led astray with strange doctrines. Just as the bodies of the animals whose blood was brought into the sanctuary by the high priest for sin were burned without the camp, Christ also suffered outside the gate as he gave up his blood that he might sanctify the people. He exhorted them to leave the camp of Judaism and go to those outside the camp, even if that meant they would be subjected to the same reproach Christ suffered *(vs. 9-13)*. He asked that they pray for him and his colleagues and prayed that the Lord make them "perfect in every good work to do his will." He also beseeched them to suffer *(i.e., endure)* the word of exhortation that he had written to them *(vs. 18-22)*. He told them that Timothy had been set free, and he hoped the two of them would soon visit them in person. He asked them to salute their church leaders and all the saints in their congregation for him. He sent them greetings from the saints in Italy *(vs. 23-24)*.

HELI

Luke 3:23. **HELI**, son of Matthat, was the father of Joseph the husband of Mary the mother of Jesus. He descended from David through Nathan. *(Note: Matt. 1:16 states that Jacob son of Matthan begat Joseph the husband of Mary. Luke 3:23 states that Heli was the father of Joseph. Thus, Joseph's lineage as given in the NT presents some confusion. Jacob descended from David through Solomon. Heli descended from David through Nathan. The BD indicates that Joseph was the son of Heli and that Mary was the daughter of his uncle Jacob. However, Mary's lineage is not given in the NT.)*

HERMAS

Rom. 16:14. **HERMAS** and several other specific disciples, "and the brethren which are with them," were sent greetings by Paul in his epistle to the Romans.

HERMES

Rom. 16:14. **HERMES** and several other specific disciples, "and the brethren which are with them," were sent greetings by Paul in his epistle to the Romans.

HERMOGENES

2 Tim. 1:15. **HERMOGENES** was one of the apostates in Asia who turned away from Paul.

HEROD

(Note: The EB vol. V, pp. 2-3, indicates there were five different Herods: (1) Herod, the Great, who ordered the massacre of the babies in Bethlehem; (2) Herod Archelaus, who Joseph feared so he settled his family in Nazareth when he left Egypt; (3) Herod Antipas, i.e., Herod the Tetrarch, who had John the Baptist beheaded, but ruled with relative competence throughout Jesus' ministry; (4) Herod (i.e., King) Agrippa I, who executed James and imprisoned Peter; (5) Herod Agrippa II, the last of the Herods.

Herod the Great was born 73 B.C and died A.D. 4. When he died, his lands were divided among three sons: Archelaus, (born 22 B.C. and died about A.D. 18); Antipas (born 21 B.C. and died A.D. 39); and Philip (died, A.D. 33). Eventually, the lands were reunited under the reign of Herod's grandson, Agrippa I (born about 10 B.C., died A.D. 44). Agrippa II, Herod's great-grandson (born A.D. 27, died about A.D. 93) succeeded to only a small part of his father's dominions.)

HEROD (I), THE GREAT

Matt. 2:1-8, 13-16, 19. **HEROD** was king when Jesus was born in Bethlehem. He was troubled when he learned that wise men from the east had come to Jerusalem seeking him that was "born King of the Jews." Herod inquired as to where Christ should be born and asked the wise men when it was that they had seen the star appear. He asked them to bring him word when they had found him so that he, too, could go worship him. When the wise men did not return, Herod slew all the children two years old and under who were in Bethlehem and the surrounding coasts. However, the angel of the Lord had appeared to Joseph in a dream and had instructed him to take Jesus and flee into Egypt. When Herod was dead, an angel of the Lord appeared to Joseph in a dream and instructed him to take Jesus from Egypt and return to the land of Israel.

Luke 1:5-13. Herod was king of Judæa when Zacharias was a priest and Zacharias and Elisabeth became parents of John the Baptist.

HEROD II (Archelaus)

Matt. 2:22. **ARCHELAUS** was the son of Herod the Great and Malthace, a Samaritan. He was a brother of Antipas (Herod the tetrarch). He reigned over Judæa, Idumaea and Samaria following his father's death. Because Joseph feared Archelaus, he took Mary and Jesus and dwelled in Nazareth in Galilee rather than in Judæa. *(Note: Archelaus was deposed by Augustus after a reign of nine years. Judæa, which he governed, was then attached to the Roman province of Syria which was being governed by a Procurator. See both the BD and the EB)*

HEROD (III) THE TETRARCH, (Antipas (1), Antipater)

Matt. 14:1-12; Mark 6:14-29; Luke 9:7-9. **HEROD THE TETRARCH** (**Antipas**) was the son of King Herod and Malthace, a Samaritan. When Jesus was preaching in the area, Herod (Antipas) thought perhaps he was John the Baptist *(whom he had had beheaded),* risen from the dead. He had cast John into prison earlier because John had declared that it was unlawful for Herod to have his brother Philip's wife, Herodias, whom Herod had married. Herod feared putting John to death because he was regarded as a prophet. However, on his birthday, Herodias' daughter, Salome, danced before him and pleased him. He promised to give her whatever she asked for. Prompted by her mother, she asked for John the Baptist's head. He complied with her wishes and had John beheaded. His head was presented to her in a charger *(i.e., on a platter).* She, in turn, gave it to her mother.

Luke 3:1. Herod was tetrarch of Galilee when Tiberius Cæsar was in the fifteenth year of his reign and John the Baptist came into the country about Jordan, preaching the baptism of repentance for the remission of sins.

Luke 13:31, 34. Herod, the Pharisees warned Jesus, desired to kill him, and told him, "Get thee out, and depart hence: for Herod will kill thee." Jesus lamented, "How often would I have gathered thy children together as a hen doth gather her brood under her wings, and ye would not!"

Luke 23:6-11. Herod, when Jesus was sent to him by Pilate, found no wrong in him. The people had taken Jesus to Pilate to be judged, but Pilate sent him to Herod because Jesus was a Galilæan and that was part of Herod's jurisdiction. However, when Herod found no wrong in him, he returned him to Pilate. *(Note: Herod was deposed by Emperor Caligula and banished to Lugdunum in Gaul in A.D. 39.)*

Acts 4:27-28. Peter and John acknowledged before God that Herod, Pontius Pilate, the Gentiles and the people of Israel, "were gathered together for to do whatsoever thy hand and thy counsel determined before to be done."

Acts 13:1. Herod the tetrarch and Manaen, one of the prophets and teachers serving in Antioch with Barnabas and Saul, were brought up together.

HEROD IV (Agrippa I)

Acts 12. **HEROD**, i.e., **Agrippa I**, who was allowed to assume the title of king, decided to vex the church and killed James, the brother of John, with a sword *(vs. 1-2).* Then, because it pleased the Jews, he arrested Peter and threw him in prison where he had him heavily guarded *(vs. 3-4).* When Herod went to get Peter following Easter, Peter was gone, having been led to freedom by an angel. Herod was so angry he commanded that the keepers should be put to death *(vs. 6-10, 19).* As Herod sat upon the throne, dressed in royal apparel, he was struck dead by the angel of the Lord because he "gave not God the glory; and he was eaten of worms, and gave up the ghost" *(vs. 21-23).*

HEROD V (Agrippa II)

Acts 23:35. **HEROD**'s judgment hall was where Felix the governor confined Paul until he could hear from both him and his (Paul's) accusers.

Acts 25:13-27. **King Agrippa** and Bernice visited Festus, procurator over Judæa, and Festus discussed with them his dilemma regarding Paul: the Jews' complaints didn't amount to anything worthy of death, and Paul had appealed to be heard by Augustus. Agrippa said he wanted to hear Paul himself. Festus agreed that on the morrow they would hear Paul. When Festus, King Agrippa, Bernice, and others present were ready, Festus explained that, because he found nothing worthy of death in Paul, he had determined to send him to Augustus. However, he felt he should send a letter detailing the crimes laid against him and hoped that perhaps they, after hearing Paul, could help him come up with what to include in the letter.

Acts 26. Agrippa gave Paul permission to speak for himself *(v. 1).* King Agrippa, according to Paul, was "expert in all customs and questions which are among the Jews." After Paul recounted his former persecution of the followers of Christ and of his conversion on the road to Damascus, he asked King Agrippa if he believed the prophets, and said he knew he did. King Agrippa told Paul, "Almost thou persuadest me to be a Christian" *(vs. 2-28).* After Paul's presentation, King Agrippa, Bernice, the governor and those who were with them drew aside and conferred. They concluded that Paul had done nothing worthy of death nor of bonds. Agrippa told Festus that if Paul had not appealed unto Cæsar, he might have been set free *(vs. 30-32).*

HERODIANS

Matt. 22:16-21; Mark 12:13-17; Luke 20:20-26. **HERODIANS**, supporters of the Herodian family, were a political party among the Jews *(BD).* The Pharisees sent their disciples with the Herodians to ask Jesus whether or not it was lawful to pay tribute to Cæsar. Jesus' response was that they should rended unto Cæsar that which is Cæsar's and unto God that which is God's.

Mark 3:6. The Herodians were approached by the Pharisees to take counsel together against Jesus after his disciples plucked ears of corn and he healed a man's withered hand on the Sabbath.

HERODIAS

Matt. 14:3-11; Mark 6:17-28; Luke 3:19-20. **HERODIAS** was the wife of Philip, brother of Antipas, i.e., Herod the tetrarch. John the Baptist declared that it was unlawful for Herod to have Herodias so Herodias desired to have him killed. She had her daughter dance before Herod for his birthday, which pleased him. When Herod promised to give her whatever she wanted in return, Herodias' daughter requested John's head *(having been counseled by her mother).* Thus, Herod had John beheaded and had his head given to the damsel, i.e. , Salome, who in turn gave it to Herodias.

HERODION

Rom. 16:11. **HERODION** was Paul's kinsman. Paul sent greetings to him in his epistle to the Romans.

HEROD'S SOLDIERS/KEEPERS OF THE PRISON

Acts 12:4, 6, 18-19. **HEROD'S SOLDIERS/KEEPERS OF THE PRISON** were placed in charge of Peter, whom Herod (Agrippa I) had arrested and thrown in prison. When Herod went to get Peter after Easter, Peter was gone, having been led to freedom by an angel of the Lord. Herod was so angry that Peter was gone that he had the keepers of the prison put to death.

HEROD THE TETRARCH (See Herod III, Antipas (1), Antipater)

HEZEKIAH (See Ezekias in Appendix A)

HEZRON (See Esrom in Appendix A)

HOSEA (See Osee)

HYMENÆUS

1 Tim. 1:6, 19-20. **HYMENÆUS** was an apostate in the early church. Paul told Timothy that some members had turned away "unto vain jangling" and had made a "shipwreck" out of their faith and good conscience. He named Hymenæus and Alexander, and said he had delivered them unto Satan, "that they may learn not to blaspheme."

2 Tim. 2:16-17. Hymenæus and Philetus were named by Paul as two apostates whose words destroyed their faith. Paul warned that those who engage in profane and vain babblings increase in ungodliness, "and their word will eat as doth a canker."

NAMES THAT BEGIN WITH "I"

ISAAC (See Appendix A)

ISAIAH (See Esaias in Appendix A)

NAMES THAT BEGIN WITH "J"

JACOB (1) (See Appendix A)

Matt. 1:2; 8:11-12; 22:32; Luke 3:34; 13:28; Acts 7:8-16; Rom. 9:13; Heb. 11:20.

JACOB (2)

Matt. 1:15-16. **JACOB** was the son of Matthan and the father of Joseph who was the husband of Mary, the mother of Jesus. *(Note: Luke 3:23-24 states that Joseph's father was Heli the son of Matthat.)*

JAILER/KEEPER OF THE PRISON

Acts 16. The **JAILER/KEEPER OF THE PRISON** in Philippi was instructed to keep Paul and Silas "safely" following their being beaten publicly, uncondemned. The keeper of the prison thrust them into the inner prison and secured their feet in the stocks *(vs. 23-24).* Suddenly, an earthquake shook the foundation of the prison: the prison doors were opened and the bands on all the prisoners were loosed. The keeper of the prison, thinking the prisoners had escaped, went to kill himself with a sword; but Paul stopped him. The keeper of the prison became converted and he and all his house were baptized that same night. He took Paul and Silas to his house and fed them *(vs. 26-34).* The following morning, the keeper of the prison was given word to release Paul and Silas. However, they refused to be discharged privily and insisted the magistrates come and release them *(vs. 35-37).*

JAIRUS, A Certain Ruler

Mark 5:22-24, 35-43; 9:18-19; Luke 8:41-42, 49-55. **JAIRUS [A Certain Ruler]** was one of the rulers of the synagogue. He came and worshiped Jesus. He beseeched Jesus to heal his gravely ill twelve-year-old daughter. He said his daughter was dead but that if Jesus would come and lay his hand upon her he knew she would live. As they journeyed toward his house, he was informed that his daughter had died. People and minstrels were making a noise when they arrived at the ruler's house. Jesus told the man not to fear, that his daughter was not dead but "sleepeth." The people laughed at him. Jesus took the girl's father and mother, and Peter, James and John in where the girl lay. He took her by the hand and told her to arise. Immediately, she arose and walked. Jesus instructed the people to get her something to eat.

JAIRUS' DAUGHTER, A Certain Ruler's Daughter

Matt. 9:18-19, 23-26; Mark 5:23, 35-43; Luke 8:41-42, 49-56. **JAIRUS' DAUGHTER [A Certain Ruler's Daughter]** was gravely ill. He beseeched Jesus to heal her. As they journeyed toward his house, Jairus was informed that his daughter had died. Jesus told him to fear not, that his daughter was not dead but "sleepeth." Jesus took the girl's father and mother, and Peter, James and John, in where the girl lay. He took her by the hand and told her to arise. Immediately, she arose and walked. Jesus instructed the people to get her something to eat.

JAIRUS' WIFE

Mark 5:40. **JAIRUS' WIFE** is not mentioned by name, just that Jesus took the father (Jairus) and the mother of the sick girl into the room where she lay dead. Jesus then took the twelve-year-old girl by the hand and told her to arise. She arose, and Jesus instructed the people to get her something to eat.

JAMES (1) (James, according to the BD, is an English form of the Hebrew name Jacob.)

Matt. 4; Mark 1; Luke 5. **JAMES**, the brother of John, was a son of Zebedee. *(According to the EB, he was called James the Great.)* James and John were mending their fishing nets with their father when Jesus called them to come follow him. They left their nets and their father and followed Jesus *(vs. 21- 22; Mark 1:19-20; Luke 5:10).* He and John were with Jesus, Peter and Andrew when they went into the housc of Peter and Andrew and Jesus healed Peter's mother-in-law *(Mark 1:29-31).*

Matt. 10; Luke 9. Jesus called 12 disciples: Simon Peter, Andrew, James, John, Philip, Bartholomew; Thomas, Matthew, James, Lebbæus (Thaddæus), Simon the Canaanite, and Judas Iscariot *(vs. 2-4).* Jesus empowered these apostles and sent them forth to teach, but instructed them that they should not go to the Gentiles nor to the Samaritans. They were to go to the lost sheep of the house of Israel. They were to heal the sick and cast out devils. They were to travel without purse or scrip. They were instructed to leave their peace upon those who received them, but to shake the dust off their feet when leaving the houses of those who reject them *(vs. 5-14; Luke 9:1-5).* They were told they would be persecuted for Christ's sake, but that "he that endureth to the end shall be saved." They are of more value than the sparrows for which the Father provides. The hairs of their heads are even numbered *(vs. 16-32).*

Matt. 17; Mark 9; Luke 9. James and his brother John, along with Peter, went with Jesus into a high mountain where they were transfigured, saw Moses and Elias, and heard a voice proclaiming, "This is my beloved Son, in whom I am well pleased; hear ye him." Peter suggested making three altars: one each for Jesus, Moses and Elias *(vs. 1-12; Mark 9:2-13; Luke 9:28-35).* When they had come unto a multitude, none of the disciples were able to heal a certain man's son who was "lunatick." Jesus said this was because of lack of faith—the kind of faith that comes from fasting and prayer *(vs. 14-21).* The disciples were grieved when Jesus again told them he would be betrayed and killed; however, he assured them he would rise again on the third day *(vs. 22-23).*

Matt. 20:20-28; Mark 10:35-45. James' mother petitioned Jesus to allow her sons, James and John, to sit on his left and right sides in his kingdom. Jesus responded that it was not his to give, but that it would be "given to them for whom it is prepared of my Father." The other ten disciples were "moved with indignation against the two brethren," and Jesus then taught that "whosoever will be great among you, let him be your minister. . . let him be your servant." *(Note: In the account recorded in Mark, James and John made the request of Jesus, not their mother.)*

Matt. 26:37-44; Mark 14:33-41; Luke 22:39-46. Jesus took Peter, James and John—the sons of Zebedee—with him as he went further into the garden of Gethsemane and asked them to wait and watch with him. Nevertheless, while he went a way off to pray, they repeatedly fell asleep. *(Note: The account in Luke does not specify that Jesus took three disciples—James, John and Peter—an additional distance with him.)*

Mark 3:17. James and John were given the surname of **BOANERGES**—The sons of thunder—by Jesus.

Mark 5:37; Luke 8:51. James and John, along with Peter, accompanied Jesus to the house of Jairus where he went to heal Jairus' twelve-year-old daughter.

Mark 13; Matt. 24; Luke 17, 21. James, John, Andrew and Peter asked Jesus what calamities would precede the Second Coming. Jesus told them there would be false Christs, wars and rumors of wars, nation would rise against nation and kingdom against kingdom; there would be earthquakes and famines and troubles. The prophets would be persecuted for Christ's sake. Brother would betray brother and fathers would betray their sons; children shall rise against their parents. The desolation prophesied by Daniel will come to pass. The sun shall be darkened, the moon will not give its light, and the stars of heaven shall fall. Then the Son of Man will come in the clouds in great power and glory *(vs. 3-27).* Jesus said to watch for the signs: just as we know summer is near when the fig tree puts forth her tender branches, so the signs will signal the Second Coming. Nevertheless, Jesus stressed that no man knows the day, time, nor place. We should be prepared and not caught "sleeping" *(vs. 28-37; Luke 21:29-36; Matt. 24:32-34; also see Luke 17:20-37 for a variation on this subject).*

Mark 14. See the entry for Matt. 26.

Luke 8:51. See the entry for Mark 5.

Luke 9:54. James and John asked Jesus if they should call down fire from heaven as Elias did to consume Jesus' detractors. Jesus forbade them and said they didn't understand God's plan.

John 21. James and John, Simon Peter, Thomas, Nathanael of Cana, and two other disciples were fishing on the sea of Tiberias when Jesus showed himself to his disciples a third time following his resurrection. Jesus stood on the shore and asked if they had any meat. They did not recognize Jesus but responded that they had none. He told them to cast their nets on the right side of the ship. They did; and their nets were so full they were unable to draw them. John declared to Peter, "It is the Lord." Peter quickly put something on and cast himself into the sea. When the disciples were gathered together on shore, Jesus dined with them on bread and fishes *(vs. 1-14).*

Acts 1:13-14. Following Jesus' ascension into heaven, Jesus' disciples, including James, met together in an upper room, along with several women *(including Mary the mother of Jesus)* and his brethren, where they continued in prayer and supplication.

Acts 12:2. James was killed by Herod with a sword. *(Note: The EB, vol. V, p. 507, states that he was beheaded by Herod in A.D. 44, and that he is the only apostle whose martyrdom is recorded in the NT. The BD included with the King James version of the Bible also states that James was beheaded. However, the scripture, itself, merely says he was killed with a sword.)*

1 Cor. 15:7. James saw the Savior following his resurrection.

Gal. 2:9. James, Cephas (Peter) and John, the leaders of the church, extended their right hands of fellowship to Paul and Barnabas when Paul and Barnabas went to Jerusalem to assure them that the doctrine they were teaching was the same doctrine the church leaders were teaching.

James 1-5. (Note: See James, the brother of Jesus. It is not clear which James is the author of this General Epistle of James. Many Biblical scholars believe it was written by James, the brother of Jesus.)

JAMES (2)

Matt. 10; Luke 9. **JAMES**, the son of Alphæus, was one of Jesus' 12 disciples: Simon Peter, Andrew, James, John, Philip, Bartholomew; Thomas, Matthew, James, Lebbæus (Thaddæus), Simon the Canaanite, and Judas Iscariot *(vs. 2-4).* Jesus empowered these apostles and sent them forth to teach, but instructed them that they should not go to the Gentiles nor to the Samaritans. They were to go to the lost sheep of the house of Israel. They were to heal the sick and cast out devils. They were to travel without purse or scrip. They were instructed to leave their peace upon those who received them, but to shake the dust off their feet when leaving the houses of those who reject them *(vs. 5-14; Luke 9:1-5).* They were told they would be persecuted for Christ's sake, but that "he that endureth to the end shall be saved." They are of more value than the sparrows for which the Father provides. The hairs of their heads are even numbered *(vs. 16-32).*

Mark 3:18; Luke 6:15. James was among the 12 men whom Jesus ordained as apostles and sent forth with power to heal sicknesses and cast out devils.

Acts 1:13-14. Following Jesus' ascension into heaven, Jesus' disciples, including James the son of Alphæus, met together in an upper room, along with several women *(including Mary the mother of Jesus)* and his brethren, where they continued in prayer and supplication. *(The BD indicates that some Biblical scholars think James (2) and James (4) may be one and the same.)*

JAMES (3)

Matt. 13:55; Mark 6:3. **JAMES** *(died about A.D. 62 in Jerusalem)* was the brother of Jesus. He also had other brothers: Joses, Simon and Judas (Juda); and sisters whose names are not given.

Acts 12:17. James occupied an important place in the church in Jerusalem. After angels helped Peter escaped from Herod's prison, Peter went to the house of Mary the mother of John Mark where the people were gathered together praying and asked them to inform James and his brethren about his escape.

Acts 15:13-22. James, when the apostles were discussing the contentious issue of circumcision, "was the chief spokesman for the Jerusalem Church at the Council of Jerusalem regarding Paul's mission to the Gentiles" *(EB, vol. V, p. 507)* and suggested that they write an epistle to the Gentile members of the church indicating that circumcision was not necessary but that they should "abstain from pollution of idols, and from fornications, and from things strangled, and from blood." The apostles agreed with James.

Acts 21:18-25. James and all the elders met with Paul and his companions after they arrived in Jerusalem. James and the brethren told Paul of the rumors that were circulating claiming Paul was teaching the Jews who were among the Gentiles that they didn't need to be circumcised and to forsake Moses. They said the Jews would all gather together when they heard that Paul was there and they suggested to him that he purify himself with four men "which have a vow on them" so the Jews would know the rumors were nothing and that Paul kept the law. They acknowledged that the Gentiles only needed to "keep themselves from things offered to idols, and from blood, and from strangled, and from fornication."

1 Cor. 15:7. James, Paul testified to the Corinthian saints, saw the risen Savior after Christ had shown himself to Cephas (Peter), then the Twelve, and then 500 brethren together. "After that, he was seen of James; then of all the apostles."

Gal. 1:19. James the Lord's brother was a leader in the church in Jerusalem.

Gal. 2:9-12. James, Peter and John were pillars in the church. They extended their right hands of fellowship to Paul: they would go and minister unto those of the circumcision; and Paul and Barnabus would go unto the heathen: those not of the circumcision. Previously, James had defended the doctrine that the heathen did not need to be circumcised.

James 1. *(Note: It is not clear which James wrote this General Epistle of James. According to the DNTC, vol. 111, p. 245, Biblical scholars seem to believe that it was written by James, the brother of Christ. However, no indication is given in the Bible, itself.)* James wrote this General Epistle to the twelve tribes of Israel who had been scattered abroad. *(Note: The location of the scattered tribes of Israel was not known in the days of James. Nor was there a way to distribute James epistle to them if he had known where they were. It would appear that he is writing this epistle to the dispersed members of the house of Israel who would be gathered in the latter days and to others who would be gathered to the fold of Christ. He addresses the readers as brethren, so he apparently was writing to those who would have received the gospel. (Ibid., pp. 244-245.))* He encouraged them to find joy in their afflictions because the trying of their faith worked patience *(vs. 1-2)*. He advised them to seek answers from God through prayer: "If any of you lack wisdom, let him ask of God, that giveth to all men liberally, and upbraideth not; and it shall be given him. But let him ask in faith, nothing wavering" *(vs. 5-6)*. *(Note: Joseph Smith, who later translated the Book of Mormon and became the first president and prophet of the Church of Jesus Christ of Latter-day Saints, acted upon James' counsel and, finding a secluded spot in a grove of trees, prayed to God to find out which church he should join. In response, God the Father and his Son, Jesus Christ, appeared to Joseph, answered his question, and gave him further instruction. See JSH, 1:15-19.)* James counseled them to be single-minded in the Lord, to beware of riches for, he said, ". . . also shall the rich man fade away in his ways" *(vs. 8-11)*. Those who resist temptation will be blessed. God does not tempt man *(vs. 12-16)*. Every good gift comes from above *(v. 17)*. People should be quick to hear, slow to speak, and slow to become angry. James admonished people to get rid of all filthiness and become doers of the word and not hearers only. He who fails to bridle his tongue deceives his own heart and his religion is vain *(vs. 19-26)*. James defined pure, undefiled religion: "To visit the fatherless and widows in their affliction, and to keep himself unspotted from the world" *(v. 27).*

James 2. James admonished the people not to be a respecter of persons: i.e., not to favor the rich man over the poor man. If they do, they become partial judges and become evil in their thoughts. And he reminded them that the rich men are the ones who have oppressed them. Additionally, he reminded them of the "royal law," "Thou shalt love thy neighbour as thyself." If they followed that, they would do well. If they are a respecter of persons, they sin, even if they observe all the rest of the gospel *(vs. 1-9).* Those who sin in one aspect of the law are guilty of breaking all of the law. To illustrate his point, James referred to two commandments: not to kill, not to commit adultery. A person who broke either point of the law, was guilty of breaking the law *(vs. 10-11).* Those who judge without mercy shall also be judged without mercy *(v. 13).* James elaborated on the issue of faith and works and stressed that faith alone cannot save a man: faith without works is dead *(vs. 14-26).*

James 3. James expounded on the need and wisdom of controlling one's tongue. If a man does not offend in word, the same is a perfect man. He illustrated how a small thing, i.e., a bit in a horse's mouth or the helm of a ship, can turn about a large thing. Likewise, the tongue, a little member of the body, has great power for good or ill. Blessings and cursing come out of the same mouth, and James said that should not be happening. A fountain cannot yield both salt and fresh water. He instructed, "Who is a wise man and endued with knowledge among you? Let him shew out of a good conversation his works with meekness of wisdom" *(vs. 1-13).* He counseled the people to avoid envying and strife. "Wisdom that is from above is peaceable, gentle . . . without hyprocrisy. And the fruit of righteousness is sown in peace of them that make peace" *(vs. 14-18).*

James 4. James chastised the people for their lusts and for engaging in wars and fighting that resulted from their lusts. He chided them for asking for things amiss, for asking for things based upon lust *(vs. 1-3).* Adulterers and adulteresses were reminded that those who are friends of the world are enemies of God *(v. 4).* He urged the people to submit themselves to God, who will draw near unto them if they do, and resist the devil, who will flee from them if they resist him *(vs. 7-8).* They were encouraged to humble themselves before God and not speak evil of one another. Those who speak evil of another sets himself up as a judge, but there is just one lawgiver who has the power to save or destroy *(vs. 10-12).* They should do what the Lord wants them to do and not worry about tomorrow: they don't know what the morrow shall hold. Even their lives are but a vapour that can vanish away. It is a sin to know to do go and not do it *(vs. 13-17).*

James 5. The wealth of the rich, who use it in a corrupt fashion, will stand as a witness against the rich *(vs. 1-3).* James rebuked the rich who got wealthy from the labor of those whom they defrauded. They condemned and killed the just *(vs. 4-6).* He admonished the people to be patient, not to bicker and backbite, but to look to the prophets as examples of how to suffer affliction and be patient, citing Job, specifically *(vs. 7-11).* They should not swear by heaven nor earth, but merely yea or nay *(v. 12).* The afflicted should pray; the merry should sing. The sick should be administered to by the elders and anointed with oil in the name of the Lord *(vs. 13-14).* We should confess our sins and pray for one another. The prayers of the righteous avail much. James illustrated his point on the effectiveness of prayer by reminding them that Elias (Elijah) had prayed for the heavens to be sealed, and they were sealed for three-and-a-half years and there was no rain. He prayed for the heavens to be unsealed, and it rained *(vs. 16-18)*. When people err and are reclaimed from their sin, both the sinner and the one who reclaimed him are saved. Engaging in such saving activity "shall hide a multitude of sins" *(vs. 19-20)*.

Jude 1:1. James was the brother of Jude which Jude was a "servant" of Jesus Christ. *(Note: He was known in later records as "the Just." Jewish tradition indicates that James was put to death by Ananus the high priest, either by stoning—according to the Jewish historian Josephus—or by being thrown from a temple tower—according to St. Hegesippus, another early Christian writer (EB, vol. V, p. 507).)*

JAMES (4)

Matt. 27:56. **JAMES** was the son of one of the Marys and the brother of Joses (Joseph). *(Note: The BD attributes this scripture to James (4). However, James the brother of Jesus also had a brother named Joses and a mother named Mary, so it is not clear to which James this refers.)*

Mark 15:40. James the less, and Joses' mother Mary was with Mary Magdalene, Salome, and several other people as they watched from a distance as Christ was crucified.

Luke 24:10. James' mother Mary was with Mary Magdalene, Joanna, and other women who went to the sepulchre early in the morning of the third day after Christ was crucified and found the stone rolled away and the tomb empty. *(Note: James may be the brother or father of Jude, but nothing more is known of this James (EB, vol. V, p. 508). "Nothing further is known of him, unless he is, as some think, the same as number 2, above" (BD).)*

JASON

Acts 17:5-9. **JASON**, of Thessalonica, was a follower of Christ. Non-believing Jews assaulted Jason's home looking for Paul and Silas. When they couldn't find them, they took Jason and some of the other brethren before the rulers of the city. After Jason and the others posted security, they were released.

Rom. 16:21. Jason, one of Paul's kinsmen, joined Paul and others in sending greetings to the saints in Rome.

JESUS CHRIST (1)

Luke 1:27-44. **JESUS** was the name the angel Gabriel told Mary *(a virgin espoused to Joseph)* she should name the baby she would have. The angel told her that she had found favor with God and that she would conceive and bear a son. She should call him Jesus. The Holy Ghost would come upon her, and the power of the Highest would overshadow her. Jesus would be called the Son of God. Mary was also told by the angel that her cousin Elisabeth was with child. Mary went to her. The infant in Elisabeth's womb *(i.e., John the Baptist)* was filled with the Holy Ghost and recognized that the infant in Mary's womb was the Son of God and jumped with joy when Mary saluted Elisabeth.

Matt. 1:1, 16-25; Luke 3. Jesus was the firstborn son of Mary. His genealogy from Abraham *(Matt. 1:2-16, through David's son Solomon, and from Adam in Luke 3:23-38, through David's son Nathan)* through Joseph the husband of Mary is given. An angel told Joseph he needn't fear to take Mary, a virgin who was espoused to him, as a wife when he learned that she was with child because the baby she had conceived was of the Holy Ghost. Joseph was to name the child Jesus. This fulfilled Isaiah's prophecy, "Behold, a virgin shall conceive, and bear a son, and shall call his name Immanuel" *(Isa. 7:14).* Joseph did as the angel instructed and knew not Mary until she had brought forth her firstborn son and they called him JESUS.

Luke 2:4-33. Jesus was born in a stable because there was no room for them in an inn when Joseph and Mary traveled to Bethlehem to be taxed after Cæsar Augustus decreed that all the world should be taxed *(vs. 4-7).* Angels told the good news to shepherds who quickly went to Bethlehem and found the baby lying in a manger *(v. 16).* When the infant was eight days old, he was circumcised and named JESUS *(v. 21).* When Joseph and Mary took Jesus to Jerusalem to present him to the Lord, a devout man named Simeon *(who had been promised by the Holy Ghost that he should not die before seeing the Lord's Christ)* was in the temple. He immediately took the infant up in his arms and acknowledged that the infant was the Christ and that now he could die in peace. Joseph and Mary marveled at the things that were spoken of Jesus *(vs. 22-33).*

Matt. 2:1, 11-14, 19-23. Jesus was born in Bethlehem in the days of king Herod. When the wise men came into the house where Jesus was, they fell down and worshiped him and gave him presents. Because Herod sought to kill the child, the angel of the Lord appeared to Joseph in a dream and instructed him to take the child and flee into Egypt. Upon Herod's death, an angel of the Lord appeared to Joseph in a dream and instructed him to bring the child back to Israel because those who sought his life were dead. However, Joseph feared Herod's son Archelaus so he turned aside and went to Galilee and dwelled in Nazareth rather than in Judæa, fulfilling the prophecy that Jesus would be called a Nazarene.

Luke 2:42-51. When Jesus was twelve years old, he went with Joseph and Mary to Jerusalem for the feast of the Passover. As Joseph and Mary left Jerusalem, Jesus was not with them and they assumed he was with other members of the family. However, he was not to be found among them. Joseph and Mary returned to Jerusalem and, after three days of searching, found him teaching in the temple. When they asked him why he had dealt with them so, he asked, "How is it that ye sought me? Wist ye not that I must be about my Father's business?"

Matt. 3:13-17; Mark 1:9-11; Luke 3:22. Jesus went from Galilee to Jordan to be baptized of John. John forbade him, saying he had need to be baptized of Jesus, not Jesus of him. However, Jesus said to suffer it to be so that they might fulfill all righteousness. Thus, John baptized Jesus. When Jesus came up out of the water, "the heavens were opened unto him, and he saw the Spirit of God descending like a dove, and lighting upon him: And lo a voice from heaven, saying, 'This is [Thou art] my beloved Son, in whom [in thee] I am well pleased.'"

Matt. 4; Mark 1; Luke 4-5. Jesus was led into the wilderness where he fasted 40 days and 40 nights. Satan then tried to tempt him by taunting him, "If thou be the Son of God, command that these stones be made bread." However, Jesus responded that "Man shall not live by bread alone, but by every word that proceedeth out of the mouth of God" *(vs. 1-4; Mark 1:12-13; Luke 4:1-4).* Jesus was then set on the pinnacle of the temple. Again, the devil tried to tempt him by saying, "If thou be the Son of God, cast thyself down: for it is written, 'He shall give his angels charge concerning thee: and in their hands they shall bear thee up, lest at any time thou dash thy foot against a stone.'" Jesus responded, "It is written again, 'Thou shalt not tempt the Lord thy God'" *(vs. 5-7; Luke 4:9-12).* Jesus was then taken up into a high mountain and the devil came to him again and tried to tempt him by offering him all the kingdoms of the world along with their glory if he would fall down and worship him. Jesus rebuffed him again and said, "Get thee hence, Satan: for it is written, 'Thou shalt worship the Lord thy God and him only shalt thou serve'" *(vs. 8-10; Luke 4:5-8).* The devil departed and angels ministered unto Jesus *(v. 11; Luke 4:13).* Jesus heard that John was in prison so he left and went into Galilee. From this time forward, Jesus began to preach *(vs. 12-17).* As he walked by the Sea of Galilee, he saw two brothers—Simon called Peter, and Andrew—fishing. He asked them to follow him and he would make them fishers of men. He then saw two other brothers—James and John—sons of Zebedee, mending their nets with their father. He called them to follow him, too, and they did *(vs. 18-22; Mark 1:16-18; Luke 5:1-11). (Note: The account in Luke 5 does not include Andrew; however, it provides greater detail.)* Jesus preached and healed the sick. Great multitudes followed him *(vs. 23-25).*

Matt. 5; Luke 6, 12. Jesus preached his sermon on the mount: the poor in spirit shall receive the kingdom of God; those who mourn shall be comforted; the meek shall inherit the earth; those who hunger and thirst after righteousness shall be filled; the merciful shall obtain mercy; the pure in heart shall see God; peacemakers shall be called the children of God; those who are persecuted for righteousness' sake shall receive the kingdom of heaven; those who are reviled and persecuted for Christ's sake should rejoice for great will be their reward *(vs. 1-12; Luke 6:20-26).* He taught: "Ye are the salt of the earth" *(v. 13);* "Ye are the light of the world" *(v. 14);* He came not to destroy the law but to fulfill it *(v. 17);* those who break the commandments and teach others to do so shall be called the least in the kingdom of heaven, but those who keep and teach the commandments shall be called great in the kingdom of heaven *(v. 19);* not only those who kill, but those who are angry with their brother without a cause shall be in danger of the judgment; therefore, people should make amends with their brother before making an offering unto the Lord *(vs. 21-24);* agree with thine adversary when thou art in the way with him *(vs. 25-26; Luke 12:58-59; 16:9);* one who lusts after a woman commits adultery with her in his heart *(v. 28);* if thy eye offend thee, pluck it out; if thy hand offend thee, cut it off *(vs. 29-30);* those who put away their wife for any reason other than fornication cause her to commit adultery; whosoever marries her that is divorced commits adultery *(vs. 31-32; Luke 16:18);* swear not at all—let thy communications be "Yea, yea; Nay, nay" *(vs. 33-37);* an "eye for an eye" is replaced with "turn" the other cheek; if a man sues for thy coat, give him your cloke also; if a man compels you to go a mile with him, go two; give to him that asketh *(vs. 38-42; Luke 6:30);* love your enemies, bless those who curse you, do good to them that hate you, pray for them which despitefully use you and persecute you, and you will be blessed *(vs. 43-47; Luke*

6:27-28, 35); be perfect [merciful], even as your Father which is in heaven is perfect [merciful] *(v. 48; Luke 6:36).*

Matt. 6; Luke 11. Jesus continued his sermon on the mount and taught his disciples about prayer: they should not pray to be seen nor should they use vain repetitions. As an example of how one should pray, Jesus offered a prayer, now known as the Lord's Prayer, which taught them the order of prayer: i.e., a salutation, gratitude expressed, blessings requested, closure *(vs. 9-13; Luke 11:2-4).* He taught them regarding forgiveness *(vs. 14-15; Luke 17:3-4),* fasting *(vs. 16-18),* the futility of laying up earthly treasures and the blessing of laying up treasures in heaven *(vs. 19-21);* people cannot serve two masters at the same time *(v. 24);* trust in the Lord who even provides for the fowls of the air, etc. *(vs. 25-32);* people should seek first the kingdom of God and his righteousness, and all other things shall be added unto them *(v. 33).*

Matt. 7; Luke 6, 11. Jesus concluded his sermon on the mount. He taught his disciples to judge not—that they would be judged as they judged; when they see a mote in another's eye, they should consider the beam in their own eye; they should not give that which is holy to dogs nor cast their pearls before swine *(vs. 1-5; Luke 6:37-42).* He taught them to ask, and it shall be given; those who seek, shall find; to those who knock, it shall be opened unto them *(vs. 6-11; Luke 11:5-13).* Whatsoever a person would have men do unto him, he should do unto others *(v. 12; Luke 6:31).* He taught strait is the gate and narrow the way that leadeth unto life *(vs. 13-14).* People should beware of false prophets. By their fruits, people can recognize them *(vs. 15-23; Luke 6:43-45).* People should build their house upon the rock and not upon the sand. The wise man is compared to one who builds upon the rock. The foolish man is compared to the man who built upon the sand *(vs. 24-28; Luke 6:46-49).* Jesus taught as one having authority *(v. 29).*

Matt. 8; Mark 1; Luke 4, 7, 8. Jesus healed a leper *(vs. 2-4)* and the servant of a centurion *(vs. 5- 13; Luke 7:2-10).* Jesus, James, John, Andrew and Simon (Peter) went into the house of Simon and Andrew. Simon's mother-in-law lay ill. Jesus took her by the hand and lifted her up and she was healed *(vs. 14-15; Mark 1:29-31; Luke 4:38-39).* He cast out devils and healed many others who were brought to him *(v. 16).* This fulfilled Esaias' (Isaiah's) prophecy that he (the Savior) would take our infirmities and bare our sicknesses *(v. 17).* He warned the scribe who wanted to follow him that he had no place to call home, and told another disciple to follow him and let the dead bury their dead *(vs. 19-22).* As Jesus and his disciples crossed the sea, a storm arose and began to swamp the ship as Jesus slept. His disciples woke him and asked him to save them before they perished. He calmed the sea *(vs. 23-27).* Jesus arrived in Gadarenes and met a man who dwelled among the tombs who was filled with an unclean spirit, which said his name was Legion. Jesus cast the unclean spirit out, but gave leave for the devils to enter into a herd of about 2,000 swine which immediately ran violently down a steep place into the sea and were drowned *(vs. 28-32; Mark 5:1-13; Luke 8:27-33).* The townspeople asked him to leave their coasts *(v. 34; Mark 5:17; Luke 8:37).*

Matt. 9; Mark 2; 5; Luke 5; 8. Jesus healed a man who was brought to him, sick with palsy and lying on a bed. He said, "Thy sins be forgiven thee." Jesus, then, rebuked the scribes who thought he blasphemed by asking them whether it was easier to say, "Thy sins be forgiven thee; or to say, Arise, and walk?" He told the man who was sick with palsy to take up his bed and go home *(vs. 2-7; Luke 5:18-26)*. Jesus called Matthew (Levi), a custom collector and son of Alphæus, to come follow him. He sat at meat with many publicans and sinners. The scribes and Pharisees were appalled that Jesus would eat with publicans and sinners. Jesus taught, "They that are whole have no need of the physician, but they that are sick: I came not to call the righteous but sinners to repentance" *(v. 9-13; Mark 2:14-17; Luke 5:27-32)*. John's disciples asked Jesus why they and the Pharisees fasted often, observing that Jesus' disciples did not fast. Jesus said as long as they had the bridegroom with them, the "children of the bridechamber" had no reason to mourn. However, he told them that when the bridegroom is gone, they will also fast *(vs. 14-15; Luke 5:33-35)*. Jesus taught that no one puts old wine into new bottles nor sews a new piece of cloth onto an old piece. They put them into new bottles and onto new cloth so they both are preserved: the bottle and the wine, etc. *(vs. 16-18; Luke 5:36-38)*. A certain ruler (Jairus) came and worshiped Jesus. He said his daughter was dead but that if Jesus would come and lay his hand upon her he knew she would live. Jesus and his disciples followed the man. People and minstrels were making a noise when they arrived at the ruler's house. Jesus said the maid was not dead: she was sleeping. The people laughed at him. When the people left, Jesus took the girl by her hand and she arose *(vs. 18-19, 23-26; Mark 5:22-24, 35-43; Luke 8:41-42, 49-55)*. A woman who had had an issue of blood for 12 years had faith that if she could just touch Jesus' garment she would be healed. Jesus sensed when she touched his garment and told her that her faith had made her whole *(vs. 20-22; Mark 5:25-34; Luke 8:43-48)*. Two blind men asked Jesus to have mercy on them and heal them. Jesus asked them if they believed that he could do that. When they said yes, he touched their eyes and healed them according to their faith. Then they spread his fame abroad in the country *(vs. 27-31)*. A dumb man possessed with a devil was brought to Jesus and the devil was cast out. The Pharisees claimed Jesus cast out devils through the prince of the devils *(vs. 32-34)*.

Matt. 10; Mark 3; Luke 6, 9. Jesus called 12 disciples: Simon Peter, Andrew, James, John, Philip, Bartholomew; Thomas, Matthew, James, Lebbæus (Thaddæus), Simon the Canaanite, and Judas Iscariot *(vs. 2-4; Mark 3:16-19; Luke 6:13-16)*. *(Note: The listing of the apostles in Luke differs slightly from the listings in Matthew and Mark: instead of Thaddæus, Luke lists Judas the brother of James, and Simon the Canaanite is listed as Simon called Zelotes.)* Jesus empowered these apostles and sent them forth to teach, but instructed them that they should not go to the Gentiles nor to the Samaritans. They were to go to the lost sheep of the house of Israel. They were to heal the sick and cast out devils. They were to travel without purse or scrip. They were instructed to leave their peace upon those who received them, but to shake the dust off their feet when leaving the houses of those who reject them *(vs. 5-14; Luke 9:1-5)*. They were told they would be persecuted for Christ's sake, but that "he that endureth to the end shall be saved." They are of more value than the sparrows for which the Father provides. The hairs of their heads are even numbered *(vs. 16-32)*.

Matt. 11; Luke 7. After Jesus instructed his disciples, he went to teach and preach in their cities. Two of John the Baptist's disciples were sent to inquire if the person John heard about while in prison was Christ. Christ acknowledged that it was he whom John was hearing about. Christ testified that John was more than just a reed shaken with the wind or a man clothed in soft raiment. John was a prophet—yea, even more than a prophet *(vs. 2-15; Luke 7:19-28)*. Jesus upbraided the cities of Chorazin, Bethsaida and Capernaum for unbelief and refusing to repent *(vs. 20-24)*. Everything is revealed unto Jesus by the Father. No man knows the Father save the Son and those to whom the Son will reveal himself *(vs. 25-27)*. The Lord's yoke is easy and his burden is light *(v. 30)*.

Matt. 12; Mark 2, 3; Luke 6, 11. Jesus plucked corn on the Sabbath so his disciples could assuage their hunger. When the Pharisees complained that Christ's disciples were breaking the Sabbath, Jesus said he was the Lord of the Sabbath *(vs. 1-9; Mark 2:23-28; Luke 6:1-5)*. He healed a man's withered hand on the Sabbath. Again the Pharisees complained, and Jesus responded that it is lawful to do well on the Sabbath *(vs. 10-13; Mark 3:1-5; Luke 6:6-10)*. A man possessed with a devil, blind and dumb was brought to Jesus, and Jesus healed him. The Pharisees claimed he cast out devils by the power of Beelzebub, the prince of devils. Jesus reminded them that a house divided against itself cannot stand. If Satan cast himself out, he could not stand *(vs. 22-28; Mark 3:22-26; Luke 11:14-20)*. Men can be forgiven for all manner of sin except blasphemy against the Holy Ghost which cannot be forgiven unto men, neither in this world nor in the world to come. *(vs. 31-32; Mark 3:28-29)*. A tree is known by its fruit; men shall be either justified or condemned by their words *(vs. 33-37; Luke 6:43-45)*. The scribes and Pharisees sought a sign and were told that an evil and adulterous generation seeketh after a sign. Jesus said the only sign they would have was the sign of the prophet Jonas (Jonah) who was in the belly of the whale three days and three nights. Likewise, the Son of Man would be three days and three nights in the heart of the earth. The men of Nineveh and the queen of Sheba would rise in judgment against these people. The men of Nineveh repented at the preaching of Jonah and the queen of Sheba sought wisdom from Solomon. One greater than Jonah or Solomon was with them and they refused to accept him *(vs. 38-42; Luke 11:16, 29-32)*. When informed that his mother and brethren desired to speak to him, he asked, "Who is my mother? and who are my brethren?" Those who do the will of the Father constitute Christ's family, his mother, brother and sister *(vs. 46-50; Mark 3:31-35; Luke 8:19-21)*.

Matt. 13; Mark 4; Luke 8; 13; 17. Jesus taught in parables and explained why, saying, ". . . all these things are done in parables: That seeing they may see, and not perceive; and hearing they may hear, and not understand; lest at any time they should be converted, and their sins should be forgiven them" *(vs. 10-17, 34-35; Mark 4:2, 11-12; Luke 8:9-10)*. He taught the parable of the sower: some seeds fell by the wayside *(when people have heard the word, Satan comes and takes away the word that was sown in their hearts)*; some fell on stony ground *(have no root in themselves so only endure for a short time, but fall away due to affliction, persecution, other offenses)*; some seeds are sown among thorns *(cares of the world, riches, choked out the word)*; some seeds are sown on good ground *(the people receive it and bring forth good fruit: 30, 60, 100 fold) (vs. 3-9; Mark 4:3-9; Luke 8:5-8)*; and gave the explanation *(vs. 18-23; Mark 4:14-20; Luke 8:11-15)*. He taught another parable of the sower and the tares *(vs. 24-30)*; and gave the explanation *(vs. 36-43).* He taught the parable of the mustard seed *(vs. 31-32; also see Mark 4:30-32; Luke 13:18-19; Luke 17:5-6);* the leaven *(v. 33);* the treasure hid in a field *(v. 44);* the pearl of great price *(vs. 45-46);* the net cast into the sea *(vs. 47-48);* and gave the explanation *(vs. 49-50).* Jesus was the son of a carpenter. His mother was Mary. His brethren were James, Joses, Simon, and Judas (Juda). His sisters are not named *(vs. 55-56; Mark 6:3).* A prophet is without honor among his own people *(v. 57; Mark 6:4).*

Matt. 14; Mark 6; Luke 9; John 6. Jesus' fame reached Herod the tetrarch and Herod thought perhaps John the Baptist *(whom he had beheaded in prison)* had risen from the dead and that it was he of whom he heard *(vs. 1-2; Mark 6:16; Luke 9:7-9).* When Jesus was informed by his disciples that John was dead, he left by ship and went to a desert place. The people followed him and he healed their sick. As evening approached, his disciples suggested he send the people away so the people could get themselves some food. Instead, Jesus had his disciples give him the five loaves and two fishes they had. He blessed and brake it and fed about 5,000 men plus women and children. Twelve baskets full of fragments remained *(vs. 15-21; Mark 6:35-44; Luke 9:10-17; John 6:5-14). (Note: the account recorded in John says a lad had the five loaves and two fishes.)* As Jesus sent the multitude away, he had his disciples sail ahead of him to the other side. After taking time to pray, he went to join them, walking upon the water. Peter left the ship and began walking on the water toward Jesus but became frightened and began to sink. Jesus caught him *(vs. 22-31; Mark 6:45-51). (Note: The account of Peter walking on the water is not included in the account recorded in Mark.).* The men of Gennesaret brought their diseased to Jesus and had faith that those who touched the hem of Christ's garment would be made whole, and it was so *(vs. 34-36; Mark 6:53-56).*

Matt. 15; Mark 7; 8; Luke 11. Jesus, when confronted by the scribes and Pharisees who asked why Jesus' disciples violated the tradition of the elders by not washing their hands before eating, stressed that it isn't what goes into a person's mouth that defiles him but that which comes out of the mouth because that which comes out of the mouth comes from the heart. He also chastised them for not honoring their fathers and mothers *(vs. 1-20. See Mark 7:1-5, 13-22; Also Luke 11:37-41).* He traveled to the coasts of Tyre and Sidon and was approached by a woman from Canaan whose daughter was "vexed with a devil." She pleaded with the Lord to heal her daughter. He ignored her at first, but finally, after her pleadings, he told her that because her faith was so great, she would be healed. And she was from that very hour *(vs. 21-28).* Jesus went to the Sea of Galilee where he was followed by a multitude. He healed their sick, lame, blind, etc. The people stayed with him three days without food. Jesus refused to send them away fasting and inquired of his disciples as to how much bread they had. They had seven loaves and a few fishes. Jesus gave thanks for the loaves and fishes, broke them and fed 4,000 men plus women and children; and there were seven baskets full left over. He sent the multitudes away and took a ship to Magdala *(vs. 29-39; Mark 8:1-9).*

Matt. 16; Mark 8; Luke 9. Jesus rebuked the Pharisees and Sadducees who tried to tempt him by asking for a sign from heaven. He chastised them for being able to recognize the signs of the weather but unable to discern the signs of the times *(vs. 1-3; Luke 12:54-57).* The only sign they would be given was the sign of Jonas *(i.e., Jonah, who was in the belly of the whale three days, representing the three days Christ would be in the earth before his resurrection) (v. 4; Luke 11:16, 29-30)*. Jesus taught his disciples to beware the leaven *(i.e., the doctrine)* of the Pharisees and Sadducees *(i.e., of Herod), (vs. 5-12; Mark 8:14- 18; Luke 12:1)*. He asked his disciples who the people said he was. They said that some said he was John the Baptist, others Elias, and still others said Jeremias. When he asked who they said he was, Peter responded, "Thou art Christ, the Son of the living God." Jesus told him that flesh and blood had not revealed that to him but his Father who was in heaven. He told Peter that upon that rock *(i.e., the rock of revelation, also Christ is the Stone, the Rock, of Israel)*, he would establish his church. He would give Peter the keys of the priesthood. He told Peter that that which he sealed on earth would be sealed in heaven and that which he loosed on earth would be loosed in heaven *(vs. 13-19; Mark 8:27-30; Luke 9:18-22). (Note: the accounts in Mark and Luke are abbreviated.)* When Jesus comes again in the glory of his Father with the angels, he will reward people according to their works *(v. 27)*.

Matt. 17; Mark 9; Luke 9. Jesus was transfigured before Peter, James and John. While on the mountain, Moses and Elias appeared and spoke to Jesus. While Peter was speaking, suggesting they make three altars: one each for Jesus, Moses and Elias, a voice spoke out of a cloud saying, "This is my beloved son, in whom I am well pleased; hear ye him." When Peter questioned Jesus regarding the prophecies that Elias must first come, Jesus taught them that Elias had already come *(i.e., John the Baptist)*, but that another Elias *(i.e., Elijah)* would come to restore all things as the prophets had written *(see Mal. 4:5-6) (v. 1-12; Mark 9:2-13; Luke 9:28-35). (Note: These scriptures in Matthew and modern-day revelation records the fulfillment of the prophecy in Malachi.)*

> *Malachi's prophecy was fulfilled when Elias (Elijah), a translated being, appeared on the mount of transfiguration with Moses who was also translated, and conferred the keys of the priesthood on Peter, James and John. He appeared again on April 3, 1836, along with Moses and others, in the Kirtland Ohio Temple and conferred those keys upon Joseph Smith and Oliver Cowdery. Without this sealing power, families would be disbanded at death and the plan of the Lord, the plan that provides for eternal families, the Plan of Exaltation, would be null and void (D&C 27:5-14.)*

Jesus healed the "lunatick" son of a certain man who petitioned Jesus in behalf of his son. The disciples could not heal him because of lack of faith—the kind of faith that comes by fasting and prayer *(vs. 14-21; Mark 9:17-29)*. Jesus again taught his disciples that he would be betrayed, killed, and would rise again on the third day *(vs. 22-23; Mark 9:31)*. The tax collectors in Capernaum questioned whether or not Jesus paid tribute. Jesus responded by having Peter catch a fish, and retrieve a piece of money from the fish's mouth. He instructed Peter to give it to the tax collectors "for thee and me" *(vs. 24-27)*.

Matt. 18; Mark 9; Luke 9, 17. Jesus taught that those who are the greatest in the kingdom of heaven are those who are converted and become as little children. It would be better to be drowned in the sea than to offend a little child *(vs. 1-6; Mark 9:33-37, 42; Luke 9:46-48; 17:2)*. Every sheep is dear to the heart of the shepherd. Likewise, it is the will of Heavenly Father that not one of his little ones should perish, even if we must leave the ninety and nine to search for the one that has gone astray *(vs. 10-14)*. Jesus told his disciples that whatsoever they bound on earth would be bound in heaven and whatsoever they loosed on earth would be loosed in heaven. Whenever two or three are gathered in his name, he will be there, also *(vs. 18-20)*. We should forgive those who offend us seventy times seven. Jesus taught the parable of the servant who was forgiven his debts but who refused to forgive a fellowservant of his debts. If we do not forgive others, Heavenly Father will not forgive us either *(vs. 21-35; see also Luke 17:3-4)*.

Matt. 19; Mark 10:1-25; Luke 18. Jesus traveled from Galilee to the coasts of Judæa. When the Pharisees queried him about marriage and divorce, he told them that what God hath joined together, man should not put asunder. The Pharisees pointed out that Moses had commanded that a letter of divorcement could be written and the wife could be put away. Jesus replied that that was because of the hardness of their hearts, but that "from the beginning it was not so" and that those who did, "except for fornication," and married another committed adultery, and whosoever married the woman who had been put away also committed adultery. ("And if a woman shall put away her husband, and be married to another, she committeth adultery") *(vs. 1-9; Mark 10:2-12; Luke 16:18)*. Jesus instructed his disciples to let the little children come unto him because "of such is the kingdom of heaven" *(vs. 13-14; Mark 10:13-16)*. When asked how one could obtain eternal life, Jesus said that those who forsake all things for his name's sake and follow him shall inherit everlasting life, but that a "rich man *(i.e., one who loves his possessions more than the Savior)* shall hardly enter into the kingdom of heaven" *(vs. 16-30; Mark 10:17-25; Luke 18:18-25)*.

Matt. 20; Mark 10:28-52. Jesus taught a parable about laborers in a vineyard: each man who serves the Lord will be recompensed according to agreement. Those who hire on at the eleventh hour may receive the same reward as those who hire on the first hour. The Lord has a right to "do what I will with mine own" and should not be criticized for being good *(vs. 1-16)*. As Jesus and his disciples traveled to Jerusalem, he told them that the Son of Man would be betrayed into the hands of the chief priests and scribes and would be condemned and crucified, but that he would rise again on the third day *(vs. 17-19; Mark 10:32-34)*. The mother of two of Jesus' disciples—James and John—asked Jesus to grant that her sons could sit on his left and on his right side in his kingdom. He asked if they were able to "drink of the cup" that he would drink and be baptized with the baptism with which he was baptized. They said yes. Nevertheless, Jesus said that it was not his to give who would sit on his left on his right, "but it shall be given to them for whom it is prepared of my Father." When the other disciples complained about James and John, Jesus taught them all that "whosoever will be great among you, let him be your minister. . . let him be your servant." He then reminded them that he came into the world not to be ministered unto but to serve and to give his life as a ransom for many *(vs. 20-28; Mark 10:28-31, 35-45)*. *(Note: In the account recorded in Mark, it says James and John made the request of Jesus, not their mother.)* They left Jerusalem followed by a multitude. Two blind men cried out for his mercy. He touched their eyes and they could see. "And they followed him" *(vs.*

30-34; Mark 10:46-52). (Note: The account recorded in Mark indicates there was one blind man, and his name was Bartimæus, the son of Timæus.)

Matt. 21; Mark 11; Luke 19, 20; John 12. Jesus instructed two of his disciples to go into a nearby village and get an ass and colt and bring them to him. If questioned, they were to say, "The Lord hath need of them." This was in fulfillment of the prophecy spoken of by Zechariah in the Old Testament: "Tell ye the daughter of Sion, Behold, thy King cometh unto thee, meek, and sitting upon an ass, and a colt the foal of an ass" *(see Zech. 9:9; John 12:14-15).* As Jesus rode into Jerusalem, the multitude spread their garments and branches down before him. They praised him, crying, "Hosanna to the Son of David," and proclaimed him to be Jesus the prophet of Nazareth of Galilee *(vs. 1-11; Mark 11:1-11; Luke 19:28-40; John 12:12- 13).* He went into the temple and cast out the money-changers *(vs. 12-13; Mark 11:15-17; Luke 19:45-46).* He healed the blind and the lame. The chief priests and scribes were displeased when they saw what he did *(vs. 14-15; Mark 11:18).* He journeyed to Bethany and condemned a fig tree that yielded no fruit to assuage his hunger. His disciples marveled at how quickly the fig tree withered away. Jesus taught them that if they have faith, they would be able to do the same thing and even more—that "all things, whatsoever ye shall ask in prayer, believing, ye shall receive" *(vs. 17-22; Mark 11:12-14, 20-24).* The chief priests and elders of the people demanded to know by what authority Jesus did what he did. Because they said they could not tell whether John's baptism was from heaven or of men, Jesus said he would not tell by what authority he did what he did *(vs. 23-27; Mark 11:27-33; Luke 20:1-8).* Jesus taught two parables: one about two sons—the first son said he wouldn't work in his father's vineyard, but repented and did; the other son said he would but didn't. Then Jesus told the chief priests and Pharisees that the publicans and harlots would enter into God's kingdom before they would *(vs. 28-32).* The second parable was about a wicked husbandman who killed the servants of the householder and then killed the heir of the householder. The chief priests and Pharisees concluded that the householder would destroy the wicked husbandman and his men and let out his vineyard to another. Jesus responded, "Therefore say I unto you, The kingdom of God shall be taken from you, and given to a nation bringing forth the fruits thereof. They feared to lay hands on Jesus because the people esteemed him as a prophet *(vs. 33-46; Mark 12:1-12; Luke 20:9-19).*

Matt. 22; Mark 12; Luke 20. Jesus gave the parable about the marriage of the king's son: those who were invited to the wedding refused to come so the king sent his armies forth and destroyed them. The king then sent his servants out into the highways to gather all they could find and bring them into the wedding. One man who came was not dressed in a wedding garment and the king had him cast out into outer darkness. "Many are called, but few are chosen" *(vs. 1-14).* The Pharisees sought to entangle him and asked if it was lawful to pay tribute unto Cæsar. Jesus said they should render unto Cæsar that which is Cæsar's and unto God that which is God's *(vs. 15-22; Mark 12:13-17; Luke 20:20-26).* The Sadducees, who did not believe in the resurrection, queried Jesus about marriage and whose wife a particular woman would be in the resurrection since she had been married to a man who died and then in turn to each of his six brothers—one after another as each died. Christ taught that worldly marriages endure in this life only and that she wouldn't be a wife to any of them in the resurrection *(vs. 23-30; Mark 12:18-27)*. The Pharisees asked Jesus which was the greatest commandment. Jesus said the first commandment is to love the Lord and the second is like unto it, to love thy neighbor as thyself. "On these two commandments hang all the law and the prophets" *(vs. 34-40; Mark 12:28-34)*. The Pharisees said Jesus was the Son of David. Jesus countered that David in spirit *(in the book of Psalms)* called him Lord. If David called him Lord, how could he be his son *(vs. 41-46; Mark 12:35-37; Luke 20:41-44)*.

Matt. 23; Luke 11. Jesus condemned the scribes and Pharisees and called them hypocrites. The people were counseled to follow their teachings but not their works because "they say, and do not" *(v. 3)* and appear beautiful and righteous on the outside but inside they are full of iniquity and hypocrisy *(v. 28)*. They, along with their forefathers, kill the prophets and will not escape the damnation of hell *(vs. 29-35; Luke 11:45-42)*. Jesus lamented, "O Jerusalem, Jerusalem, . . . how often would I have gathered thy children together, even as a hen gathereth her chickens under her wings, and ye would not!" *(v. 37)*

Matt. 24; Mark 13; Luke 17, 21. Jesus' disciples asked him when his Second Coming would be and what the signs would be to indicate the end of the world. Jesus said that no man, not even the angels of heaven, knew the day and hour of his coming, only his Father in Heaven. However, certain signs would precede that day: there would be false Christs and false prophets, wars and rumors of wars, famines, pestilences and earthquakes, nation would rise against nation, people would betray and hate one another, and his gospel would "be preached in all the world for a witness unto all nations; and then shall the end come" *(vs. 1-12, 36; also see Luke 21)*. He reminded them that Daniel *(see the OT)* had spoken of the desolation that would precede his coming. Jesus gave the parable of the fig tree: just as people recognize that summer is nigh when the fig tree begins to leaf, likewise when the signs spoken of appear, the Second Coming will be nigh. He also said that just as the people in the days of Noe (Noah) did not know when the flood would occur but needed to be ready and watchful, so it will be with the Second Coming *(vs. 32-51; also see Luke 17:20-37; 21:29-36)*.

Matt. 25. Jesus taught three parables. (1) The parable of the 10 virgins. Five were wise and kept their lamps full of oil. Five were foolish and let their lamps burn dry; thus, when the bridegroom came, they were unable to join the wedding party *(vs. 1-13)*. We must always be prepared because we don't know the day nor hour when the Savior will come. (2) The parable of the talents. Three servants were entrusted with five, two and one talents respectively. The servants having received five and two talents invested them and returned them doubled to their master. They were rewarded by being made ruler over many things. The one with one talent buried it and returned only what he had been given. His master was wroth with him for being an unprofitable servant and he was cast out into outer darkness *(vs. 14-30. Also see Luke 19:11-27)*. (3) The parable of the sheep and goats. When the Son of Man comes again, he will gather the sheep on his right hand and the goats on his left. The sheep are those who fed the hungry, clothed the naked, healed the sick. The goats are those who refused to clothe the naked, heal the sick or feed the hungry. "Inasmuch as ye have done it unto one of the least of these my brethren, ye have done it unto me . . . Inasmuch as ye did it not to one of the least of these, ye did it not to me" *(vs. 31-46).*

Matt. 26; Mark 14; Luke 22; John 13. Jesus warned his disciples that following the Passover, two days hence, he would be betrayed to be crucified *(vs. 1-2).* When Jesus was in the home of Simon the leper, a woman poured oil on his head. The disciples objected at the "wasting" of such precious oil. Jesus gently rebuked them, saying they would always have the poor with them. The woman had anointed his body for burial. Wherever the gospel was preached, people were to be told of her deed as a memorial of her *(vs. 6- 13; Mark 14:3-9). (Note: John 11:2, identifies the woman as Mary the sister of Martha and Lazarus.)* Judas Iscariot, one of Jesus' disciples, promised to betray him for thirty pieces of silver *(vs. 14-16; Mark 14:10-11; Luke 22:3-6).* Jesus kept the Passover with his disciples in the home of a certain man. He instituted the sacrament. He told his disciples that one of them would betray him. They all promised they never would deny him. Jesus warned Peter that before the cock crowed [twice], he would deny him three times *(vs. 17-35; Mark 14:12-31; Luke 22:31-34; John 13:37-38).* Jesus and his disciples went to a place called Gethsemane. He asked the disciples to sit and wait, but he took Peter, James and John—the sons of Zebedee—with him as he went into the garden. He asked them to tarry with him while he went a little way further to pray. When he returned Peter, James and John were asleep. He woke them and asked them to watch and pray. He went to pray a second time and they were asleep again when he returned. He left them sleeping and prayed a third time, "O my Father, if this cup may not pass away from me, except I drink it, thy will be done" *(vs. 36-45; Mark 14:32-41; Luke 22:39-46). (Note: The account recorded in Luke states that an angel from heaven ministered unto him and strengthened him.)* Judas betrayed Jesus with a kiss, a prearranged signal *(vs. 47-50; Mark 14:43-46; Luke 22:47-48; see John 18 for a modified version).* Jesus was taken to Caiaphas, the high priest, and the scribes and elders. Peter followed. Jesus was tried and found guilty of blasphemy when two false witnesses testified against him. Three times people accused Peter of being one of Jesus' disciples. Three times he denied knowing Jesus, and immediately the cock crowed. Peter went out and wept bitterly *(vs. 57-75; Mark 14:53-72; Luke 22:54-62). (Note: The record in Mark states that the cock first crowed after Peter's first denial. It crowed the second time immediately after his third denial.)*

Matt. 27; Mark 15; Luke 23. Jesus was taken to Pontius Pilate, the governor, by the chief priests and elders who conspired to have Jesus put to death *(vs. 1-2; Mark 15:1; Luke 23:1).* The chief priests and elders accused Jesus, but he answered nothing *(v. 12; Mark 15:2-5).* Pilate wanted to release Jesus, but the chief priests and elders persuaded the multitude to request the release of Barabbas and not Jesus *(vs. 13-26; Mark 15:6-15; Luke 23:2-25). (Note: The account in Luke states that the people took Christ to Pilate, who subsequently sent him to Herod. Herod returned him again to Pilate, who wanted to release Jesus, but finally acquiesced to the people's demands.)* The soldiers took Jesus, stripped him, put on him a scarlet robe, a crown of platted thorns and spit upon him and mocked him *(vs. 27-31; Mark 15:16-20).* The soldiers compelled Simon from Cyrene to bear Jesus' cross. Above his head, on the cross, a sign was placed which read, "THIS IS JESUS THE KING OF THE JEWS" *(vs. 32-37; Mark 15:21-26; Luke 23:26,*

38). Two thieves were also crucified with Jesus, one on his left hand and one on his right. They and the chief priests, scribes and elders mocked Jesus *(vs.38-44; Mark 15:27-32; Luke 23:32-33, 39-43). (Note: The account in Luke states that just one malefactor railed on Christ. The other rebuked his fellow thief, and asked Jesus to remember him when he came into his kingdom. Christ told him, "Today shalt thou be with me in paradise.")* From the sixth to the ninth hour, darkness covered the land. And then Jesus cried out, "My God, my God, why hast thou forsaken me?" And then he yielded up the ghost *(vs. 45-50; Mark 15:33-37; Luke 23:44-46).* The earth quaked, the veil of the temple was torn, rocks were broken up, and graves were opened and saints came out of the graves after Jesus' resurrection *(vs. 51-53; Mark 15:38).* The centurion who watched and saw the earthquake declared that Jesus truly was the Son of God. Many women followed after Jesus and observed from afar: Mary Magdalene; Mary the mother of James (the less) and Joses, and the mother of Zebedee's children [and Salome] [and the women who followed him] *(vs. 54-56; Mark 15:39-41; Luke 23:47-49). (Note: The account in Matt. includes "the mother of Zebedee's children." The account in Mark includes "Salome" rather than "the mother of Zebedee's children." The account in Luke does not name the women.)* Joseph of Arimathæa begged Pilate for the body of Jesus. He wrapped Christ in clean linen and placed him in a new tomb, and then he rolled a stone to the door of the sepulchre *(vs. 57-60; Mark 15:42-46; Luke 23:50-54). (Note: John 19:39 indicates that Nicodemus assisted Joseph of Arimathæa in retrieving Christ's body and wrapping it in linen, etc.)* Mary Magdalene and the other Mary [and Mary the mother of Joses] sat over by the sepulchre [beheld where he was laid] *(v. 61; Mark 15:47; Luke 23:55-56).* Meanwhile, the chief priests and Pharisees went to Pilate and asked him to make sure the tomb was secure so Jesus' disciples could not steal the body *(vs. 62-66).*

Matt. 28; Mark 16; Luke 24. Jesus was not in the sepulchre when Mary Magdalene and the other Mary [Mary Magdalene, and Mary the mother of James, and Salom] went there at the end of the Sabbath following his crucifixion. An angel of the Lord told them to fear not, [two men in shining garments said . . .] that he had risen as he had said he would. As the women went to tell the disciples as instructed, Jesus appeared to them. He also told them not to be afraid, but to go and tell his brethren they would see him in Galilee *(vs. 5-10; Mark 16:6-7; Luke 24:1-10). (Note: Mark 16:9 says Jesus "appeared first to Mary Magdalene, out of whom he had cast seven devils.")* Jesus met his eleven disciples in Galilee and they worshiped him. However, some doubted. He instructed his disciples to go into all the nations and baptize people "in the name of the Father, and of the Son, and of the Holy Ghost" *(vs. 16-20).* Signs shall follow those who believe *(Mark 16:16-20).*

Mark 1. See entry for Matt. 3. Part of Mark 1 also follows entry for Matt. 4.

Mark 1; Luke 4-5. Jesus taught in the synagogue as one with authority, not as the scribes *(vs. 21-22).* He cast out an unclean spirit from a man in the synagogue *(vs. 23-26; Luke 4:34-35). (Note: See entry for Matt. 8 for the healing of Simon's mother-in-law. Mark 1:29-31; Luke 4:38-39.)* Jesus healed all that were diseased and possessed with devils who were brought to him *(vs. 34-39; Luke 4:40-42).* The following morning as they journeyed to another town, he healed a leper who beseeched him. The leper spread it around and, as a result, "Jesus could no more openly enter into the city, but was without in desert places: and they came to him from every quarter" *(vs. 40-45; Luke 5:12-15).*

Mark 2. Jesus went to Capernaum and was immediately surrounded by so many people there was not room in the house. Four men brought one who was sick with palsy. They could not get into the house with him so they made a hole in the roof of the house and lowered him through the hole. When Jesus saw their great faith, he said to the sick man, "Son, thy sins be forgiven thee." Certain of the scribes found fault with Jesus for saying the man's sins were forgiven. However, Jesus taught that it was just as easy to say, "Thy sins be forgiven thee," as it was to say, "Arise, and take up thy bed, and walk," but that they should know that the Son of Man had power on earth to forgive sins *(vs. 3-11).* Jesus called Levi (Matthew) to come follow him *(vs. 14-17; see Matt. 9:9). (Note: The BD states that Matthew was known as Levi prior to his conversion.)* Jesus' disciples had no need to fast as long as he was with them. When the bridegroom is taken from them, then they will fast *(vs. 18-20).* You don't sew new cloth onto old nor pour new wine into old bottles *(vs. 21-22).* Jesus' disciples plucked ears of corn on the Sabbath day. "The Sabbath was made for man, and not man for the Sabbath." The Son of Man is also Lord of the Sabbath *(vs. 23-28).*

Mark 3. Jesus and his disciples withdrew from the people as the Pharisees plotted with the Herodians against Jesus. He requested that a small boat should wait on him because of the multitude, "lest they should throng him" *(v. 7).* He ordained the twelve apostles *(vs. 16-19; see entry for Matt. 10:2-4).* The scribes claimed he had Beelzebub *(vs. 22-26; see entry for Matt. 12:22-28).* Blasphemy against the Holy Ghost cannot be forgiven *(vs. 28-29; see entry for Matt. 12:31-32).* Those who do the work of his Father are his mother, brother and sister *(vs. 31-35; see entry for Matt 12:46-50).*

Mark 4; Luke 8, 13. (See the entry for Matt. 13 for the parable of the Sower.) He gave the parable of the candlestick *(vs. 21-22; Luke 8:16-17; 11:33-36);* the parable of the seed growing in secret *(vs. 26-29);* and the parable of the mustard seed *(vs. 30-32; Matt. 13:31-32; Luke 13:18-19; also see Luke 17:5-6).* Jesus and his disciples decided to cross over to the other side of the lake in several boats. While Jesus slept, a windstorm arose and began to swamp the boat. His disciples awakened him and asked, "Master, carest thou not that we perish?" Jesus rebuked the wind and calmed the sea *(vs. 36-41; Luke 8:22-25).*

Mark 5; Luke 8. Jesus cast out devils which entered swine. *(vs. 1-13, 17. See entry for Matt. 8.). (For the stories of Jairus and the woman who touched Jesus' garment, see the entry for Matt. 9.)*

Mark 6. See Matt. 13-14.

Mark 7. Jesus chastised the Pharisees for following false traditions such as the excessive washing of hands. That which goes into a man's mouth is not what defiles the man [for it comes out in the "draught"], but that which comes forth out of the mouth [which originates from out of the heart]—evil thoughts, adulteries, murders, thefts, etc.—are what defile a man *(vs. 1-5, 13-22; also see Matt. 15:1-20; Luke 11:37-41).* Esaias (Isaiah) had correctly prophesied of them: "This people honoureth me with their lips, but their heart is far from me" *(v. 6).* A certain woman who was a Greek, a Syrophenician, asked Jesus to cast a devil out of her daughter. Jesus responded that the children of the kingdom should first be cared for: "for it is not meet to take the children's bread, and to cast it unto the dogs" *(i.e., give that which belongs to the children of the kingdom of God to those who are unworthy).* Her response was that the dogs under the table eat of the children's crumbs. Because of her response, Jesus told her to go her way and that the devil was gone from out of her daughter, and it was so *(vs. 25- 30).* A man who was deaf and had a speech impediment was brought to Jesus, and he healed both his ears and his speech impediment *(vs. 32- 35).*

Mark 8 (See Matt. 15; 16). Jesus fed the multitude *(which numbered about 4,000)* who had been with him for three days without eating. His disciples had seven loaves and a few small fishes. After they had eaten, there were seven baskets of broken "meat" left *(vs. 1-9; Matt. 15:29-39).* The Pharisees sought a sign of him. He said no sign would be given unto that generation *(vs. 9-12; Matt. 16:1-4).* Jesus counseled his disciples to beware of the leaven of the Pharisees and of Herod *(vs. 14-18; see Matt. 16:5-12; Luke 12:1).* He healed a blind man *(vs. 22-26).* Christ asked, "Whom do men say that I am?" *(v. 27; see Matt. 16:19).* When Christ tried to teach his disciples that he would be rejected and killed but would rise again in three days, Peter began to rebuke him. Jesus chastised Peter because he did not "savour" that which was of God. Jesus called the people to come follow him. "Whosoever will save his life shall lose it; but whosoever shall lose his life for my sake and the gospel's, the same shall save it" *(vs. 31-38; Matt. 16:24-25).*

Mark 9. (See Matt. 18:6; Luke 17:2.) Jesus took a little child and stressed, "Whosoever shall humble himself like one of these children, and receiveth me, ye shall receive in my name. And whosoever shall receive me, receiveth not me only, but him that sent me, even the Father" *(vs. 36-37; JST vs. 34-35).* Jesus condemned those who offend children. Better to cut off a hand if it offend thee than to go into hell with two hands *(vs. 42-50).*

Mark 10. See entries for Matt. 19-20.

Mark 11. Jesus taught that we must forgive others or our Father in Heaven will not forgive us our trespasses *(vs. 25-26). (Also see entry for Matt. 21.)*

Mark 12; Luke 21. Jesus cautioned people to beware of hypocritical scribes *(vs. 38-40).* The widow who gave two mites into the treasury gave more than the wealthy because she gave of her want; they gave of their abundance *(vs. 41-44; Luke 21:1-4). (For verses 1-37, see entries for Matt. 21, 22.)*

Mark 13; Matt. 24; Luke 17. Jesus explained to Peter, James, John and Andrew what calamities would precede the Second Coming. There would be false Christs, wars and rumors of wars, nation would rise against nation and kingdom against kingdom; there would be earthquakes and famines and troubles. The prophets would be persecuted for Christ's sake. Brother would betray brother and fathers would betray their sons; children shall rise against their parents. The desolation prophesied by Daniel will come to pass. The sun shall be darkened, the moon will not give its light, and the stars of heaven shall fall. The Son of Man will then come in the clouds in great power and glory *(vs. 3-27).* Jesus said to watch for the signs: just as we know summer is near when the fig tree puts forth her tender branches, so the signs will signal the Second Coming. Nevertheless, Jesus stressed that no man knows the day, time, nor place. We should be prepared and not caught "sleeping" *(vs. 28-37; also see Matt. 24:37-51; Luke 17:20-37).*

Mark 14. See entry for Matt. 26.

Mark 15. See entry for Matt. 27.

Mark 16. See entry for Matt. 28.

Luke 4. Jesus went to Nazareth and taught in the synagogue on the Sabbath from the book of Esaias (Isaiah). And he told them that the Spirit of the Lord was upon him because he had been anointed to preach the gospel to the poor, heal the broken-hearted, preach deliverance to the captives and others, etc. "This day is this scripture fulfilled in your ears." He knew the people would say unto him, "Physician heal thyself," and he told them "No prophet is accepted in his own country." He told them that when the heavens were shut up for three and a half years, Elias (Elijah) was sent only unto a widow. Likewise, there were many lepers in the time of Eliseus but only Naaman the Syrian was cleansed. The people were then angry with Jesus *(vs. 16-29). (See entry for Matt. 4:1-11 for Luke 4:1-13.)*

Luke 5. See entries for Matt. 4 and Mark 1.

Luke 6. See entries for Matt. 12 and Matt. 7.

Luke 7. Jesus had compassion on a widow woman and restored the life of her only son, saying, "Young man, I say unto thee, Arise." And he did *(vs. 11-18)*. Jesus was invited by Simon, a Pharisee, to have dinner with him. A woman who was a sinner, when she heard that Jesus was having dinner in the home of Simon, brought an alabaster box of ointment and anointed Jesus' feet, washing his feet with her tears, wiping his feet with her hair, and kissing his feet. *(See Matt. 26:7-13 and Mark 14:3-9 for a similar account when Mary, the sister of Martha and Lazarus, anointed the Savior with ointment and washed his feet with her tears and wiped them dry with her hair. See John 11:2.)* When Simon disapproved, Jesus gave a parable about two debtors who were forgiven by their master. The one who was most in debt was forgiven the most, and that debtor loved his master the most. Jesus forgave the woman of her sins and reminded Simon that since he had entered Simon's house, Simon had not shown him any of the love the woman had *(vs. 36-50). (For Luke 7:1-10, see entry for Matt. 8. For Luke 7:18-28, see entry for Matt. 11.)*

Luke 8. As Jesus went throughout the villages preaching, many followed after him, including several women: Mary Magdalene, Joanna and Susanna who ministered unto him *(vs. 1-3). (Note: For the parable of the Sower, see entry for Matt. 13. For the parable of the candlestick and Christ's calming the sea, see the entry for Mark 4. For Christ's casting out the devils who entered the swine, see entry for Matt. 8; the healing of Jairus' daughter and the woman who had had an issue of blood twelve years, see the entry for Mark 5.)*

Luke 9. A man who cast out devils in the name of Christ was forbidden to do so by John and other of Christ's disciples. When John told Jesus about the man, Jesus told them they should not forbid him, "for he that is not against us is for us" *(vs. 49-50)*. Three different men offered to follow Jesus. Jesus told the first that he had no place to even lay his head. The second wanted to bury his father first. Jesus said to let the dead bury the dead. The third wanted to tell his family farewell first. Jesus said that he that puts his hand to the plough and then looks back is not fit for the kingdom of God *(vs. 57-62)*.

Luke 10. Jesus called seventy and sent them two and two into the cities and towns to do missionary work. He told them to go without purse or scrip. They were to bless the houses of those who accept them, but to wipe the dust of their feet off into the streets as a curse against those who reject them. They were given authority to teach and heal and to have power over the power of the enemy *(vs. 1-20).* Jesus rejoiced in the Spirit. The Father is revealed only through the Son *(vs. 21-22).* A certain lawyer tried to tempt Jesus by asking what he should do to inherit eternal life. Jesus asked him what the law said, and said to follow the law. The lawyer asked, "And who is my neighbor?" Jesus then taught the parable of the good Samaritan. The man who helped the injured man showed himself to be neighbor unto that man. Jesus told the lawyer to go and do likewise *(vs. 25-37).* Martha and Mary were sisters who were friends of Jesus. Martha tended to duties while Mary sat at Christ's feet. When Martha complained to the Savior, he said, "Martha, Martha, thou art careful and troubled about many things; But one thing is needful: and Mary hath chosen that good part, which shall not be taken away from her" *(vs. 38-42).*

Luke 11. Christ again taught, "He that is not with me is against me" *(v. 23).* A certain woman, recognizing that Jesus was the Son of God, indicated that Christ's mother was a blessed woman. Christ, however, indicated that giving birth to him was not what makes one blessed, but keeping the word of God *(vs. 27-28).* Jesus taught that he was greater than Jonas and Solomon *(vs. 31-32).* When the Pharisees complained that Jesus did not wash before sitting to dine, Jesus chastised the Pharisees for being hypocrites, cleaning the outside of the vessel but leaving the inside "full of ravening and wickedness" *(vs. 37-44). (Also see Mark 7:1-5, 13-22.) (Note: For verses 2-4, see Matt. 6:9-13; verses 9-13, see Matt 7:6-11; verses 14-20, Matt. 12:22-28; verses 16, 29-32, Matt. 12:38-42; verses 33-36, Mark 4:21-22; verses 37-44, Matt. 15:13-22.)*

Luke 12. Christ taught his disciples not to fear those who had power to kill their bodies, just to fear God, i.e., the One who had power to not only kill the body but also afterward cast them into hell *(vs. 4-5).* God is omniscient—the birds are not forgotten before God; the hairs on their own heads are numbered. God values people more than sparrows *(vs. 6-8).* Therefore, the disciples were not to worry about what to eat or drink, etc., but to seek the kingdom of God, "and all these things shall be added unto you." Where your treasure is, there, also is your heart *(vs. 22-34).* All sins can be forgiven except the sin against the Holy Ghost *(v. 10).* A man asked Jesus to intervene in an inheritance dispute with his brother. Christ counseled against covetousness and gave the parable of a certain rich man who gathered wealth so someday he could eat, drink and be merry. However, the man died and never got to enjoy any of that material wealth. Jesus taught we should lay up treasures in heaven, not on earth *(vs. 13-21).* We must always be prepared for the coming of the Lord because no man knows when he will come. "He will come at an hour when ye think not" *(vs. 35-40).* Jesus taught his disciples the parable of the wise servant who was prepared and the unwise servant who was not prepared when their master came suddenly. Where much is given, much is required *(vs. 41-48).* Christ acknowledged that preaching the gospel would bring division *(vs. 49-53).* Agree with thine adversary so that he will not deliver you to the judge and have you cast into prison *(v. 58).*

Luke 13; Matt. 13; Mark 4. Christ taught that those who perished did not necessarily suffer because they were more wicked than other people, but that if the rest of the people did not repent, they would likewise perish *(vs. 1-5).* He taught the parable of the fig tree. Rather than cut it down, the servant asked for time to nurture it so it would bear good fruit. If, then, it failed to bear good fruit, the master could still cut it down *(vs. 6-9).* The Savior, on the Sabbath, healed a woman who had been afflicted eighteen years. When the ruler of the synagogue complained, Jesus reminded him that he cared for his animals on the Sabbath and that it was right that the woman should also be freed from her bond on the Sabbath *(vs. 11-17).* Christ likened the kingdom of God unto a grain of mustard seed *(vs. 18-19, Matt. 13:31-32; Mark 4:30-32)* and also to leaven hidden in three measures of meal, causing the whole to be leavened *(vs. 20-21).* In response to someone's query, Christ discussed whether few or many will be saved in the kingdom of God. The Pharisees instructed him to leave town "for Herod will kill thee." Jesus lamented how oft he would have gathered Jerusalem as a mother hen gathers her brood, but she would not *(vs. 23-35).* Christ taught that if people did not repent, they would be cast out and there would be weeping and gnashing of teeth when they see Abraham, Isaac, and Jacob and all the prophets in the kingdom of God, while they themselves are excluded *(v. 28).*

Luke 14. Jesus, on the Sabbath, healed a man afflicted with dropsy as he challenged the lawyers and Pharisees as to whether or not they would rescue an ass or an ox if it fell into a pit on the Sabbath *(vs. 1-5).* Christ taught about humility through a parable about which room a person should choose to sit in when invited to a wedding *(vs. 7-11).* We should do things for people who can not recompense us rather than for friends and family who will return the favor bestowed upon them *(vs. 12-14).* Christ used another parable to teach the people that those who follow him must be willing to forsake all other things *(vs. 16-33).* If salt loses its savor, it is good for nothing *(vs. 34-35).*

Luke 15. Christ surrounded himself with sinners; and the Pharisees and scribes murmured because of it *(vs. 1-2).* Thus, Christ took the opportunity to teach them of the great joy that comes when that which is lost is found again, and he illustrated that message through three parables: (1) the parable of the lost sheep *(vs. 3-7);* (2) the parable of the piece of silver *(vs. 8-10);* and (3) the parable of the prodigal son *(vs.11-32).*

Luke 16. Christ gave a parable about an unjust steward. The unjust steward made friends with other unrighteous people. The lord of the unjust steward commended him and said, "And I say unto you, Make to yourselves friends of the mammon of unrighteousness; that, when ye fail, they may receive you into everlasting habitations" *(vs. 1-9; also see Matt. 5:25; Luke 12:58).* People who are unfaithful over minor responsibilities will be unfaithful over major responsibilities. Those who are faithful over that which is minor will be faithful over that which is major *(vs. 10-12).* No man can serve two masters *(v. 13).* Until Christ came, the teachings of the law according to the Old Testament prophets governed, but with the coming of Christ, which had been prophesied from the beginning, the kingdom of God was preached *(vs. 14-17).* Christ condemned divorce *(v. 18).* Christ taught a parable about the rich man and Lazarus, a beggar, to illustrate that our works on earth *(or lack thereof)* will be reflected in the rewards we receive in heaven; and that now is the time to heed the warnings of the prophets, for if the people won't accept Moses and the prophets, neither would they accept someone even if he were risen from the dead *(vs. 19-31)*.

Luke 17. Christ condemned those who offend little children *(v. 2; also Matt. 18:6; Mark 9:42)*. People need to forgive others unendingly *(vs. 3-4; also see Matt 18:21-22)*. Christ taught that people should have the faith of a grain of mustard seed *(vs. 5-6)*. No matter how completely we serve the Lord, we will still be unprofitable servants, for we have only done that which was our duty to do *(vs. 7-10)*. Christ healed ten lepers; only one returned to thank him *(vs. 12-19)*. In response to demands made by the Pharisees to know when the kingdom of God should come, Christ said the kingdom of God is within you and that no man knows when the Son of Man will come again. First, he must be rejected by the people. Then, things will be like in the days of Noe (Noah) and in the days of Lot *(vs. 20-37)*.

Luke 18. Christ taught a parable about a widow who petitioned a judge to avenge her of her adversary. The judge said no, but decided that she would bother him incessantly if he didn't, so he changed his mind and avenged her. If this unrighteous judge was willing to avenge this woman, surely we can expect God to avenge his own elect *(vs. 1-8)*. Christ taught a parable about a Pharisee and a publican to certain people who were puffed up as to their own importance. The Pharisee prayed, thanking God he was not as other men. The publican acknowledged his own weaknesses. The Pharisee will ultimately be abased and the publican will be exalted for his humility *(vs. 9-14)*. Christ said his disciples should not forbid the children to come unto him for of such is the kingdom of God *(vs. 15-17)*. Christ explained to a certain ruler what he had to do to gain eternal life; i.e., keep the commandments. The ruler had done that. Christ told him to sell what he had and give to the poor. The man was very sorrowful for he was rich *(vs. 18-23)*. It will be difficult for the rich to enter into the kingdom of God *(vs. 24-25)*. Christ promised Peter and the apostles that there is no one who has given up all things for him who will not "receive manifold more in this present time, and in the world to come life everlasting" *(vs. 26-30)*. Jesus spoke to the Twelve about his pending death and resurrection *(vs. 31-34)*. On the way to Jericho, Jesus healed a blind man *(vs. 35-43)*.

Luke 19. As Jesus passed through Jericho, Zacchæus, a rich man who was too short to see over the crowd, ran and climbed a tree so he could see Christ. Jesus saw him there and had him come out of the tree because he said he needed to abide in Zacchæus' house that day. Jesus blessed him, saying that this day salvation was come unto his house because he also was a son of Abraham, and that he had come to save that which was lost *(vs. 1-10)*. Jesus taught the people an important lesson about stewardship as he told the parable of the ten pounds: those who are faithful stewards will be added upon; those who are unfaithful stewards will lose that which they had been given previously; those who reject the Savior will be cast away *(vs. 11-27)*. *(Also see Matt. 25:14-30 for the parable of the talents). (See entry for Matt. 21:1-11 for verses 28-40, the two disciples sent into a village to get a certain colt for Jesus to ride upon.)* Jesus wept over Jerusalem as he rode into the city upon an ass *(v. 41)*. *(Also, see entry for Matt. 21:12-13 for verses 45-47,*

Christ cleansed the temple of money-changers again.) Christ taught daily in the temple *(v. 47)*.

Luke 20. See the entries for Matt. 21, 22.

Luke 21:5-28. Christ was asked what signs would precede his Second Coming. He said there would be wars and commotions; nation would rise against nation; earthquakes, famines and pestilences would be in divers places. Prior to that time, the disciples would be persecuted and cast into prisons. They would be betrayed by family and friends. Some of them would be put to death. They would be hated for Christ's sake. However, not a hair of their heads will perish. There will be signs in the heaven and upon the earth. *(Also see entry for Matt. 24:32-51; Mark 13:28-37; and Luke 17:20-37.)* Jesus taught in the temple in the daytime and abode in the mount of Olives at night *(v. 37)*. *(For verses 1-4, the widow's mite, see Mark 12:41-44.)*

Luke 24; Mark 16. Christ's body was not in the sepulchre when Mary Magdalene, Joanna, and Mary the mother of James and the other women went there with their spices. Two men in shining garments told them that he was not there because he was risen as he had said. [A young man sitting on the right side of the sepulchre told them to be not afraid.] They quickly went to tell the apostles that the sepulchre wherein Jesus was laid was empty and that they had been told he was risen. Peter immediately ran to the sepulchre and looked inside. He beheld the linen clothes that were lying there *(v. 12)*. As Cleopas *(this could possibly be Peter, i.e., Cephas)* and another disciple went to Emmaus, Jesus drew near unto them and walked with them *(see Mark 16:12-13)*. They did not recognize the resurrected Christ. Cleopas asked the man if he were a stranger and whether or not he was aware of all that had recently occurred. Cleopas told him about the women coming to tell the disciples that the tomb was empty and that they had seen angels who said Christ was alive. As they drew nigh unto the village, Jesus acted as though he would have gone further, but they constrained him to abide with them because it was evening. He took bread, blessed it and brake it, and gave it to them. Their eyes were then opened and he vanished out of their sight. The disciples acknowledged that they had felt a burning within themselves while Jesus was with them. They returned to Jerusalem and found the eleven apostles and told them what had happened and how Jesus had appeared to Simon *(i.e. Peter/Cephas) (vs. 13-33)* and how he was known of them in breaking of bread. *(Note: Jesus changed Simon Peter's name to Cephas when Peter was called to be a disciple. John 1:42. It would appear from verses 32-35 that the disciple referred to as Cleopas in verse 18 could be Simon Peter.)* As they spoke, Jesus came and stood in the midst of them. He ate meat with them and blessed and taught them *(vs. 36-53)*.

John 1. Christ was in the beginning with God and was the Word of God. He created all things. In him was life *(vs. 1-4)*. John was sent as a witness to testify of Christ: the Word was made flesh; he came into the world; the world rejected him; his own rejected him; those who believed him were given the power to become sons of God *(vs. 6-14)*. Christ would take away the sins of the world *(v. 29)*. Christ would come, following John, and would baptize with the Holy Ghost *(vs. 30-33)*. John declared Jesus to be the Lamb of God *(v. 36)*. Andrew brought his brother Simon Peter to hear Jesus. Jesus changed Peter's name to Cephas *(vs. 40-42)*. Jesus called Philip to follow him. Philip found Nathanael and told him they had found Jesus, of whom Moses and the prophets had written. Jesus recognized Nathanael as one in whom there was no guile. When Nathanael wondered how Jesus knew that, Jesus said he had seen him under the fig tree before Philip called him. Because of Nathanael's belief, Jesus told him he would see heaven open and the angels of God ascending and descending upon the Son of Man *(vs. 43-51).*

John 2. Jesus performed his first miracle at a wedding in Cana when he turned water into wine *(vs. 1-11).* He, his mother, brethren, and disciples then went to Capernaum. Jesus went to Jerusalem for the Passover. While there, he drove the money changers out of the temple *(vs. 12-17).* The Jews asked for a sign. Christ told them, "Destroy this temple, and in three days I will raise it up." They thought he was referring to the building that had taken 46 years to build but he was referring to his body which he would raise from the dead following his crucifixion *(vs. 18-22).*

John 3. Jesus was approached at night by Nicodemus, a Pharisee and a ruler of the Jews. Nicodemus acknowledged that Christ was a great teacher. He was puzzled by Jesus' teaching that a man must be born again, and wondered how that was possible. Jesus taught that a man must be born of water and of the spirit or he cannot enter into the kingdom of God. Jesus chided Nicodemus for being a leader in Israel and still not knowing the things of which Christ spoke. Jesus asked him, "If ye have not believed the earthly things I have taught, how will ye believe of heavenly things?" *(vs. 1-13).* Christ's eventual death and resurrection are foreshadowed: just as Moses lifted up the serpent, so must the Son of Man be lifted up *(vs. 14-15).* God so loved the world that he gave his only begotten Son that the world through him might be saved *(vs. 16-17).* John the Baptist testified that Jesus is the Light: everyone who does evil, hates the Light; those who do truth, come to the Light *(vs. 18-21).* Jesus and his disciples went to Judæa and performed baptisms *(v. 22).* John again testified that he was not Christ: he was sent before him *(vs. 28-34).* The Father loves the Son, and he has given the Son all things. He that believeth on the Son, hath everlasting life *(vs. 35-36).*

John 4. Jesus' disciples performed baptisms, not Jesus *(vs. 1-2).* Jesus went to Samaria, where he asked a woman to draw him some water. She was puzzled since the Jews would have nothing to do with the Samaritans. In the interchange that ensued, Jesus taught her that whosoever drank of the water he gave them would never thirst again. When the woman said she had no husband, Jesus agreed, saying she had had five husbands but that the man she now lived with was not her husband. True worshippers must worship the Father in spirit and in truth. When she said she knew that the Messias, called Christ, cometh, Jesus said, "I that speak unto thee am he" *(vs. 3-26).* The woman went into the city and told the men of the city, and said, "Is not this the Christ?" *(vs. 28-29).* Many Samaritans believed because of the woman. Others believed because they heard Jesus speak *(vs. 39-42).* When Jesus' disciples offered him meat to eat, he said he had meat of which they knew not. His meat was to do the will of the Father. He pointed out that the disciples recognized that in four months it would be harvest time. However, he pointed out that, as far as the gospel was concerned, the field was already ripe and ready for harvest *(vs. 31-38).* Jesus returned to Cana. The son of a certain nobleman was ill. The nobleman asked Jesus to heal his son. Jesus told him to go his way, that his son liveth. The man believed. As he journeyed home, his servants met him along the way and told him his son was well. The man wanted to know what hour he had begun to get better. They said it was the seventh hour of the previous day. That was the same hour Jesus had told him that his son liveth. This was Jesus' second miracle when he came out of Judæa into Galilee *(vs. 46-54).*

John 5. Jesus, on a Sabbath day, was at the pool of Bethesda where many ill and infirm people waited for the chance to be healed in the water. There by the pool, Jesus saw a certain man who had had an infirmity for 30 years. He had compassion on him and healed him and instructed him to take up his bed and walk *(vs.2- 9).* The Jews said it was not lawful for the man to carry his bed on the Sabbath and demanded to know who told him to do it. After seeing Jesus in the temple, the man told the Jews that Jesus had healed him and had told him to take up his bed and walk *(vs. 10-15).* Thus, the Jews sought to slay Jesus. They hated him even more when he said God was his Father *(vs. 16-18).* He said the Son can do nothing of himself, only what he seeth the Father do. The Father loves the Son and shows him all things that he himself does. The Father raised the dead and the Son also "quickeneth whom he will." The Father has committed all judgment unto the Son; therefore, all men should honor the Son just as they honor the Father. The dead will hear Christ's voice. He that hears the word and believes will receive everlasting life. All men will be resurrected and will be rewarded according to that which they have done: the righteous unto the resurrection of life; the wicked, unto the resurrection of damnation *(vs. 19-29).* Jesus testified of the divine law of witnesses *(vs. 31-47).*

John 6. When Jesus went across the Sea of Galilee, many followed because they saw the miracles of healing that he did. Jesus and his disciples went up into a mountain, and he sat with them *(vs. 1-2). (For the miracle of the loaves and the fishes, see entry for Matt. 14:5-14.)* While Jesus was by himself up in a mountain, the disciples set sail toward Capernaum. As they got partway there, a great wind arose. As they looked, they saw Jesus walking toward them on the water. They gladly received him, and "immediately the ship was at the land whither they went" *(vs. 15-21).* When the people saw that Jesus and his disciples had crossed the sea, they followed. Jesus told them that they didn't seek him because of the miracles they had seen, but because they ate of the loaves and were filled. He then taught that he is the living manna sent from God—that he is the bread of Life: ". . . he that cometh to me shall never hunger; and he that believeth on me shall never thirst." Those who believe on him will have everlasting life *(vs. 22-40).* The Jews murmured against him, saying he was the son of Joseph and that they knew his parents. How, therefore, could he claim to be the bread that came down from heaven? Jesus said he was the bread of life. He explained how men eat his flesh and drink his blood *(vs. 41-59).* Many followers apostatized at that time. Jesus asked the Twelve if they, too, would go away. Peter, speaking for the group, testified that Jesus is the Messiah. Nevertheless, Jesus reminded them that one of them *(i.e., Judas Iscariot)* would betray him *(vs. 60-71)*

John 7. Jesus abode in Galilee because the Jews sought to kill him. He did not go up to the feast of tabernacles when his brethren did because he said his time had not yet come. Jesus' own brethren did not believe in him *(vs. 1-9).* Jesus secretly attended the feast. People covertly disputed over whether he was a good person or a bad one, fearing to speak openly for fear of the Jews *(vs. 10-13).* Jesus taught in the temple, indicating that the doctrine he taught was not his own but his Father's who is in heaven. He proclaimed his divine Sonship *(vs. 14-31)*. The Pharisees sought to take him, but no one laid hands on him because his time was not yet come. Nevertheless, Jesus told them the time was near when he would no longer be among them and that they would be unable to find him—that where he went they could not come. He offered living waters unto all men. The Holy Ghost was not yet given because Jesus was not yet glorified *(vs. 32-39)*. The people continued to dispute among themselves regarding just who Jesus was. Nicodemus reminded the people that under their law a man should be heard before being judged *(vs. 40- 53)*.

John 8. While Jesus was teaching in the temple, the scribes and Pharisees brought a woman to him who was taken in adultery. Jesus stooped down and seemingly ignored their questions as he wrote on the ground. After repeated questioning by the Pharisees, Jesus suggested, "He that is without sin among you, let him first cast a stone at her." One-by-one the accusers all quietly left. When Jesus finally looked up, he asked the woman where her accusers were. She told him that no one had condemned her. Jesus told her that neither did he, and "go and sin no more" *(vs. 2-11)*. Jesus is the light of the world *(v. 12)*. The Pharisees challenged Christ's claim of divine Sonship because he testified of himself. However, Christ reminded them that it was written in the law that the testimony of two men is true and that both he and the Father bore witness that Jesus is the Christ *(vs. 12-19)*. The people were puzzled over Christ's saying that where he was going they could not come *(vs. 21-22)*. Jesus again proclaimed his Messiahship. When you know the truth, the truth will make you free *(vs. 23-32)*. When the people claimed to be sons of Abraham, Jesus countered that if they were sons of Abraham they would do the works of Abraham *(vs. 33-40)*. The people then claimed they had one father, even God. Jesus again countered their claim saying that if God were their Father, they would love him because the Father sent him *(vs. 41-43)*. Rather than being children of God, they were children of the devil *(v. 44)*. Before Abraham was, Christ said, "I am" *(v. 58)*.

John 9. Jesus, on the Sabbath, healed the eyes of a man who had been blind from birth. When his disciples asked who had sinned—the man or his parents—since he had been blind from birth, Jesus said neither of them; but rather, he was born blind so the works of God could be manifest in him *(vs. 1-7)*. Later, when the Jews cast the man out because he defended Christ as a righteous man, Jesus asked if he believed on the Son of God. When he said yes, Jesus told him he was the Son of God, and the man believed *(vs. 35-38)*. Jesus came into the world for judgment. He lectured the Pharisees about being spiritually blind *(vs. 39-41)*.

John 10. Jesus taught the parable of the sheep and the shepherd. Sheep know their shepherd's voice and follow him. The shepherd calls his sheep by name. Jesus is the good Shepherd. A hireling will not give his life to save the sheep, but the good shepherd will give his life for the sheep. Jesus taught that he had other sheep which were not of this fold and that they, too, must hear his voice. There will be one fold and one shepherd *(vs. 1-18, 26-27)*. *(Note: The record of the fulfillment of this scripture is found in the BM when Christ appeared to the Nephites on the American continent following his death and resurrection. He declared, "And verily I say unto you, that ye are they of whom I said: Other sheep I have which are not of this fold; them also I must bring, and they shall hear my voice; and there shall be one fold, and one shepherd" (3 Nephi 15:11-24).)* Jesus and his Father are one *(i.e., they are united in purpose) (v. 30).* When the Jews requested that Jesus tell them plainly whether or not he was truly the Christ, he reminded them that they had seen the works he had done and those works were a witness of him *(vs. 24-25).* The Jews claimed they didn't stone him for his works but because he "makest thyself God." Jesus reminded them that it was written in the law that "Ye are gods," and asked how they could then condemn him for saying he was the Son of God *(vs. 31-36).* Jesus went to the place beyond Jordan where John first baptized and abode there. Many came and believed, acknowledging that John did not perform any miracles but that everything he said about Christ was true *(vs. 40-42).*

John 11. Jesus was good friends with Mary *(that Mary who had anointed him with oil and wiped his feet with her hair)* and Martha and their brother Lazarus. When Lazarus became ill, Mary and Martha sent for Jesus, but Jesus tarried for a few days before going to them. Lazarus died. When Jesus received word of his death, he told his disciples that Lazarus "sleepeth" and that he was going to go to him so he could awaken him. The disciples thought Jesus meant he was resting in sleep, but Jesus made it clear that Lazarus was dead. Jesus said he was glad for the sake of his disciples that he was not there when Lazarus became ill and died, "to the intent ye may believe" *(v. 15).* By the time Jesus arrived, Lazarus had been in the grave four days. Jesus comforted Mary and Martha and told them that he (Jesus) was the resurrection and the life; he that believed in him, though he were dead, would yet live: and that whosoever liveth and believeth in him shall never die *(vs. 25-26).* Jesus wept when he saw the sorrow of his friends. He had the stone removed from the tomb and thanked his Father in heaven for hearing him; [and he said he knew he always heard him, but that he said it in order to help those who stood by and heard know that heavenly Father had sent him], and then he cried with a loud voice, "Lazarus, come forth," and Lazarus came forth from the tomb *(vs. 35-44).* The chief priests and Pharisees met in council to decide what to do regarding Jesus, saying that, while he performed many miracles, if they left Jesus alone, too many people would believe him and then the Romans would come and take away their place and their nation. Caiaphas, the high priest, spoke prophetically to them about the imminent death of Jesus: "that Jesus should die for that nation; and not for that nation only, but that also he should gather together in one the children of God that were scattered abroad" *(vs. 47-52).* From that day forth, they counseled how to have Jesus put to death. And from that day forth, Jesus no longer walked openly among the Jews. When the Passover drew near, the chief priests and Pharisees issued a command that if any one knew where Jesus was, they were to report it to them so they could take him *(vs. 53-57).*

John 12. Jesus went to Bethany six days before the Passover and ate supper *(in the house of Simon the leper) (Matt. 26:6)* with Lazarus *(whom he had raised from the dead)* and his disciples. Martha served. When Mary anointed Jesus with oil, bathed his feet with her tears and wiped his feet with her hair, Judas Iscariot, Simon's son, complained about Mary wasting the oil when it could have been sold and the proceeds given to the poor. Jesus reminded them they would have the poor with them always, but they would not always have him *(vs. 1-8). (See Matt.*

26:22.) The chief priests wanted to not only put Jesus to death but Lazarus also because too many people were beginning to believe on Jesus because Lazarus had been brought back to life. *(For verses 12-15 regarding Jesus' riding on the colt of an ass, etc., and the people strewing palm leaves before him, see entry for Matt 21:1-11.)* Certain Greeks came to worship at the feast of the Passover and told Philip that they wished to see Jesus *(vs. 20-22)*. Jesus again foretold of his death and why it was necessary: "Except a corn of wheat fall into the ground and die, it abideth alone: but if it die, it bringeth forth much fruit" *(vs. 23-36)*. Christ petitioned the Father "to glorify thy name." The Father responded, and the people heard a voice from heaven say, "I have both glorified it, and will glorify it again" *(v. 28)*. Jesus told the people that the voice came not because of him, but for the sake of those who heard it *(v. 30)*. In spite of all the miracles Jesus performed, many still did not believe on him that the words of Esaias (Isaiah) might be fulfilled *(vs. 37-41)*. *(See Isa. 53:1; 6:10)*. Many leaders believed but did not admit it because they feared being removed from the synagogue and loved the praise of men more than the praise of God *(vs. 42-43)*. Jesus taught that those who loved him, loved the Father; those who hated him, hated the Father. He spoke nothing of himself—only that which the Father had commanded him to speak *(vs. 44-50)*.

John 13. Prior to the feast of the Passover, Jesus washed the disciples' feet and dried them with a towel. As he reached Simon Peter, Peter declined to have him wash his feet. Jesus responded, "If I wash thee not, thou hast no part with me." Then Peter told him he could wash all of him. Jesus said that the feet were sufficient *(vs. 1-10)*. He explained that he had washed their feet as an example of service. He said, "Ye should do as I have done to you . . . the servant is not greater than his lord; neither he that is sent greater than he that sent him" *(vs. 13-16)*. Jesus identified Judas the son of Simon as the one who would betray him *(vs. 2, 10-11, 21, 26-30)*. Jesus taught his disciples a new commandment: "Love one another as I have loved you" *(vs. 34-35)*. When Peter desired to go where Jesus was going and said he would lay down his life for him, Jesus gently admonished him and said that Peter would deny him three times before the cock crowed *(vs. 36-38; also see entry for Matt. 26)*.

John 14. Jesus promised that in his Father's house are many mansions and that he was going there to prepare a place for those who follow him—that where he is, his followers may be also *(vs. 1-3)*. Thomas queried as to how he and his fellow disciples could know the way. Jesus said he was "the way, the truth, and the life, no man cometh unto the Father but by me" *(vs. 5-6)*. Philip asked Jesus to show them the Father. Jesus said he that hath seen him hath seen the Father, that he is in the Father and the Father is in him *(vs. 8-11)*. Those who believe on Jesus Christ will do his works. Whatsoever they ask in his name, he will do *(vs. 12-13)*. Jesus taught, "If ye love me, keep my commandments" *(v. 15)*. Jesus told Judas *(not Iscariot)* that the Father will love those who love Jesus *(vs. 22-23)*. He promised to send two comforters: (a) the Spirit of truth "whom the world cannot receive, because it seeth him not, neither knoweth him: but ye know him; for he dwelleth with you, and shall be in you;" and (b) the Holy Ghost "whom the Father will send in my name, he shall teach you all things, and bring all things to your remembrance, whatsoever I have said unto you" *(vs. 16-17, 26)*. Jesus gives peace unto the world, but not as the world giveth *(v. 27)*. Jesus said if his disciples loved him they would rejoice that he was going away because he would be going unto his Father, "who is greater than I" *(v. 28)*. Satan, who would soon come, has no power over Jesus, but he does have power over mankind *(v. 30)*.

John 15. Jesus taught that he is the true vine; his Father is the husbandman; the disciples are the branches *(vs. 1-5)*. Jesus loved his disciples just as the Father loved him. He commanded his disciples to love one another as he had loved them *(vs. 9-12, 17)*. Jesus taught the great law of love: "Greater love hath no man than this, that a man lay down his life for his friends. He called the disciples "friends," not servants. He chose and ordained them—they did not choose him *(vs. 13-16)*. If the world hates them *(the disciples)*, it is because the world hates Jesus; and if the world hates Jesus, it is because they also hate the Father. If Christ had not come and taught the truth, the world would not have had sin; but having been taught, they have no cloak with which to hide their sin *(vs. 18-24)*. The Comforter, the Spirit of truth, will testify of Christ *(v. 26)*.

John 16. Jesus discussed the role and mission of the Holy Ghost *(vs. 7-15)*. He referred to his death and resurrection: "A little while, and ye shall not see me: and again, a little while, and ye shall see me, because I go to the Father. His disciples failed to understand Christ's saying. He compared his death and resurrection to a woman in labor who as soon as she is delivered remembers the pain no longer, but rejoices in the birth of the infant *(vs. 16-22)*. Jesus came forth into the world from the Father and, as he leaves the world, he will return to the Father *(v. 28)*. Christ has overcome the world *(v. 33)*.

John 17. Jesus offered a great intercessory prayer to Heavenly Father in behalf of "them which thou has given me; for they are thine" *(v. 9)*. Christ stated that "This is life eternal, that they might know thee the only true God, and Jesus Christ, whom thou hast sent" *(v. 3)*. None of those whom the Father gave to Christ was lost save the son of perdition *(v. 12)*. Jesus prayed that his disciples and those who believe through their teachings would be one "as thou, Father, art in me, and I in thee, that they also may be one in us; that the world may believe that thou hast sent me . . . that they may be one, even as we are one" *(vs. 20- 22)*. The Father loved Jesus before the foundation of the world *(i.e., in the pre-existence) (v. 24)*.

John 18. (Note: John 18 provides an expanded version of Judas' betrayal of Jesus. Compare Matt. 26:36-67.) Jesus and his disciples went over the brook Cedron to a garden which Jesus entered. Judas was familiar with the place because Jesus and his disciples went there often. Judas brought a band of men and officers from the chief priests and Pharisees to the garden. Jesus asked whom they sought. When they said, "Jesus," he acknowledged that he was Jesus. When they fell back, Jesus asked again whom they were seeking, knowing all the time what their purpose was. They responded again, "Jesus." He told them he was Jesus and told them to, therefore, "let the others go" *(vs. 1-9)*. Peter drew a sword and sliced off the ear of Malchus, one of the servants. Jesus told him to put the sword away, indicating that he needed to drink the cup which his Father had given him *(vs. 10-11; Matt. 26:51-52)*. Jesus was taken captive to Annas, the father-in-law of Caiaphas the High Priest *(vs. 12-13)*, who sent him to Caiaphas *(v. 24)*. The high priest interrogated Jesus. An officer, taking offense at Christ's response, struck him with the palm of his hand. Jesus challenged the officer to bear witness of the evil he attributed to Christ or to explain why he struck him *(v. 23)*. Jesus was led from Caiaphas to the hall of judgment. Pilate ascertained the charges and then questioned Jesus. He told the Jews that he found no fault in Christ. Because it was the custom to release a prisoner at the time of the Passover, Pilate asked whom they would have released, hoping they would have him release Jesus, the King of the Jews. The Jews rejected Jesus and had Pilate release Barabbas, a robber *(vs. 28-40).*

John 19. Jesus was scourged by Pilate and, after the soldiers put a platted crown of thorns on Christ's head and smote him with their hands, Pilate took him before the people and told them again that he found no fault in Jesus. The chief priests and officers demanded that Pilate crucify Jesus, and the Jews said their laws required it "because he made himself the Son of God" *(vs. 1-7).* Pilate questioned Jesus again, but Jesus did not respond. In frustration, Pilate reminded Jesus that he had the power to free him. Jesus told him that the only power Pilate could have against him was that which was given to him from above and that the greater sin was upon those who had delivered Jesus to Pilate. Pilate continued to try to release Jesus, but the Jews said that if he did he was not a friend of Cæsar's *(vs. 8-13).* When the people continued to demand that Jesus be crucified, Pilate delivered him to them. Jesus bore his cross to Golgotha where the people proceeded to crucify him along with two others—one on each side of him *(vs. 13-18).* Pilate wrote a title in three languages—Hebrew, Greek and Latin—and had it placed on the cross. It read: "JESUS OF NAZARETH THE KING OF THE JEWS." The chief priests asked Pilate to change it and write, "He said, I am King of the Jews." Pilate refused and said, "What I have written, I have written" *(vs. 19-22).* After Christ was crucified, the soldiers parted his garments four ways. Since Christ's coat was made without a seam, they decided to cast lots for it rather than tear it. Thus, the prophecy recorded in *Psalm 22:18* was fulfilled: "They part my garments among them, and cast lots upon my vesture" *(vs. 23-24).* As Jesus saw his mother Mary standing by the cross, along with Mary the wife of Cleophas and Mary Magdalene, he spoke to her and to his beloved disciple who was nearby and said, "Woman, behold thy son!" and to his disciple he said, "Behold thy mother!" Then he said, "I thirst." Jesus was given a sponge filled with vinegar. He said, "It is finished," bowed his head and gave up the ghost *(vs. 25-30).* Because it was nearing the Sabbath and bodies were not to remain on the cross during the Sabbath, the people wanted Pilate to let them break the legs of those whom they had crucified so as to hasten their deaths. The soldiers broke the legs of the two thieves who had been crucified with Jesus, but when they came to him, they found that he was already dead so they did not break his legs. Nevertheless, one of the soldiers pierced his side with a sword. This fulfilled the scriptures recorded in *Exodus 12:46:* ". . . neither shall ye break a bone thereof;" in *Numbers 9:12:* "They shall leave none of it unto the morning, nor break any bone of it: according to all the ordinances of the Passover they shall keep it;" and in *Zechariah 12:10:* " . . . and they shall look upon me whom they have pierced . . ." *(vs. 31-37).* Joseph of Arimathæa got permission from Pilate to take Jesus' body. Nicodemus aided Joseph of Arimathæa and they wound Christ's body in linen clothes with spices and placed him in a sepulchre in the garden near where he was crucified *(vs. 38-42). (See entry for Matt. 27:57-59.)*

John 20. After Christ's crucifixion, Mary Magdalene came early on the first day of the week and found the sepulchre empty. *(Also see Matt. 27:61; 28:1; Mark*

16:1 for different versions.) As she wept, Jesus appeared to her in the garden *(see Mark 16:9)*. She thought he was the gardener, but when he called her by name she called him Rabboni, i.e., Master. Jesus told her to touch him not because he had not yet ascended to his Father, and to "your Father; and to my God, and your God" *(vs. 1-17)*. That evening, as the disciples were assembled in seclusion for fear of the Jews, Jesus came and stood in their midst and said, "Peace be unto you." He showed them the wounds in his hands and side, and "breathed on them" and said, "Receive ye the Holy Ghost" *(vs. 19-22)*. Thomas was not with the rest of the disciples at the time. When they told Thomas they had seen the Lord, he would not believe them, "Except I shall see in his hands the print of the nails, and put my finger into the print of the nails, and thrust my hand into his side." Eight days later, the Lord again appeared unto his disciples and told Thomas to feel the wounds for himself. He admonished Thomas, "Thomas, because thou hast seen me, thou hast believed: blessed are they that have not seen and yet have believed" *(vs. 24-29)*. Jesus performed many other signs in the presence of his disciples. He is Christ, the Son of God *(vs. 30-31)*.

John 21. Jesus showed himself to his disciples a third time following his resurrection. Peter, Thomas, Nathanael of Cana, James and John and two other disciples were fishing on the sea of Tiberias. Jesus stood on the shore and asked if they had any meat. They did not recognize Jesus, but responded that they had none. He told them to cast their nets on the right side of the ship. They did; and their nets were so full they were unable to draw them. John declared to Peter, "It is the Lord." When they were gathered together on shore, Jesus dined with them on bread and fishes *(vs. 1-14)*. After eating, Jesus asked Simon Peter, "Simon, son of Jonas, lovest thou me more than these?" Peter said he did. Christ asked him the same question three times. Each time Peter said he did. And each time, Christ told him, "Feed my lambs" or "Feed my sheep" *(vs. 15-17)*. Jesus foretold Peter's martyrdom *(vs. 18-19)*. Jesus foretold of John the Beloved's translation *(20-23)*. If everything Jesus did was recorded, the world could not contain all the books *(v. 25)*.

Acts 1:3-9. Jesus ministered among his disciples 40 days following his resurrection. He promised the apostles that they would soon be baptized with the Holy Ghost. He instructed them that after they received the baptism of the Holy Ghost they were to bear witness of him throughout the world—"to the uttermost part of the earth." He then ascended into heaven while the apostles watched until he was received by a cloud.

Acts 2:22-36. "Jesus is the Christ," Peter testified on the day of Pentecost, and said that David had also testified to that in his day.

Acts 3. 20-21. Before the Second Coming of Christ, there would be a restitution of all things spoken of by the holy prophets since the world began.

Acts. 4:10. Jesus' name was the name by which a certain lame man had been healed, Peter and John testified.

Acts 9. Jesus, following his death, resurrection and ascension into heaven, spoke to Saul as Saul traveled to Damascus to persecute the saints there, saying, "Saul, Saul, why persecutest thou me?" Saul inquired as to who was speaking and then asked, "What wilt thou have me to do?" Jesus told him to go into the city and he would learn what it was he should do *(vs. 4-6)*. The Lord in a vision directed

Ananias, a disciple dwelling in Damascus, to go to the house of Judas and ask for Saul, who had seen in a vision a man named Ananias coming in and restoring his sight. Ananias was fearful of Saul because he knew Saul hated the followers of Christ. However, the Lord told him to go to him because Saul was "a chosen vessel unto me, to bear my name before the Gentiles, and kings, and the children of Israel." Ananias did as the Lord commanded *(vs. 9-17).*

Acts 13:23. Jesus, the Savior, was of David's seed as was prophesied anciently *(v. 23).* Jesus was slain in fulfillment of all that had been written of him. He was raised from the dead, and was seen many days by various people *(vs. 30-31).* While David's body saw corruption, Christ's body did not suffer corruption because he was raised up by the Father *(vs. 34-37).*

Acts 22:7-16. Jesus appeared to Saul as Saul was on the road to Damascus. The account is retold by Paul to the brethren in Jerusalem.

Acts 26:14, 22-23. When Jesus spoke to Saul (Paul) on the road to Damascus, he spoke in the Hebrew tongue. *(The account is retold to King Agrippa, Bernice and Festus, by Paul with a little elaboration from earlier accounts.)* Jesus told Saul, "It is hard for thee to kick against the pricks." The prophets and Moses had all testified of things which should come: "Christ should suffer, and that he should be the first that should rise from the dead, and should shew light unto the people, and to the Gentiles."

Rom. 1-16. Paul reminded the saints in Rome that Jesus Christ, the Son of God, was of the seed of David *(1:1-3).* The gospel of Jesus Christ is the power of God unto salvation to everyone who believeth *(1:16).* Though all have sinned, all are justified freely by his grace through the redemption that is in Jesus Christ and made possible through his atoning sacrifice *(3:23-24).* Christ died for us, and we are justified by his blood *(5:8-9).* Just as death was brought upon all mankind when one man (Adam) fell, so it is that through the atonement of one man (Jesus Christ), all mankind may be saved *(5:12-19).* Baptism is a similitude of the death, burial and resurrection of Jesus Christ *(6:3-5)* The wages of sin is death, but righteousness brings eternal life through Jesus Christ *(6:21-23).* Just as Christ was raised from the dead, so shall our mortal bodies be resurrected *(8:11).* Christ was the firstborn of the Father. Heavenly Father knew us in a pre-existent state and foreordained those who would become his leaders here on earth *(8:29-30).* Christ is at the right hand of God and makes intercession for us *(8:34).* Christ's love for us is constant. No outside influence can separate us nor cut us off from his love *(8:35-39).*

1 Cor. 11:3, 11. Christ is head of the man; the man is head of the woman; God is head of Christ in the Lord's eternal plan of leadership. Nevertheless, man is not without the woman, nor is the woman without the man.

1 Cor. 12:3. Only by the power of the Holy Ghost can one know that Jesus is the Lord. No one speaking by the power of the Holy Ghost can deny Jesus is the Lord.

1 Cor. 15. Christ died for our sins, was buried and was resurrected on the third day *(vs. 3-4).* He was seen by many people following his resurrection: Cephas (Paul), the twelve, 500 brethren at once, James, the apostles, Paul *(vs. 5-9).* Christ taught that he would be resurrected. If he was not resurrected, the apostles are all false witnesses and people's faith is in vain and their hope is for in this life only *(vs. 12-19).* Christ was the firstfruits of the resurrection. As in Adam all men die, even so in Jesus Christ will all men be made alive *(be resurrected).* After Christ, all those who are made Christ's at his coming will be resurrected. All things, except the Father, will be under Christ's feet. "Then shall the Son also himself be subject unto him that put all things under him, that God may be all in all" *(vs. 20-28).* Victory over death comes through the Lord Jesus Christ *(v. 57).*

Gal. 1:1, 12. Paul was called to preach by Jesus Christ and God the Father, not by man. Paul was taught the gospel by the revelation of Jesus Christ.

Gal. 2:16. Man is not justified by the law *(i.e., the law of Moses),* but by faith in the Lord Jesus Christ.

Eph. 1:3, 20. Jesus Christ is the son of God the Father. The Father wrought his power in Christ, "when he raised him from the dead, and set him at his own right hand in the heavenly places."

Eph. 2:5, 8, 20. We are saved by grace through faith in Jesus Christ. The Church is built upon the foundation of apostles and prophets, with Jesus Christ being the chief cornerstone.

1 Thes. 3:11. Paul testified to the Thessalonians that God the Father and the Lord Jesus Christ direct his way unto them.

2 Tim. 4:1. Christ shall judge the quick and the dead at the Second Coming.

Heb. 12:2. 24. Jesus is the author and finisher of our faith. He endured the cross knowing the joy that lay in store for him. He now sits on the right hand of the throne of God. He is the mediator of the new covenant.

Heb. 13:8. He is the same yesterday, today and forever.

1 Jn. 1. Christ is the Word of life and was from the beginning *(v. 1).* The righteous shall have fellowship with the Father and with his Son, Jesus Christ *(v. 3).* We are cleansed through the blood of Christ *(v. 7).* He will forgive those who confess their sins *(v. 9).*

1 Jn. 2:1-2. Jesus Christ is our advocate with the father when we sin. He is the propitiation *(will make conciliation, atone)* for our sins.

1 Jn. 4:9-10, 14. Christ was sent into the world, the only Begotten Son of God, that we might live through him. He was sent to be the propitiation *(make atonement)* for our sins; to be the Savior of the world.

1 Jn. 5:16-20. To know Jesus Christ and God the Father is eternal life.

Rev. 1:5, 8, 11, 12-18. Jesus Christ gave John a revelation in which he identified himself as the first begotten of the dead and the prince of the kings of the earth, who washed us from our sins in his own blood. He is Alpha and Omega, the beginning and the end, the Almighty. John saw him in the midst of the seven candlesticks *(the seven churches of Asia),* holding seven stars in his right hand *(i.e., the seven stars are the leaders over the seven churches in Asia).* He is the first and the last; he that liveth, and was dead. He has the keys of hell and death.

Rev. 2-3. The Savior identified himself to the leaders over the seven churches in Asia in a variety of ways: (1) as "he that holdeth the seven stars in his right hand, who walketh in the midst of the seven golden candlesticks" to the leader of the church in Ephesus *(2:1);* (2) as "the first and the last, which was dead, and is alive" to the leader of the church in Smyrna *(2:8);* (3) as "he which hath the sharp sword with two edges" to the leader of the church in Pergamos *(2:12);* (4) as the Son of God "who hath his eyes like unto a flame of fire, and his feet are like fine brass" to the leader of the church in Thyatira *(2:18);* (5) as "he who hath the seven stars, which are the seven servants of God" to the leader of the church in Sardis *(JST 3:1);* (6) as "he that is holy, he that is true, he that hath the key of David, he that openeth, and no man shutteth; and shutteth and no man openeth" to the leader of the church in Philadelphia *(3:7);* and (7) as "the Amen, the faithful and true witness, the beginning of the creation of God" to the leader of the church of the Laodiceans *(3:14).*

Rev. 5:5. The Savior is called the Lion of the tribe of Juda (Judah), the Root of David.

JESUS (2) (See Justus)

JESUS' BRETHREN

Matt. 12:46-50; Mark 3:31-35; Luke 8:19-21. **JESUS' BRETHREN**, along with Jesus' mother, wished to speak to Jesus as he was talking to the people. Jesus stretched forth his hand toward his disciples and declared that those who do the will of his Father in heaven are his brother, sister and mother.

Matt. 13:55-56; Mark 6:3. Jesus' brethren are named: James, Joses, Simon, and Judas (Juda). Unnamed sisters are also mentioned.

John 2:12. Jesus' brethren, mother and disciples went with him to Capernum following the miracle he performed at the wedding feast in Cana where he turned water into wine.

John 7:5. Jesus' brethren did not believe in him.

Acts 1:13-14. Following Jesus' ascension into heaven, his brethren and his mother Mary and several women, along with Jesus' disciples, met together in an upper room where they continued in prayer and supplication.

1 Cor. 9:5. Referring to the brothers of the Lord and Peter as examples, Paul indicated that even though he was an apostle, he was still free to eat and drink and enjoy family relationships the same as Peter *(i.e., Cephas)* and the brothers of the Lord.

Gal. 1:19. One of the Lord's brothers was James, who was one of the apostles. Paul said he saw him when he (Paul) stayed with Peter for 15 days in Jerusalem.

JESUS' DISCIPLES (Christians)

Matt. 8:23-27. **JESUS' DISCIPLES** were on a ship with Jesus. While Jesus was asleep, a strong tempest arose covering the ship with waves, and they were frightened. They awoke Jesus and asked him to save them. He rebuked the winds and calmed the sea.

Matt. 9:14-15; Mark 2:18-20; Luke 5:33-35. Jesus' disciples were not required to fast while he was with them. Jesus explained that as long as the bridegroom was with them, there was no need to fast; however, when he was gone, then they would fast.

Matt. 10:1-5; Mark 3:14-19; Luke 6: 13-16. Jesus' twelve apostles were: Simon Peter and Andrew his brother; James and John *(sons of Zebedee),* Philip, Bartholomew; Thomas, Matthew the publican, James the son of Alphæus, Lebbæus *(whose surname was Thaddæus),* Simon the Canaanite, and Judas Iscariot. *(Note: The listing of the apostles in Luke differs slightly from the listings in Matthew and Mark: instead of Thaddæus, Luke lists Judas the brother of James, and Simon the Canaanite is listed as Simon called Zelotes.)* Jesus gave them power against unclean spirits, the power to heal sicknesses and to do other things, and commanded them to go forth and teach. However, they were not to go unto the Gentiles nor into any city of the Samaritans. *(Note: Mark wrote that Jesus gave Zebedee's sons the surname: Boanerges, which means, The sons of thunder. He also refers to Lebbæus only as Thaddæus.)*

Matt. 14; Mark 6; Luke 9; John 6. Jesus' disciples took John the Baptist's body and buried it after Herod the tetrarch had him beheaded in prison. Then they went and told Jesus *(v. 12; Mark 6:30).* As Jesus healed the sick of the multitude who followed him, his disciples urged him to send the multitude away so the people could buy food and have some dinner. Instead, Jesus had his disciples give him what they had: five loaves and two fishes. He blessed and brake the loaves and fishes and fed about 5,000 men plus women and children. Twelve baskets full of fragments remained *(vs. 15-21; Mark 6:35-44; Luke 9:10-17; John 6:9-13). (Note: The account in John says that a lad had the five loaves and two fishes.)* Jesus had his disciples sail to the other side ahead of him while he sent the multitudes away and went up into a mountain apart to pray. He went to rejoin them and walked upon the water. The disciples were frightened and thought it was a spirit. Jesus calmed their fears. Peter left the ship and began walking on the water to meet Jesus. However, he became fearful and began to sink. Jesus caught hold of him. The disciples on the ship worshiped Jesus, saying, "Of a truth thou art the Son of God" *(vs. 22-33; Mark 6:45-51). (Note: The account in Mark does not include the account of Peter walking on the water to meet Jesus.)*

Matt. 16; Mark 8; Luke 12. Jesus' disciples followed him to "the other side," but they forgot to take bread. Jesus warned them to beware of the leaven of the Pharisees and Sadducees, i.e., beware of their doctrine *(vs. 6-12; Mark 8:14-18; Luke 12:1).* Jesus asked his disciples who people thought he was. They said some said John the Baptist, Elias, or Jeremias or other prophets. He then asked who they thought he was *(vs. 13-19).* Jesus charged his disciples not to tell anyone that he was Jesus the Christ *(v. 20).* Jesus taught his disciples that soon he would be killed but that he would rise again on the third day. He also taught them that when the Son of Man comes again in the glory of his Father, with angels, every man will be rewarded according to his works *(vs. 21-28).*

Matt. 17:14-21; Mark 9:17-29. Jesus' disciples could not heal the "lunatick" son [son which hath a dumb spirit] of a certain man due to lack of faith, the kind of faith, according to Jesus, that comes by fasting and prayer.

Matt. 18; Mark 9; Luke 9. Jesus' disciples inquired of him as to who was the greatest in the kingdom of heaven. Jesus responded that those who humble themselves as a little child are the greatest in the kingdom of heaven *(vs. 1-6; Mark 9:33-37; Luke 9:346-48).* He also told his disciples that whatsoever they bound on earth would be bound in heaven: and whatsoever they loosed on earth would be loosed in heaven. Whenever two or three are gathered together in his name, he will be in the midst of them *(vs. 18- 20).*

Matt. 19. Jesus taught the multitudes and his disciples about marriage and divorce *(vs. 3-12; Mark 10:11-12; Luke 16:18).* He taught them to let the little children come unto him because "of such is the kingdom of heaven" *(vs. 13-15).*

He taught them that in order to inherit everlasting life, one must be willing to give up all things "for my name's sake" *(i.e., keep the commandments and follow him),* and that it would be difficult for a rich man *(one who loved possessions more than the Savior)* to enter into the kingdom of heaven *(vs. 16-30; Mark 10:17-25; Luke 18:18-25).* As for the disciples, specifically, he said, "That ye which have followed me . . . ye also shall sit upon twelve thrones, judging the twelve tribes of Israel" *(vs. 26-30).*

Matt. 20; Mark 10. The twelve disciples were instructed by Jesus as they were going up to Jerusalem that the Son of Man would be betrayed into the hands of the chief priests and scribes, condemned to death and crucified, but that he would rise again on the third day *(vs. 17-19; Mark 10:32-34).* The mother of two of his disciples, James and John, [James and John] petitioned Jesus to allow her sons [them] to sit on his left and right hand sides in his kingdom. Jesus said that was not his to give. The other ten disciples "were moved with indignation against the two brethren" *(vs. 20-24; Mark 10:35-41).* Jesus used the opportunity to teach them that whosoever is greatest among them "let him be your minister . . . your servant" just as he had come to serve and not be ministered unto *(vs. 25-28; Mark 10:42-45).*

Matt. 21:1-7; Mark 11:1-7; Luke 19:29-35. Two of Jesus' disciples were sent to a little village to get an ass that was tied up along with her colt that the prophecy might be fulfilled spoken of Zechariah that said ". . . thy King cometh unto thee, meek, and sitting upon an ass, and a colt the foal of an ass" *(see Zech. 9:9).*

Matt. 24. Jesus' disciples showed him the buildings of the temple. Jesus told them that not one stone of the temple would be left standing—they would all be thrown down *(vs. 1-2).* They asked him to tell them when the end of the world would be, when the Second Coming would be, and what the signs indicating the time would be. Jesus told them what the signs would be, but stressed that no man, not even the angels of heaven, knew the time when it would occur, only his Father in Heaven *(vs. 3-36).* Just as the people in the days of Noe (Noah) did not know the day and hour of when the flood would occur, but needed to be prepared and watchful, so it will be with the Second Coming of the Son of Man *(vs. 37-44; also see Mark 13:28-37; Luke 17:20-37; 21:29-36).*

Matt. 26; Mark 14; Luke 22; John 11; 12; 13. Jesus warned his disciples that following the Passover, two days hence, he would be betrayed to be crucified *(vs. 1-2).* When Jesus was in the home of Simon the leper *(John 12:2),* a woman *(Mary the sister of Martha: John 11:2; 12:3)* poured oil on his head. The disciples objected at the "wasting" of such precious oil. Jesus gently rebuked them, saying they would always have the poor with them. The woman had anointed his body for burial. Wherever the gospel was preached, people were to be told of her deed as a memorial of her *(vs. 6-13; Mark 14:3-9; John 12:3-8).* Judas Iscariot *(Simon's son: John 12:4),* one of Jesus' disciples, promised to betray him for thirty piece of silver *(vs. 14-16, 46-50; Mark 14:10-11; Luke 22:3-6).* Jesus kept the Passover with his disciples in the home of a certain man. He instituted the sacrament. He told his disciples that one of them would betray him. They all promised they never would deny him. Jesus warned Peter that before the cock crowed, he would deny him three times *(vs. 17-35; Mark 14:12-31; Luke 22:31-34; John 13:37-38).* Jesus and his disciples went to a place called Gethsemane. He asked the disciples to sit and wait *(v. 36; Mark 14:32),* but he took Peter, James and John—the sons of Zebedee—with him as he went into the garden. He asked them to tarry with him while he went a little way further to pray *(v. 37; Mark 14:33-34; Luke 22:39-46). (Note: The account in Luke does not specify that Peter, James and John went an additional distance with Jesus.)* Judas betrayed Jesus with a kiss, a prearranged signal. One of Jesus' disciples (Peter) took a sword and cut off the ear of a servant of the high priest *(vs. 47-51; Mark 14:43-47; Luke 22:47-50; see John 18:2-12 for a modified version).*

Matt. 28:16-20. Following Jesus' resurrection, Jesus met with eleven disciples in a mountain where he had appointed them to go. The disciples worshiped him, although some doubted. They were instructed to go into every nation and baptize "in the name of the Father, and of the Son, and of the Holy Ghost," and to do all things which he had commanded them to do.

Mark 4; Luke 8. Jesus' disciples were taught parables by Jesus, who said, "Unto you it is given to know the mystery of the kingdom of God: but unto them that are without, all these things are done in parables: That seeing they may see, and not perceive; and hearing they may hear, and not understand; lest at any time they should be converted, and their sins should be forgiven them." He taught them the parables of the sower *(vs. 3-9, 14-20),* the candle under a bushel *(vs. 21-22),* the seed growing secretly *(vs. 26-29),* and the parable of the mustard seed *(vs. 30-32; Matt. 13:31-32; Luke 13:18-19; also see Luke 17:5-6).* Jesus and his disciples decided to cross over to the other side of the lake in several boats. While Jesus slept, a windstorm arose and began to swamp the boat. His disciples awakened him and asked, "Master, carest thou not that we perish?" Jesus rebuked the wind and calmed the sea *(vs. 36-41; Luke 8:22-25).*

Mark 5:31; Luke 8:43-45. Jesus' disciples were with Jesus when the woman who had had an issue of blood 12 years touched his garment and was healed. When Jesus asked who had touched his garment, they were taken aback because he was being pressed by a whole crowd, and they asked, "'Thou seest the multitude thronging thee, and sayest thou, Who touched me?'" *(Also see Matt. 9:20-22.)*

Mark 6. See Matt. 14.

Mark 7:17-23. Jesus' disciples asked him to explain what he meant when he said that nothing that enters a man's mouth defiles him, just that which comes out of his mouth. Jesus explained that the food that enters a man's mouth "goeth out into the draught," but that which comes out of man's mouth proceeds from out of the heart: murder, adulteries, evil thoughts, etc., and those are what defile a man.

Mark 11:1-7. See Matt. 21:1-7.

Luke 12:41-48. John asked Jesus if the lesson regarding being prepared was just to the disciples or to all people. In response, Jesus taught the parable of the wise servant who was prepared and the unwise servant who was not prepared when their master came suddenly. Where much is given, much is required.

Luke 18:31-34. As the twelve disciples went with Jesus to Jerusalem, he explained to them about his pending death and resurrection, but they understood none of what he was trying to tell them.

Luke 24:12. When Mary Magdalene, Joanna, and Mary the mother of James and the other women told the apostles that the sepulchre wherein Jesus was laid was empty and that they had been told he was risen, they did not believe them.

John 2. Jesus' disciples, along with Jesus and his mother, attended a wedding feast. When they wanted wine, Mary told Jesus that there was no wine. Jesus asked what she would have him do, and she told the servants to do whatever Jesus told them to do. He had them fill six waterpots with water which he then turned into wine *(vs. 3-5)*. Following the wedding, Mary, Jesus, his brethren and his disciples journeyed to Capernaum *(v. 12)*.

John 3:22. Jesus' disciples went with Jesus to Judæa where he tarried with them and performed baptisms. *(John 4:2 states that the disciples performed the baptisms, not Jesus.)*

John 4:31. Jesus' disciples entreated him to eat. Jesus responded that he had meat to eat which they knew not of, and explained that his meat was to do the will of the Father and to finish the Father's work.

John 6:15-21. While Jesus was by himself up in a mountain, the disciples set sail toward Capernaum. As they got partway there, a great wind arose. As they looked, they saw Jesus walking toward them on the water. They gladly received him, and "immediately the ship was at the land whither they went."

John 11:8. Jesus' disciples thought to discourage Jesus from going to Judæa when their friend Lazarus was ill because the Jews had sought to stone him when he was there before. Nevertheless, Jesus was not dissuaded.

John 12:16. Jesus' disciples failed to understand much of what Jesus tried to teach them just prior to his death, but after Jesus was glorified, they remembered the things that had been written of him and that had been done to him.

John 13. Jesus washed his disciples feet and told them it was an example of what they should do one to other: "The servant is not greater than his lord; neither he that is sent greater than he that sent him" *(vs. 5-16)*. When Jesus told his disciples that one of them would betray him, they wondered who it would be. Jesus identified the one *(Judas Iscariot)* by giving him a morsel of food *(vs. 18, 21-26)*. Jesus gave his disciples a new commandment: "Love one another as I have loved you" *(v. 34)*.

John 14. Jesus' disciples were promised that there are many mansions in his Father's house. Jesus was going there to prepare a place for them, "that where I am, there ye may be also" *(vs. 2-3)*. They were promised two comforters: (a) the Spirit of truth; (b) the Holy Ghost *(vs. 16-17, 26)*.

John 15. Jesus chose and ordained his disciples—they didn't choose him *(v. 16)*. If the world hates them, it is because the world hates Jesus. Those who hate Jesus also hate the Father *(vs. 18-24)*. The Comforter, whom Jesus promised to send to his disciples, will testify of him" *(v. 26)*.

John 16. The disciples could not receive the Comforter if Christ did not go away *(v. 7)*. Some of Jesus' disciples could not understand his teaching, "A little while, and ye shall not see me: and again, a little while, and ye shall see me," so Jesus explained *(vs. 17-22)*. The disciples said they now believed that Jesus knew all things and that he came forth from God" *(vs. 29-30)*.

John 17:20-22. Jesus prayed that his disciples and those who believe through their teachings would be one "as thou, Father, art in me, and I in thee, that they also may be one in us; that the world may believe that thou hast sent me . . . that they may be one, even as we are one."

John 20. Following Christ's resurrection and the discovery that his body was not in the sepulchre, Christ's disciples met together in seclusion for fear of the Jews. That evening, Jesus appeared to them as they were thus assembled and showed them the wounds in his hands and side and told them to "Receive ye the Holy Ghost." However, Thomas was not with them *(vs. 19-24)*. The other disciples told Thomas they had seen the risen Lord, but Thomas refused to believe until he saw for himself. Christ appeared to his disciples again eight days later, at which time Thomas was present *(vs. 25-26)*.

Acts 1. Jesus' apostles saw Jesus following his resurrection. Jesus ministered among them for 40 days and then ascended into heaven. Jesus promised them that they would soon be baptized by the Holy Ghost. They were then to bear witness of him unto the "uttermost part of the earth" *(vs. 1-8)*. As they stood gazing into heaven following Jesus' ascension, two men dressed in white told them that Jesus' eventual return would be in a like manner *(vs. 10-11)*. The apostles returned from mount Oliver and gathered in an upper room along with many others, including Mary the mother of Jesus, his brethren, and other women. In those days, Peter pointed out to the disciples that there was a vacancy in the Twelve that needed to be filled. Judas had not only fallen from his office, but had died. The apostles considered two possible replacements and prayed to know which one should be selected. Matthias was the person chosen to replace Judas *(vs. 12- 26)*.

Acts 2:1-12. The apostles spoke in tongues on the day of Pentecost. There was a sound as of a mighty rushing of wind. Cloven tongues like as of fire, sat upon each of them. They were all filled with the Holy Ghost. In Jerusalem there dwelled devout men from every nation, and they were all amazed to hear the apostles testify of Christ in their own languages.

Acts 5. The apostles wrought many signs and wonders among the people. Many people joined the church, and they brought forth their sick, hoping that even a bit of Peter's shadow would fall upon them *(vs. 12-16)*. The apostles were arrested by the high priest and his followers (of the sect of the Sadducees) and cast into the common prison. However, an angel of the Lord opened the prison doors and set them free. When the high priest and the council sent for them the next day, the officers reported that they were not in prison, even though the prison doors had been shut and guarded. Someone came and reported that the apostles were standing in the temple, preaching to the people. When the apostles were brought before the high priest, they were asked, "Did not we straitly command you that ye should not teach in this name?" Peter and the other apostles replied that they ought to obey God rather than men. They then testified of Christ, "whom ye slew and hanged on a tree" *(vs. 17-30)*.

Acts 6:3-6. The apostles chose seven men to assist them in the work. They were: Stephen, Philip, Prochorus, Nicanor, Timon, Parmenas and Nicolas. After praying, the apostles placed their hands on them *(to confirm their new callings upon them and to anoint them or set them apart for their positions)*.

Acts 11. When the apostles and brethren in Judæa heard that the Gentiles *(Cornelius and his kinsmen and friends)* had received the word from Peter, they contended with Peter for going in to uncircumcised men. Peter explained about the vision he had had and that Cornelius had seen an angel of the Lord in a vision. He told how the Holy Ghost had fallen upon all of them. He recalled how the Lord said that John would baptize with water but "ye shall be baptized with the Holy Ghost." Then he admonished them, "Forasmuch then as God gave them the like gift as he did unto us, who believed on the Lord Jesus Christ; what was I, that I could withstand God?" The apostles and brethren then held their peace and glorified God, saying, "Then hath God also to the Gentiles granted repentance" *(vs. 1-18)*. The disciples were first called **Christians** in Antioch *(v. 26)*.

1 Cor. 15:5. The Twelve saw the Savior following his resurrection.

JESUS' SISTERS

Matt. 13:56; Mark 6:3. **JESUS' SISTERS** are mentioned but no names are given.

JEWS

John 2:18-22. The **JEWS** asked for a sign when Christ drove the money changers out of the temple. Christ told them, "Destroy this temple, and in three days I will raise it up." They thought he was referring to the building that had taken 46 years to build, but he was referring to his body which he would raise from the dead following his crucifixion.

John 3:25-36. A question arose between the Jews and some of John's disciples about purifying. They questioned John about the fact that Jesus was also baptizing. John reminded them that he had told them he was not Christ, and that a man can receive nothing except it be given him from heaven. John testified to them of the divinity of the Savior.

John 4:16-18. The Jews sought to slay Jesus when he healed a man on the Sabbath who was waiting by the pool of Bethesda for the chance to be healed of the infirmity he had had for 30 years. When Christ said he was the Son of God, the Jews sought even more to slay him.

John 6:41-42. The Jews murmured against Jesus, saying he was the son of Joseph and that they knew his parents. How, therefore, could he claim to be the bread that came down from heaven?

John 7:1-15. The Jews sought to kill Jesus. People dared not speak openly of Jesus at the feast of tabernacles for fear of the Jews. When Jesus taught in the temple, the Jews marveled how someone so unschooled as Jesus could be so knowledgeable.

John 8. The Jews were puzzled over Christ's saying that where he was going they could not come *(vs. 21-22)*. Jesus again proclaimed his Messiahship. When you know the truth, the truth will make you free *(vs. 23-32)*. When the Jews claimed to be sons of Abraham, Jesus countered that if they were sons of Abraham, they would do the works of Abraham *(vs. 33-40)*. They claimed they had one father, even God. Jesus again countered their claim saying that if God were their Father, they would love him because the Father sent him *(vs. 41-43)*. Rather than being children of God, they were children of the devil *(v. 44)*. Before Abraham was, Christ said, "I am" *(v. 58)*.

John 9. The Jews did not believe that the man who Jesus healed had been blind from birth and demanded an explanation from the man's parents. They feared the

Jews and told them to ask their son: he was old enough to speak for himself *(vs. 18-23)*. When the man defended Jesus as a righteous man, the Jews cast him out *(vs. 24-34)*.

John 10. When the Jews heard Jesus' parable about the sheep and heard him declare that he was the good Shepherd, there was a division among them *(vs. 1-19)*. When they requested that Jesus tell them plainly whether or not he was truly the Christ, he reminded them that they had seen the works he had done and those works were a witness of him *(vs. 24-25)*. The Jews claimed they didn't stone him for his works but because he "makest thyself God." Jesus reminded them that it was written in the law that "Ye are gods," and asked how they could then condemn him for saying he was the Son of God *(vs. 31-36)*.

John 11. Some of the Jews went to comfort Mary and Martha when their brother Lazarus died, and they wept along with Mary *(vs. 31, 33)*. When they saw Jesus also weep, they exclaimed, "Behold how he loved him!" *(v. 36)*. Many of the Jews who had been with Mary and saw what Jesus did, believed, but others went and told the Pharisees *(vs. 45-46)*. Because the chief priests and Pharisees sought to take Jesus and have him put to death, Jesus no longer walked openly among the Jews *(vs. 53-55)*.

John 12:9-11. Many Jews believed Jesus because he raised Lazarus from the dead, and many came to where Jesus, Lazarus and the disciples ate supper prior to the Passover so they could not only see Jesus, but Lazarus, also.

John 18:31, 38-40. The Jews did not want Pilate to release Jesus into their jurisdiction for judgment because, they said, "It is not lawful for us to put any man to death." When Pilate offered to release a prisoner at the time of the feast of the Passover as was customary, the Jews insisted he release Barabbas and not Christ. They demanded Pilate crucify Jesus.

John 19. The Jews insisted that their law required that Jesus die ". . . because he made himself the Son of God" *(v. 7)*. When Pilate continued to try to get the people to have him release Jesus, the Jews told him that, if he did, he was no friend of Cæsar's *(v. 12)*. The Jews besought Pilate that they might break the legs of the three on the cross because it was the Sabbath and they wanted to hasten their deaths so they could be taken down from their crosses in compliance with Sabbath law. The legs of the two thieves were broken, but when the soldiers came to Jesus, he was already dead so it was not necessary to break his legs. This fulfilled the prophecy in *Numbers 9:12:* "They shall leave none of it unto the morning, nor break any bone of it . . ." *(v. 31)*.

Acts 9:22-25. The Jews in Damascus sought to kill Saul after Saul's conversion because he was preaching so forcefully among the people, confounding the Jews and proving that Jesus was the Christ. They waited and watched by the gates to catch him, but the disciples lowered him over the wall at night in a basket and he joined the disciples in Jerusalem.

Acts 13:42-51. The Jews, after listening to Barnabas and Paul teaching in the synagogues, left. However, many of the Jews and religious proselytes asked the apostles to give the same message the following week. When the Jews saw the multitudes that gathered to hear the apostles, they were envious and spoke against Barnabas and Paul and their teachings. Paul reminded them that it was necessary that the gospel first be preached to them, but since they rejected it, the Lord commanded that it be preached to the Gentiles. The Jews stirred up the women and chief men of the city, persecuted the apostles and expelled them out of their coasts. Barnabas and Paul shook off the dust of their feet against them as they left the city.

Acts 14. The Jews stirred the people up against Paul and Barnabas when they preached in the synagogue in Iconium. The apostles fled to Lystra and Derbe when they learned the people planned to stone them *(vs. 1-5)*. Certain Jews came from Antioch and Iconium and persuaded the people in Lystra to turn against the apostles. They stoned Paul and drew him out of the city, thinking he was dead. However, the disciples stood around him, and he rose the next day *(vs. 19-20)*.

Acts 21. The Jews in Jerusalem, the prophet Agabus warned Paul, would bind and deliver Paul to the Gentiles *(v. 11)*. The Jews from Asia stirred the Jews up in Jerusalem, and they drew Paul out of the temple and beat him. Paul was rescued by the chief captain of the band, his soldiers and the centurions *(vs. 27-32)*. Paul requested permission to speak to the Jews, and spoke to them in the Hebrew tongue *(vs. 39- 40)*.

Acts 22. When the Jews heard Paul speak in the Hebrew tongue, they were silent *(v. 2)*. They listened as Paul recounted his conversion, but were not appeased and wanted him dead *(v. 22)*.

Acts 23:12-33. Forty Jews plotted to kill Paul and made an agreement to neither eat nor drink until they had accomplished their deed. They discussed their plan with the chief priests and elders. Paul's nephew, his sister's son, reported the plot to Paul. Paul had the young man taken to Claudius Lysias, the chief captain. When he learned of the plot, he had Paul escorted out of town in the middle of the night. He was taken to Felix, the governor.

Acts 24:1-9. The Jews that accompanied Tertullus, Ananias and the elders as they went to lodge their complaints against Paul with Felix assented to the false testimony given by Tertullus, their spokesman.

JOANNA (1)

Luke 3:27. See **Joanna (1)** in Appendix A.

JOANNA (2)

Luke 8:2-3. **JOANNA** was the wife of Chuza, Herod's steward. She and Mary Magdalene, out of whom Jesus sent seven devils, and Susanna, were among the women who followed Jesus and ministered unto him as he went throughout the villages and towns preaching.

Luke 24:1-11. Joanna, Mary Magdalene, Mary the mother of James, and other women went to the sepulchre wherein Jesus had been laid and found the tomb empty. Two men in shining garments *(i.e., angels)* told them not to be afraid, Jesus was risen as he had said. The women quickly went to tell the apostles. The disciples did not believe them.

JOHN (1) (the son of Zebedee)

Matt. 4; Mark 1; Luke 5. **JOHN**, the brother of James, was a son of Zebedee. John and James were mending their fishing nets with their father when Jesus called them to come follow him. They left their nets and their father and followed Jesus *(Matt. 4:21-22; Mark 1:19-20; Luke 5:10-11)*. He and James were with

Jesus, Peter and Andrew when they went into the house of Peter and Andrew and Jesus healed Peter's mother-in-law *(Mark 1:29-31)*.

Matt. 10; Luke 9. Jesus called 12 disciples: Simon Peter, Andrew, James, John, Philip, Bartholomew; Thomas, Matthew, James, Lebbæus (Thaddæus), Simon the Canaanite, and Judas Iscariot *(Matt. 10:2-4)*. Jesus empowered these apostles and sent them forth to teach, but instructed them that they should not go to the Gentiles nor to the Samaritans. They were to go to the lost sheep of the house of Israel. They were to heal the sick and cast out devils. They were to travel without purse or scrip. They were instructed to leave their peace upon those who received them, but to shake the dust off their feet when leaving the houses of those who reject them *(Matt. 10: 5-14; Luke 9:1-5)*. They were told they would be persecuted for Christ's sake, but that "he that endureth to the end shall be saved." They are of more value than the sparrows for which the Father provides. Even the hairs of their heads are numbered *(Matt. 10:16- 32)*.

Matt. 17; Mark 9; Luke 9. John and his brother James, along with Peter, went with Jesus into a high mountain where they were transfigured, saw Moses and Elias, and heard a voice proclaiming, "This is my beloved Son, in whom I am well pleased; hear ye him." Peter suggested making three altars: one each for Jesus, Moses and Elias *(vs. 1-12; Mark 9:2-13; Luke 9:28-35)*. When they had come unto a multitude none of the disciples was able to heal a certain man's son who was "lunatick." Jesus said this was because of lack of faith—the kind of faith that comes from fasting and prayer *(vs. 14-21)*. The disciples were grieved when Jesus told them he would be betrayed and killed but would rise again on the third day *(vs. 22- 23)*.

Matt. 20:20-28; Mark 10:35-45. John's mother petitioned Jesus to allow her sons, James and John, to sit on his left and right sides in his kingdom. Jesus responded that it was not his to give, but that it would be "given to them for whom it is prepared of my Father." The other ten disciples were "moved with indignation against the two brethren," and Jesus then taught that "whosoever will be great among you, let him be your minister. . . let him be your servant." *(Note: In the account recorded in Mark, James and John made the request of Jesus, not their mother.)*

Matt. 26:37-44; Mark 14:33-41; Luke 22:39-46. Jesus' disciples followed him when he went to the Garden of Gethsemane. He had them wait while he went off to pray, but he took Peter and the sons of Zebedee—James and John—with him as he went further into the garden of Gethsemane and asked them to wait and watch with him. Nevertheless, while he went a way off to pray, they repeatedly fell asleep. *(Note: The account in Luke does not specify that Jesus took John, James and Peter an additional distance with him.)*

Mark 3:17. John and James were given the surname of <u>BOANERGES</u>—The sons of thunder—by Christ.

Mark 5:37; Luke 8:51. John and James, along with Peter, accompanied Jesus to the house of Jairus where he healed Jairus' twelve-year-old daughter.

Mark 9:38-40; Luke 9:49-50. John told Jesus that he and the disciples had observed someone casting out devils in Jesus' name and so they forbade him to do it because the man didn't follow them. Jesus told them not to forbid the man because no one can perform any miracle in his name and still speak evil of him, and he that is not against him is with him.

Mark 10:35-41. See entry for Matt. 20:20-28.

Mark 13. John, James, Peter and Andrew asked Jesus what calamities would precede the Second Coming. Jesus told them there would be false Christs, wars and rumors of wars, nation would rise against nation and kingdom against kingdom; there would be earthquakes and famines and troubles. The prophets would be persecuted for Christ's sake. Brother would betray brother and fathers would betray their sons; children shall rise against their parents. The desolation prophesied by Daniel will come to pass. The sun shall be darkened, the moon will not give its light, and the stars of heaven shall fall. Then the Son of Man will come in the clouds in great power and glory *(vs. 3-27)*. Jesus said to watch for the signs, just as we know summer is near when the fig tree puts forth her tender branches, so the signs will signal the Second Coming. Nevertheless, Jesus stressed that no man knows the day, time, nor place. We should be prepared and not be caught "sleeping" *(vs. 28-37; also see Matt. 24:37-51; Luke 21:29-36; also see Luke 17:20-37 for a variation on this subject)*.

Mark 14. See the entry for Matt. 26.

Luke 8:51. See the entry for Mark 5.

Luke 9:54. *(See Mark 9:38-40 for verses 49-50.)* John and James asked Jesus if they should call down fire from heaven to consume the Samaritans who refused to receive him as he traveled to Jerusalem because his time had come. The Savior rebuked them and indicated they failed to understand that he had come to save lives, not destroy them.

Luke 22:8-13. John and Peter were sent into the city by Jesus to prepare the Passover. Jesus told them they would find a man with a pitcher of water whom they should follow and he would show them to a large upper room. *(Also see Mark 14:13-16.)*

John 19:26-27. John, the disciple whom Jesus loved, was standing by the cross upon which Jesus hung. Jesus, referring to John, told his mother, "Woman, behold thy son!" To John, he said, "Behold thy mother!" The disciple took Mary into his home from then on.

John 20. John *(i.e., the other disciple whom Jesus loved)* and Simon Peter dashed to the sepulchre wherein Christ's body had been placed after Mary Magdalene reported that Jesus' body was gone. John beat Peter to the Sepulchre but stood outside peering in when Peter arrived. Peter went inside the sepulchre and saw the linen clothes lying there. After seeing for themselves and believing he was gone, the disciples returned to their homes *(vs. 2-10)*. That evening Jesus appeared to his disciples as they were assembled in seclusion for fear of the Jews and showed them the wounds in his hands and side and told them to "Receive ye the Holy Ghost" *(vs. 19-22)*. He appeared to them again eight days later *(v. 26)*.

John 21. John and James, Peter, Thomas, Nathanael of Cana, and two other disciples were fishing on the sea of Tiberias when Jesus showed himself to his disciples a third time following his resurrection. Jesus stood on the shore and asked if they had any meat. They did not recognize Jesus, but responded that they had none. He told them to cast their nets on the right side of the ship. They did; and their nets were so full they were unable to draw them. John declared to Peter, "It is the Lord." Peter quickly put something on and cast himself into the sea. When the disciples were gathered together on shore, Jesus dined with them on bread and fishes *(vs. 1-14).* Jesus foretold John's translation *(vs. 20-23).*

Acts 1:13-14. Following Jesus' ascension into heaven, Jesus' disciples, including John, met together in an upper room, along with several women (including Mary the mother of Jesus) and his brethren, where they continued in prayer and supplication.

Acts. 3. When John and Peter went to the temple to pray, a man lame from birth asked for alms. Peter told him they had neither silver or gold, but would give them what they did have, and then he told him, "In the name of Jesus Christ of Nazareth rise up and walk," and the man was healed. When the people gathered around John and Peter in amazement, Peter admonished them and said the God of Abraham had glorified his Son by healing the man *(vs. 1-11).*

Acts 4. John and Peter were arrested by the priests, captain of the temple and the Sadducees as they spoke unto the people about Christ. Peter, filled with the Holy Ghost, spoke boldly and testified of Christ, saying that it was through Christ's name that a certain lame man was healed. The rulers, elders, scribes, Annas the high priest, Caiaphas, John and Alexander, and as many kindred of the high priest as there were, met to confer as to what to do about John and Peter. The healed man was with the apostles so they could not deny he had been healed, and they feared the people. They resolved to threaten them and let them go. They commanded John and Peter not to speak or teach in the name of Jesus. They responded with a question: "Was it better to hearken unto them or unto God?" *(vs. 1-22).* They returned to their fellow apostles and they all praised God, quoting David *(Ps. 1-2).* As they finished praying, the building shook and they were all filled with the Holy Ghost. All their followers were of one heart and they had all things in common *(vs. 31-37).*

Acts 8. John and Peter went to Samaria when the apostles heard that the people there were being converted. While the people had been baptized by Philip, they had not received the laying on of hands for the gift of the Holy Ghost. Thus, John and Peter "laid their hands on them, and they received the Holy Ghost" *(vs. 14-17).* A man named Simon, who had been baptized by Philip, offered to pay them money if they would give him the power to lay hands on people and give them the Holy Ghost. Peter rebuked him and told him to repent for his heart was not right before God. Simon asked Peter to pray to the Lord that the things Peter said would not come upon him. John and Peter, after preaching and testifying, returned to Jerusalem *(vs. 18-25).*

Acts 13:5, 13. John ministered to the people at Salamis along with Barnabas and Saul. From Salamis, the apostles went to Paphos where they encountered Barjesus, a Jew who was a false prophet and sorcerer. When Paul and Barnabas left Paphos, John left also. He returned to Jerusalem.

Gal. 2:9. John, James, and Cephas (Peter) were pillars in the church and extended the right hand of fellowship to Paul and Barnabas. Paul and Barnabas were to go unto the heathen, those of the uncircumcision, to preach: the apostles were to go unto those of the circumcision.

1 Jn. 1. (Note: The BD states that even though the writer of the three epistles attributed to John never identifies himself by name, tradition assigns them to John, and points out there is similarity in the language between these epistles and the fourth Gospel.) John testifies Christ was from the beginning and that he and his colleagues have seen and handled the risen Christ, the Word of life. They declare unto the people that which they have seen and heard so that the people may also have fellowship with them and with God the Father and his Son, Jesus Christ. The message they declare is this: God is light and there is no darkness in him at all *(vs. 1-5)*. We are cleansed through the blood of Christ *(v. 7)*. Christ will forgive those who confess their sins. Those who say they have no sins deceive themselves *(vs. 8-9)*.

1 Jn. 2. Christ is our advocate with the Father. We show that we know him by keeping his commandments, walking as he walked *(vs. 1-6)*. He reminded the people of the Lord's commandment to love our brothers *(vs. 7-11)*. John addressed all ages in the church—little children, fathers, young men—and said their sins were forgiven for Christ's name's sake *(i.e., when baptized, they take upon themselves the name of Christ and receive forgiveness upon repentance) (vs. 12-14)*. He admonished them not to love the world. They cannot love both God and the world. Those who love God abideth forever *(vs. 15-17)*. He warned them about the apostasy that was already beginning to occur and the many antichrists who would preach false doctrines *(vs. 18-19)*. His purpose in writing to these saints was not because they didn't know the truth, they did. They knew lies are not of truth and that liars deny Jesus Christ; thus, liars also deny Heavenly Father. He encouraged them to remain true to the teachings they had received from the beginning, ultimately receiving eternal life as promised by God *(vs. 21-25)*. John acknowledged that they did not need to be taught by man because they had the Holy Ghost to teach them of all things *(v. 27)*. He encouraged them to be faithful so they would not be ashamed at his coming. Those who are righteous are born of Christ *(vs. 28-29)*.

1 Jn. 3. John taught that Heavenly Father showed his great love by providing a way for people to become sons of God. The world does not know the sons of God because it knows not God. Though the faithful are sons of God now, what they ultimately will become is not yet fully known, but when he shall appear, they will be like him and they shall see him as he is *(vs. 1-2)*. Those who sin transgress the law. Those who abide in Christ do not sin. Those who commit sin are of the devil. Those who do not love their brother are of the devil. We have been commanded from the beginning to love our brother. Cain followed the devil and killed his brother because his works were evil and his brother's works were righteous. Those who do not love their brother abideth in death. Because Christ laid down his life for us, we should be willing to lay down our life for the brethren. The love of God does not abide in those who have the ability to help a brother who is in need and fails to do so. We must love in deed and truth, not just in word *(vs. 4-18)*. If our hearts are pure before God, they will commend us; if not, they will condemn us. If we keep the commandments, the Lord will answer our prayers. We must love one another as he commanded. Those who keep the commandments dwell in him and him in them *(vs. 19-24)*.

1 Jn. 4. John admonished the saints to test those who profess to be of God, saying that those who are of God testify of Christ. Those who testify against Christ are antichrists. Those who are of the world, speak of the world and the world listens to them. Those who are of God, speak of God and are heard by those who also know God *(vs. 1-6)*. John continued to expound upon the subject of love. We must love one another. Love is of God. God sent his only Begotten Son into the world that we might live through him. Because God so loved us, we ought to love one another. "No man hath seen God at any time, except them who believe" *(v. 12, JST)*. Heavenly Father sent his son into the world to be the Savior of the world. God is love. Those who dwell in love, dwell in God and God in them. Those who claim to love God but hate their brothers are liars. John poses this question: "For he that loveth not his brother whom he hath seen, how can he love God whom he hath not seen?" He who loves God must love his brother, also *(vs. 7-21)*.

1 Jn. 5. Those who believe that Jesus is the Christ are born of God. Those who love God and keep his commandments show that they also love the children of God. Those who are born of God are able to overcome the world *(vs. 1-5)*. Three things testify of Christ: the Spirit, water and blood *(vs. 6-8)*. One must believe in Christ and have a testimony that he is the Son of God in order to gain eternal life *(vs. 9-13)*. John stressed that those who pray, "according to his will," will receive answers to their prayers *(vs. 14-15)*. "There is a sin unto death" *(i.e., denying the testimony of the Holy Ghost) (v. 16)*. All unrighteousness is sin, but some sin is not unto death. Satan is unable to touch those who are begotten of God and keep the commandments. John testified that the Son of God had come and had given them an understanding. To know Jesus Christ and God the Father is eternal life *(vs. 17-20)*.

2 Jn. 1:1-13. John, an elder and apostle in the church, addressed this epistle "unto the elect lady and her children." John rejoiced in that the children were walking in truth; and he counseled her and her household to continue to keep the commandment to love one another. He cautioned them about those who seek to deceive the members of the church, the antichrists, who confess not that Christ had indeed come to earth in the flesh, and instructed them not to receive such into their homes. He withheld writing all he wanted to say to them, and expressed his hope to come to them soon. He sent greetings from the children of her elect sister. *(Note: There is no explanation as to who the elect lady is that he is addressing. She obviously is a very righteous woman to be regarded as an "elect lady"—one who is worthy to be chosen as a daughter of God in this life and who is qualified to be an heir of God and a member of his household. It might possibly be his wife and his children. DNTC, vol. III, p. 410.)*

3 Jn. 1. John addressed this epistle to his beloved Gaius, whom he commended for walking in the truth and for his charity which was evident in the help he gave to both those in and out of the church *(vs. 1-6)*. He referred to Diotrephes, who had apparently apostatized, and counseled Gaius not to follow evil, only that which is good *(vs. 9-11)*. He informed Gaius that Demetrius had good report of all men and of the truth, of which John said he and his colleagues also bore record *(v. 12)*. He declined to write more and indicated that he hoped to see him face to face shortly *(vs. 13-14)*.

Rev. 1. (Note: According to the BD, the revelation John received can be divided into two parts: chapters 1-3 deal with John's day and is addressed to the members of the Church living at that time in seven cities in Asia; chapters 4-22 are prophetic writings that relate to future events. The EB, vol. VIII, p. 537, adds the following insight into the Revelation of John: chapters 2-3 contain moral admonitions but no visions or symbolism; chapters 4-22, however, include visions, allegories and symbols that are largely left unexplained, leading to a variety of interpretations.) This revelation was given by Christ unto John via an angel for the benefit of the saints. Those who read, hear and understand the words of this prophecy, and keep them, will be blessed. Through Christ's blood and his atonement for our sins, we are made kings and priests unto God and his Father. *(i.e., "They are they who received the testimony of Jesus, and believed on his name and were baptized after the manner of his burial, being buried in the water in his name. . . and who overcome by faith, and are sealed by the Holy spirit of promise . . . They are they who are the church of the Firstborn . . . into whose hands the Father has given all things They are they who are priests and kings, who have received of his fulness, and of his glory . . ." D&C 76:51-56.)* John identifies himself and states that he has also suffered tribulation and was banished to the isle of Patmos for the gospel's sake. The Lord is Alpha and Omega, the beginning and the end. He instructed John to write the revelation in a book and send it to the seven churches—Ephesus, Smyrna, Pergamos, Thyatira, Sardis, Philadelphia and Loadicea—which were in Asia, for the time is at hand *(vs. 1-11). (Note: Joseph Smith, a latter-day prophet was also commanded by the Lord "To lift up your voice as with the sound of a trump . . . For behold . . . the time is soon at hand that I shall come in a cloud with power and great glory. D&C 34:6-7.)* As John turned to see who spoke to him, he saw seven candlesticks *(which he was informed represented the seven churches in Asia);* in the midst of the seven candlesticks, he saw a person like unto the Son of Man who had seven stars in his right hand *(which, he was informed, represented the angels; i.e., servants, of the seven churches).* When John saw this person, he fell at his feet as though dead, and the person said, "Fear not; I am the first and the last; I am he that liveth, and was dead; and, behold, I am alive for evermore, Amen; and have the keys of hell and of death." John was commanded to write what he saw, what was, and what he would yet see *(vs. 12-20).*

Rev. 2. John was instructed to write to the "angel of the church at Ephesus" in the name of "he that holdeth the seven stars in his right hand" and say that the Lord knows his works, commend him for abhorring the Nicolaitans and those who did evil, and to chastise him for not following through on certain other aspects of the gospel *(vs. 1-7).* John was instructed to inform the "angel of the church in Smyrna" that the Lord, i.e., "the first and the last, which was dead, and is alive," was aware of his works, tribulation and poverty; of the blasphemy of those who claimed to be Jews but were actually of Satan's synagogue. This leader was admonished not to fear the opposition; Satan would try him and some of the saints would be cast into prison; he would have tribulation ten days; those who are faithful unto death will receive a crown of life *(i.e., the gift of salvation; D&C 6:13)*; he that overcomes evil shall avoid the second death *(vs. 8-11).* To the angel *(servant)* of the church in Pergamos, John was to write that "he which hath the sharp sword with two edges" knew of his works and where Satan's seat is. He was commended for not denying the faith, even in the days of strong persecution when Antipas was martyred, but he was also chastised for allowing apostates into their group: those that held to the doctrine of Balaam and the doctrine of the Nicolaitans. He was told to repent, or the Lord would come against him. Those who overcome evil would be given to eat of "the hidden manna," *(i.e., Jesus Christ, the bread of life);* and would receive a white stone *(i.e., the Urim and Thummim, see the footnote to this verse in the N.T.),* wherein a new name would be written "which no man knoweth saving he that receiveth it *(vs. 12-17).* The angel of the church in Thyatira was to be told that the Son of God knew of his works and charity, patience, faith and service. Nevertheless, he was to be chastised for allowing Jezebel, a false prophetess, to lead people astray through fornication and by eating things sacrificed unto idols. Those who commit adultery with her would be cast into great tribulation and her children *(i.e., her followers)* killed. To the righteous who did not follow Jezebel, the Lord admonished them to hold fast to that which they already had "til I come." He would put no more upon them. Those who endure faithfully to the end will be given power over many kingdoms *(i.e., will inherit the celestial kingdom and rule over many kingdoms) (vs. 18-29).*

Rev. 3. John was instructed to write to the church in Sardis where many members were members in name only, but were, in fact, spiritually dead. The "angel, i.e., servant, of the church in Sardis" was counseled to be watchful *(i.e., looking forth for the signs of Christ's Second Coming, D&C 39:23)* and strengthen those who were still faithful but were close to losing their faith. The Lord knew of his works and said he had not found them *(his works)* to be perfect before God. He told him to repent; otherwise, he *(the Lord)* would come upon him as a thief, "and thou shalt not know what hour I will come upon thee." There were still a few church members in Sardis who had not defiled their garments. They were worthy to someday walk with the Lord, dressed in white raiment. Those who repent and are found worthy will also have their names written in the book of life and shall be clothed in white and walk with the Lord *(vs. 1-6).* To the angel in Philadelphia, John was told to write that "he that hath the key of David" knows his works and knows that he has kept his *(the Lord's)* word and not denied his name. The Lord will cause those who say they are Jews but who are of the synagogue of Satan to worship before his servant in Philadelphia, but he will keep him *(the angel of the church in Philadelphia)* from the hour of temptation which will come upon all the world. The Lord will come quickly when he comes, and admonished this servant to hold fast that which he had so that no man could rob him of his crown. Those who overcome temptation and keep the commandments will receive eternal glory in the house of God. The Lord will write upon him "the name of my God, and the name of the city of my God . . . and I will write upon him my new name" *(vs. 7-13).* To the angel of the church of the Laodiceans, John was instructed to write that the Amen *(i.e., the Lord)* knew his works and knew that he was neither hot nor cold, and wished that he were either hot or cold. Since he is lukewarm, the Lord will spew him out of his mouth. He is caught up in his own riches and fails to recognize his own state of wretchedness. The Lord told him to repent and counseled him to buy of him things that would lead unto eternal life. The Lord chastens those whom he loves. He knocks at the door. He will enter whenever people hear his voice and open their doors and "will sup with them" and they with him. Those who overcome unrighteousness will sit with the Lord in his throne just as Christ overcame and "am set down with my Father in his throne" *(vs. 14-22).*

Rev. 4. After John saw the seven candlesticks and received instructions from the Lord pertaining to the seven servants over the seven churches in Asia, he looked and a door was opened into heaven and John was permitted to gaze into heaven. He heard a voice telling him to come so he could be shown all things which were yet to come. John saw (a) the throne of God; (b) one sitting on the throne whose countenance he described as being like precious gems; (c) 24 seats round about the throne upon which were sitting 24 elders, clothed in white and wearing gold crowns upon their heads; (d) thunderings, lightnings and voices proceeding out of the throne; (e) seven lamps of fire, representing seven servants of the Lord, burning before the throne; (f) a sea of glass like unto crystal was also before the throne; (g) 24 elders in the midst of the throne; (h) four beasts full of eyes both before and behind round about the throne *(vs. 1-6)*. The first beast was like a lion; the second like a calf; the third had the face of a man; the fourth was like a flying eagle. They each had six wings. They were full of eyes. They praised the Lord day and night without rest. *(Note: The Old Testament prophet Ezekiel was also shown a vision with four beasts: one with the face of a lion; the second like an ox (rather than calf); the third the face of a man; and the fourth had the face of an eagle. Ezek. 1:4-28.)* As the beasts praised God, the 24 elders fell down and worshiped God as he sat upon his throne *(vs. 7-11)*.

Note: Modern-day revelation contained in D&C 77 provides an interpretation of what John saw. The sea of glass is the earth in its sanctified, immortal, and eternal state" (v. 1). The four beasts are figurative expressions used by John in describing heaven; the paradise of God; the happiness of man; and of beasts, and of creeping things, and of the fowls of the air; that which is spiritual being in the likeness of that which is temporal," and vise versa (v. 2). They represent the glory of the classes of beings in their destined order or sphere of creation," (v. 3). The eyes represent light and knowledge, and the wings represent power to move and act (v. 4). The 24 elders were elders who had belonged to the seven churches and had been faithful in the ministry but who were now dead and were in the paradise of God (v. 5).

Rev. 5. The vision continued. John saw (a) a book in the right hand of the one *(i.e., God the Father)* sitting on the throne; (b) the book was written within and on the backside and was sealed with seven seals; and (c) a strong angel asking in a loud voice if anyone was worthy to loose the seals of the book. No one was found who could open the book and John wept. One of the 24 elders comforted John and told him that the Lion of the tribe of Juda (Judah), the Root of David *(i.e., Jesus Christ, the Savior)* had prevailed to open the book and loose the seven seals *(vs. 1-5)*. John saw (a) a Lamb in the midst of the throne, the four beasts and the 24 elders, standing as it had been slain; (b) the Lamb had seven *(12)* horns and seven *(12)* eyes which are the seven *(12)* servants of God sent forth into all the earth *(Rev. 5:6, JST, says 12 not seven) (v. 6)*. The Lamb took the book from the right hand of God and the four beasts and 24 elders, having harps and vials full of odours *(i.e., the prayers of the saints)*, fell down before the Lamb and sang a new song, acknowledging that he was worthy to open the seals; that he had been slain and had redeemed all mankind by his blood, making us kings and priests unto God, to reign on the earth. John heard the voice of many angels—ten thousand times ten thousand, and thousands of thousands—praising the Lamb *(vs. 7-14)*.

D&C 77 continues to explain this vision. The <u>*book with seven seals*</u> *represents "the revealed will, mysteries, and the works of God; the hidden things of his economy concerning this earth during the seven thousand years of its continuance, or its temporal existence" (v. 6). The* <u>*first seal*</u> *represents the things of the first thousand years; the* <u>*second seal*</u> *represents the things of the second thousand years, and so on (v. 7).*

Rev. 6. <u>John saw</u> the Lamb (the Savior) open the seven seals. When the <u>first seal</u> was opened, John heard one of the four beasts telling him to come and see. John saw someone wearing a crown and holding a bow, sitting astride a white horse, going forth to conquer *(vs. 1-2).* When the <u>second seal</u> was opened, John heard the second beast inviting him to come and see. He saw someone upon a red horse, given a sword, and he was given the power to take peace from the earth, that the people should kill one another *(vs. 3-4). ("I . . . will that all men shall know that the day speedily cometh; the hour is not yet, but is nigh at hand, when peace shall be taken from the earth, and the devil shall have power over his own dominion" (D&C 1:35).)* When the <u>third seal</u> was opened, the third beast invited John to come and see. He saw someone sitting on a black horse holding a pair of balances in his hand. A voice in the midst of the four beasts said, "A measure of wheat for a penny, and three measures of barley for a penny; and see thou hurt not the oil and the wine" *(vs. 5-6).* When the <u>fourth seal</u> was opened, the voice of the fourth beast beckoned John. He beheld a pale horse upon which sat one whose name was Death, and Hell followed him. They were given powers of terrible destruction over the fourth part of the earth *(vs. 7-8).* When the <u>fifth seal</u> was opened, John saw under the altar, the souls of those who had been slain for their faith, crying out for justice. They were given white robes and told to rest for a season—until the time was fulfilled when other of their brethren, who were also to be killed as they had been, were killed *(vs. 9-11).* When the Lamb opened the <u>sixth seal</u>, John witnessed many things: (a) there was a great earthquake; (b) the sun became black as sackcloth of hair, and the moon became as blood; (c) the stars fell unto the earth; (d) the heavens opened like a scroll being rolled together; (e) every mountain and island was moved out of its place; (f) every man—rich and poor, bond and free—hid in the dens and rocks of the mountains praying that the rocks would fall on them and hide them from the face of God and from the wrath of the Lamb, for the day of his wrath is come *(vs. 12-17). (Note: The Lord revealed the events recorded in the Revelation given to John to Joseph Smith.)*

The things spoken of in this chapter are to be accomplished in the sixth thousand years, or the opening of the sixth seal (D&C 77:10).

For not many days hence and the earth shall tremble and reel to and fro as a drunken man; and the sun shall hide his face, and shall refuse to give light; and the moon shall be bathed in blood; and the stars shall become exceedingly angry, and shall cast themselves down as a fig that falleth from off a fig-tree." (D&C 88:87. Compare Rev. 6:12.)

. . . and immediately after shall the curtain of heaven be unfolded, as a scroll is unfolded after it is rolled up, and the face of the Lord shall be unveiled." (D&C 88:95. Compare Rev. 6:14.)

Rev. 7. Continuation of what John saw: (g) John saw four angels standing on the four corners of the earth, holding back the winds so they could not blow; (h) he saw another angel ascending from the east, having the seal of the living God, crying unto the four angels *(to whom it was given to hurt the earth and the sea)* not to hurt the earth, the sea, nor the trees until the servants of God had been sealed in their foreheads; (I) the number sealed was 144,000 of the tribes of the children of Israel, 12,000 per tribe *(vs. 1- 8).* (j) John then saw a great multitude—too great to be numbered—from all the nations of the world, clothed in white robes and carrying palms in their hands, praising God and the Lamb; (k) all the angels stood round the throne, the beasts and the elders, and fell down and worshiped God *(vs. 9-12).* (l) One elder asked John who they were who came in white robes and from whence they came, to which John responded that the angel knew the answer; (m) the angel said they were those who had suffered great tribulation and had washed their robes and made them white in the blood of the Lamb; therefore, they were before the throne of God and served him night and day in the temple; God would dwell among them. They shall neither hunger nor thirst, and the Lamb shall feed them and lead them unto living fountains of waters. God shall wipe away all their tears *(vs. 13-17).*

> *The explanation of this vision continues in D&C 77. The four angels referred to in 7:1 "are four angels sent forth from God, to whom power is given over the four parts of the earth, to save life and to destroy; these are they who have the everlasting gospel to commit to every nation, kindred, tongue, and people; having power to shut up the heavens, to seal up unto life, or to cast down to the regions of darkness" (v. 8). "The angel ascending from the east is he to whom is given the seal of the living God over the twelve tribes of Israel; wherefore, he crieth unto the four angels having the everlasting gospel, saying: Hurt not the earth, neither the sea, nor the trees, till we have sealed the servants of our God in their foreheads. And, if you will receive it, this is Elias which was to come to gather together the tribes of Israel and restore all things" (v. 9). These things will take place in the sixth thousand years, or the opening of the sixth seal (v. 10). "Those who are sealed are high priests, ordained unto the holy order of God, to administer the everlasting gospel; for they are they who are ordained out of every nation, kindred, tongue, and people, by the angels to whom is given power over the nations of the earth, to bring as many as will come to the church of the Firstborn" (v. 11).*

Rev. 8. When John opened the seventh seal, there was silence for about half an hour *(v. 1).* Other things were shown unto John: (a) the seven angels which stood before the altar were given seven trumpets; (b) another angel, having a golden censer, came and stood before the altar and was given incense to offer with the prayers of all saints upon the golden altar; (c) the smoke of the incense ascended up before God; (d) the angel took the censer, filled it with the fire of the altar, and cast it into the earth; (e) there were thunderings, lightnings and an earthquake; (f) the seven angels prepared themselves to sound the trumpets *(vs. 2-6).* When the first angel sounded, there was hail and fire mingled with blood. They were cast upon the earth. One-third of the trees and all green grass were burned up *(v. 7).* When the second angel sounded, a great burning mountain was cast into the sea, and one-third of the sea became blood; one-third of the creatures in the sea, died; and one-third of the ships were destroyed *(vs. 8-9)*. The third angel sounded and a great star, burning as a lamp, fell from heaven upon the third part of the rivers, and upon the fountains of waters. The name of the star was Wormwood. One-third of the waters became wormwood, and many men died from the bitter waters *(vs. 10-11)*. The fourth angel sounded, and one-third of the sun, moon and stars, were smitten and darkened so one-third of both the day and night did not shine. And John saw and heard another angel flying through the midst of heaven crying woe unto the people of the earth "by reason of the other voices of the trumpets of the three angels which had not yet sounded" *(vs. 12-13)*. *(Note: Revelation given to Joseph Smith supports, complements and provides some insight into the meaning of the revelation given to John.)*

> *"And there shall be silence in heaven for the space of half an hour . . ." (D&C 88:95. Compare Rev. 8:1.)*
>
> *Regarding the trumpets: "God made the world in six days, and on the seventh day he finished his work, and sanctified it, and also formed man out of the dust of the earth, even so, in the beginning of the seventh thousand years will the Lord God sanctify the earth, and complete the salvation of man, and judge all things, and shall redeem all things, except that which he hath not put into his power, when he shall have sealed all things, unto the end of all things; and the sounding of the trumpets of the seven angels are the preparing and finishing of his work, in the beginning of the seventh thousand years—the preparing of the way before the time of his coming." (D&C 77:12. Compare Rev. 8:2.)*
>
> *"Also cometh the testimony of the voice of thunderings, and the voice of lightnings, and the voice of tempests, and the voice of the waves of the sea heaving themselves beyond their bounds. . . And angels shall fly through the midst of heaven, crying with a loud voice, sounding the trump of God, saying: Prepare ye, prepare ye, O inhabitants of the earth; for the judgment of our God is come. Behold, and lo, the Bridegroom cometh; go ye out to meet him." (D&C 88:90, 92. Compare Rev. 8:5, 13.)*

Rev. 9. The fifth angel sounded, and John saw a star fall from heaven unto the earth: and to him *(the star which fell from heaven)* was given the key of the bottomless pit. He opened the bottomless pit. A dark smoke arose out of the pit as from a great furnace, and darkened the sun and the air. Locusts, with the power of scorpions, came out of the smoke. They were commanded not to hurt any plant life, "only those men which have not the seal of God in their foreheads." These men were to be tormented five months, not killed. Men shall seek to die, but death will not come *(vs. 1-6)*. The locusts were shaped like unto horses prepared for battle. They appeared to wear crowns of gold on their heads. Their faces were as the faces of men; hair as of the hair of women; teeth as of the teeth of lions. They were wearing breastplates as of iron; the sound of their wings was as the sound of many chariots; they had tails with stingers like unto scorpions *(vs. 7-10)*. They were ruled over by a king, the angel of the bottomless pit. His name in Hebrew is Abaddon; in Greek, Apollyon *(v. 11)*. The sixth angel sounded and John heard a voice from the four horns of the golden altar telling the sixth angel with the trumpet to loose the four angels which are bound in the great river Euphrates. *(Note:*

The JST reads "bottomless pit" rather than "great river Euphrates.") The angels were loosed which had been prepared to slay one-third of the part of men. Their army numbered 200,000,000. The horsemen wore breastplates of fire, jacinth and brimstone. The heads of the horses were as the heads of lions; and fire, smoke and brimstone issued forth out of their mouths, which fire, smoke and brimstone killed one-third of the host of men *(vs. 13-19)*. Those who were not killed by the plagues still failed to repent of their evil doings and idol worship *(vs. 20-21)*. *(Note: The things written in chapter 9 of Revelation shall be accomplished after the opening of the seventh seal, before the coming of Christ (D&C 77:13).)*

Rev. 10. John saw another mighty angel come down from heaven, clothed with a cloud, a rainbow upon his head, his face as it were the sun, and his feet as pillars of fire. He had a little open book in his hand. His right foot was upon the sea and his left foot upon the earth. He cried with a voice like a roaring lion. When he cried, seven thunders *(i.e., the seven angels, DNTC, III, p. 505)* uttered their voices. As John prepared to write, a voice from heaven told him not to write because the things the seven thunders uttered were sealed up *(vs. 1-4)*. The angel which had one foot on the sea and the other on the earth, lifted his hands to heaven, and declared that there should be time no longer. In the days of the seventh angel, the mystery of God should be finished as he hath declared to his servants the prophets *(vs. 5-7)*. *(And he will "swear in the name of him who sitteth upon the throne, that there shall be time no longer; and Satan shall be bound, that old serpent, who is called the devil, and shall not be loosed for the space of a thousand years (D&C 88:110).)* The voice from heaven instructed John to take the little open book from the angel. The angel told him to eat it up: that it would taste sweet in his mouth, but would be bitter in his belly; and it was so *(vs. 8-10)*. *(The little book eaten by John represents a "mission, and an ordinance, for him to gather the tribes of Israel; behold, this is Elias, who, as it is written, must come and restore all things" (D&C 77:14).)* The angel told John that he must yet prophesy again before many peoples, and nations, and tongues, and kings *(v. 11)*. *(John was commissioned to participate in the restoration of all things in the latter days.)*

Rev. 11. (The Revelation concerning the latter days continues.) John was given a reed like unto a rod and commanded to measure the temple, the altar and those who worship therein, but not to measure the courtyard, for it was given unto the Gentiles who would tread upon the holy city 42 months *(vs. 1-2)*. The Lord will send two prophets to Jerusalem who will prophesy 1260 days dressed in sackcloth. These two prophets are the two olive trees and the two candlesticks standing before the God of the earth which John saw earlier. The prophets will have the power to destroy anyone who tries to hurt them and the power to shut the heavens so no rain will fall. They will have power to turn water into blood and smite the earth with plagues *(vs. 3-6)*. *(They are two prophets that are to be raised up to the Jewish nation in the last days, at the time of the restoration, and to prophesy to the Jews after they are gathered and have built the city of Jerusalem in the land of their father (D&C 77:15).)* After they have completed their mission, they shall be slain. Their dead bodies will lie in the street of Jerusalem for three and one-half days as the people rejoice; after which, they shall be resurrected, causing great fear in those who beheld them. John saw them ascend up into heaven in a cloud; and their enemies saw them *(vs. 7-12)*. Within the hour, a great earthquake came, killing 7,000 men, frightening the rest who then gave glory to God *(v. 13)*. Thus, passed the second woe. The third was yet to come *(v 14)*. The seventh angel sounded. Great voices in heaven proclaimed that the kingdoms of this world are become the kingdom of our Lord, and he would reign forever upon the earth. The 24 elders fell down and worshiped God. It was now time for the judgment: to reward those who had been faithful, and destroy those who destroyed the earth *(vs. 15-18)*. *("For a trump shall sound both long and loud, even as upon Mount Sinai, and all the earth shall quake, and they shall come forth—yea, even the dead which died in me, to receive a crown of righteousness, and to be clothed upon, even as I am, to be with me, that we may be one" (D&C 29:13).)* The temple of God was opened in heaven. The ark of his testament was seen in his temple. There were lightnings, voices, thunderings, an earthquake and great hail *(v. 19)*. *("And there shall be a great hailstorm sent forth to destroy the crops of the earth (D&C 29:16).)*

Rev. 12 (JST). John was shown a great sign in heaven, represented by the likeness of things here on earth: (1) A woman clothed with the sun *(i.e., "The Church in its glory, beauty, power and perfection." See DNTC, III, p. 516)*, (2) with the moon under her feet *(i.e., "As the moon shines by reflected light, so do all earthly churches and kingdoms. They are under, beneath and lower than the true Church." Ibid, p. 517)*, (3) wearing a crown of 12 stars *(i.e., The 12 apostles of the Lamb, who are at the head and preside over the Church, and who with "the saints, . . . small and great, shall have place in the promised kingdom. Ibid.) (v. 1)*. *(This is ". . . the beginning of the rising up and the coming forth of my church out of the wilderness—clear as the moon, and fair as the sun, and terrible as an army with banner" (D&C 5:14).)* The woman was with child and cried, travailing in birth, and pained to be delivered. She brought forth a man child who would rule over all the earth with a rod of iron *(i.e., the priesthood)*. He was caught up unto God and his throne *(vs. 2-3)*. Another sign appeared: a great red dragon (Satan) with seven heads and ten horns wearing seven crowns upon his heads. His tail drew one-third of the stars of heaven and cast them down to the earth. *("And it came to pass that Adam, being tempted of the devil—for, behold, the devil was before Adam, for he rebelled against me, saying, Give me thine honor, which is my power; and also a third part of the hosts of heaven turned he away from me because of their agency; And they were thrust down, and thus came the devil and his angels; and Behold, there is a place prepared for them from the beginning, which place is hell" (D&C 29:36-38).)* The dragon stood before the woman, waiting to devour her child after it was born. The woman *(the church)* fled into the wilderness to a place which God had prepared, where she would be fed for 1260 years *(vs. 4-5)*. *(John saw the imminent apostasy of the church. "And after they have fallen asleep the great persecutor of the church, the apostate, the whore, even Babylon, that maketh all nations to drink of her cup, in whose hearts the enemy, even Satan, sitteth to reign—behold he soweth the tares; wherefore, the tares choke the wheat and drive the church into the wilderness" (D&C 86:3).)* John saw that there was a war in heaven wherein Michael and his angels fought against the dragon (Satan) and his angels. Satan was defeated and he and his angels were cast out *(vs. 7-8)*. With the defeat of Satan, a loud voice proclaimed, "Now is come salvation, and strength, and the kingdom of our God, and the power of his Christ" *(vs. 9-10)*. John saw the continuation of the war in heaven here on earth: "They have overcome him by the blood of the Lamb" and by being faithful to their testimony, even unto death *(v. 11)*. John heard another voice warning the people of the earth of Satan's presence and the persecution he would heap upon the church, knowing his time was limited *(vs. 12-13)*. The woman *(church)* fled *(was taken from the earth for a time) (vs. 14-15)*. The earth again welcomed the woman, *(the church was restored to earth)* causing the dragon (Satan) to become wroth with her. Thus, Satan went to make war with those who are obedient, faithful, and have the testimony of Jesus Christ *(vs. 16-17)*.

Rev. 13. John saw a beast rise up out of the sea, having seven heads and ten horns, and upon his horns ten crowns. Upon his heads was the name of blasphemy *(i.e., John saw beasts that symbolize earthly kingdoms controlled by Satan, and their dealings with people)*. The beast (Satan) had the power to perform miracles, including healing deadly wounds. Thus, he enticed people to worship him. He was also given great power to speak blasphemy against God and other holy things in heaven, and to make war against the righteous on the earth and to overcome all "whose names are not written in the book of life of the Lamb slain from the foundation of the world" *(vs. 1-8)*. He that leadeth into captivity shall go into captivity. He that killeth with the sword, shall be killed with the sword *(vs. 9-10)*. *(Those who lead others into the captivity of sin, will themselves become captives in hell. Those who slay the saints shall themselves be slain spiritually by the sword of the Lord (DNTC, III, pp. 522-523).)* John saw another beast come up out of the earth. It had two horns like a lamb and spake as a dragon. He had all the power the first beast had and caused the earth and those who dwelled therein to worship the first beast whose deadly wound was healed, using miracles to deceive the people of the earth. He caused his followers to put a mark, or the name of the beast, or the number of his name, in their right hands or in their foreheads. That number is 666 *(vs. 11-18)*. *(Note: Satan, also known as the Great Imitator, patterns his kingdom after the kingdom of God, and has the power to imitate many miracles. The servants of God are sealed in their foreheads, Rev. 7:3. Satan uses a mark on the hand or forehead, real and figuratively, to designate his followers, as well. The Lord told Joseph Smith, "And again, I will give unto you a pattern in all things, that ye may not be deceived; for Satan is abroad in the land, and he goeth forth deceiving the nations" (D&C 52:14).)*

Rev. 14. John saw the Lamb standing upon mount Sion (Zion), with 144,000 having his Father's name written in their foreheads. He heard a voice from heaven, and the voice of harpers playing their harps, singing as it were a new song before the throne, the four beasts and the elders. Only the 144,000 who were redeemed from the earth could learn the new song. The 144,000 were those who were not defiled with women, who followed the Lamb wherever he went, and were the firstfruits unto God and to the Lamb. They were without guile and without fault before the throne of God *(vs. 1-5)*. *(Note: "Those who are sealed are high priests, ordained unto the holy order of God, to administer the everlasting gospel; for they are they who are ordained out of every nation, kindred, tongue, and people, by the angels to whom is given power over the nations of the earth, to bring as many as will come to the church of the Firstborn" (D&C 77:11). Refer back to Rev. 7:3-8.)* John saw six angels, one after another. First angel: John saw an angel fly in the midst of heaven, having the everlasting gospel to preach unto all the inhabitants of the earth, crying, "Fear God, and give glory to him; for the hour of his judgment is come . . ." *(Note: John saw the promised restoration of the gospel which would come by angelic ministration (D&C 88:104).)* Second angel: Another angel followed saying that Babylon is fallen. *(Note: The restoration of the gospel will cause Babylon to fall (ibid, v. 105).)* The third angel, in a loud voice, proclaimed the wrath of God that is poured out upon those who worship the beast and have his mark on their hands or foreheads *(vs. 6-12)*. John heard a voice from heaven commanding him to write, "Blessed are the dead which die in the Lord from henceforth: Yea, saith the Spirit, that they may rest from their labours; and their works do follow them *(v. 13)*. John saw one like unto the Son of Man, wearing a golden crown, holding a sharp sickle in his hand, sitting on a white cloud *(v. 14)*. A fourth angel emerged from the temple and cried out to the one sitting on the cloud, "Thrust in thy sickle, and reap: for the time is come for thee to reap; for the harvest of the earth is ripe." The one on the cloud thrust in his sickle and reaped the earth *(vs. 15-16)*. A fifth angel exited the temple, carrying a sharp sickle. The sixth angel came out from the altar, which had power over fire; and cried to the one having a sharp sickle, "Thrust in the sharp sickle, and gather the clusters of the vine of the earth; for her grapes are fully ripe." The angel did so, gathering the vine of the earth and casting it into the great winepress of the wrath of God. "Blood came out of the winepress, even unto the horses' bridles, by the space of a thousand and six hundred furlongs" *(vs. 17-20)*.

Rev. 15. John saw another sign in heaven: seven angels having seven last plagues. He saw as it were a sea of glass mingled with fire *(i.e., the earth in its celestial glory)*, and those who had victory over the beast *(i.e., the exalted saints)*, singing songs and praising God *(vs. 1-4)*. The temple of the tabernacle of the testimony in heaven was opened and the seven angels which had the seven plagues came out, clothed in white. Their breasts were girded with golden girdles. One of the four beasts gave the seven angels seven golden vials full of the wrath of God. No man was able to enter into the temple until the seven plagues of the seven angels were fulfilled *(vs. 5-8)*. *(God shall pour out plagues in the latter days which will sweep many of the unrighteous from off the earth in preparation for the final Millennial cleansing needed to prepare the earth for its sanctified, immortal, and eternal state as the abode of the righteous (DNTC, p. 539).)*

Rev. 16. John heard a great voice out of the temple commanding the seven angels to pour out the vials of the wrath of God upon the earth. The seven plagues John saw are: (1) noisome and grievous sores upon those who followed the beast *(vs. 1-2)*; (2) the sea became as the blood of a dead man, killing every living creature in the sea *(v. 3)*; (3) the fountains and rivers became blood *(v. 4)*; (4) the sun scorched men with fire and with great heat *(v. 8-9)*; (5) darkness *(i.e., wickedness and probably spiritual darkness)*, pain and sores, spread over the seat of the beast *(i.e., the kingdoms of the earth) (vs. 10-11)*; (6) the river Euphrates was dried up and Satan and his false prophets perform false miracles for the purpose of gathering together the armies of the world for the "battle of that great day of God Almighty" at Armageddon; *(vs. 12-16)*; (7) the elements of the earth were in upheaval with thunders, lightnings and a mighty earthquake; the great city was divided into three parts; cities of the nations fell and Babylon came in remembrance before God; every island fled away and the mountains were not found; and there was a great hail storm with each stone weighing a talent *(vs. 17-21). (Note: The following explanation by Bruce R. McConkie, provides insight into events surrounding the seventh plague.)*

> *Three natural changes in the earth—all apparently growing out of one transcendent happening—are here named as attending our Lord's Second Coming. They are: (1) Earth's land masses shall unite; islands and continents shall become one land. (2) Every valley shall be exalted and every mountain shall be made low; the rugged terrain of today shall level out into a millennial garden. (3) Such an earthquake as has never been known since man's foot was planted on this planet shall attend these changes in the earth's surface and appearance" (DNTC, III, p. 543).*
>
> *In a revelation given to Joseph Smith and recorded in the D&C, we are also given to know that "He shall command the great deep, and it shall be driven back into the north countries, and the islands shall become one land . . . and the earth shall be like as it was in the days before it was divided" (D&C 133:23-24). (Note: The earth was divided in the days of Peleg.. (Gen 10:25; 1 Chr. 1:19.)*

Rev. 17. One of the seven angels having one of the seven vials spoke to John and carried him away in the spirit into the wilderness so he could show unto him "the judgment of the great whore *(i.e., Babylon)* that sitteth upon many waters." John saw a woman sit upon a scarlet colored beast, full of names of blasphemy, having seven heads and ten horns. The woman was arrayed in purple and scarlet colors, decked with precious gems, and held a golden cup in her hand full of abominations and filthiness of her fornication. Written upon her forehead was: MYSTERY, BABYLON THE GREAT, THE MOTHER OF HARLOTS AND ABOMINATIONS OF THE EARTH. John saw the woman *(Babylon)* drunken with the blood of saints and martyrs *(vs. 1-6).* The angel volunteered to explain the mystery of the woman and the beast with seven heads and ten horns. Explanation: The seven heads are seven mountains on which Babylon sits. There are seven kings: five are fallen, one is, and one is yet to come. When the seventh king comes, he will continue for a short space. The beast that was, and is not, is the eighth and is of the seventh, and goeth into perdition. The ten horns are ten kings which have no kingdom as yet, but after one hour with the beast they receive power as kings. They are united and give their power and strength to the beast. They shall make war with the Lamb, but the Lamb shall overcome them. The waters upon which the whore sits are peoples, multitudes, nations and tongues. The ten horns *(kings)* shall hate the whore *(Babylon)* and will unite in giving their strength to the beast, and will destroy her, that the words of God shall be fulfilled. The woman John saw was that great city *(Babylon)* which reigneth over the kings of the earth *(vs. 7-18).*

Rev. 18. John saw another angel come down from heaven, and the earth was lightened *(shined)* with his glory. He proclaimed the fall of Babylon, and said it is become the habitation of devils and every other evil and vile thing. All nations have joined with her in her abominations *(vs. 1-3).* He heard another voice from heaven calling the saints to leave Babylon lest they become partakers of her sins and receivers of her plagues *(v. 4).* Babylon shall be visited with death, mourning, famine and fire. Kings and merchants and shipmasters shall lament for her. All her riches shall come to naught in just an hour, and she will be made desolate *(vs. 8-19)*. *("For after today cometh the burning—this is speaking after the manner of the Lord—for verily I say, tomorrow all the proud and they that do wickedly shall be as stubble; and I will burn them up, for I am the Lord of Hosts; and I will not spare any that remain in Babylon (D&C 64:24).)* Heaven, the holy apostles and the prophets were told to rejoice over the fall of Babylon, "for God hath avenged you on her" *(v. 20)*. A mighty angel picked up a stone like a mighty millstone and threw it into the sea, indicating that Babylon shall be thrown down with like violence and found no more, nor will any of her inhabitants be found for "in her was found the blood of prophets and of saints, and of all that were slain upon the earth" *(vs. 21-24)*.

Rev. 19. John heard a great voice of many people praising the Lord our God: His judgments are true and righteous and he hath judged the great whore that corrupted the earth *(vs. 1-3)*. *("And the great and abominable church, which is the whore of all the earth, shall be cast down by devouring fire, according as it is spoken by the mouth of Ezekiel the prophet, who spoke of these things, which have not come to pass but surely must, as I live, for abominations shall not reign" (D&C 29:21).)* The 24 elders and four beasts fell down and worshiped God. A voice came out of the throne calling upon the people, both great and small, to praise God *(vs. 4-5)*. He heard another voice proclaiming that the Lord God omnipotent reigneth and that the marriage of the Lamb is come. His wife *(i.e., the church composed of the faithful saints who have waited and watched for the Savior's return (DNTC, vol., III, p. 563))* was granted to be arrayed in white, "for the fine linen is the righteousness of the saints." John was instructed to write, "Blessed are they which are called unto the marriage supper of the Lamb" *(vs. 6-9)*. *("And after that cometh the day of my power; then shall the poor, the lame, and the blind, and the deaf, come in unto the marriage of the Lamb, and partake of the supper of the Lord, prepared for the great day to come" (D&C 58:11).)* John fell at the feet of the one speaking to him, but was told not to because he was his fellow servant. He told John to worship God, "for the testimony of Jesus is the spirit of prophecy" *(v. 10)*. John saw the heavens open, and he beheld a white horse upon which sat one *(i.e., Christ)* who was called "Faithful and True." In righteousness he judges and makes war. His eyes were as a flame of fire. He wore many crowns upon his head. He had a name written that nobody knew but he himself. He was clothed with a vesture dipped in blood *("And the Lord shall be red in his apparel, and his garments like him that treadeth in the wine-vat" (D&C 133:48).)*. His name is called "The Word of God." The armies in heaven which followed him were clothed in white, clean, fine linen, and rode upon white horses *(vs. 11-14)*. The word of God proceeded out of his mouth, and with it he would smite the nations and rule over them with the word of his mouth. "He treadeth the wine-press in the fierceness and wrath of Almighty God" *(JST v. 15)*. *("And again, another angel shall sound his trump, which is the seventh angel, saying: It is finished! It is finished! The Lamb of God hath overcome and trodden the wine-press alone, even the wine-press of the fierceness of the wrath of Almighty God" (D&C 88:106).)* A name was written on his clothing and on his thigh: KING OF KINGS, AND LORD OF LORDS *(v. 16)*. John saw an angel standing in the sun, beckoning the birds to gather themselves together unto the supper of the great God, that they might eat the flesh of all those who fight against the Lamb *(JST v. 18)*. John saw the beast and his followers gathered together to fight against the Lamb and his army. The beast and his false prophet were taken and cast into a lake of fire burning with brimstone. The rest of the wicked "were slain with the word of him that sat upon the horse, which word proceeded out of his mouth . . . and all the fowls were filled with their flesh" *(vs. 19- 21)*.

Rev. 20. John saw an angel come down from heaven, having with him the key to the bottomless pit and a great chain, with which he bound Satan for 1,000 years. Satan was then cast into the bottomless pit and locked up. *("Wherefore, the end, the width, the height, the depth, and the misery thereof, they understand not, neither any man except those who are ordained unto this condemnation" (D&C 76:48).)* A seal was set upon Satan so that he could not deceive the nations until 1,000 years had passed, after which time he would be loosed again for a season *(vs. 1-3)*. *("For Satan shall be bound, and when he is loosed again he shall only reign for a little season, and then cometh the end of the earth" (D&C 43:31).)* John saw those of the first resurrection. They shall be priests of God and of Christ and reign with him 1,000 years. The second death has no power over those who have part in the first resurrection. The rest of the dead shall not live again until after the 1,000 years are finished *(vs. 4-6)*. After the 1,000 years, Satan will be loosed to deceive the nations which are in the four corners of the earth, Gog and Magog, to gather them together to battle. John saw them compassed about the camp of the saints and the beloved city. God sent fire down from heaven and devoured them. "The devil that deceived them was cast into the lake of fire and brimstone, where the beast and the false prophet are, and shall be tormented day and night for ever and ever" *(vs. 7-10)*. John saw a great white throne "and him that sat on it," from whose face the earth and heaven fled *("For all old things shall pass away, and all things shall become new, even the heaven and the earth, and all the fulness thereof, both men and beasts, the fowls of the air, and the fishes of the sea. . ." (D&C 29:24))*: and the dead, great and small, stood before God. And the books were opened, and the people were judged out of the books according to their works. The sea, death and hell, all delivered up their dead, and every man was judged according to his works *(vs. 11-13)*. Death and hell were cast into the lake of fire. This is the second death. Whosoever was not found in the book of life was cast into the lake of fire *(vs. 14-15)*.

Rev. 21. John saw a new heaven and a new earth, for the old had passed away, and there was no more sea. *(Again, John sees that the earth shall be like it was in the days before it was divided: the islands shall be gathered together into one land mass and the waters shall be gathered together (D&C 133:23:24).)* He saw the holy city, the new Jerusalem, descending from God out of heaven, prepared as a bride for her bridegroom. One of the seven angels who had the vials containing the last seven plagues, carried John away in the spirit and showed him the bride—the lamb's wife: that great city, holy Jerusalem, having the glory of God *(vs. 1-2, 9-10)*. Those who dwell in the holy city shall be God's people, and he shall dwell with them and wipe away all tears. There shall be no more death, sorrow, crying or pain. These things are passed away: he will make all things new. Those who overcome shall inherit all things, "And I will be his God, and he shall be my son" *(vs. 3-7)*. The fearing and unbelieving, the abominable, murderers, etc., "shall have their part in the lake which burneth with fire and brimstone: which is the second death" *(v. 8).* John saw that the new Jerusalem had twelve gates, with twelve angels at the gates, upon which were written the names of the twelve tribes of the children of Israel. Three gates were on each of the north, east, south and west sides of the city wall. The wall had twelve foundations in which were the names of the twelve apostles of the Lamb. An angel measured the city. The city street was pure gold, like unto clear glass, and the foundation was garnished with all manner of precious stones. *("I saw the transcendent beauty of the gate through which the heirs of that kingdom will enter, which was like unto circling flames of fire; Also the blazing throne of God, whereon was seated the Father and the Son. I saw the beautiful streets of that kingdom, which had the appearance of being paved with gold" (D&C 137:2-4).)* There was no temple therein for the Lord God is the temple of it. There was no need for sun nor moon for the glory of God lightened it and the Lamb is the light thereof. The kings of the earth shall bring glory and honor into it. There shall be no night there. Nothing that can defile it or work abomination or make a lie will be able to enter into it: only those who are written in the Lamb's book of life *(vs. 12-27). (Note: Ether, an ancient Book of Mormon prophet, prophesied concerning both the new Jerusalem and the old Jerusalem.)*

> *Referring to the American continent, he prophesied, "And that it was the place of the New Jerusalem, which should come down out of heaven, and the holy sanctuary of the Lord.*
>
> *"Behold, Ether saw the days of Christ, and he spake concerning a New Jerusalem upon this land.*
>
> *"And he spake also concerning the house of Israel, and the Jerusalem from whence Lehi should come—after it should be destroyed it should be built up again, a holy city unto the Lord; wherefore, it could not be a new Jerusalem for it had been in a time of old; but it should be built up again, and become a holy city of the Lord; and it should be built unto the house of Israel—*
>
> *"And that a New Jerusalem should be built up upon this land, unto the remnant of the seed of Joseph, for which things there has been a type.*
>
> *"For as Joseph brought his father down into the land of Egypt, even so he died there; wherefore, the Lord brought a remnant of the seed of Joseph out of the land of Jerusalem, that he might be merciful unto the seed of Joseph that they should perish not, even as he was merciful unto the father of Joseph that he should perish not..*
>
> *"Wherefore, the remnant of the house of Joseph shall be built upon this land; and it shall be a land of their inheritance; and they shall build up a holy city unto the Lord, like unto the Jerusalem of old, and they shall no more be confounded, until the end come when the earth shall pass away.*
>
> *"And there shall be a new heaven and a new earth; and they shall be like unto the old save the old have passed away, and all things have become new.*
>
> *And then cometh the New Jerusalem;; and blessed are they who dwell therein, for it is they whose garments are white through the blood of the Lamb; and they are they who are numbered among the remnant of the seed of Joseph, who were of the house of Israel.*
>
> *"And then also cometh the Jerusalem of old; and the inhabitants thereof, blessed are they, for they have been washed in the blood of the Lamb; and they*

are they who were scattered and gathered in from the four quarters of the earth, and from the north countries, and are partakers of the fulfilling of the covenant which God made with their father, Abraham." (Ether 13:3-11).

The Savior, when he appeared to the Nephites here upon the American continent following his resurrection, told the people, "And behold, this people will I establish in this land, unto the fulfilling of the covenant which I made with your father Jacob; and it shall be a New Jerusalem. And the powers of heaven shall be in the midst of this people; yea, even I will be in the midst of you" (3 Ne. 20:22). (Also see 3 Ne. 21:23-24.)

Rev. 22. The angel showed John a pure river of water of life. *(Jesus offers living water to all men. In Rev. 21:6, the Lord said he would give unto him that is athirst of the fountain of the water of life freely. The Old Testament prophet Ezekiel spoke of the water that issued from the house of the Lord and healed the Dead Sea. Ezek. 47:1-8.)* John was shown the tree of life, which yielded 12 manner of fruits, yielding her fruit each month. The leaves of the tree were for the healing of the nations. There shall be no more curse: the throne of God and of the Lamb shall be present *(vs. 1-3) (Note: The earth was cursed for Adam's sake so that it brought forth weeds instead of fruit spontaneously. When the earth receives its celestial splendor, the curse will be removed (DNTC, vol III, p. 589).)* The saints shall reign in celestial glory and see the face of God and his name shall be in their foreheads. *("But the day soon cometh that ye shall see me, and know that I am; for the veil of darkness shall soon be rent, and he that is not purified shall not abide the day" (D&C 38:8).)* There will be no need for candles, nor for the sun: the Lord giveth light; and they shall reign for ever and ever *(vs. 4-5). ("Then shall they be gods, because they have no end; therefore shall they be from everlasting to everlasting, because they continue; then shall they be above all, because all things are subject unto them. Then shall they be gods, because they have all power, and the angels are subject unto them" (D&C 132:20).)* The Lord sent his angels unto his servants to show them the things which must shortly come to pass. He will come quickly. Those who keep the sayings of the prophecy given to John will be blessed. John fell down to worship before the feet of the angel who showed him these things. The angel forbade him, saying he was a fellow servant and of John's brethren the prophets and of those who keep the sayings of the book. He told John to worship God. John was instructed not to seal the prophecy up because the time is at hand *(vs. 6-10).* Every man will be judged according to his works: the unjust will be unjust still, the filthy will be filthy, the righteous will be righteous and the holy, holy. Blessed are those who keep the commandments. *("For verily I say unto you, blessed is he that keepeth my commandments, whether in life or in death; and he that is faithful in tribulation, the reward of the same is greater in the kingdom of heaven" (D&C 58:2).)* They have a right to the tree of life and may enter into the celestial city. The wicked are without *(vs. 11-15).* Jesus, the root and the offspring of David, sent his angel to testify of these things. Jesus invites all who are athirst, and whosoever will, to come and take of the water of life freely *(vs. 16-17).* A warning is issued to anyone who adds or takes away from the words of the book of this prophecy. To those who add, God shall add unto him the plagues written in the book. To him who takes away from the words of this prophecy, God will remove him from the book of life and from out of the holy city. The Lord testified that the revelation given to John is true *(vs. 18-21)*.

JOHN (2)

Acts 4:6. **JOHN** was with Annas the high priest, Caiaphas and Alexander and as many of the kindred of the high priest as there were gathered together at Jerusalem to confer about what to do with or to Peter and John for preaching and teaching about Christ. *(Note: Nothing else seems to be known about him.)*

JOHN'S DISCIPLES

Matt. 9:14-15; Mark 2:18-20; Luke 5:33-35. **JOHN'S DISCIPLES** asked Jesus why they and the Pharisees fasted often, observing that Jesus' disciples did not fast. Jesus said as long as they had the bridegroom with them, the children of the bridechamber had no reason to mourn. However, he told them that when the bridegroom is gone, they will also fast.

John 3:25-36. A question arose between some of John's disciples and the Jews about purifying. They questioned John about the fact that Jesus was also baptizing. John reminded them that he had told them that he was not Christ, and that a man can receive nothing except it be given him from heaven. John testified to them of the divinity of the Savior.

JOHN THE BAPTIST

Luke 1:13-17, 44, 60-62, 80. **JOHN THE BAPTIST** was the son of Zacharias and Elisabeth. His father was of the course of Abia (Abijah). Both of his parents were of the lineage of Aaron. His parents were well-stricken in years when an angel of the Lord told Zacharias that Elisabeth would conceive and bear a son, whom they were to name John. The angel said the child would be filled with the Holy Ghost, even from his mother's womb; that he would be great in the sight of the Lord; and that he would drink neither wine nor strong drink. He would go forth in the spirit and power of Elias *(i.e., Elijah)* to turn the hearts of the parents to the children and the disobedient to the wisdom of the just. When Mary *(who was to be the mother of Jesus)* went to Elisabeth's house, John, while yet in the womb, was filled with the Holy Ghost and leaped for joy because of the baby Mary was carrying. When John was eight days old, they came to circumcise him and give him a name. They wanted to name him Zacharias after his father. Elisabeth said it was to be John. They didn't want to name him that because it was not a family name. Zacharias confirmed that the baby was to be named John. The child grew strong in the spirit and lived in the desert until the day of his ministry was to begin.

Luke 3. When John the Baptist came into the country about Jordan preaching the baptism of repentance for the remission of sins, Annas and Caiaphas were the high priests, Tiberius Cæsar was in the fifteenth year of his reign, Pontius Pilate was governor of Judæa and Herod was tetrarch of Galilee *(vs. 1-3)*. As the people listened to John, they wondered whether he was the Christ. John told them that one mightier than he would come and baptize with the Holy Ghost and with fire *(vs. 15-16)*.

Matt. 3; Mark 1; Luke 3. John the Baptist preached in the wilderness of Judæa. He said he was the one spoken of by the prophet Esaias (Isaiah) saying, "The voice of one crying in the wilderness, 'Prepare ye the way of the Lord, make his paths straight'" *(See Isaiah 40:3)*. John's raiment was made of camel's hair and he wore a leather girdle about his loins. His meat was locusts and wild honey. People from Jerusalem, Judæa, and all the region around Jordan went to him to be baptized in Jordan and to confess their sins. However, when the Pharisees and Sadducees came to him, he chastised them and called them a "generation of vipers" and said they needed to bring forth fruits worthy of repentance. Just because they claimed lineage to Abraham was not sufficient *(vs. 1-11; Mark 1:4-6; Luke 3:4-8)*. He said that while he baptized with water, there would come after him someone who "is mightier than I, whose shoes I am not worthy to bear: he shall baptize you with the Holy Ghost, and with fire" *(v. 11; Mark 1:7-8; Luke 3:16)*. When Jesus came to him to be baptized, John forbade him, saying that he had need to be baptized of Jesus, not Jesus of him. Nevertheless, Jesus said to suffer it to be so that he might fulfill all righteousness. Then, John baptized Jesus *(vs. 13-15);* and the heavens opened and the Spirit of God descended like a dove, lighting upon Jesus; and a voice from heaven declared, "This is my beloved Son, in whom I am well pleased" *(vs. 16-17; Mark 1:9-11.)*.

Matt. 4:12; Mark 1:14. John was cast into prison. When Jesus heard that John was cast into prison, he went to Galilee, preaching the gospel of the kingdom.

Matt. 11:2; Luke 7:19-28. While John was in prison, he heard of a man doing great works. He sent two of his disciples to inquire if the works were of Christ. Christ said they were; and he testified that John was more than a prophet, he was the one of whom it had been written, "Behold, I send my messenger before thy face, which shall prepare thy way before thee" *(vs. 2-14)*. *(Note: Jesus refers to John the Baptist as Elias. Elias is a Greek word for Elijah. The ancient prophet Elijah is sometimes referred to as Elias, as well. According to the BD, Elias is also a title applied to many others for specific missions or restorative functions that they are to fulfill.)*

Matt. 14:1-12; Mark 6:14-30; Luke 3:19-20. When Herod the tetrarch heard of Christ preaching in the area, he thought it was John, whom he had beheaded, risen from the dead. Herod had cast John into prison because John rebuked him for taking his brother Philip's wife, Herodias *(vs. 1-5; Mark 14-20; Luke 3:19-20)*. The daughter of Herodias (Salome) danced before Herod for his birthday, and pleased him. He offered to give her anything she wanted in return. Having been counseled by her mother, she asked for John's head. Herod granted her wish and presented it to her in a charger. She gave his head to her mother. His disciples took his body and laid it in a tomb and went and told Jesus *(vs. 6-12; Mark 6:21-30)*.

Matt. 16:13-14; Mark 8:27-28. When Jesus asked his disciples whom people said he was, they responded that some said he was John the Baptist and others said he was Elias or Jeremias . . ."

Matt. 17:12. John the Baptist was the Elias who it was prophesied would come before Jesus to prepare the way for him. Another Elias would come later to restore all things as also written by the prophets.

John 1. John testified that Christ was in the beginning with God and was the Word of God and that he created all things. In him was life *(vs. 1-4)*. John was sent as a witness to testify of Christ. He testified that the Word was made flesh; he came into the world; the world rejected him; his own rejected him; those who believed him were given the power to become sons of God *(vs. 6-14)*. Christ would take away the sins of the world *(v. 29)*. John said that Christ would come after him and would baptize with the Holy Ghost *(vs. 30-33)*. John declared Jesus to be the Son of God and the Lamb of God *(vs. 34, 36)*.

John 3. John was baptizing in Aenon near Salim when Jesus and his disciples went to Judæa where Jesus performed baptisms *(vs. 22-23)*. John again testified that he was not Christ: he was sent before him *(vs. 28-34)*. The Father loves the Son, and he has given the Son all things. He that believeth on the Son, hath everlasting life *(vs. 35-36)*.

John 10:41. The people acknowledged that John performed no miracles, but said that everything he spoke about Jesus was true.

Acts 13:24-25. John preached of the baptism of repentance before the coming of the Savior. He testified that "there cometh one after me, whose shoes of his feet I am not worthy to loose."

Acts 19:3-4. John's baptism was the baptism of repentance and pointed people to believe on Jesus Christ who would follow after John.

JOHN (Whose Surname Was Mark; See Mark)

JONA (Jonas (2))

Matt. 16:17. John 1:42; 21:15-17. **JONA (Jonas)** was the father of Simon Peter.

JONAS (1) (Jonah)

Matt. 12:39-41; Luke 11:16, 29-32. See **Jonas (1)** in Appendix A.

JONAS (2)

Matt. 16:17; John 1:42; 21:15-17. See **Jona.**

JOSEPH (1)

Matt. 1:16, 18-25. **JOSEPH** was the son of Jacob and the husband of Mary, the mother of Jesus Christ. *(Note: Joseph's genealogy through the lineage of David's son Solomon is given in verses 1-16 where his father is listed as Jacob, the son of Matthan. However, his genealogy through the lineage of David's son Nathan is given in Luke 3:23-38 where his father is listed as Heli. The BD indicates that his father was Heli and that Mary was the daughter of his uncle Jacob.)* When Joseph, to whom Mary was espoused, learned that Mary was with child, he thought to put her away privately rather than hold her up to public ridicule. An angel of the Lord appeared to him in a dream and instructed him that he needn't fear taking Mary to wife, that her child was of the Holy Ghost, that she would bring forth a son and they were to call his name Jesus because he would save the people from their sins. This fulfilled the prophecy wherein it was written that "a virgin shall be with child, and shall bring forth a son and they shall call his name Emmanuel" *(Isaiah 7:14)*, which means, "God with us." Joseph took Mary for his wife and he "knew her not till she had brought forth her firstborn son: and he called his name Jesus."

Luke 2:4-33. Joseph and Mary traveled to Bethlehem to be taxed when Cæsar Augustus decreed that all the world should be taxed. There was no room for them in the inn; thus, they found refuge in a stable where Mary gave birth to Jesus and placed him in a manger *(vs. 4-7)*. Angels told the good news to shepherds who quickly went to Bethlehem and found Joseph and Mary, and the baby lying in a manger *(v. 16)*. When Joseph and Mary took Jesus to Jerusalem to present him to the Lord, a devout man named Simeon (who had been promised by the Holy Ghost that he should not die before seeing the Lord's Christ) was in the temple. He immediately took the infant up in his arms and acknowledged that the infant was the Christ and that now he could die in peace. Joseph and Mary marveled at the things that were spoken of Jesus *(vs. 22-33)*.

Matt. 2:13-23. Joseph was warned in a dream by the angel of the Lord to take Jesus and Mary and flee into Egypt because Herod sought the child's life. After Herod was dead, an angel of the Lord appeared to Joseph in a dream and instructed him to take Mary and Jesus into Israel because those who had sought the child's life were dead. Joseph feared Archelaus, the son of Herod, so he turned aside and went into the part of Galilee called Nazareth rather than to Judæa.

Luke 2:42-51. Joseph and Mary went to Jerusalem every year at the feast of the Passover. They went from Nazareth to Jerusalem when Jesus was twelve years old. As they left Jerusalem, Jesus was not with them and they assumed he was with other members of the family. However, he was not to be found among them. Joseph and Mary returned to Jerusalem and, after three days of searching, found him teaching in the temple. When they asked why he had dealt with them so, he responded, "How is it that ye sought me? Wist ye not that I must be about my Father's business?"

Luke 3:23. Joseph was the son of Heli through the lineage of David's son Nathan.

JOSEPH (2) OF ARIMATHÆA

Matt. 27:57-60; Mark 15:42-46; Luke 23:50-54; John 19:38-42. **JOSEPH OF ARIMATHÆA** was a rich man and a follower of Jesus. When Jesus was crucified, he petitioned Pilate to allow him to take Jesus' body. He wrapped it in a clean linen cloth and laid it in a newly-hewn tomb in a rock. He then rolled a great stone to the door of the sepulchre and left. *(Note: The account in John states that Nicodemus helped Joseph take Jesus' body; helped him prepare it by wrapping it in linen clothes with spices; and then helped place it in the sepulchre in the garden.)*

JOSEPH (3)

Luke 3:24. See **Joseph (3)** in Appendix A.

JOSEPH (4)

Luke 3:26. See **Joseph (4)** in appendix A.

JOSEPH (5)

Luke 3:30. See **Joseph (5)** in Appendix A.

JOSEPH (6) CALLED BARSABAS (See Barsabas (1))

JOSEPH (7) (son of Jacob)

Acts 7:9-18; Heb. 11:21-22. See **Joseph (7)** (son of Jacob) in Appendix A.

JOSES (1)

Matt. 13:55; Mark 6:3. **JOSES** was the brother of Jesus. He also had other brothers: James (the Just), Simon and Judas; and sisters whose names are not given.

JOSES (2)

Matt. 27:56; Mark 15:40, 47. **JOSES** (Joseph) was the son of Mary. His brother was James (4), i.e., James the less. *(Note: There is some confusion between the entry in the BD for James (4) and the BD entry for Joses. The entry for Joses indicates all references for Joses (1) and Joses (2) refer to one person, i.e., Joses, the brother of Jesus. However, the entry for James (4) indicates that James (4) and James (2), the son of Alphæus, may be one and the same; however, those James are not the James who is the brother of Jesus. If Joses (1) and Joses (2) are one and the same, then James (4) and James (3), it seems, would be the same, rather than James (4) and James (2).)*

JOSES (3) (Surnamed Barnabas) (See Barnabas (2))

JUDAS (2) ISCARIOT

Matt. 10; Luke 9. **JUDAS ISCARIOT** was one of Jesus' 12 disciples: Simon Peter, Andrew, James, John, Philip, Bartholomew; Thomas, Matthew, James, Lebbæus (Thaddæus), Simon the Canaanite, and Judas Iscariot *(vs. 2-4)*. Jesus empowered these apostles and sent them forth to teach, but instructed them that they should not go to the Gentiles nor to the Samaritans. They were to go to the lost sheep of the house of Israel. They were to heal the sick and cast out devils. They were to travel without purse or scrip. They were instructed to leave their peace upon those who received them, but to shake the dust off their feet when leaving the houses of those who reject them *(vs. 5-14; Luke 9:1-5)*. They were told they would be persecuted for Christ's sake, but that "he that endureth to the end shall be saved." They are of more value than the sparrows for which the Father provides. Even the hairs of their heads are numbered *(vs. 16-32)*.

Matt. 26; Mark 14; Luke 22; John 12. Judas Iscariot was the son of Simon the leper. When Mary anointed Jesus' feet with expensive oil, bathed his feet with her tears and wiped them dry with her hair, Judas complained and wanted to know why the oil wasn't sold and the proceeds given to the poor. Jesus reminded the disciples that they would have the poor with them always, but they would only have him for a short time and that she had poured the ointment on him for his burial *(vs. 6-13; John 12:3-8)*. Judas offered to betray Jesus unto the chief priests for thirty pieces of silver *(vs. 14-16; Mark 14:10-11; Luke 22:3-6)*. At the feast of the Passover, Jesus told his disciples that one of them would betray him *(vs. 21-22; Mark 14:18-19)*. When Judas asked if it was he, Jesus replied, "Thou hast said" *(v. 25)*. After Jesus prayed in the garden of Gethsemane, he and his disciples were leaving when Judas and a multitude sent from the chief priests and elders of the people came. Judas kissed Jesus on the cheek, a prearranged signal that he was the one they wanted, and they "laid hands on Jesus, and took him" *(vs. 47-50; Mark 14:43-46; Luke 22:47-48; see John 18 for a modified account).*

Mark 3:19. Judas Iscariot and the other eleven disciples were ordained by Jesus Christ so he could send them forth to preach, to have power to heal sicknesses and to cast out devils.

Luke 6:16. Judas Iscariot was a traitor to Christ.

John 6:70-71. Jesus reminded his disciples that, in spite of the fact Peter acknowledged that he was Christ the Son of the living God, one of them *(i.e., Judas Iscariot)* would betray him.

John 12:4 (3-8). See entry for Matt. 26.

John 13:2, 21, 26-30. Satan entered into the heart of Judas Iscariot, Simon's son, who Jesus identified as the one who would betray him. Jesus gave Judas a morsel and then Judas left, taking the money purse with him. The other disciples merely thought he was going off to purchase items they needed.

John 18:1-19. Judas was familiar with the garden where Jesus and the other disciples were because they went there often. Judas brought a band of men and officers from the chief priests and Pharisees to the garden. Jesus asked whom they sought. When they said, "Jesus," he acknowledged that he was Jesus. They fell back, and Christ asked again whom they sought. Again, they said, "Jesus."He told them a second time that he was Jesus and to let his disciples go.

Acts 1:18, 26. After Jesus' ascension into heaven following the 40 days he ministered among the people, the remaining apostles met to discuss Judas' replacement. Following his betrayal of Jesus, Judas "purchased a field with the reward of iniquity; and falling headlong, he burst asunder in the midst, and all his bowels gushed out." The man chosen to replace Judas was Matthias.

JUDAS (3) (Juda, Jude)

Matt. 13:55; Mark 6:3. **JUDAS** (**Juda**) was the brother of Jesus. His also had other brothers: James, Joses and Simon; and sisters whose names are not given. *(The BD indicates that Judas was the writer of the epistle of Jude. Thus, Judas was apparently also called* ***Jude*** *as well as Juda.)*

Jude 1. Jude referred to himself as a servant of Jesus Christ and the brother of James in this epistle which he addressed to the members of the church. The implication is that he had written previously about salvation which is available to all mankind. *(Note: Whatever Jude wrote previously has been lost along with other lost scriptures.)* He exhorted them to earnestly contend for the faith and warned them against evil men who had "crept in unawares," who denied the Lord God and also Jesus Christ *(vs. 1-4).* Jude reminded the people of things they already knew: the Lord led his people out of Egypt; those who reviled against Moses *(i.e., against the Lord)* were destroyed by the Lord; and the angels which kept not their first estate *(i.e., were not valiant in the preexistence)* are "reserved in everlasting chains under darkness unto the judgment of the great day" *(vs. 5-6).* Jude referred to a disputation between Michael the archangel and Satan over the body of Moses. Michael chose not to bring a railing accusation against Satan, reserving judgment to the Lord *(v. 9). (Note: This account is not recorded in the Bible; how-*

ever, Jude obviously had some scriptures wherein it was recorded. Modern revelation tells us that Moses, like Elijah, was taken up into heaven without tasting death, in order that he might fulfill yet other responsibilities. Satan, always striving to thwart the will of God, apparently wanted Moses to die so that he would not have a tangible body with which he could perform these additional acts (DNTC, vol. 111, pp. 420-423).) Jude condemned the "filthy dreamers" who defile the flesh and engage in other evil works and said they follow in the paths of Cain *(who killedAbel),* Balaam *(who divined for money),* and Core *(i.e., Korah, who rebelled against Moses and Aaron in the desert) (vs. 10-13).* Jude reminded the people that Enoch had prophesied of the latter days and that Christ would come with 10,000 saints to execute judgment upon the whole earth. The prophets had also prophesied that mockers would come in the latter days and walk after their own ungodly lusts *(vs. 14-18).* He praised the Savior, the only one "able to keep you from falling, and to present you faultless before the presence of his glory with exceeding joy" *(vs. 24-25).*

JUDAS (4) (not Iscariot) (See Thaddæus)

JUDAS (5) OF GALILEE

Acts 5:37-39. **JUDAS OF GALILEE**, "in the days of the taxing," apparently drew many followers only to perish. His followers got dispersed. Gamaliel referred to Judas of Galilee to illustrate to the council who sat against the apostles that if what the apostles said was false, time would bear that out, but that if what they taught was true, time would also bear that out.

JUDAS (6)

Acts 9:11. **JUDAS** was the man whose home the sightless Saul was led to after the Lord spoke to him on the road to Damascus. Ananias was sent there by the Lord to restore Saul's vision to him.

JUDAS (7), Surnamed Barsabas (2)

Acts 15:22, 32-33. **JUDAS**, surnamed Barsabas, was one of the men the apostles in Jerusalem sent to Antioch with Paul, Barnabas and Silas to deliver their epistle to the Gentile converts regarding circumcision. Judas and Silas were also prophets and exhorted the brethren "with many words." After delivering the epistle, Judas left to return to the apostles.

JUDE (See Judas (3))

JULIA

Rom. 16:15. **JULIA** and several other named disciples, "and all the saints which are with them," were sent greetings by Paul in his epistle to the Romans.

JULIUS

Acts 27. **JULIUS** was a centurion of Augustus' band. Paul, along with other prisoners, including Aristarchus, was put on a ship set to sail to Italy and placed in Julius' charge. Paul was treated courteously by Julius, who gave him liberty to mingle with his friends to refresh himself *(vs. 1-3)*. *(Note: See the entry for Paul for an account of the trip.)* Sailing eventually became dangerous "because the fast was now already past," and Paul offered some forewarning of pending danger, but the centurion ignored it, choosing to believe the master and the owner of the ship *(vs. 4-9)*. On the 14th night of the storm, thinking they were near some country, the shipmen were about to flee out of the ship, but Paul warned the centurion and soldiers that, unless they stayed aboard ship, they would die. They stayed. The ship got stuck and the hinder part was broken by violent waves. The soldiers wanted to kill the prisoners so none could escape, but the centurion wouldn't let them. The centurion told those who could swim to cast themselves into the sea and swim toward shore. Others clung to boards or to broken pieces of the ship and made it to shore. All escaped safely to land *(vs. 27-44)*.

Acts 28:16. The centurion, when the group reached Rome, delivered the prisoners to the captain of the guard.

JUNIA

Rom. 16:7. **JUNIA** was one of Paul's kinsmen. He and Andronicus were fellow prisoners with Paul, and were "of note among the apostles." They apparently were followers of Christ prior to Paul's conversion.

JUSTUS (1)

Acts 18:7 (6-7). **JUSTUS** lived adjacent to the synagogue and worshiped God. Paul entered into his house after the Jews blasphemed and "he shook his raiment, and said unto them, Your blood be upon your own heads; I am clean: from henceforth I will go unto the Gentiles."

JUSTUS (2) (Jesus (2))

Col. 4:11. **JUSTUS**, (also called **Jesus**), was a fellow worker with Paul in Rome. He was "of the circumcision." He sent his greetings to the saints in Colosse, along with Paul and others, in Paul's epistle to the Colossians.

NAMES THAT BEGIN WITH "K"

KEEPERS (of the Sepulchre)

Matt. 28:4. The **KEEPERS of the Sepulchre** wherein Jesus lay were frightened when an angel of the Lord descended from heaven in an earthquake and rolled the stone away. They shook and became as dead men.

KING AGRIPPA (See Agrippa, King)

KINSMAN OF MALCHUS, Servant of the High Priest

John 18:26. **KINSMAN OF MALCHUS**. One of the servants of the high priest, whose relative (Malchus) had had his ear cut off by Peter, asked Peter if he had not been in the garden with Jesus. For the third time, Peter denied it. "And immediately the cock crew."

KISH (See Cis in Appendix A)

KORAH (See Core in Appendix A)

NAMES THAT BEGIN WITH "L"

LAD, A

Mark 6:35-44; Luke 9:12-17; John 6:5-13. **A LAD** was among the multitude that followed Jesus because he healed their sick. As evening approached, Christ's disciples suggested he send the people away so the people could get themselves some food. Instead, Jesus had his disciples give him five loaves and two fishes that they said they had. He blessed and brake it and fed about 5,000 men plus women and children. Twelve baskets full of fragments remained. *(Note: The account of the miracle of the five loaves and two fishes as recorded in John says a lad had the loaves and the fishes.)*

LAODICEANS

Col. 2:1; 4:16. **LAODICEANS** were citizens of Laodicea. In Paul's epistle to the Colossians, he expressed his concern for the Laodiceans as well as the Colossians and asked them to give his greetings to the members of the church in Laodicea and requested that his epistle be read in the church there. He also requested that the epistle he sent to the Laodiceans be read to the Colossian saints. *(Note: This epistle is apparently lost and unknown.)*

Rev. 1:11. The church in Laodicea was one of the seven churches to whom John's revelation was to be sent.

Rev. 3:14-16. The Laodiceans were neither cold nor hot, and the Lord said he would spew them out of his mouth because they were lukewarm in their faithfulness.

LAZARUS (1)

John 11:1-44. **LAZARUS** was the brother of Mary and Martha. He and his sisters were beloved friends of Jesus. He became ill. Mary and Martha sent for Jesus, but Jesus tarried for a few days before going to them. Lazarus died. When Jesus received word of his death, he told his disciples that Lazarus "sleepeth" and that he was going to go to him so he could awaken him. Jesus said he was glad for the sake of his disciples that he was not there when Lazarus became ill and died, "to the intent ye may believe" *(v. 15).* By the time Jesus arrived, Lazarus had been in the grave four days. Jesus comforted Mary and Martha and told them that he was the resurrection and the life; he that believed in him, though he were dead, would yet live: and that whosoever liveth and believeth in him shall never die *(vs. 25-26).* Jesus wept when he saw the sorrow of his friends. He had the stone removed from the tomb and spoke to his Father in heaven; and then he cried with a loud voice, "Lazarus, come forth;" and Lazarus came forth from the tomb.

John 12. Lazarus sat at supper with Jesus and the disciples six days prior to the Passover *(vs. 1-2).* Many people came, not only to see Jesus but to see Lazarus who had been raised from the dead *(v. 9).* The chief priests wanted to put Lazarus to death *(along with Jesus)* because too many people were beginning to believe Jesus due to his having brought Lazarus back to life *(vs. 1-10-11).* After Jesus was glorified, the people who witnessed his bringing Lazarus back to life, bore record that it was so *(v. 17).*

LAZARUS (2)

Luke 16:29-25. **LAZARUS** means, "Helped of God." Jesus used the name to teach the people that those who will not listen to Moses and the prophets will not listen to one raised from the dead.

LEBBÆUS (Judas (4) "Not Iscariot") (See Thaddæus)

LEPER, A

Matt. 8:2-4; Mark 1:40-45; Luke 5:12-15. **A LEPER** fell down and worshiped Jesus and asked him to make him clean, and Jesus did. Jesus told him to go and tell no man but to show himself to the priest and to offer a gift according to the teachings of Moses. However, the leper told everyone and, as a result, Jesus couldn't openly enter the city anymore, "but was without in desert places: and they came to him from every quarter."

LEPERS, TEN

Luke 17:12-19. **TEN LEPERS** stood afar off as Jesus entered a certain city. Jesus had mercy on them and told them to go show themselves unto the priest. They did and were cleansed. Only one, a Samaritan, turned back and fell down on his face to thank the Lord, who asked, "Were there not ten cleansed? But where are the nine?" He told the man to rise and go his way and said his faith had made him whole.

LEVI (1) THE SON OF ALPHÆUS (Matthew)

Mark 2:14-17. See **Matthew.**

LEVI (2)

Luke 3:24. See **Levi (2)** in Appendix A.

LEVI (3)

Levi 3:29. See **Levi (3)** in Appendix A.

LIBERTINES

Acts 6:9. **LIBERTINES**, freedmen, were among the opponents of Stephen who stirred up the people against him so that he was brought before the council where false witnesses testified against him and opponents ultimately stoned him to death.

LINUS

2 Tim. 4:21. **LINUS**, a Christian at Rome and friend of Paul and Timothy, joined Paul and all the brethren in sending greetings to Timothy. *(Note: The BD indicates that historians Irenaeus and Eusebius speak of him as bishop of Rome, A.D. 68-80.)*

LOIS

2 Tim. 1:5. **LOIS** was Timothy's (Timotheus') grandmother and apparently the mother of Eunice, Timothy's mother. Paul indicated that he knew Lois and Eunice had unfeigned faith in Jesus Christ and the gospel.

LUCAS (See Luke)

LUCIUS

Acts 13:1. **LUCIUS** of Cyrene was one of the prophets and teachers preaching in Antioch with Barnabas and Saul.

Rom. 16:21. Lucius, Jason and Sosipater were Paul's kinsmen, and joined Paul and others in sending salutations to the saints in Rome.

LUKE (Lucas)

2 Cor. Postscript. **LUKE (Lucas)** was a companion of Titus. Paul's second epistle to the Corinthians was written from Philippi and carried to the saints in Corinth by Lucas and Titus.

Col. 4:14. Luke was the beloved physician. He, apparently, was in Rome with Paul and sent his greetings, along with Paul and others, in Paul's epistle to the Colossians.

2 Tim. 4:11. Only Luke remained with Paul as Paul wrote his second epistle to Timothy.

Phil. 1:24. Lucus, Paul's "fellowlabourer," was named among others who sent salutations to Philemon along with Paul. *(Note: Luke was the writer of the third Gospel and the Acts. He was with Paul during Paul's second imprisonment and martyrdom in Rome. It is assumed that when the plural pronoun is used in Acts, it refers to Paul and Luke. For more information on Luke, see the BD and EB, vol. 11, p. 177.)*

"LUNATICK" SON OF A CERTAIN MAN, THE (A Son with a Dumb Spirit)

Matt. 17:15-18; Mark 9:17-29; Luke 9:38-42. **THE "LUNATICK" SON OF A CERTAIN MAN** [**A Son with a Dumb Spirit**] was healed by Jesus, who rebuked the devil and it departed out of him. He was cured from that very hour. Meanwhile, Jesus chastised his disciples for having insufficient faith to heal the child. When they asked Jesus why they could not cast the foul spirit out, Jesus told them, "This kind can come forth by nothing, but by prayer and fasting."

LYDIA

Acts 16. **LYDIA**, a seller of purple who was of the city of Thyatira, worshiped God, believing what Paul taught. She and her household were all baptized. She constrained Paul and Silas and their brethren to abide in her house *(vs. 14-15).* After Paul and Silas were released from prison and told to leave the city, they first went to Lydia's house to see their brethren and comfort them. Then they departed *(v. 40).*

LYSANIAS

Luke 3:1. **LYSANIAS** was tetrarch of Abilene when Tiberius Cæsar was in the fifteenth year of his reign and John the Baptist came into the country about Jordan, preaching the baptism of repentance for the remission of sins.

NAMES THAT BEGIN WITH "M"

MAGI (See "Wise Men")

MAGISTRATES AND SERJEANTS IN PHILIPPI

Acts 16. The **MAGISTRATES IN PHILIPPI** rent Paul's and Silas' clothes off them and had them beaten and cast into prison. They charged the keeper of the prison to keep them safely *(vs. 20-23)*. Later, they sent SERJEANTS to the prison with word to let them go free, but Paul would not because they were Romans and had been beaten openly, uncondemned, and Paul insisted the magistrates themselves come and set them free. The Serjeants reported Paul's words to the magistrates. When they heard that they were Romans, they were fearful, and quickly went to the prison to have Paul and Silas released. They asked them to depart out of the city *(vs. 35-39)*.

MALCHUS

Matt. 26; Mark 14; Luke 22, John 18. **MALCHUS** [A Servant of the High Priest] had his ear smitten off by one of Jesus' disciples (Peter) when the servant and others sent by Caiaphas came to capture Jesus when Judas betrayed him *(v. 51; Mark 14:47; Luke 22:50; John 18:10)*. Jesus admonished his disciple (Peter) and indicated that he needed to drink the cup which his Father had given him. The servants of the High Priest spit on Jesus and struck him with the palms of their hands *(v. 67; Mark 14:65; Luke 22:63-65; John 18:11)*.

MANAEN

Acts 13:1. **MANAEN**, who was brought up with Herod the tetrarch, was one of the prophets and teachers preaching in Antioch with Barnabas and Saul.

MAN BLIND FROM BIRTH, A

John 9. **A MAN BLIND FROM BIRTH** was healed by Jesus on the Sabbath. Jesus' disciples asked who had sinned—the man or his parents—since he had been blind from birth. Jesus said neither of them: he was born blind so the works of God could be manifest in him *(vs. 1-7)*. Neighbors demanded to know how he had gained his sight. When he told them, they didn't believe him *(vs. 8-12)*. They brought him before the Pharisees, who also demanded to know how he gained his sight. When he told them, they claimed Jesus was a sinner *(vs. 13-17)*. The Jews still did not believe that he used to be blind and demanded an explanation from his parents. They said he could speak for himself. He continued to defend Christ as a righteous person. Later, when the Jews cast the man out because he defended Christ, Jesus asked if he believed on the Son of God. When he said yes, Jesus told him he was the Son of God, and the man believed *(vs. 18-38)*.

MAN POSSESSED WITH A DEVIL, BLIND AND DUMB, A

Matt. 12:22. **A MAN POSSESSED WITH A DEVIL, BLIND AND DUMB**, was brought to Jesus and he healed him. He both saw and spoke. Thus, the Pharisees claimed that Jesus was the prince of the devils.

MAN SEEKING HIS SHARE OF AN INHERITANCE, A

Luke 12:13-21. **A MAN SEEKING HIS SHARE OF AN INHERITANCE** requested that Jesus speak to his brother about dividing an inheritance with him. Jesus took the opportunity to teach a parable about a certain rich man who stored up treasures so someday he could eat, drink and be merry, only to die and not have anything at all. Christ taught people to lay up treasures in heaven, not upon earth.

MAN SICK WITH PALSY, A

Matt. 9:2-7; Mark 2:3-12; Luke 5:18-25. **A MAN SICK WITH PALSY** was [lowered through a hole in the roof and] brought on a bed to Jesus. He healed him and said, "Thy sins be forgiven thee." Jesus rebuked the scribes who thought he blasphemed by asking them whether it was easier to say, "Thy sins be forgiven thee; or to say, Arise, and walk?" He then told the man who was sick with palsy to take up his bed and go home.

MAN WHO CAST OUT DEVILS, A

Luke 9:49-50. **A MAN WHO CAST OUT DEVILS** in the name of Christ was forbidden to do so by Christ's disciples. When John told Jesus about it, Jesus told them not to forbid the man, "for he that is not against us is for us."

MAN WITH AN EVIL SPIRIT, A

Acts 19:16. **A MAN WITH AN EVIL SPIRIT** leaped on the seven sons of Sceva as they unsuccessfully tried to exorcize him. They ran from the house naked and wounded.

MAN WITH AN UNCLEAN SPIRIT, A (1)

Mark 1:23-26; Luke 4:33-35. **A MAN WITH AN UNCLEAN SPIRIT** was in the synagogue when Jesus entered there. The unclean spirit cried out for Jesus to let them alone. The unclean spirit acknowledged, "I know thee who thou art, the Holy One of God." Jesus cast out the unclean spirit.

MAN WITH AN UNCLEAN SPIRIT, A (2)

Mark 5:2-21. **A MAN WITH AN UNCLEAN SPIRIT** dwelled among the tombs. No man could bind him, and he spent night and day in the tombs crying and cutting himself. When Jesus came, the unclean spirit said his name was Legion, "for we are many." Jesus cast the unclean spirit out and gave leave for the devils to enter into a herd of about 2,000 swine, which immediately ran down a steep incline into the sea and were drowned.

MAN WITH A WITHERED HAND, A

Matt. 12:10-14; Mark 3:1-6; Luke 6:6-10. **A MAN WITH A WITHERED HAND** was brought to Jesus on the Sabbath; and Jesus healed him. The [scribes and Pharisees] criticized Jesus. Jesus responded that it is lawful to do good on the Sabbath.

MAN WITH DROPSY, A

Luke 14:1-4. **A MAN WITH DROPSY** was healed by Jesus on the Sabbath. When the lawyers and Pharisees found fault with that, Christ chided them and asked who of them would not rescue an ass or an ox that fell into a pit on the Sabbath.

MARK (Marcus, John whose surname was Mark)

Acts 12:12, 25. **MARK [John, Whose Surname Was Mark]**, son of Mary (4), went with Barnabas and Saul after their return from Jerusalem upon completion of their ministry there.

Acts 13:5, 13. John (**Mark**), Saul, Barnabas and others ministered together in the church at Cyprus. They continued on to Paphos, where they encountered a false prophet, Bar-jesus. When they left Paphos, they went to Perga in Pamphylia, where John left the group and returned to Jerusalem.

Acts 15:37-39. Mark went with Barnabas to Cyprus when Barnabas and Paul parted ways in a dispute over who should accompany them to visit the church in the cities where they had been previously. Paul was opposed to Mark because Mark had "departed from them from Pamphylia, and went not with them to the work." Paul took Silas with him.

Col. 4:10. **Marcus** was a kinsman of Barnabas. He sent his greetings, along with Paul and others, in Paul's epistle to the Colossians.

Philem. 1:24. Marcus and other fellow laborers with Paul sent their salutations to Philemon along with Paul.

1 Pet. 5:13. Marcus, Peter said, sent his greetings along with Peter's and the members of the church at Babylon to the members of the church who were scattered throughout Pontus, Galatia, Cappadocia, Asia, and Bithynia. Peter referred to Marcus as "my son."

2 Tim. 4:11. Paul asked Timothy to bring Mark with him when he came to see him in Rome, saying, "For he is profitable to me for the ministry." *(Mark's Gospel was possibly written under the direction of Peter (BD).)*

MARTHA

Luke 10:38-42. **MARTHA** and Mary were sisters, and were friends of Jesus. Martha tended to duties while Mary sat at Christ's feet. When Martha complained to the Savior, he said, "Martha, Martha, thou art careful and troubled about many things; But one thing is needful: and Mary hath chosen that good part, which shall not be taken away from her."

John 11:1-44. Martha and Mary and their brother Lazarus were good friends with Jesus. When Lazarus became ill, Martha and Mary sent for Jesus, but Jesus tarried for a few days before going to them. Lazarus died. When Jesus received word of his death, he told his disciples that Lazarus "sleepeth" and that he was going to go to him so he could awaken him. By the time Jesus arrived, Lazarus had been in the grave four days. Martha told Jesus that if he had been there, her brother would not have died. Jesus comforted Martha and told her that he was the resurrection and the life; he that believed in him, though he were dead, would yet live: and that whosoever liveth and believeth in him shall never die. Martha said she did believe. Jesus wept when he saw the sorrow of his friends. He had the stone removed from the tomb and thanked his Father in heaven for hearing him (and said he knew he always heard him, but that he said it in order to help those who stood by and heard know that heavenly Father had sent him), and then he cried with a loud voice, "Lazarus, come forth," and Lazarus came forth from the tomb.

John 12:2. Six days before the Passover, as Jesus, Lazarus and the disciples ate supper in the home of Simon the leper *(see Matt. 26:6),* Martha served while Mary anointed Jesus' feet, bathed them with her tears and dried them with her hair.

MARY (1), the mother of Jesus

Luke 1. **MARY**, of Nazareth, a virgin, was espoused to Joseph when an angel of the Lord, Gabriel by name, told her that she had found favor with God and that she would conceive and bear a son whom she should call JESUS. The Holy Ghost would come upon her, and the power of the Highest would overshadow her. The infant born of her would be called the Son of God. Mary was also told by the angel that her cousin Elisabeth was with child. Mary went to her. The infant in Elisabeth's womb jumped with joy when Mary saluted Elisabeth *(vs. 27-44).* Mary praised the Lord and rejoiced in her Savior. She stayed with Elisabeth for about three months and then returned home *(vs. 46-55).*

Matt. 1:16, 18-25. When Mary was espoused to Joseph, she was found to be with child. When Joseph learned that she was with child, he thought to put her away privately rather than hold her up to public ridicule. An angel of the Lord appeared to him in a dream and instructed him that he needn't fear taking Mary to wife, that her child was of the Holy Ghost, that she would bring forth a son and they were to call him Jesus because he would save the people from their sins. This fulfilled the prophecy wherein it was written, "Behold a virgin shall be with child, and shall bring forth a son and they shall call his name Emmanuel" *(Isaiah 7:14),* which means, God with us. Mary became Joseph's wife; and he "knew her not till she had brought forth her firstborn son: and he called his name Jesus."

Luke 2. Mary and Joseph traveled to Bethlehem to be taxed when Cæsar Augustus decreed that all the world should be taxed. There was no room for them in the inn; thus, they found refuge in a stable where Mary gave birth to Jesus and placed him in a manger *(vs. 4-7).* Angels told the good news to shepherds who quickly went to Bethlehem and found Joseph and Mary, and the baby lying in a manger *(v. 16).* When the days of Mary's purification according to the law of Moses were accomplished, she and Joseph took Jesus to Jerusalem to present him to the Lord. A devout man named Simeon who had been promised by the Holy Ghost that he should not die before seeing the Lord's Christ was in the temple. He immediately took the infant up in his arms and acknowledged that the infant was the Christ and that now he could die in peace. Joseph and Mary marveled at the things that were spoken of Jesus *(vs. 22-33).*

Matt. 2:11-23. Mary was with the child Jesus when the wise men came into the house and fell down and worshiped him. After the wise men left, Joseph took Mary and Jesus by night and fled into Egypt as instructed by the angel of the Lord. They stayed there until an angel of the Lord instructed them that it was safe to return to Israel. However, Joseph took Mary and Jesus and went to Nazareth in Galilee instead of Judæa because he feared Archelaus, the son of Herod, fulfilling the prophecy that Christ would be called a Nazarene.

Luke 2:42-51. Mary and Joseph went to Jerusalem every year at the feast of the Passover. When Jesus was twelve years old they went from Nazareth to Jerusalem. As they left Jerusalem, Jesus was not with them and they assumed he was with other members of the family. However, he was not to be found among them. Joseph and Mary returned to Jerusalem and, after three days of searching, found him teaching in the temple. When they asked him why he had dealt with them so, he asked, "How is it that ye sought me? Wist ye not that I must be about my Father's business?"

Matt. 12:46-50; Mark 3:31-35; Luke 8:19-21. Mary and Jesus' brethren wished to speak to Jesus as he was talking to the people. Jesus stretched forth his hand toward his disciples and declared that those who do the will of his Father in heaven are his brother, sister and mother.

Matt. 13:55; Mark 6:3. Mary was the mother of Jesus. The scriptures indicate that Jesus had brothers: James, Joses, Simon and Judas (Juda), and sisters who are not mentioned by name.

John 2. Mary was attending a wedding at which Jesus was also present. When Jesus and the disciples wanted a drink, Mary told Jesus there was no wine. Jesus asked what she would have him do, and she told the servants to do whatever Jesus bid them do. He had them fill six waterpots with water which he then turned into wine *(vs. 3-5).* Following the wedding, Mary, Jesus, his brethren and his disciples journeyed to Capernaum *(v. 12).*

John 19:25-27. Mary, Mary's sister, Mary the wife of Cleophas and Mary Magdalene, were standing by the cross upon which Jesus was hanging. Jesus looked at his mother and at John, his beloved disciple, and said to Mary, "Woman, behold thy son!" Then to his disciple he said, "Behold thy mother!" From then, Mary resided with Jesus' beloved disciple. *(Note: It is not clear who Mary's sister is and there is no other mention of her.)*

Acts 1:13-14. Following Jesus' ascension into heaven, Jesus' disciples met together in an upper room, along with several women (including Mary the mother of Jesus) and his brethren, where they continued in prayer and supplication.

MARY (2), the sister of Martha

Matt. 26:7-13; Mark 14:3-9; John 12:3-8. **MARY** [A WOMAN] *(John 11:2 identifies the woman as Mary, the sister of Martha)* came to the house of Simon the leper and anointed Jesus with expensive ointment. When Jesus' disciples complained about her wasting such precious oil when it could have been sold to help the poor, Jesus told them they would always have the poor with them, but she had anointed his body for burial. Wherever the gospel was preached, the people should be told of what she did as a memorial of her. *(Note: See "A WOMAN WHO WAS A SINNER" for a similar experience of a woman going to the home of Simon the*

Pharisee and anointing the Savior with oil, washing his feet with her tears and wiping them dry with her hair. Luke 7:37-50.)

Luke 10:39-42. Mary and Martha were friends of Jesus. Martha tended to duties while Mary sat at Christ's feet. When Martha complained to the Savior, he said, "Martha, Martha, thou art careful and troubled about many things; But one thing is needful: and Mary hath chosen that good part, which shall not be taken away from her."

John 11:1-44. Mary and Martha and their brother Lazarus were good friends with Jesus. It was Mary who had anointed Jesus with ointment and wiped his feet with her hair. When Lazarus became ill, Mary and Martha sent for Jesus, but Jesus tarried for a few days before going to them. Lazarus died. When Jesus received word of his death, he told his disciples that Lazarus "sleepeth" and that he was going to go to him so he could awaken him. By the time Jesus arrived, Lazarus had been in the grave four days. Mary told Jesus that if he had been there, Lazarus would not have died. Jesus wept when he saw Mary and the Jews who had come to comfort her weeping. He had the stone removed from the tomb and thanked his Father in heaven for hearing him (and said he knew he always heard him, but that he said it in order to help those who stood by and heard know that heavenly Father had sent him), and then he cried with a loud voice, "Lazarus, come forth," and Lazarus came forth from the tomb.

John 12:2-3. Six days before the Passover, as Jesus, Lazarus and the disciples ate supper in the home of Simon the leper *(see Matt. 26:6-13),* Mary anointed Jesus' feet, bathed them with her tears and dried them with her hair while her sister Martha served.

MARY (3) Also referred to as: the mother of James the less and Joses (Joseph), the "other Mary;" the wife of Cleophas

Matt. 27:56, 61; Mark 15:40-41, 47; Luke 23:47-49, 55-56. **MARY** the mother of James [the less] and Joses and Mary Magdalene [and Salome] were among the women who followed Jesus and ministered unto him who observed from a distance that which occurred when Jesus was crucified. The "other Mary" [Mary the mother of Joses] and Mary Magdalene sat over against the sepulchre wherein Jesus was laid. *(Note: The women are not mentioned by name in the account recorded in Luke.)*

Matt. 28:1-10; Mark 16:1-8; Luke 24:1-10. The "other Mary" [Mary the mother of James] and Mary Magdalene [and Salome or Joanna, depending upon the scripture] came to the sepulchre at the end of the Sabbath following Jesus' crucifixion. There was a great earthquake as an angel of the Lord descended from heaven. He told the women to fear not, that Jesus was not there, but to go and tell his disciples that he had risen from the dead. As they went, Jesus met them, and they held him by the feet and worshiped him. He also told them to go and tell his brethren that they would see him in Galilee. *(Note: Different women are named in the different records. The account in Luke is modified quite a bit.)*

Luke 24:1-11. When Mary the mother of James, Mary Magdalene, Joanna and the other women went with their spices to the sepulchre following Christ's crucifixion, Christ's body was not in the sepulchre. Two men, i.e., angels, told them that he was not there because he was risen as he had said. The angels told the women not to be afraid. They quickly went to tell the apostles that the sepulchre wherein Jesus was laid was empty and that they had been told he was risen. The disciples did not believe them.

John 19:25. Mary the wife of Cleophas was with Mary the mother of Jesus, Jesus' mother Mary's sister, and Mary Magdalene as they all stood by the cross on which Jesus hung.

MARY (4)

Acts 12:12. **MARY** was the mother of John, whose surname was Mark. When Peter was freed from prison by an angel of the Lord, he went to Mary's house where many were gathered together praying.

MARY (5)

Rom. 16:6. **MARY** had bestowed much labor on Paul and his colleagues. Paul sent greetings to her in his epistle to the Roman saints.

MARY MAGDALENE

Matt. 27:56, 61; Mark 15:40-41, 47; Luke 23:47-49, 55-56. **MARY MAGDALENE**, Mary the mother of James [the less] and Joses, and the mother of Zebedee's children [and Salome] were some of the women who followed Jesus and ministered unto him who observed from a distance that which occurred when Jesus was crucified. Mary Magdalene and "the other Mary" [Mary the mother of Joses] sat over against the sepulchre wherein Jesus was laid. *(Note: The mother of Zebedee's children is not mentioned in Mark, but Salome is named. In Luke, the women are not mentioned by name at all, just as "the women who followed him. . .")*

Matt. 28:1-10; Mark 16:1-8, 9-10; Luke 24:1-11; John 20. (See the entries for Luke 24 and John 20 for varied versions of the same incident.) Mary Magdalene and the "other Mary" [Mary the mother of James, and Salome] came to the sepulchre at the end of the Sabbath following Jesus' crucifixion. There was a great earthquake as an angel of the Lord descended from heaven. He told the women to fear not, that Jesus was not there, but to go and tell his disciples that he had risen from the dead. As they went, Jesus met them, and they held him by the feet and worshiped him. He also told them to go and tell his brethren that they would see him in Galilee. *(Note: The record in Matthew names Mary Magdalene, and "the other Mary" as going to the sepulchre, and that the risen Savior appeared to both of them. Mark 16:1, records that Mary Magdalene, Mary the mother of James, and Salome went to the sepulchre early in the morning the first day of the week. Mark 16:9, however, states that the Savior first appeared to Mary Magdalene and does not mention the other women as seeing the Savior. Luke 24:10, lists Mary Magdalene, Joanna, and Mary the mother of James and "other women" as going to the sepulchre that first morning and discovering the Savior's body missing. John's record of this incident only mentions Mary Magdalene as going to the sepulchre and seeing the Savior.)*

Luke 8:2-3. Mary Magdalene, out of whom Jesus sent seven devils; Joanna, the wife of Chuza, Herod's steward; and Susanna were among the women who followed Jesus and ministered unto him as he went throughout the villages and towns preaching.

Luke 24:1-11 When Mary Magdalene, Joanna, and Mary the mother of James and the other women went with their spices to the sepulchre following Christ's crucifixion, Christ's body was not in the sepulchre. Two men *(i.e., angels),* told them that he was not there because he was risen as he had said. The angels told the women not to be afraid. They quickly went to tell the apostles that the sepulchre wherein Jesus was laid was empty and that they had been told he was risen. The disciples did not believe them.

John 19:25. Mary Magdalene was with Mary the mother of Jesus, Mary's sister, and Mary the wife of Cleophas as they stood by the cross on which Jesus hung.

John 20:1-18. Mary Magdalene went to the sepulchre early on the first day of the week and found it empty. She quickly ran and told Peter and John *(i.e., the other disciple whom Jesus loved).* They ran to the sepulchre to see for themselves. After the disciples left, Mary stood outside the sepulchre weeping. She saw two angels sitting where the body of Christ had lain, one at the head and one at the foot. They asked her why she wept. She responded that it was because they had taken away her Lord and she didn't know where he had been taken. When she turned away, she saw Jesus but did not recognize him. Thinking he was the gardener, she asked if he had taken Christ away and, if so, where had he taken him? She offered to take him away. Jesus called her by name, and she said, "Rabboni; which is to say, Master." Jesus told her to touch him not because he had not yet ascended unto his Father. Mary Magdalene then went and told the disciples that she had both seen and spoken with the Lord.

MARY'S SISTER (i.e., the sister of Mary the mother of Jesus).

John 19:25-27. **MARY'S SISTER**, Mary the mother of Jesus, Mary the wife of Cleophas and Mary Magdalene, were standing by the cross upon which Jesus was hanging. Jesus looked at his mother and at John, his beloved disciple, and said to Mary, "Woman, behold thy son!" Then to his disciple he said, "Behold thy mother!" From then, Mary resided with Jesus' beloved disciple. *(Note: It is not clear who Mary's sister is and there is no other mention of her.)*

MATTHEW (Levi (1))

Matt. 9:9. **MATTHEW** was a custom collector. Jesus called him to follow him and he did. *(Matthew was called Levi prior to his conversion (BD).)*

Mark 2:14-17; Luke 5:27-32. Levi the son of Alphæus was a tax collector, a publican. He and other publicans and sinners were invited to have dinner with Jesus. This was contrary to Jewish custom. Jesus said he didn't come to call the righteous to repentance but the sinner.

Matt. 10; Luke 9. Matthew the publican was one of Jesus' 12 disciples: Simon Peter, Andrew, James, John, Philip, Bartholomew; Thomas, Matthew, James, Lebbæus (Thaddæus), Simon the Canaanite, and Judas Iscariot *(vs. 2-4).* Jesus empowered these apostles and sent them forth to teach, but instructed them that they should not go to the Gentiles nor to the Samaritans. They were to go to the lost sheep of the house of Israel. They were to heal the sick and cast out devils. They were to travel without purse or scrip. They were instructed to leave their peace upon those who received them, but to shake the dust off their feet when leaving the houses of those who reject them *(vs. 5-14; Luke 9:1-5).* They were told they would be persecuted for Christ's sake, but that "he that endureth to the end shall be saved." They are of more value than the sparrows for which the Father provides. Even the hairs of their heads are numbered *(vs. 16-32).*

Acts 1:13-14. Following Jesus' ascension into heaven, Jesus' disciples, including Matthew, met together in an upper room, along with several women (including Mary the mother of Jesus) and his brethren, where they continued in prayer and supplication.

MATTHIAS

Acts 1:21-26. **MATTHIAS** was one of the two men (having been a disciple throughout the Lord's ministry) considered to fill the vacancy in the Twelve left by Judas' removal from the apostleship. Joseph called Barsabas was the other man. The lot fell upon Matthias. *(Tradition states that Matthias preached the gospel and suffered martyrdom in Ethiopia (BD).)*

MEN OF GENNESARET

Matt. 14:34-36. The **MEN OF GENNESARET** brought all their diseased to Jesus and had faith that, if they might only touch the hem of his garment, they would be healed; and it was so.

MERCURIUS

Acts 14:12. **MERCURIUS** was the Roman equivalent of the Greek god Hermes who was the herald of the gods. After Paul healed a certain man's feet at Lystra, the men of Lystra called Paul "Mercurius" because he was the chief speaker. *(They called Barnabas "Jupiter.")*

MNASON

Acts 21:16. **MNASON** was an old *(i.e., elderly)* disciple of Cyprus. A group of disciples of Cæsarea brought him with them as they journeyed with Paul and his companions to Jerusalem. Paul and his companions were to lodge with him.

MONEY-CHANGERS

Matt. 21:12-13; Mark 11:15-17; Luke 19:45-46; John 2:12-16. Money-changers and sellers of oxen, sheep and doves were driven out of the temple by Jesus, who overthrew the tables and dumped the money out. He ordered that they not make his Father's house a house of merchandise.

MOTHER OF ZEBEDEE'S CHILDREN (See Salome (2))

NAMES THAT BEGIN WITH "N"

NARCISSUS' HOUSEHOLD

Rom. 16:11. **NARCISSUS' HOUSEHOLD** were among the followers of Christ. Paul sent greetings to them in his epistle to the Romans.

NATHANAEL (See Bartholomew)

NEREUS

Rom. 16:15. **NEREUS** and his sister, and several other specific disciples, "and all the saints which are with them," were sent greetings by Paul in his epistle to the Romans.

NEREUS' SISTER

Rom. 16:15. **NEREUS' SISTER** is not named. However, she and Nereus and several other specific disciples, "and all the saints which are with them," were sent greetings by Paul in his epistle to the Romans.

NERO (Cæsar (5))

*(Note: The BD indicates there were five Cæsars: (1) Augustus, 31 B.C. (see **Cæsar Augustus**); (2) Tiberius, A.D. 14 (see **Tiberius Cæsar**); (3) Caligula, A.D. 37 (Caligula's real name was Gaius Cæsar. He is not referred to in the N.T.); (4) Claudius, A.D. 41 (see **Claudius Cæsar**); (5) Nero, A.D. 54. (**NERO**'s original name was Lucius Domitius Ahenobarbus. He was born Dec. 15, A.D. 37, in Rome, and died A.D. 68, in Rome. He put both his mother (in A.D. 59) and his wife Octavia (in A.D. 62) to death. He is "remembered for his unstable character and his cruelty." (EB vol. VII, p. 263).)*

2 Tim. Postscript. **NERO** was the emperor before whom Paul was brought in Rome. Paul wrote his second epistle to Timothy when he was brought before Nero the second time.

NICANOR

Acts 6:5. **NICANOR** was one of the seven men the apostles chose and set apart to help them with the work.

NICODEMUS

John 3:1-13. **NICODEMUS** was a Pharisee and a ruler of the Jews. He came to Jesus by night to ask him some questions. He acknowledged that Christ was a great teacher. He was puzzled by Jesus' teaching that a man must be born again, and wondered how that was possible. Jesus taught that a man must be born of water and of the spirit or he cannot enter into the kingdom of God. Jesus chided Nicodemus for being a leader in Israel and still not knowing the things of which Christ spoke. Jesus asked him, "If you have not believed the earthly things I have taught, how will ye believe of heavenly things?"

John 7:50-51. When the Pharisees, officers and chief priests were disputing over Christ, with some seeking to lay hands on him, Nicodemus reminded them that the law provided for a man to be heard before being judged.

John 19:39-42. Nicodemus assisted Joseph of Arimathæa retrieve the body of Jesus from the cross, wrap it in linen clothes with spices, and place it in Joseph's sepulchre in the garden. *(Note: The account as recorded in Matt. 27, Mark 15, and Luke 23, does not include Nicodemus, just Joseph of Arimathæa.)*

NICOLAITANS

Rev. 2:6, 15. **NICOLAITANS**, according to the BD, were an Antinomian sect in Asia Minor who claimed license for sensual sin *(p. 738).* The Lord instructed John to write unto the "angel of the church at Ephesus" *(i.e., the leader of the church at Ephesus)* and say that "he that holdeth the seven stars in his right hand, who walketh in the midst of the seven golden candlesticks" commends him for abhorring the deeds of the Nicolaitans, which doctrine he hates.

NICOLAS

Acts 6:5. **NICOLAS**, a proselyte of Antioch, was one of the seven men the apostles chose and set apart to help with the work.

NYMPHAS

Col. 4:15. **NYMPHAS** was apparently a member of the church in Colosse. In Paul's epistle to the Colossians, he asked them to give his greetings to the members of the church in Nymphas' household.

NAMES THAT BEGIN WITH "O"

OLYMPUS

Rom. 16:15. **OLYMPUS** and several other specific disciples, "and all the saints which are with them," were sent greetings by Paul in his epistle to the Romans.

ONESIMUS

Col. 4:9, Postscript. **ONESIMUS**, a Colossian, was a faithful and beloved brother of Paul. He and Tychicus carried Paul's epistle to the Colossians.

Philem. Onesimus was Philemon's slave. He ran away from Philemon and joined Paul in Rome. Paul would have had Onesimus stay with him and minister to him in the stead of Philemon, but would not do so without first consulting Philemon *(vs. 10-14).* Paul sent Onesimus back to Philemon in Colosse with a letter, wherein he requested Philemon receive Onesimus, not as a slave, but as a brother in the gospel. He told Philemon that if Onesimus owed him anything to put it on Paul's account *(vs. 12, 16, 18).*

ONESIPHORUS

2 Tim. 1:16-18. **ONESIPHORUS** was a member of the church who showed kindness to Paul. He refreshed Paul and was not ashamed of Paul's bondage; and sought him out diligently when he was in Rome. Paul prayed the Lord would show mercy to the house of Onesiphorus because of the kindness he had shown unto him and "in how many things he ministered unto me at Ephesus."

2 Tim. 4:19. Paul asked Timothy to salute the household of Onesiphorus for him.

NAMES THAT BEGIN WITH "P"

PARMENAS

Acts 6:5. **PARMENAS** was one of the seven men the apostles chose and set apart to help with the work.

PARENTS OF A MAN BLIND FROM BIRTH, THE

John 9:18-23. **THE PARENTS OF A MAN BLIND FROM BIRTH**, when quizzed by the Jews as to how he gained his sight, fearing the Jews, told them to ask their son because he could speak for himself.

PATROBAS

Rom. 16:14. **PATROBAS** and several other specific disciples, "and the brethren which are with them," were sent greetings by Paul in his epistle to the Romans.

PAUL (Saul (1), Tertius)

Acts 7:58. **[PAUL] SAUL**, a young man, was among the people who either witnessed or participated in the stoning of Stephen, Jesus' disciple. The witnesses of the stoning laid down their clothes at Saul's feet.

Acts 8:1-3. Saul consented to Stephen's death and engaged in great persecution against the church, causing great havoc. Members of the church were forced to scatter abroad, and Saul hauled men and women into prison.

Acts 9. Saul requested letters from the high priest to give him permission to arrest any of Christ's followers he could find in Damascus and bring them bound back to Jerusalem. As he neared Damascus, he heard a voice saying, "Saul, Saul, why persecutest thou me? *(vs. 1-4).* Saul asked who was speaking and Jesus said it was he. Saul immediately asked what the Lord would have him do, and the Lord told him to go into the city and he would be told what to do. The men with Saul heard the voice but saw no one and were speechless. *(Note: Acts 9:7 in the JST reads, "And they who were journeying with him saw indeed the light, and were afraid; but they heard not the voice of him who spake to him." Acts 22:9 verifies that translation: "And they that were with me saw indeed the light, and were afraid; but they heard not the voice of him that spake to me.")* They helped Saul to his feet and led him into town because he could not see. For three days, Saul was without sight and went without food and drink *(vs. 5-9).* The Lord revealed to him in a vision that a man by the name of Ananias would come to him and he would regain his sight. The Lord told Ananias in a vision to go to Saul. Ananias put his hands on Saul, and Saul received his sight and was filled with the Holy Ghost. He arose and was baptized *(vs. 10-18).* After eating, he joined with the disciples at Damascus for a few days and then he began preaching of Christ in the synagogues. The Jews were confounded and plotted to kill him. However, Christ's disciples lowered Saul over the city wall in a basket and he went to Jerusalem. *(Note: This is also referred to in 2 Cor. 11:32-33.)* The disciples feared him because of his former behavior, but Barnabas took him to the apostles and told them about Saul's encounter with the Lord on the road to Damascus, how he then had preached boldly at Damascus in the name of Jesus, and how the people had sought to kill him. The apostles took him to Cæsarea and sent him to Tarsus. Then the church began to have rest throughout all Judæa, Galilee and Samaria *(vs. 19-31)*.

Acts 11:25-30. Saul was sought in Tarsus by Barnabas who had him go to Antioch with him where they taught for a year. It was here that the disciples were first called Christians. Because of a dearth in the land, which was prophesied by Agabus who went up to Antioch from Jerusalem, the disciples and every man, according to his means, sent relief to the brethren in Jerusalem by the hands of Barnabas and Saul.

Acts 12:25. Saul and Barnabas returned from Jerusalem after their ministry there and took John, whose surname was Mark, with them.

Acts 13. Saul and Barnabas, along with certain other prophets and teachers—Simeon (called Niger), Lucius of Cyrene and Manaen—were preaching in Antioch when the Holy Ghost indicated that Saul and Barnabas should leave Antioch. They went to Seleucia and then sailed to Cyprus. They preached in Salamis, along with John who was there. They went through the isle unto Paphos and found Bar-jesus (also called Elymas), a sorcerer and false prophet, who was with the deputy of the country, Sergius Paulius. Saul (**Paul**) rebuked Bar-jesus and said the Lord would cause him to be blind for a season. Sergius Paulius, witnessed what happened and believed Paul (Saul) and Barnabas *(vs. 1-12)*. They left Paphos and went to Perga in Pamphylia. John returned to Jerusalem. From Perga, they went to Antioch where they preached in the synagogue *(vs. 13-14)*. Following a powerful sermon by Paul wherein he reviewed some of Israel's past history and their asking for and being granted a king, and his testimony that David saw corruption but that Jesus saw no corruption because he was resurrected *(vs. 16-41)*, the Jews left but the Gentiles asked that the same words be preached again the following Sunday. Paul and Barnabas encouraged those Jews and religious proselytes who followed after them to continue in the grace of God *(vs. 42-43)*. When the Jews saw the multitudes that returned the following Sunday, they were envious and spoke against the two apostles who said that it was necessary that the word first be delivered to them, but since they rejected it, the Lord commanded that the word be given to the Gentiles. Paul and Barnabas were expelled from the land by the people who had been stirred up by the Jews. They shook off the dust of their feet against them as they left *(vs. 44-51)*.

Acts 14. Paul and Barnabas taught together in Iconium. The unbelieving Jews stirred up the people who sought to stone them so they fled to Lystra and Derbe *(vs. 1-6)*. In Lystra, they saw a man who had been crippled from birth. Paul healed him; and the people who witnessed it hailed Paul and Barnabas as gods come down from heaven. They called Paul, "Mercurius," and Barnabas, "Jupiter." The apostles quickly denied they were gods, saying, "We also are men of like passions with you . . ." Even so, they could scarcely keep the people from offering sacrifice unto them *(vs. 8-18)*. Certain Jews came from Antioch and Iconium and stirred up the people and stoned Paul. He was presumed to be dead. The disciples stood around him and he rose up the next day and departed with Barnabas to

Derbe *(19-20)*. After converting many people in Derbe, they returned to Lystra, Iconium and Antioch. They ordained elders in every church. From Pisidia, they went to Pamphylia. From Perga, they went down to Attalia and then sailed to Antioch where they stayed a long time with the disciples there *(vs. 21-28)*.

Acts 15. Paul and Barnabas and certain other men were sent to Jerusalem to inquire of the apostles and elders regarding the matter of circumcision when disputations arose after certain men came down from Judæa to Antioch preaching that every man had to be circumcised or he could not be saved. When they got to Jerusalem, some of the converted Pharisees claimed also that it was needful for them all to be circumcised so as to keep the law of Moses *(vs. 1-5)*. The apostles discussed the matter and concluded that it was not necessary for the Gentiles who joined the church to be circumcised. They were admonished to "abstain from meats offered to idols, and from blood, and from things strangled, and from fornication." And they sent Barnabas, Paul, Judas and Silas back to Antioch with letters stating the same *(vs. 6-29)*. After delivering the epistle to the multitude in Antioch, Judas decided to return to Jerusalem, but Silas decided to stay in Antioch. Some days later, Paul and Barnabas also decided to leave Antioch and see how the church members were doing in the areas where they had been previously. However, Paul and Barnabas disagreed sharply over taking John Mark with them. The disagreement was so sharp that Paul and Barnabas parted ways: Paul took Silas with him, and Barnabas took John Mark with him *(vs. 33-40)*.

Acts 16. Paul traveled to Derbe and Lystra, where he met Timotheus, the son of a Jewess, who believed, and a Greek father. Paul circumcised him and had him go forth with him. They traveled throughout Phrygia and the region of Galatia. The Spirit forbade them preaching in Asia. They traveled to Mysia and contemplated going to Bithynia, but the Spirit again indicated they should not. They passed Mysia and went to Troas, where Paul had a vision wherein a man of Macedonia was praying for him to go there. They traveled from Troas to Samothracia and Neapolis; and then on to Philippi, the chief city of that part of Macedonia. They went by the riverside where the women resorted and spoke to them. One of the women was Lydia. After her conversion and baptism, she constrained Paul and his brethren to abide in her house *(vs. 1-15)*. A certain damsel possessed with a spirit of divination followed Paul. After several days, Paul commanded the spirit in the name of Jesus Christ to come out of her. When her masters could no longer gain anything by her soothsaying, they took Paul and Silas to the rulers and the magistrates and brought charges against them. The magistrates commanded they be beaten and cast them into prison, ordering the jailer to keep them safely. He thrust them into the inner prison and held their feet fast in the stocks *(vs. 16-24)*. At midnight, Paul and Silas prayed and sang praises to God. The prisoners heard them. Suddenly, an earthquake shook the foundation of the prison, the doors were opened and everyone's bands were loosed. When the keeper of the prison went to kill himself because he thought the prisoners had fled, Paul stopped him, saying they were all still there. The jailer fell down before Paul and Silas and had them teach him. He took Paul and Silas and washed their stripes and then he and all who were his were baptized. He took them to his house and fed them *(vs. 25-34)*. The next morning the magistrates sent sergeants to the jailer with orders to release Paul and Silas. Paul refused, saying they were Romans and had been beaten openly, uncondemned, and were not going to be thrust out privily. The serjeants reported what Paul said to the magistrates who, when they heard, were fearful because they were Romans. They quickly went to the prison and personally besought them and brought them out and asked them to depart from the city. Paul and Silas went to the home of Lydia, comforted the brethren there, and then left *(vs. 35-40)*.

Acts 17. Paul, Silas and Timotheus passed through Amphipolis and Apollonia and went to Thessalonica where Paul preached in the synagogue of the Jews. A great multitude of the devout Greeks and many of the chief women believed *(vs. 1-4)*. Disbelieving Jews assaulted the house of Jason, a kinsman of Paul (*BD*), and, when they couldn't find Paul and Silas, took Jason and certain brethren before the rulers. When Jason and the others gave security, they were released. They sent Paul and Silas away by night to Berea *(vs. 5-10)*. Many of the people in Berea, including many "honourable women which were Greeks," were converted. When the Jews in Thessalonica heard that Paul and Silas were preaching in Berea, they came and stirred up the people. The brethren immediately sent Paul away, but Silas and Timotheus stayed. Paul went to Athens and sent word for Silas and Timotheus to join him *(vs. 12-15)*. Meanwhile, Paul was concerned about the idolatry he witnessed and was taken to Mars' hill (Areopagus) to answer to the civil council for preaching in the synagogue. He told them that they were too superstitious. They were praying to the "Unknown God," and so he told them of God and that we are the offspring of God. "Therefore, we ought not to think that the Godhead is like unto gold, or silver, or stone, graven by art and man's device." He also preached of a day of judgment and of the resurrection. Some people mocked him, others believed, including Dionysius the Areopagite and a woman named Damaris *(vs. 16-34)*.

Acts 18. Paul left Athens and went to Corinth. He met a Jewish couple, Aquila and Priscilla. Because he was of the same craft as they—tentmakers—he stayed with them. Silas and Timotheus came from Macedonia and joined him there. He testified of Christ. When the people opposed him and blasphemed, he shook his raiment and said their blood was upon their own heads and that, henceforth, he would go unto the Gentiles *(vs. 1-6)*. He went to the Corinthians and stayed in the house of Justus, whose house was connected to the synagogue. Crispus, the chief ruler of the synagogue, and many of the Corinthians believed and were baptized *(vs. 7-8)*. The Lord told Paul in a vision to keep preaching and not to be afraid because he had many people in that city. Paul labored in Corinth for a year and a half *(vs. 9-11)*. When Gallio was the deputy of Achaia, the Jews brought Paul before him; however, Gallio said the matter was not one that should come before him and he sent them from the judgment seat *(vs. 12-16)*. Paul sailed to Syria and took Priscilla and Aquila with him. He took leave of them in Ephesus and went to preach in the synagogue. He sailed from Ephesus to Cæsarea, checked up on the church and then went down to Antioch. After spending time there, he went all over the country of Galatia and Phrygia, strengthening all the disciples *(vs. 18-23)*.

Acts 19. Paul traveled to Ephesus and found many disciples there who had been baptized with the baptism of John (the baptism of repentance). He baptized them in the name of the Lord Jesus Christ and laid his hands upon them and conferred upon them the gift of the Holy Ghost *(vs. 1-6)*. Paul then spent three months preaching in the synagogue. However, because of those who opposed him, he left and "disputed daily" in the school of Tyrannus for two years *(vs. 8-10)*. During this time, God performed many miracles through Paul: the sick were healed and evil spirits were cast out. The seven sons of Sceva tried to exorcize a man, and the evil spirit acknowledged that it knew Jesus and Paul, and asked, "but who are ye?" The man in whom the evil spirit was lept upon the exorcists and overcame them, and they fled out of the house naked and wounded. As word of this spread, "the name of the Lord Jesus was magnified" *(vs. 11- 20)*. Paul stayed in Asia for a season but sent Timotheus and Erastus to Macedonia. At this time, a group of craftsmen who made their living making silver shrines unto Diana raised the people up against Paul (saying not only their craft was at stake but also the worship of Diana was at stake). Thus, the people caught Gaius and Aristarchus, Paul's companions who were of Macedonia, and rushed them into the theatre. Paul's other associates discouraged him from entering the theatre. The town clerk calmed the people down and talked to them about the proper legal recourse they had if there was a problem, and then he dismissed the assembly *(vs. 22-41)*.

Acts 20. Paul called the disciples unto him after the uproar, embraced them, and then departed for Macedonia. From there, he traveled to Greece where he stayed for three months. The Jews laid in wait for him as he was about to sail to Syria so he went to Macedonia, instead. His traveling companions at this time were Sopater of Berea, Aristarchus and Secundus of the Thessalonians, Gaius of Derbe, Timotheus, Tychicus and Trophimus of Asia. They joined together at Troas and stayed there for seven days *(vs. 1-6)*. They met together on the first day of the week to break bread; and Paul preached to them for a long time, even until midnight. Eutychus, a young man, was sitting in the window and fell asleep. He fell down from the third loft and was killed. However, Paul embraced him and said they shouldn't be troubled because the young man's life was in him. After breaking bread and talking until daybreak, Paul departed. And the disciples were comforted because the young man was alive *(vs. 7-12)*. Paul met his traveling companions at Assos and joined them aboard ship for the journey to Mitylene. They went to Chios, Samos, Trogyllium (where they tarried), and went the next day to Miletus. Paul wanted to sail past Ephesus and not spend time in Asia because he hoped to be in Jerusalem the day of Pentecost *(vs. 13-16)*. While in Miletus, Paul sent for the elders of the church in Ephesus. He reviewed with them his three years of faithful service in the ministry and told them that he was going to Jerusalem, not knowing what would befall him there, but that he was not concerned for his life, even though the Holy Ghost witnessed to him in every city that bonds and afflictions would be his lot. Then he told them that they would see his face no more, and instructed them to "record this day, that I am pure from the blood of all men. For I have not shunned to declare unto you all the counsel of God" *(vs. 17-27)*. He cautioned them to be watchful because "grievous wolves *(shall)* enter in among you, not sparing the flock," and men from within their own group would arise who would try to draw away disciples after them. After he finished speaking to them, they all kneeled down and prayed. They wept and kissed him. Then, they accompanied him to the ship *(vs. 28-38)*.

Acts 21. Paul and his company traveled via Coos, Rhodes, Patara, Phenicia, Cyprus into Syria, landing at Tyre where they tarried for seven days and met with the disciples they found there. Paul was warned by the Spirit that he should not journey on to Jerusalem. As he and his companions prepared to depart, the disciples in Tyre accompanied them until they were out of the city. They all kneeled down on the shore and prayed, and then Paul and his traveling companions and the disciples in Tyre went their separate ways *(vs. 1-6).* From Tyre, they went to Ptolemais where they stayed with the brethren for a day, and then they journeyed on to Cæsarea. The group stayed with Philip the evangelist, who was one of the seven. While at Philip's home, the prophet Agabus came. He took Paul's girdle and used it to bind his own hands and feet. He prophesied that the Jews at Jerusalem would bind the man who owned the girdle and would deliver him into the hands of the Gentiles. Paul's companions tried to get him to refrain from going to Jerusalem, but Paul told them he was not only ready to be bound, if necessary, but also to die, if necessary, for the name of the Lord. When Paul could not be persuaded to change his mind, they took their journey to Jerusalem *(vs. 7-15).* He took Mnason, an old disciple from Cæsarea, with him. Paul and his companions went to see James. All the elders were present. They told Paul of the rumors that were circulating and instructed him that he should purify himself with four other men who have a "vow on them." Paul agreed to do so. As the seven days of purification neared an end, the people were stirred up by the Jews from Asia, and they drew Paul out of the temple and tried to kill him. They were stopped by the chief captain of the band and his soldiers and the centurions who all responded to the tumult as soon as they heard about it. The chief captain had Paul bound in chains and demanded to know who he was and what he had done. The soldiers bore him into the castle. Paul requested that the chief captain allow him to speak. Paul explained that he was a Jew of Tarsus of Cilicia and asked permission to speak unto the people. He spoke unto them in the Hebrew tongue *(vs. 16-40).*

Acts 22. Paul spoke to the people in the Hebrew tongue and recounted the story of his conversion on the road to Damascus: his having been taught at the feet of Gamaliel, the Lord's speaking to him, his blindness, and subsequent healing by Ananias. He told them of his seeing Jesus in a vision in Jerusalem as he prayed in the temple, and of the charge Jesus gave him. He told of his protestations to the Lord because he had persecuted the believers and had agreed to Stephen's death *(vs. 1-21).* The people were not persuaded. The chief captain commanded he be brought into the castle and scourged. However, Paul asked the centurion if it was lawful to scourge a man who was a Roman and who was uncondemned. When the centurion told the chief priest, the chief priest was afraid, knowing Paul was a Roman and that he had bound him. He had the bands loosed on Paul, called the council together, and set Paul down before them *(vs. 22-30).*

Acts 23. Paul appealed earnestly to the council. However, Ananias, the high priest, commanded those standing by Paul to smite him across the mouth. Paul called him a "whited wall" for sitting in judgment of him according to the law, but commanding that he be smitten contrary to the law. Paul was chastised for speaking against "God's high priest." He said he didn't know he was the high priest, and acknowledged that it was written that "Thou shalt not speak evil of the ruler of thy people" *(vs. 1-5).* Paul perceived that part of the council was comprised of Sadducees and part of Pharisees. He appealed to the Pharisees and spoke of the hope and resurrection of the dead (in which the Pharisees believed). Part of the scribes of the Pharisees cried out in support of Paul and said they found no evil in him. A great dissension followed and the chief captain, fearing that Paul would be pulled in pieces, commanded the soldiers take him by force from among the people and take him to the castle *(vs. 6-10)*. The Lord appeared to Paul and told him that just as he had testified of him in Jerusalem, he also needed to testify of him in Rome *(v. 11)*. Forty Jews plotted to kill Paul and bound themselves to neither eat nor drink until they had accomplished the deed. However, Paul's nephew (his sister's son) reported the plan to Paul, and Paul asked a centurion to take the young man to the chief captain because he had something to tell him. After the chief captain learned of the plan, he gave orders to two centurions to prepare 200 soldiers, 70 horsemen, and 200 spearmen to go to Cæsarea at the third hour of the night. They were to be given beasts for Paul to ride on, and they were to escort him to Felix the governor *(vs. 12-24)*. The chief captain, Claudius Lysias, wrote a letter to Felix. The soldiers took Paul by night to Antipatris and left Paul with the horsemen to journey on to Cæsarea. They delivered both Paul and the chief captain's letter to the governor *(vs. 25-33)*. After reading the letter, Felix asked of what province Paul was from. When he learned he was from Celicia, he agreed to hear him when his accusers could also be there, and ordered that Paul be kept in Herod's judgment hall *(vs. 34-35)*.

Acts 24. Five days after Paul was delivered safely to Felix the governor, Ananias the high priest, the elders, and an orator by the name of Tertullus, arrived, ready to lodge their complaints against Paul. Tertullus was their spokesman. Tertullus accused Paul of sedition and of profaning the temple. He said that they had planned to judge Paul according to their law but that Claudius Lysias, the chief captain, had, with great violence, taken Paul away and commanded they present their accusations to Felix. The Jews in the group assented to what Tertullus said *(vs. 1-9)*. Paul responded in defense of his life and his teachings, and denied that he had disputed with any man in the temple, nor had he raised up the people in the synagogues nor in the city. Furthermore, he said, his accusers could not prove any of the charges they made against him. After hearing both sides, Felix deferred making a decision until he could hear from Lysias. He instructed a centurion to keep Paul, but to let Paul have his liberty and not deny him association with his acquaintances *(vs. 10-23)*. Felix came with his wife Drusilla and had Paul explain about his faith. When Paul spoke of righteousness, temperance and judgment to come, Felix trembled and sent Paul on his way, saying he would call for him again when he had "a convenient season." Hoping Paul would give him money to free him, he sent for him frequently. Two years passed, and Porcius Festus came into Felix' room (i.e., succeeded Felix as procurator of Judæa). In order to please the Jews, Felix left Paul bound *(vs. 24-27)*.

Acts 25. Paul was brought before Festus as Festus sat on the judgment seat. Ananias and other Jews had informed Festus about Paul during the previous ten days when Festus was in Jerusalem. They had hoped Festus would agree to send Paul to Jerusalem to be tried, and they planned to lay in wait and kill him. However, Festus had declined and said Paul should remain in Cæsarea. They could make their complaint there. They laid before Festus "many and grievous complaints against Paul, which they could not prove." Paul offered his own defense, saying he had not offended against the law of the Jews, nor against the temple, nor against Cæsar, and he appealed to Cæsar. Festus agreed to send him to Cæsar *(vs. 1-12)*. Festus discussed the dilemma he had regarding Paul with King Agrippa and Bernice when they came to visit. Agrippa said he wanted to hear Paul himself. Festus agreed. The following day, as Festus, Agrippa, Bernice and other men were ready, Festus commanded that Paul be brought forth. He told the group that the Jews cry that Paul ought not to live any longer, but that he hadn't been able to find anything against Paul that was worthy of death. Because Paul had appealed to Augustus, Festus said he planned to send him there, but felt he should also send a letter detailing the crimes laid against him. However, he couldn't find any "certain thing to write" to Augustus. He hoped that after this group examined Paul, perhaps they could determine what he should write in the letter *(vs. 13-27)*.

Acts 26. Paul was given permission by King Agrippa to speak in his own defense *(v. 1)*. He recounted his former persecution of the saints as he lived the life of a Pharisee *(vs. 4-11)*. He testified of his conversion on the road to Damascus of Christ's appearance to him and of the charge Christ gave him to be a minister and witness to both the Jews and the Gentiles. He said he testified only of those things the prophets and Moses said would come to pass: that Christ would suffer, and that he would be the first to rise from the dead and would show light unto the people and to the Gentiles *(vs. 12-23)*. Festus said Paul was mad. Paul denied the accusation, saying he spoke forth the words of truth and soberness. King Agrippa said that Paul "almost" persuaded him to be a Christian. Paul said he wished that all who heard him that day would "almost and altogether" be as he was, only without the bonds *(vs. 24-29)*. King Agrippa, Bernice, Festus and those with them, drew aside and conferred, concluding that Paul had done nothing worthy of death or of bonds. Agrippa then indicated that if Paul hadn't appealed unto Cæsar, he might have been set free *(vs. 30-32)*.

Acts 27. Paul, along with other prisoners, including Aristarchus, was put on a ship set to sail to Italy and placed in the charge of Julius, a centurion. Paul was treated courteously by Julius, who gave him liberty to mingle with his friends to refresh himself. They sailed by or "touched" several places: Sidon; under Cyprus; over the sea of Cilicia and Pamphylia; and Myra, a city of Lycia. At Myra, the centurion placed them on a ship of Alexandria sailing into Italy. Travel was slow. After many days, they were near Cnidus, " . . . the wind not suffering us, we sailed under Crete, over against Salmone;" then near the city of Lasea. Sailing now became dangerous "because the fast was now already past," and Paul offered some forewarning of pending danger, but the centurion ignored it, choosing to believe the master and the owner of the ship. They decided to try to winter in Phenice, a haven of Crete. Encouraged by a soft wind, they sailed close by Crete. However, a terrible wind called Euroclydon came up. The ship tossed; they lightened the ship; they cast out with their own hands the tackling of the ship. They saw no sun or stars for many days. They began to lose hope that they would even be saved. After a long abstinence, Paul finally stood in their midst and told them they should have listened to him earlier, but to be of good cheer because an angel of God had stood by him that night and said that Paul needed to be brought before Cæsar and that he and all aboard ship would be saved. However, they would be cast upon a certain island *(vs. 1-26)*. On the 14th night of the storm, thinking they were near some country, the shipmen were about to flee out of the ship but Paul warned the centurion and soldiers that unless they stayed aboard ship they would die. They stayed. As day approached, Paul encouraged them all to eat because they had been fasting for 14 days. This was for their health, he said, and he promised them that not a hair would fall from their heads. Paul took bread, gave thanks to God, broke it and they all ate. Then they also ate meat. There were 276 people aboard ship. After eating, they lightened the ship, in part by tossing the wheat overboard. The next morning, they didn't recognize the land they were near, but there was a creek (bay) with a shore which they hoped to sail into. The ship got stuck and the hinder part was broken by violent waves. The soldiers wanted to kill the prisoners so none could escape but the centurion wouldn't let them. The centurion told those who could swim to cast themselves into the sea and swim toward shore. Others clung to boards or to broken pieces of the ship and made it to shore. All escaped safely to land *(vs. 27-44)*.

Acts 28. Paul and the other people from the ship were treated kindly by the people of Melita. The islanders built a fire so they could get warm. As Paul gathered sticks for the fire, he was bitten by a viper which fastened on his hand. The "barbarians" thought that Paul must be a murderer because vengeance was upon him, even though he had escaped the sea. However, Paul shook the viper off and was totally unharmed by the viper's bite. Then the barbarians thought Paul must be a god *(vs. 1-6)*. The father of Publius, the chief man of the island, became ill. Paul laid his hands upon him and healed him. He then healed others on the island who were ill. The islanders honored them with many honors and supplied them with all they needed when they departed three months later in a ship of Alexandria *(vs. 7-11)*. They landed at Syracuse and stayed there for three days. They traveled to Rhegium (spent a day there); to Puteoli (where they met brethren and stayed with them for seven days); and on toward Rome *(vs. 12-15)*. In Rome, the centurion delivered the prisoners to the captain of the guard. However, Paul was placed alone with a soldier who kept him. After three days, Paul called the chief of the Jews together and told them why he was there and that he had done no wrong. They said they had not received any letter nor word against Paul, and they desired to hear from him. Paul taught them concerning Jesus, "both out of the law of Moses, and out of the prophets." Some believed, some did not. After preaching to the Jews, the gospel was "sent unto the Gentiles." During this time, Paul rented his own house and lived there two years *(vs. 16-31)*.

Rom. 1-16; Postscript. (Note: See Romans for a synopsis of Paul's epistle to them.) Paul referred to himself as **Tertius** *(Rom. 16:22)*. The epistle to the saints in Rome was delivered to them by Phebe, a servant of the church at Cenchrea *(Postscript)*.

1 Cor. 1-16; 2 Cor. 1-13. (Note: See Corinthians for a synopsis of Paul's epistles to them) Paul wrote both epistles to the Corinthians from Philippi, a city of Macedonia. He sent the first epistle to them via the hands of Stephanas, Fortunatus, Achaicus and Timotheus . He sent the second by Titus and Lucas. Several years prior to when Paul wrote his second epistle to the Corinthians, he was caught up into the third heaven *(i.e., the celestial kingdom)*. Paul prayed the Lord would remove his weakness, his "thorn in the flesh." However, the Lord told Paul, "My grace is sufficient for thee: for my strength is made perfect in weakness." Paul gloried in his infirmities because it is through our infirmities that God is able to manifest the power of Christ. Paul told the saints, "When I am weak, then am I strong" *(2 Cor. 12:1-10)*.

Gal. 1-6. (Note: See Galatians for a synopsis of Paul's epistle to them.) Paul wrote his epistle to the Galatians from Rome.

Eph. 1-6. (Note: See Ephesians for a synopsis of Paul's epistle to them.) Paul wrote his epistle to the Ephesians from Rome and sent it to them by Tychicus.

Philip. 1-4. (Note: See Philippians for a synopsis of Paul's epistle to them.) Paul wrote his epistle to the Phillippians from Rome and sent it to them by Epaphroditus.

Col. 1-4. (Note: See Colossians for a synopsis of Paul's epistle to them.) Paul wrote his epistle to the Colossians from Rome and sent it to them by Tychicus and Onesimus.

1 Thes. 1-5; 2 Thes.1-3. (See Thessalonians for a synopsis of Paul's epistles to them.) Paul wrote both of his epistles to the Thessalonians from Athens.

1 Tim. 1-6; 2 Tim. 1-4. (See Timotheus for a synopsis of Paul's epistles to Timothy.) Paul wrote his first epistle to Timothy from Laodicea, the chiefest city of Phrygia Pacatiana. He wrote his second epistle to Timothy from Rome when he was brought before Nero the second time.

Titus 1-3. (See Titus for a synopsis of Paul's epistle to Titus.) Paul wrote to Titus from Nicopolis of Macedonia.

Philem. (See Philemon for a synopsis of Paul's epistle to Philemon.) Paul wrote to Philemon from Rome and sent it to him by the hand of Onesimus, Philemon's slave.

Heb. 1-13. (See Hebrews for a synopsis of Paul's epistle to the Hebrews.) Paul wrote his epistle to the Hebrews from Italy and sent it to them via Timothy.

2 Pet. 5:15. Paul, Peter said in his second epistle to the saints, had written to them of the same teachings of salvation that Peter was writing to them about.

PAUL'S (Saul's) COMPANIONS

Acts 9:7-8. **SAUL'S COMPANIONS** on the road to Damascus heard the voice of the Lord speak to Saul, but they saw no man. They led the sightless Saul by hand into the city. *(Note: Modern-day revelation records the account as follows:)*

> *"And they who were journeying with him saw indeed the light, and were afraid; but they heard not the voice of him who spake to him" (Acts 9:7, JST).*

Acts 22:9. Paul's Companions saw the light and were afraid, but they heard not the voice that spoke to Paul. *(Note the contradiction to Acts 9:7 and the corroboration of the JST of Acts 9:7.)*

PAUL'S MOTHER

Rom. 16:13. **PAUL'S MOTHER** was sent greetings by Paul in his epistle to the saints in Rome.

PAUL'S NEPHEW

Acts 23:16-33. **PAUL'S NEPHEW,** his sister's son, warned Paul of the plan whereby 40 Jews conspired to kill Paul. Paul asked a centurion to take the young man to the chief captain because he had something to tell him. After the chief captain learned of the plot, he had his soldiers and spearmen take Paul away during the night and deliver him safely to Felix, the governor.

PERSIS

Rom. 16:12. **PERSIS** labored much in the Lord, according to Paul, who referred to him as the "beloved Persis." Paul sent greetings to him in his epistle to the Romans.

PETER (Simon Called Peter, Cephas, Cleopas?, Simeon)

Matt. 4:18-20; Mark 1:16-18; Luke 5:1-11; John 1:40-42. **SIMON CALLED PETER** was the brother of Andrew. They were fishermen. When Jesus saw them fishing in the Sea of Galilee, he called them to come follow him, saying he would make them fishers of men. The brothers immediately left their nets and followed Jesus. *(Note: The account in the different Gospels varies. Luke 5 does not include Andrew; however, it provides greater detail. The account in John indicates that Andrew, a disciple of John the Baptist, went seeking Peter to tell him that they (he and another disciple) had found the Messias, i.e., the Christ, and that Andrew brought Peter to see Jesus, who then said to Peter, "Thou art Simon the son of Jona; thou shalt be called* ***Cephas,*** *which is by interpretation, A stone.")*

Matt. 8:14; Mark 1:30-31; Luke 4:38-39. Peter's [Simon's] mother-in-law was sick. When Jesus went into Peter's house, he touched her hand and she was healed. *(Note: Matthew used the name Peter. Mark and Luke used the name Simon.)*

Matt. 10; Luke 9. Jesus called 12 disciples: Simon Peter, Andrew, James, John, Philip, Bartholomew, Thomas, Matthew, James, Lebbæus (Thaddæus), Simon the Canaanite, and Judas Iscariot *(vs. 2-4).* Jesus empowered these apostles and sent them forth to teach but instructed them that they should not go to the Gentiles nor to the Samaritans. They were to go to the lost sheep of the house of Israel. They were to heal the sick and cast out devils. They were to travel without purse or scrip. They were instructed to leave their peace upon those who received them, but to shake the dust off their feet when leaving the houses of those who reject them *(vs. 5-14; Luke 9:1-5).* They were told they would be persecuted for Christ's sake, but that "he that endureth to the end shall be saved." They are of more value than the sparrows for which the Father provides. Even the hairs of their heads are numbered *(vs. 16-32).*

Matt. 14:22-31. Peter and Jesus' other disciples sailed to the other side of the water ahead of Jesus while Jesus sent the multitudes of people away and took time to pray. When Jesus went to rejoin them, he walked on the water toward the ship. The disciples thought it was a spirit and were frightened. After Jesus calmed the fears of the disciples, Peter left the ship and started to walk on the water toward Jesus. However, he became fearful and began to sink. When he cried out for help, Jesus stretched forth his hand and caught him.

Matt. 15:15-20. Peter asked Jesus what he meant when he told the Pharisees and scribes that it is not what goes into the mouth that defiles a person but that which comes out of the mouth; and Jesus explained the parable to his disciples.

Matt. 16:16-19; Mark 8:27-29, 31-33; Luke 9:18-22. Peter and the disciples, when asked by Jesus who the people said he was, said that some people said he was John the Baptist, some Elias, and other Jeremias. When Jesus asked, "But whom say ye that I am?" Peter answered, "Thou art the Christ, the Son of the living God." Jesus said that flesh and blood had not revealed that to Peter, but his Father who is in heaven. Then Peter was told that on that rock *(i.e., the rock of revelation; also, Jesus is the Rock or Stone)* Christ would build his church, and that Christ would give unto Peter the keys of the priesthood to guide the church—that whatsoever he bound on earth would be bound in heaven, and that whatsoever he loosed on earth would be loosed in heaven. When Christ said he would soon be killed but would rise again on the third day, Peter rebuked him. Christ corrected him. *(Note: The accounts in Mark and Luke are abbreviated.)*

Matt. 17; Mark 9; Luke 9. Peter, James and John went with Jesus into a high mountain where they were transfigured, saw Moses and Elias, and heard a voice proclaiming, "This is my beloved Son, in whom I am well pleased; hear ye him." Peter suggested making three altars: one each for Jesus, Moses and Elias *(vs. 1-12; Mark 9:2-13; Luke 9:28-35).* When they had come unto a multitude, none of the disciples was able to heal a certain man's son who was "lunatick" [son, which hath a dumb spirit] [a man's only child]. Jesus said this was because of lack of faith—the kind of faith that comes from fasting and prayer *(vs. 14- 21; Mark 9:17-29; Luke 9:38-42).* The disciples were grieved when Jesus again told them he would be betrayed and killed, but Christ assured them he would rise again on the third day *(vs. 22-23; Mark 9:31; Luke 9:44).* When tax collectors in Capernaum queried Peter regarding Jesus' payment of tribute, Jesus had him catch a fish, retrieve a coin from its mouth, and pay the tax collectors *(vs. 24-27).*

Matt. 18; Luke 17. Peter inquired of the Lord as to how many times a person ought to be forgiven. Jesus told him that we should forgive those who offend us seventy times seven *(vs. 21-22; also see Luke 17:3-4).* Jesus then taught the parable of the servant who was forgiven his debts but who refused to forgive a fellow servant of his debts. He stressed that if we do not forgive others, Heavenly Father will not forgive us either *(vs. 23-35).*

Matt. 19:27; Luke 18:28-30. Peter, speaking to Jesus, said that the disciples had forsaken everything and had followed Jesus, and inquired, "What shall we have therefore?" Jesus responded that when the Son of Man sits upon his throne of glory, they would also sit upon thrones and judge the twelve tribes of Israel.

Matt. 26; Mark 14; Luke 22; John 13, 18. Peter promised he would never deny Jesus. Jesus gently chided him and said that before the cock crowed [twice], Peter would deny him three times *(vs. 33-34; Mark 14:29-30; Luke 22:31-34; John 13:37-38). (Note: The account in Luke states that Jesus told Peter that Satan desired to have him, and that he, Jesus, had prayed for him that his faith would not fail.)* Jesus took Peter, James and John, the sons of Zebedee, with him as he went further into the garden of Gethsemane and asked them to wait and watch with him. Nevertheless, while he went a way off to pray, they repeatedly fell asleep *(vs. 37-44; Mark 14:33-41; Luke 22:39-46). (Note: The account in Luke does not specify that Jesus took Peter, James and John an additional distance with him.)* When Jesus was tried before Caiaphas and the scribes and elders, Peter followed and "sat with the servants, to see the end." When he was outside the palace a damsel, a maid, and a group of people at various times approached him and accused him of being one of Jesus' men. Each time, Peter vehemently denied it. Immediately following the third denial, the cock crowed. "And he went out, and wept bitterly" *(vs. 57-75; Mark 14:54, 66-72; Luke 22:54-62; see entry for John 18 for an expanded account).*

Mark 5:37; Luke 8:51. Peter, James and John accompanied Jesus to the house of Jairus where he went to heal Jairus' twelve-year-old daughter.

Mark 8. See entry for Matt. 16.

Mark 11:21. Peter pointed out the withered fig tree as he recalled that Jesus had condemned it earlier. Jesus used that as an opportunity to teach Peter and the disciples about faith.

Mark 13. Peter, James, John and Andrew asked Jesus what calamities would precede the Second Coming. Jesus told them there would be false Christs, wars and rumors of wars, nation would rise against nation and kingdom against kingdom; there would be earthquakes and famines and troubles. The prophets would be persecuted for Christ's sake. Brother would betray brother and fathers their sons; children shall rise against their parents. The desolation prophesied by Daniel will come to pass. The sun shall be darkened, the moon will not give its light, and the stars of heaven shall fall. Then the Son of Man will come in the clouds in great power and glory *(vs. 3-27).* Jesus said to watch for the signs: just as we know summer is near when the fig tree puts forth her tender branches, so the signs will signal the Second Coming. Nevertheless, Jesus stressed that no man knows the day, time, nor place. We should be prepared and not caught "sleeping" *(vs. 28-37; Luke 21:29-36; also see Matt. 24:32-34, 37-51 and Luke 17:20-37 for a variation on this subject).*

Mark 14. See the entry for Matt. 26.

Luke 8:51. See entry for Mark 5.

Luke 12:41-48. Peter asked Jesus if the lesson regarding being prepared was just to the disciples or to all people. In response, Jesus taught the parable of the wise servant who was prepared and the unwise servant who was not prepared when their master came suddenly. Where much is given, much is required.

Luke 24. Peter immediately ran to the sepulchre and looked inside when Mary Magdalene, Joanna, and Mary the mother of James and the other women told the apostles that the sepulchre wherein Jesus was laid was empty and that they had been told he was risen. He beheld the linen clothes that were lying there *(v. 12). (See entry for John 20:2-10.)* **Cleopas** and another disciple went to Emmaus. As they walked along, Jesus drew near unto them and walked with them. They did not recognize the resurrected Christ. Cleopas asked the man if he were a stranger and whether or not he was aware of all that had recently occurred. Cleopas told him about the women coming to tell the disciples that the tomb was empty and that they had seen angels who said Christ was alive. As they drew nigh unto the village, Jesus acted as though he would have gone further, but they constrained him to abide with them because it was evening. He took bread, blessed it and brake it, and gave it to them. Their eyes were then opened and he vanished out of their sight. The disciples acknowledged that they had felt a burning within themselves while Jesus was with them. They returned to Jerusalem and found the eleven apostles and told them what had happened and how Jesus had appeared to Simon *(vs. 13-33). (Note: It is not clear who Cleopas is. It is conceivable that Cleopas and Cephas are varied spellings of the same name and refer to Simon Peter. The resurrected Christ visited with Cleopas on the road to Emmaus, and broke bread with him and others. After Christ vanished from their sight, those with whom he broke bread rushed to tell the eleven apostles who were together about the risen Lord having appeared to Simon and that he had broken bread with them. However, the footnote to verse 18 cross-references Cleopas with John 19:25, which refers to Cleopas, the husband of a woman named Mary. The BD indicates there is no certainty as to whether or not these references refer to two different people named Cleopas or whether they are one and the same person. Meanwhile, the footnote to verse 34 cross-references Simon with 1 Cor. 15:5, Cephas, one of the twelve. Jesus changed Simon Peter's name to Cephas when Peter was called to be a disciple. John 1:42.)* As they spoke, Jesus came and stood in the midst of them. He ate meat with them and blessed and taught them *(vs. 36-53).*

John 1:40-42. See entry for Matt. 4:18-20.

John 6:68-70. When many of Christ's followers apostatized following his exposition regarding the bread of life and eating of his flesh and drinking of his blood, Christ asked the Twelve if they, too, would leave. Peter, speaking for the group, testified that Jesus is the Messiah. Jesus reminded them that, nevertheless, one of them would betray him.

John 13. Peter declined to have Jesus wash his feet, but Jesus told him if he didn't, Peter would have no part with him. Peter quickly volunteered to have Jesus wash all of him. Jesus told him that the feet were enough *(vs. 6-10).* When Jesus told his disciples that one of them would betray him, they wondered who it was. Peter asked if it would be he. Jesus said it would be the one to whom he gave a morsel of food (i.e., Judas Iscariot) *(vs. 21-26).* Peter questioned Jesus as to why he could not go where Jesus said he was going and offered to lay down his life for Jesus. Jesus told Peter that he would deny him three times before the cock crowed *(vs. 36-38; see entry for Matt. 26).*

John 18. Peter smote off the ear of Malchus, a servant of the high priest Caiaphas, when the band of men and officers from the chief priests and Pharisees came to arrest Jesus when Judas betrayed him. Jesus told Peter to put away his sword—that he needed to drink the cup which his Father had given him *(vs. 10-11).* When the officers took Jesus away, Peter and another disciple followed. While the one disciple who knew the high priest followed the group indoors, Peter remained outside. When this disciple came to bring Peter inside, the damsel at the door asked Peter if he was not also one of Jesus' disciples. Peter said he was not. As the servants and officers warmed themselves beside a fire, Peter stood with them *(vs. 15-18).* When these men asked if Peter was not also one of Jesus' disciples, Peter again denied it. One of the servants of the high priest, whose relative had had his ear cut off by Peter, also asked Peter if he had not been in the garden with Jesus. For the third time, Peter denied it. "And immediately the cock crew *(vs. 25-27). (See entry for Matt. 26.)*

John 20. Peter and the other disciple whom Jesus loved *(i.e., John)* dashed to the sepulchre wherein Christ's body had been placed after Mary Magdalene reported that Jesus' body was gone. John beat Peter to the Sepulchre but stood outside peering in when Peter arrived. Peter went inside the sepulchre and saw the linen clothes lying there. After seeing for themselves and believing he was gone, Peter and John returned to their homes *(vs. 2-10)*. That evening Jesus appeared to his disciples as they were assembled in seclusion for fear of the Jews and showed them the wounds in his hands and side and told them to "Receive ye the Holy Ghost" *(vs. 19-22)*. He appeared to them again eight days later *(v. 26)*. *(See entry for Luke 24.)*

John 21. Peter, Thomas, Nathanael of Cana, James and John and two other disciples were fishing on the sea of Tiberias when Jesus showed himself to his disciples a third time following his resurrection. Jesus stood on the shore and asked if they had any meat. They did not recognize Jesus, but responded that they had none. He told them to cast their nets on the right side of the ship. They did; and their nets were so full they were unable to draw them. John declared to Peter, "It is the Lord." Peter quickly put something on and cast himself into the sea. When the disciples were gathered together on shore, Jesus dined with them on bread and fishes *(vs. 1-14)*. After eating, Jesus asked Simon Peter, "Simon, son of Jonas, lovest thou me more than these?" Peter said he did. Christ asked him the same question three times. Each time Peter said he did. And each time, Christ told him, "Feed my lambs" or "Feed my sheep" *(vs. 15-17)*. Jesus foretold Peter's martyrdom *(vs. 18-19)*. Peter wondered what would become of John. Jesus indicated that it really shouldn't matter to Peter. Peter's responsibility was to follow Jesus *(v. 21)*.

Acts. 1:15-26. After Jesus' ascension into heaven, the apostles met and Peter reminded them that the scripture, "Yea, mine own familiar friend, in whom I trusted, which did eat of my bread, hath lifted up his heel against me" *(Ps. 41:9)*, had to be fulfilled; and now that Judas was no longer an apostle, in fact, Judas had died, there was a vacancy in the Twelve that needed to be filled. The remaining eleven apostles presented two names—Joseph called Barsabas, and Matthias—to the Lord in prayer. The lot fell upon Matthias to replace Judas.

Acts 2. Peter and the other apostles spoke in tongues on the day of Pentecost. There was a sound as of a mighty rushing of wind. Cloven tongues like fire sat upon each of them. They were all filled with the Holy Ghost. In Jerusalem, there dwelled devout men from every nation; and they were all amazed to hear the apostles testify of Christ in their own languages. Peter testified that they were not drunken, but they were fulfilling the prophecy of Joel who said that in the last days God would pour out his Spirit upon all flesh, "and your sons and your daughters shall prophesy . . . and it shall come to pass, that whosoever shall call on the name of the Lord shall be saved" *(vs. 17-21; Joel 2:28-32)*. Peter testified of Jesus and reminded the people that David also testified of Jesus *(vs. 22-36)*. Approximately 3,000 souls were baptized. They had all things in common. More people were added to the church daily *(vs. 41-47)*.

Acts 3. When Peter and John went to the temple to pray, a man lame from birth asked for alms. Peter told him they had neither silver nor gold but would give them what they did have; and then they told him, "In the name of Jesus Christ of Nazareth rise up and walk;" and the man was healed. When the people gathered around in amazement, Peter admonished them and said the God of Abraham, Isaac and Jacob had glorified his Son by healing the man. And he reminded them that they had killed the Son of God and had desired a murdered to live instead *(vs. 1-16)*. Peter indicated that what the people had done, they did because of ignorance, but that now they needed to repent and be converted *(vs. 17-19)*. There will be a time of "restitution of all things, which God hath spoken by the mouth of all his holy prophets since the world began" before the Second Coming *(vs. 20-21)*. Christ is the prophet of whom Moses spoke when he said, "A prophet shall the Lord your God raise up unto you of your brethren, like unto me . . ." *(v. 22)*. Other prophets, from Samuel on, also foretold of "these days," Peter said *(v. 24)*.

Acts 4. Peter and John were arrested by the priests, the captain of the temple and the Sadducees as they spoke unto the people about Christ. Peter, filled with the Holy Ghost, spoke boldly, testifying of Christ and saying that it was through Christ's name that the lame man was healed. The rulers, elders, scribes, Annas the high priest, Caiaphas, John and Alexander, and as many kindred of the high priest as there were, met to confer as to what to do about Peter and John. The healed man was with the apostles so they could not deny he had been healed, and they feared the people. They resolved to threaten them and let them go. They commanded Peter and John not to speak or teach in the name of Jesus. They responded with a question: "Was it better to hearken unto them or unto God?" *(vs. 1-22)*. They returned to their fellow apostles and they all praised God, quoting David *(Ps. 1-2)*. As they finished praying, the building shook and they were all filled with the Holy Ghost. All their followers were of one heart and they had all things in common *(vs. 31-37)*.

Acts 5. Peter, at the time when the congregation had all things in common, asked Ananias why he had kept back part of the proceeds from the sale of his land, and reminded Ananias that he had not lied unto men, but unto God. Ananias then fell down and died. Three hours later, Peter asked Sapphira, Ananias' wife, about the price of the property. She also lied. When Peter chastised her for lying to the Lord, she, too, fell down and died *(vs. 1-10)*.

Acts 8. Peter and John went to Samaria when the apostles heard that the people there were being converted. While the people had been baptized by Philip, they had not received the laying on of hands for the gift of the Holy Ghost. Thus, Peter and John "laid their hands on them, and they received the Holy Ghost" *(vs. 14-17)*. A man named Simon, who had been baptized by Philip, offered to pay Peter and John money if they would give him the power to lay hands on people and give them the Holy Ghost. Peter rebuked him and told him to repent for his heart was not right before God. Simon asked Peter to pray to the Lord that the things Peter said would not come upon him. Peter and John, after preaching and testifying, returned to Jerusalem *(vs. 18-25)*.

Acts 9:32-43. As Peter taught, he traveled to Lydda where he found a man named Aeneas who had been sick in bed for eight years with the palsy. Peter healed the man, who arose immediately from his bed. Another disciple, a woman named Tabitha, also called Dorcas, lived in Joppa which was near Lydda. The disciples in Joppa sent for Peter so he could bless Dorcas. When he arrived, Dorcas was already dead and her body had been washed and she had been laid in an upper chamber. Peter sent the people out of the room, kneeled down and prayed, and said, "Tabitha arise." Tabitha opened her eyes and sat up. Peter took her by the hand and presented her alive to the saints and widows who had been mourning her. While he tarried in Joppa, he stayed with Simon, a tanner.

Acts 10. While Peter sojourned in the home of Simon the tanner, an angel of the Lord instructed Cornelius in a vision to send for him, saying that Peter would tell him what he should do *(vs 2-6).* Peter went to the housetop to pray about the sixth hour. He fell into a trance and had a vision wherein he "saw heaven opened, and a certain vessel descending unto him, as it had been a great sheet knit at the four corners, and let down to the earth . . ." The sheet was filled with all kinds of four-footed beasts, wild beasts, creeping things, and fowls. A voice told him to kill and eat. Peter declined, saying he had never eaten any unclean or common thing. Three times the voice told him to eat, saying, "What God hath cleansed, that call not thou common" *(vs. 9-15).* The vessel was taken back up into heaven. Peter pondered the vision. Just then, Cornelius' men arrived looking for Peter. At the same time, the Spirit told Peter that three men were seeking him and he should go with them. Peter had the three men spend the night there and on the morrow they all left for Cæsarea where Cornelius awaited them. When Cornelius fell down at Peter's feet to worship him, Peter raised him up, saying he, too, was just a man *(vs. 16-26).* Cornelius told Peter about the vision he had had and asked Peter to tell him and all the kinsmen and friends he had assembled there "all things that are commanded thee of God" *(vs. 30-33).* Peter perceived that God is no respecter of persons and that those who fear God, the righteous people of every nation, are accepted by him *(vs. 34-35).* Peter preached of Christ to Cornelius and his assembled guests. They believed and the Holy Ghost fell upon those who heard the word. Those of the circumcision who believed were astonished that the Holy Ghost fell upon Gentiles as well as upon them. Peter sermonized that no one who accepted Christ and had received the Holy Ghost should be denied baptism, and commanded Cornelius and his people to be baptized. The people then prayed that Peter would tarry with them additional days *(vs. 36-48).*

Acts 11. Peter was criticized by his fellow apostles and brethren in Judæa who had heard that the Gentiles *(Cornelius and his kinsmen and friends)* had received the word from him. They contended with him for going in to uncircumcised men. Peter explained about the vision he had had and that Cornelius had seen an angel in a vision. He told how the Holy Ghost had fallen upon all of them. He recalled how the Lord said that John would baptize with water but "ye shall be baptized with the Holy Ghost." Then he admonished them, "Forasmuch then as God gave them the like gift as he did unto us, who believed on the Lord Jesus Christ; what was I, that I could withstand God?" The apostles and brethren then held their peace and glorified God, saying, "Then hath God also to the Gentiles granted repentance" *(vs. 1-18).* The disciples were first called Christians in Antioch *(v. 26).*

Acts 12:3-17. Peter was arrested by Herod and put in prison. Four squads of four men each were placed to guard him. On the night prior to when Herod planned to have him brought forth, Peter had to sleep between two soldiers, bound with two chains. Keepers before the door kept the prison. Meanwhile, the church members prayed unceasingly unto God. While Peter and the soldiers were sleeping, an angel of the Lord came and awakened him and led him to freedom. He went to the house of Mary the mother of John Mark, where many were gathered together praying. When Peter knocked at the door of the gate, a damsel named Rhoda answered, but rather than letting him in, she ran to report that Peter stood outside the gate. The people didn't believe her, but when he continued knocking, they finally opened the door and were astonished. He told them how the Lord had delivered him and told them to go tell James and the brethren. Then he went into another place.

Acts 15:7-11. Peter, when considering the question of circumcision, reminded the apostles and other brethren that the Lord put no difference between them and the Gentiles who accepted the truth, and suggested they not tempt God, "to put a yoke upon the neck of the disciples" and reminded them that it is through the "grace of the Lord Jesus Christ we shall be saved, even as they" *(and not because of circumcision). (Note: James refers to Peter as* ***Simeon*** *in verse 14.)*

1 Cor. 1:12. The saints in Corinth had contentions among them with some saying they were of Cephas (Peter), and others saying they were of Paul or Apollos or Christ.

1 Cor. 9:5. Using Peter as an example, Paul responded to those who questioned his apostleship or actions and indicated that even though he was an apostle, he was still free to eat and drink and enjoy family relationships as were the other apostles, including Cephas (*Peter*), and the brothers of the Lord.

1 Cor. 15:5. Cephas saw the Lord following his resurrection.

Gal. 2:7-16. The gospel of the circumcision was committed unto Peter while the gospel of the uncircumcision was committed unto Paul. Cephas, James and John extended their right hands of fellowship to Paul and Barnabas when Paul, Barnabas and Titas went to Jerusalem and met with the leaders of the church and satisfied them that what they were teaching was the same thing the leaders were teaching. Paul met with Peter and contended with him over a point of church policy. Peter was the head of the church and Paul was subject to his direction. Nevertheless, Paul stood firm in the belief that they should walk "uprightly according to the truth of the gospel." Peter tried to avoid offending the Jewish semi-converts by placating those who still kept the law of Moses.

1 Pet. 1. Peter addressed his first epistle to the strangers *(which, according to the BD probably meant those who were non-Israelite by birth)* scattered throughout Pontus, Galatia, Cappadocia, Asia and Bithynia. Peter explained that the elect, those who receive the gospel, were foreordained to do so according to the foreknowledge of God the Father and on condition of obedience to gospel principles. Just as Christ was raised from the dead, the faithful shall also be raised and receive an incorruptible inheritance. We are placed on earth to live by faith: to believe in Christ, to love him and follow his teachings never having seen him. The trial of our faith precedes salvation. The end goal of faith is the salvation of our souls *(vs. 1-9)*. A testimony of Jesus Christ and his teachings as taught by the prophets is confirmed by the Holy Ghost *(vs. 10-12)*. Peter admonished them to be holy in their conversation, for the Lord is holy *(vs. 15-16)*. The Father is no respecter of persons and judges every man according to his works *(v. 17)*. We are redeemed by the blood of Christ who was foreordained to be the Savior before the foundation of the world. We were not bought with silver or gold or any other corruptible thing *(vs. 18-20)*. Peter counseled them to love one another with a pure heart *(v. 22)*. Those who believe in Christ are born again, not of corruptible material (like our mortal bodies), but will receive incorruptible bodies according to the word of God. The word of the Lord endures forever *(vs. 23-25).*

1 Pet. 2. Peter compared new converts to newborn babies and encouraged them to seek after the genuine and simple truths of the gospel *(vs. 1-2).* Peter referred to Christ as the living stone who was disallowed by men, but who was made the chief corner stone of the plan of salvation. Peter referred to faithful members of the church as "lively stones" and told them they were built up as part of a spiritual house with a holy priesthood to offer up spiritual sacrifices that would be acceptable unto God by Jesus Christ *(vs. 4-5).* Those who believe on Christ will not be confounded *(will be saved),* but to those who do not believe and are rebellious, he will be a stumbling stone *(vs. 6-8).* Those who accept and follow Christ *(both anciently, in the meridian of time, and in these latter days)* are a chosen generation, a royal priesthood *(they are blessed to have the power of the priesthood),* a holy nation and a peculiar people *(peculiar in that they do not follow the ways of the world).* Formerly, they may not have been believers and were not "a people;" however, having become members of Christ's church, they "are now the people of God" *(vs. 9-10).* Peter refers to his readers as "Dearly beloved," and urges them to abstain from worldliness and to let their good works shine forth so that others seeing their good works will glorify their Father who is in heaven. He encouraged them to obey all the laws of the land, to submit to government officials, honor the king and all men, fear God; and, in the case of servants, willingly subject themselves to their masters, indicating that "by well doing ye may put to silence the ignorance of foolish men." He also stressed that it was thankworthy if a man endured grief and suffering wrongfully, because there was no glory in suffering if the suffering were for one's own faults. He reminded them that Christ suffered for no fault of his own but for our faults, and said we should follow his example *(vs. 11-21).* Without the gospel, the people were as sheep going astray, but with the gospel, they have "returned unto the Shepherd and Bishop *(overseer)* of your souls" *(v. 25).*

1 Pet. 3. Peter taught that wives should submit themselves unto their husbands just as Sara (Sarah) obeyed Abraham. He also taught that those husbands who did not accept the gospel may be won by the conduct of their wives. Women should be more concerned about adorning the spirit rather than the body *(vs. 1-6).* Husbands were also counseled to honor their wives. Husbands and wives are heirs together of eternal life *(v. 7).* The people were admonished to be of one mind; not to return evil for evil, but to return a blessing for evil; control their tongues; eschew evil and do good. The eyes of the Lord are upon the righteous and hears their prayers. His face is against those who do evil *(vs. 8-12).* It is better to suffer for doing what's right than for doing evil. Christ suffered for the sins of all people, both living and dead. After Christ's death, he went to preach to the spirits who were in prison who had rejected the truth in the days of Noah. The mere act of baptism does not save us *(the people in Noah's day were covered with water, but that did not save them because they were wicked),* we must repent of our sins. Baptism is effective in our lives because of the atonement and resurrection of Christ who has ascended into heaven and is on the right hand of God *(vs. 13-22).*

1 Pet. 4. We should be willing to suffer for righteousness sake, even as Christ did. It is a reflection of one's having turned away from the sins of the flesh and willingness to follow the will of God. Prior to accepting the gospel, the people walked in the ways of the Gentiles, and now the Gentiles think it strange that they no longer walk with them. Nevertheless, people will have to give account of their actions at the judgment bar. Christ will judge the quick and the dead *(vs. 1-5)*. The gospel is preached to the spirits of those who have already died and who are in prison so they can have the same opportunity to accept the truth just as those who are living have the opportunity to accept the truth, and can be judged accordingly *(v. 6)*. The people were admonished to have charity (charity prevents a multitude of sins); and to be hospitable to one another. Every thing they do should be done as Christ would do it: minister as good stewards and speak as the oracles of God—that God may be glorified in all things *(vs. 8-11)*. He counseled them to rejoice in their trials when they suffer for righteousness for so even did Christ. Christ is glorified in their suffering, and when his suffering is revealed, they will also be glad with exceeding joy. No one should be ashamed for suffering for the name of Christ; however, Peter admonished them not to suffer as a murderer or other evil doer *(vs. 12-19)*.

1 Pet. 5. Peter affirmed his priesthood calling as an elder in the church, and stressed that the elders should teach the gospel to their flock. They should not use force nor money; nor should they use their priesthood leadership position to control the people, but they should be examples to their people. If they fulfill their calling as the Lord directs, when Christ appears in the latter days, they shall receive a crown of glory that will not fade away *(vs. 1-4)*. The younger members of the church were counseled to obey their elders *(presumably both parents and those in authority in the church)*. Humility leads to exaltation in due time *(vs. 5-6)*. He cautioned them to be vigilant against the adversary *(the devil),* and assured them that he and his colleagues were being buffeted by Satan the same as they *(vs. 8-10)*. It would appear that Peter sent his epistle via Silvanus (Silas). He, the church at Babylon, and Marcus sent their greetings *(vs. 12-13)*.

2 Pet. 1. Peter wrote to the members of the church who had attained faith like unto his and the other apostles. He exhorted them to make their calling and election sure by adding to faith, virtue; to virtue, knowledge; to knowledge, temperance; to temperance, patience; to patience, godliness; to godliness, brotherly kindness; and to brotherly kindness, charity. Peter said if they do those things, they will be able to enter into the everlasting kingdom of our Lord and Savior, Jesus Christ *(vs. 1-11)*. Peter said as long as he was alive, he would continue to stir them up into a remembrance of those things that are so important. Acknowledging that he would shortly leave mortality, he desired to make sure that the saints would always be able to keep these things in remembrance, even after his decease *(vs. 12-15)*. He and the brethren did not teach fables. They were eyewitnesses of Christ's majesty. While in the holy mount, they heard a voice from heaven declaring, "This is my beloved Son, in whom I am well pleased." They also have a more sure word of prophecy: God sends his word through prophets who prophesy as they are moved upon by the Holy Ghost. "No prophecy of the scripture is of any private interpretation" *(vs. 16-21)*.

2 Pet. 2. Peter warned the saints that just as there were false prophets among the people, false teacher would also come among them. He condemned false teachers and reminded the saints of the destruction that came upon the angels who fought on the side of Lucifer before the world was formed and were cast down to hell; the people of Noah's day who rejected the truth (only Noah and seven others were saved from the flood); and the cities of Sodom and Gomorrha (only Lot and his two daughters were ultimately saved) *(vs. 1-7)*. Nevertheless, the Lord knows how to deliver the godly out of temptation and reserve the unjust unto the day when they will be judged and receive their punishment *(v. 9)*. The wicked, who have chosen to follow Balaam the son of Bosor (Beor) and love the wages of unrighteousness, shall perish in their own corruption *(vs. 12-15)*. The wicked promise liberty, but are the servants of corruption. It would be better for a person never to have accepted the gospel than to have a knowledge of the truth and then turn from it and go back to the ways of the world *(vs. 19-21)*.

2 Pet. 3. Peter told his beloved saints that he wanted to stir them up again to a remembrance of the teachings of the holy prophets and of the apostles. He warned that scoffers will come in the latter days, walking after their own lusts and denying continuing revelation and the Second Coming of the Savior *(vs. 1-4)*. The same God that ruled in ancient days continues to rule the universe *(vs. 5-7)*. A thousand years is but a day with the Lord *(v. 8)*. At his Second Coming, the Lord will appear as a thief in the night; the heavens will pass away with a great noise; the elements shall melt; and the earth and the works that are therein shall be burned *(v. 10)*. The Lord has promised that there will be new heavens and a new earth upon which the righteous will dwell *(v. 13)*. Peter reminded the saints that Paul had also written to them of these same teachings of salvation. For the unlearned and the unstable, some things are hard to understand unto their own destruction. However, his beloved saints knew these things. Nevertheless, he encouraged them to continue growing from grace to grace and in the knowledge of the Lord lest they fall into error and away from their own steadfastness *(vs. 15-18)*.

PETER'S MOTHER-IN-LAW

Matt. 8:14-15; Mark 1:30-31; Luke 4:38-39. **PETER'S MOTHER-IN-LAW** was sick with a fever. When Jesus entered Peter's house, he touched her hand and she was healed. She arose and ministered unto them.

PHANUEL

Luke 2:36. **PHANUEL**, of the tribe of Asher, was the father of Anna the prophetess.

PHARISEES

Matt. 3:7. **PHARISEES** and Sadducees who came to Jesus' baptism were denounced by Jesus who called them a generation of vipers.

Matt. 9; Mark 2; Luke 5. Pharisees and the disciples of John fasted oft, but Jesus' disciples did not fast. John's disciples asked Jesus why this was so. He told them that while the bridegroom was with them, they had no cause to mourn. However, he said that when the bridegroom is taken from them, they, too, would fast *(v. 14; Mark 2:18-20; Luke 5:33-35)*. When Jesus cast a devil out of a dumb man, the Pharisees claimed he cast out devils through the prince of the devils *(v. 34)*.

Matt. 12; Mark 3; Luke 6. The Pharisees criticized Jesus for plucking corn on the Sabbath *(vs. 2- 9; Mark 2:23-24; Luke 6:1-2)* and for healing a man's withered hand on the Sabbath. Jesus told them it was lawful to do good on the Sabbath *(vs. 10-13; Mark 3:1-5; Luke 6:6-10).* They held a council to devise ways they might destroy him. He withdrew from the area and told his followers not to make his whereabouts known *(vs. 14-16; Mark 3:6-7; Luke 6:11).* When Jesus cast out devils, they claimed it was by the power of Beelzebub the prince of the devils *(v. 24; Mark 3:22; Luke 11:15).* The Pharisees and scribes asked for a sign. Jesus said the only sign they would be given was the sign of Jonas (Jonah) who was in the belly of the whale three days and three nights. Likewise, the Son of Man would be in the heart of the earth three days and three nights. The men of Nineveh and the queen of Sheba will stand in judgment of this generation because of their lack of faith and refusing to listen to one greater than either Jonah or Solomon *(vs. 38-41; Luke 11:16, 29-32).*

Matt. 15:1-11; Mark 7:1-5, 13-22; Luke 11:37-44. The Pharisees and scribes asked Jesus why his disciples transgressed the tradition of the elders by not washing their hands before eating. Jesus told them that it is not what goes into the mouth that defiles a person, but that which comes out of the mouth. He also called them hypocrites and said they failed to honor their fathers and mothers. He rebuked them for honoring the Lord with their lips, and said their hearts were far from him. *(The account in Luke is worded differently, but the message is the same.)*

Matt. 16; Mark 8; Luke 11, 12. The Pharisees and Sadducees tried to tempt Jesus by asking for a sign from heaven. Jesus pointed out that they could read the signs forecasting the weather i.e., red in the morning equals bad weather, red at night equals fair weather; but that they couldn't discern the signs of the times *(vs. 1-3; Luke 12:54-57).* He reprimanded them and said a wicked and adulterous generation seeks for signs. The only sign they would be given was the sign of Jonas (i.e., Jonah), who was in the belly of the whale three days, signifying Christ would be in the earth three days before his resurrection *(v. 4; Luke 11:29).* Jesus warned his disciples to beware of the leaven (i.e., doctrine) of the Pharisees and Sadducees *(vs. 6-12; Mark 8:15; Luke 12:1).*

Matt. 19:3, 7-9; Mark 10:2-12; Luke 16:18. The Pharisees tried to entrap Jesus by asking him about divorce since Moses had commanded that a letter of divorcement could be written and a wife could be "put away." Jesus told them that it was not that way in the beginning and the only reason Moses allowed for it was because of the hardness of the hearts of the people, and that whosoever put his wife away, except for the cause of fornication, and married another committed adultery. Additionally, he said that whosoever married the woman who had been put away also committed adultery. *(Note: Mark adds: "And if a woman shall put away her husband, and be married to another, she committeth adultery.")*

Matt. 21:33-46; Mark 12:12; Luke 20:9-19. The Pharisees and chief priests recognized that Jesus' parable regarding the wicked husbandmen pertained to them. However, they didn't dare lay hands on him because the people regarded Jesus as a prophet.

Matt. 22; Mark 12; Luke 20. The Pharisees, seeking to entangle Jesus, asked him if it was lawful to pay tribute to Cæsar. Jesus said to render unto Cæsar that which is Cæsar's and unto God that which is God's *(vs. 15-21; Mark 12:13-17; Luke 20:20-26)*. Again, the Pharisees [a scribe] sought to entangle Jesus and asked him which was the greatest commandment in the law. Jesus told them the first commandment was to love God and the second was like unto it to love their neighbor as themselves, and that on these two commandments hang all the law and the prophets *(vs. 34-40)*. Jesus asked the Pharisees, "What think ye of Christ?" They responded he was the Son of David. Jesus countered that David, in spirit [in the book of Psalms], called Christ Lord, so how then could Christ be his son *(vs. 41-46; Mark 12:35-37; Luke 20:41-44)*.

Matt. 23. The Pharisees and scribes were condemned and called hypocrites by Jesus. He counseled the people to follow their teachings but not their works because "they say, and do not" *(v. 3)* and appear beautiful and righteous on the outside but inside they are full of iniquity and hypocrisy *(v. 28)*. They, along with their forefathers, kill the prophets and will not escape the damnation of hell *(vs. 29-35)*. Jesus lamented, "O Jerusalem, Jerusalem, . . . how often would I have gathered thy children together, even as a hen gathereth her chickens under her wings, and ye would not!" *(v. 37. Also see Luke 13:34 for a similar lament.)*

Matt. 27. The Pharisees and chief priests petitioned Pilate to place a guard at the sepulchre following Jesus' crucifixion so his disciples could not come in the night and steal his body away. Pilate told them to do it and they did *(vs. 62-66)*.

Mark 2. The Pharisees and certain scribes were appalled that Jesus ate meat with publicans and sinners. He taught them that he didn't come to call the righteous to repentance, but the sinner *(vs. 15-17)*. They complained that Jesus' disciples didn't fast but the disciples of John and of the Pharisees did. Jesus taught that while he was with them there was no need to fast. When the bridegroom was taken from them, then they would have need to fast *(vs. 18-20)*. The Pharisees complained that Jesus' disciples plucked ears of corn on the Sabbath. Jesus reminded them of what king David had done when he was hungry, and that the Sabbath was made for man, not man for the Sabbath. He also taught them that the Son of Man is Lord also of the Sabbath *(vs. 24-28)*.

Mark 3. See entry for Matt. 12.

Mark 7. The Pharisees were chastised by Jesus for following false traditions such as the excessive washing of hands. That which goes into a man's mouth is not what defiles the man (for it comes out in the "draught"), but that which comes forth out of the mouth (which originates from out of the heart)—evil thoughts, adulteries, murders, thefts, etc.—are what defile a man *(vs. 1-5, 13-22). (See entry from Matt. 15. Also see Luke 11:37-44.)* Esaias (Isaiah) had correctly prophesied of them: "This people honoureth me with their lips, but their heart is far from me" *(v. 6)*.

Mark 8; Matt. 16; Luke 12. The Pharisees sought a sign from heaven. Jesus said there would be no sign given unto that generation *(vs. 11-12; Matt. 16:1-4)*. Jesus warned his disciples to beware of the leaven (false teachings) of the Pharisees and Herod *(v. 15; Matt. 16:6-12; Luke 12:1)*.

Mark 10:2-12. See entry for Matt. 19.

Mark 12. See entries for Matt. 19, 21-22.

Luke 6. See entry for Matt. 12.

Luke 13:31, 34. The Pharisees came to Jesus and told him to depart from Jerusalem "for Herod will kill thee." Jesus lamented how oft he would have gathered the people like a mother hen gathers her brood, but they would not. *(See Matt. 23:37, for a similar lament.)*

Luke 14:1-6. One of the chief Pharisees hosted Jesus on the Sabbath day. As Jesus entered his home to eat bread with him, he met a man with dropsy and healed him. To counter the criticism of the Pharisees and lawyers, Christ asked if they wouldn't rescue an ass or an ox if either of them fell into a pit on the Sabbath.

Luke 15. The Pharisees and scribes murmured because Christ surrounded himself with sinners *(vs. 1-2).* Thus, Christ took the opportunity to teach them of the great joy that comes when that which is lost is found again, and he illustrated that message through three parables: (1) the parable of the lost sheep *(vs. 3-7);* (2) the parable of the piece of silver *(vs. 8-10);* and (3) the parable of the prodigal son *(vs.11-32).*

Luke 19:39-40. When some of the Pharisees wanted Jesus to rebuke his disciples because they went before him as he rode an ass into Jerusalem, praising him as the King that cometh in the name of the Lord, Christ rebuked the Pharisees and said that if the disciples should hold their peace, the stones would immediately cry out.

John 1:24-25. The Pharisees sent some of their people to inquire of John the Baptist why he was performing baptisms if he was neither Christ nor Elias.

John 4:1-3. The Pharisees heard that Jesus (his disciples, not Jesus, himself) baptized more disciples than John, so Jesus left Judæa and went to Galilee.

John 7. When the Pharisees heard the people murmuring against Christ, they and the chief priests sent officers to arrest him. However, no one laid hands on him because his time was not yet come *(vs. 32-33).* When the Pharisees, officers and chief priests were disputing over Christ, with some seeking to lay hands on him, Nicodemus reminded them that the law provided for a man to be heard before being judged *(vs. 50-51).*

John 8. While Jesus was teaching in the temple, the scribes and Pharisees brought a woman to him who was taken in adultery. Jesus stooped down and seemingly ignored their questions as he wrote on the ground. After repeated questioning by the Pharisees, Jesus suggested, "He that is without sin among you, let him first cast a stone at her." One-by-one the accusers all quietly left. When Jesus finally looked up, he asked the woman where her accusers were. She told him that no one had condemned her. Jesus told her that neither did he, and " . . . go and sin no more" *(vs. 2-11).* Jesus is the light of the world *(v. 12).* The Pharisees challenged Christ's claim of divine Sonship because he testified of himself. However, Christ reminded them that it was written in the law that the testimony of two men is true and that both he and the Father bore witness that Jesus is the Christ *(vs. 12-19).*

John 9. After Jesus healed the eyes of a man who had been blind from birth, neighbors hauled the man before the Pharisees who asked him how he had gained his vision. When he told them, some called Christ a sinner for having healed on the Sabbath; others said a sinner could not perform miracles *(vs. 13-16).* Jesus lectured the Pharisees on being spiritually blind *(vs. 39-41).*

John 11. The Pharisees were informed of Jesus' raising Lazarus from the dead by some of the Jews who had gone to comfort Mary when her brother died *(v. 46).* The Pharisees and chief priests gathered together a council and plotted how to take Jesus that they might put him to death *(vs. 47-53).* When the Jews Passover was near, they issued a command that whosoever knew where Jesus was, they were to inform them so they could take him *(v. 57).*

John 18:3-12, 22. A band of men and officers from the Pharisees and chief priests were led by Judas to the garden where Jesus and his disciples were. Peter smote the ear off of Malchus, one of the servants. *(See Matt. 26:47-51, 57; Mark 14:47; Luke 22:49-50 for variations of this same incident.)* The band and the captain and officers of the Jews bound Jesus and took him to Anna, the father-in-law of Caiaphas the high priest. When an officer took offense at Christ's response to Caiaphas' questions, he struck Jesus with his palm.

Acts 23:6-9. Because the Pharisees believed in both angels and the resurrection, Paul appealed to the portion of the council in Jerusalem comprised of Pharisees as he pleaded his case. The scribes of the Pharisees' part of the council arose and cried that they found no evil in Paul. A great dissension arose and Claudius Lysias, the chief captain, sent soldiers to rescue Paul and take him to the castle.

Acts 26:5. Prior to Paul's conversion, he lived as a Pharisee.

(Note: Pharisees are defined as "separated; a member of a school or party among the ancient Jews who were noted for strict and formal observance of rites and ceremonies of the written law and for insistence on the validity of the traditions of the elders. They believed in the immortality of the soul and in the resurrection of the body, future retribution, and a coming Messiah. Their interpretation provided the standard of observance and belief for the great majority of Jews from the 1st century A.D." (WTNID, vol II, "Pharisee," p. 1694). The BD adds that they believed in the existence of angels and spirits. They upheld the authority of oral tradition *as of equal value with* the written law."

PHEBE

Rom. 16:1, footnote. **PHEBE** was one of the women who served in the church in Cenchrea. She was the courier who delivered Paul's epistle to the saints in Rome.

PHILEMON

Philem. **PHILEMON**, a beloved and fellowlaborer with Paul, was the owner of Onesimus, the slave who ran away and joined Paul. Paul sent Onesimus back to Philemon with a letter wherein Paul requested Philemon to accept Onesimus, not as a servant but as a brother *(vs. 10-16).* He said he would have retained Onesimus "with me, that in thy stead he might have ministered unto me in the bonds of the gospel;" however, Paul said he would do nothing without consulting Philemon first *(vs. 13-14).* Paul requested that if Onesimus owed something to Philemon, to put it on Paul's account *(v. 17).* Paul asked Philemon to prepare him a place to stay because he expected to pay him a visit *(v. 22).* He sent greetings to and from others *(vs. 23-24).*

PHILETUS

2 Tim. 2:16-17. **PHILETUS** and Hymenæus were named by Paul as two apostates whose words destroyed their faith. Paul warned that those who engage in profane and vain babblings increase in ungodliness, "and their word will eat as doth a canker."

PHILIP (1)

Matt. 10; Luke 9. **PHILIP** was one of Jesus' 12 disciples: Simon Peter, Andrew, James, John, Philip, Bartholomew; Thomas, Matthew, James, Lebbæus (Thaddæus), Simon the Canaanite, and Judas Iscariot *(vs. 2-4).* Jesus empowered these apostles and sent them forth to teach, but instructed them that they should not go to the Gentiles nor to the Samaritans. They were to go to the lost sheep of the house of Israel. They were to heal the sick and cast out devils. They were to travel without purse or scrip. They were instructed to leave their peace upon those who received them, but to shake the dust off their feet when leaving the houses of those who reject them *(vs. 5-14; Luke 9:1-5).* They were told they would be persecuted for Christ's sake, but that "he that endureth to the end shall be saved." They are of more value than the sparrows for which the Father provides. Even the hairs of their heads are numbered *(vs. 16-32).*

John 1:43-45. Jesus called Philip to follow him. Philip found Nathanael and told him they had found Jesus of Nazareth, the son of Joseph, of whom Moses and the prophets had written.

John 6:5-7. Jesus, knowing what he himself planned to do, asked Philip, in order to prove him, where they could buy bread to feed the multitude. Philip responded that two hundred pennyworth of bread would not be enough to feed the crowd.

John 12:21-22. Philip was approached by certain Greeks who came to the feast of the Passover and wanted to see Jesus. Philip told Andrew and, together, they told Jesus.

John 14:8-11. Philip asked Jesus to show him and his fellow disciples the Father. Jesus said he that hath seen him hath seen the Father, that he is in the Father and the Father is in him.

Acts 1:13-14. Following Jesus' ascension into heaven, Jesus' disciples, including Philip, met together in an upper room, along with several women (including Mary the mother of Jesus) and his brethren, where they continued in prayer and supplication.

PHILIP (2)

Matt. 14:3; Mark 6:17; Luke 3:19. **PHILIP** was the brother of Herod the tetrarch and the husband of Herodias. John the Baptist rebuked Herod for taking his brother Philip's wife. He died A.D. 33.

Luke 3:1. Philip was tetrarch of Ituræa when Tiberius Cæsar was in the fifteenth year of his reign and John the Baptist came into the country about Jordan, preaching the baptism of repentance for the remission of sins. *(Note: His mother was Cleopatra. When Herod the Great died, his realm was divided between three of his sons: Antipas, i.e., Herod the tetrarch; Archelaus and Philip. Philip's area was the N.E. district of Palestine. When he died, his land was given to his half-nephew, Agrippa I (EB, vol. V, pp. 2-3, vol. VII, p. 940)).*

PHILIP (3)

Acts 6:5. **PHILIP** was one of the seven men the apostles chose and set apart to help them with the work.

Acts 8. Philip preached in Samaria, healing people with palsies and casting out unclean spirits. Many people believed and were baptized, including a man named Simon *(vs. 5-13).* Philip was instructed by an angel of the Lord to go down from Jerusalem unto Gaza. He beheld a eunuch from Ethiopia, one of great authority under Candace queen of Ethiopia, and the Spirit instructed Philip to go to the eunuch (who was reading Esaias, i.e., Isaiah, in the scriptures). Philip explained the scriptural passage to the eunuch and taught him the gospel. The eunuch believed and was baptized. Philip was then "caught away" by the "Spirit of the Lord" and the eunuch saw him no more. However, Philip was found in Azotus. He preached in the cities around until he came to Cæsarea *(vs. 26-40).*

Acts 21:8-9. Philip the evangelist hosted Paul and his company in Cæsarea, and they abode with him for many day. Philip had four daughters, virgins, who prophesied.

PHILIPPIANS

Act 16. **PHILIPPIANS** were citizens of Philippi, a city of Macedonia *(v. 12).* When Paul visited Philippi, he and Silas were beaten and cast into prison *(vs. 22-23).* A great earthquake shook the foundation of the prison and burst open the doors. When the magistrate sent word to let Paul and Silas go, Paul refused, saying they had beaten them openly uncondemned, being Romans, and that the magistrates needed to come and release them personally, which they did *(vs. 25-39). (Note: Philippi was founded by Philip, the father of Alexander the Great. It was a Roman colony which contained some Roman citizens who had been placed there for military purposes. See Philippi in the BD.)*

Philip. 1. The saints in Philippi were dear to the heart of Paul and he said he thanked the Lord "upon each remembrance of you." He commended them for their fellowship in the gospel, "from the first day until now" *(vs. 1-5).* He said that God knew how much he loved them and how he longed for them in the "bowels of Jesus Christ" *(v. 8).* As great as their love was for one another, he encouraged them to increase that love even more, "in knowlege and in all judgment" *(v. 9).* Paul assured the Philippians that everything that had happened to him (bad as well as good, in prison or out) helped further the cause of the gospel. Many of the brethren were strengthened and grew in confidence after observing Paul. Some people, he said, preached insincerely, hoping to add to his bondage, and others preached out of love knowing he was set to defend the gospel. Regardless of the purpose behind the preaching, it all preached of Christ and would turn to Paul's salvation; and Christ would be magnified whether by Paul's life or by his death *(vs. 12-20).* While Paul desired to leave this earth and go with Christ, he told the Philippians it was better for them for him to stay *(vs. 23-24).* The Philippians were encouraged to continue living and speaking in ways consistent with the gospel, "that ye stand fast in one spirit, with one mind striving together for the faith of the gospel." He counseled them not to fear their adversaries: it was given to them "not only to believe on him, but also to suffer for his sake" *(any persecution they experienced would be in place of Christ, receiving that which the wicked would have heaped upon the Savior if he were present) (vs. 27-29).*

Philip. 2. The Philippians were encouraged to be of one accord and of one mind: to esteem each other even better than themselves. Paul also counseled them to look to the welfare of others and not only to their own welfare; thus, they would be acting as Christ did *(vs. 1-5).* Christ was in the form of God: it took nothing from God for Christ to be equal with God *(v. 6).* Nevertheless, Christ chose to be a servant and humbled himself, even to the extent of allowing himself to be hung on the cross *(vs. 7-8).* Therefore, God exalted Christ, and every knee shall bow and every tongue confess that Jesus is Lord, to the glory of God the Father *(vs. 9-11).* Paul commended his beloved saints for their faithful obedience and encouraged them to be even moreso in his absence as they continued to work out their own salvation with fear and trembling *(v. 12).* He admonished them to avoid murmurings and disputation—to shine as lights in the midst of a crooked and perverse nation *(vs. 14-15).* He said he planned to send Timotheus to them shortly and that he hoped to come himself before too long *(vs. 19-24).* Paul sent his epistle to the Philippians via Epaphroditus, who had carried a message to Paul from the Philippians earlier. Epaphroditus had been ill but was now better, and Paul hoped his return to Philippi would alleviate the saints' concerns *(vs. 25-30).*

Philip. 3. Paul cautioned the Philippians to beware of false teachings and those who would try to lead them astray: "Beware of dogs, beware of evil workers, beware of the concision" *(i.e. cutting off, division) (v. 2).* Paul reminded them that circumcision was the law of the flesh, but that circumcision of the spirit is what God required of them *(v. 3).* He pointed out to them that if being born Jewish, being circumcised, conforming to the Mosaic law and ritual and persecuting the church brought salvation, than Paul had few peers. Things that previously brought him status, he said, "Those I counted loss for Christ" *(vs. 4-7).* Paul said he suffered the loss of all things that he might win Christ and attain unto the resurrection of the dead *(vs. 8-11).* His goal was "the prize of the high calling of God in Christ Jesus" *(i.e., eternal life) (v. 14).* Paul reminded his brethren to follow those whose example was the same as Paul's and not to follow those who are "the enemies of the cross of Christ" *(vs. 17-19).* Followers of Christ, in the resurrection, will receive bodies like the Savior's *(i.e. celestial bodies),* "fashioned like unto his glorious body, according to the working whereby he is able even to subdue all things unto himself" *(vs. 20-21).*

Philip. 4. The Philippian saints were dearly beloved and longed for by Paul. He beseeched Euodias and Syntyche to be of the same mind in the Lord as he and the other faithful followers. He entreated the brethren to help the women in the church who had labored with him and Clement and other fellowlaborers in the gospel *(vs. 1-3).* He encouraged them to be moderate in all things, that their moderation might be known unto all men. They should be prayerful and thankful and make their requests known unto God, and he promised them that they would then have the peace of God, "which surpasseth all understanding," to be with them *(vs. 5-7).* Paul encouraged them to seek after all things that are honest, just, pure, lovely, virtuous or of good report or praiseworthy *(v. 8).* He appreciated their concern for him, acknowledging their lack of opportunity at times to assist him. He thanked them for the gifts they sent via Epaphroditus. He and the saints with him, chiefly those of Cæsar's house, sent their greetings to all the saints in Philippi *(vs. 10-23).*

PHILOLOGUS

Rom. 16:15. **PHILOLOGUS** and several other specific disciples, "and all the saints which are with them," were sent greetings by Paul in his epistle to the Romans.

PHLEGON

Rom. 16:14. **PHLEGON** and several other specific disciples, "and the brethren which are with them," were sent greetings by Paul in his epistle to the Romans.

PHYGELLUS

2 Tim. 1:15. **PHYGELLUS** was one of the apostates in Asia who turned away from Paul.

PONTIUS PILATE

Luke 3:1. **PONTIUS PILATE** was governor of Judæa when Tiberius Cæsar was in the fifteenth year of his reign and John the Baptist came into the country about Jordan, preaching the baptism of repentance for the remission of sins.

Matt. 27; Mark 15; Luke 23; John 18; also see entry for John 19. Pontius Pilate was the governor before whom the chief priests and elders of the people took Jesus to be tried for blasphemy *(v. 2; Mark 15:1; Luke 23:1).* Pilate found no wrong in Jesus and, having been warned by his wife to have nothing to do with Jesus, he desired to release him during the feast since one prisoner could be released. He gave the people a choice between Barabbas and Jesus. The people said to release Barabbas and crucify Jesus. He washed his hands before them and said he was innocent of his blood, and they could see to it. They agreed Jesus' blood would be upon them and upon their children. Then Pilate's soldiers took Jesus *(vs. 13-27; Mark 15:6-16; Luke 23:2-25; John 18:28-40). (Note: The account in Luke states that the people took Christ to Pilate, who subsequently sent him to Herod. Herod returned him again to Pilate, who wanted to release Jesus, but finally acquiesced to the people's demands.)*

John 19. Pilate scourged Jesus and, after the soldiers put a platted crown of thorns on Christ's head and smote him with their hands, took Jesus before the people and told them again that he found no fault in him. The chief priests and officers demanded that Pilate crucify Jesus, and the Jews said their laws required it "because he made himself the Son of God" *(vs. 1-7).* Pilate questioned Jesus again, but Jesus did not respond. In frustration, Pilate reminded Jesus that he had the power to free him. Jesus told him that the only power Pilate could have against him was that which was given to him from above and that the greater sin was upon those who had delivered Jesus to Pilate. Pilate continued to try to release Jesus, but the Jews said that if he did he was not a friend of Cæsar's *(vs. 8-13).* When the people continued to demand that Jesus be crucified, Pilate delivered him to them.

Jesus bore his cross to Golgotha where the people proceeded to crucify him along with two others—one on each side of him *(vs. 13-18)*. Pilate wrote a title in three languages—Hebrew, Greek and Latin—and had it placed on the cross. It read: "JESUS OF NAZARETH THE KING OF THE JEWS." The chief priests asked Pilate to change it and write, "He said, I am King of the Jews." Pilate refused and said, "What I have written, I have written" *(vs. 19-22)*. Because it was nearing the Sabbath and bodies were not to remain on the cross during the Sabbath, the people wanted Pilate to let them break the legs of those whom they had crucified so as to hasten their deaths *(v. 31)*. *(Note: Jesus was already dead so they did not break his legs.)* Joseph of Arimathæa got permission from Pilate to take Jesus' body *(v. 38)*.

Acts 4:27-28. "Pontius Pilate, Herod, the Gentiles and the people of Israel," Peter and John acknowledged before God, "were gathered together for to do whatsoever thy hand and thy counsel determined before to be done."

Acts 13:28. Pilate, at the demands of the people, suffered Jesus to be slain.

PONTIUS PILATE'S SOLDIERS

Matt. 27; Mark 15:16-20, 23, 21, 24; also see entry for John 19. **PONTIUS PILATE'S SOLDIERS** took Jesus and, with the help of the whole band of soldiers, stripped him, clothed him in a scarlet robe, placed a platted crown of thorns on his head, mocked him and spit on him. They made Simon of Cyrene help bear his cross. They gave Jesus vinegar to drink mingled with gall and crucified him. They parted his garments among themselves and placed a sign over Jesus' head that read, "THIS IS JESUS THE KING OF THE JEWS." And they sat and watched him on the cross *(vs. 27-37)*. The chief priests and Pharisees placed some soldiers as a watch to make sure Jesus' disciples did not come by night and steal his body away *(vs. 62-64)*.

Matt. 28:11-15. Some of the guard ran into the city and reported what had happened after the angel came and rolled the stone away from the sepulchre. The chief priests and elders bribed the soldiers with money to get them to falsely state that Jesus' disciples came by night and stole his body. They promised to protect them if word got to Pontius Pilate.

John 19. The soldiers put a platted crown of thorns on Christ's head and smote him with their hands after Pilate had scourged him. After Christ was crucified, the soldiers parted his garments four ways. Since Christ's coat was made without a seam, they decided to cast lots for it rather than tear it. Thus, the prophesy recorded in Psalm 22:18 was fulfilled: "They part my garments among them, and cast lots upon my vesture" *(vs. 23-24)*. Because it was nearing the Sabbath and bodies were not to remain on the cross during the Sabbath, the people wanted Pilate to let them break the legs of those whom they had crucified so as to hasten their deaths. The soldiers broke the legs of the two thieves who had been crucified with Jesus but, when they came to Jesus, they found that he was already dead so they did not break his legs. Nevertheless, one of the soldiers pierced his side with a sword. This fulfilled the scriptures recorded in Exodus 12:46: ". . . neither shall ye break a bone thereof;" in Numbers 9:12: "They shall leave none of it unto the morning, nor break any bone of it: according to all the ordinances of the passover they shall keep it;" and in Zechariah 12:10: " . . . and they shall look upon me whom they have pierced . . ." *(vs. 31-37).*

PONTIUS PILATE'S WIFE

Matt. 27:19. **PONTIUS PILATE'S WIFE** encouraged her husband to have nothing to do with judging Jesus, "that just man: for I have suffered many things this day in a dream because of him."

POOR WIDOW, A

Mark 12:41-44; Luke 21:1-4. **A POOR WIDOW** threw two mites into the treasury. Jesus, observing, declared that she gave more than all those who were rich because she gave of her want while they gave of their abundance.

PORCIUS FESTUS

Acts 24:27. **PORCIUS FESTUS** succeeded Felix as the procurator of Judæa, where Paul was still kept bound.

Acts 25. Festus went to Jerusalem three days after arriving in Cæsarea. The high priest and chief of the Jews informed him against Paul and requested that he be sent to Jerusalem where they planned to lay in wait for him so as to kill him. Festus declined and said that Paul should remain in Cæsarea where he himself would be going shortly. He suggested that those who had complaint against Paul should go to Cæsarea with him and accuse Paul there, "if there be any wickedness in him." Ten days later, when he returned to Cæsarea and sat upon the judgment seat, he sent for Paul. The Jews made their complaints, which they could not prove *(vs. 1-7).* Paul answered for himself and said that he had not offended against the law of the Jews, nor against the temple, nor against Cæsar. When Festus asked if Paul would be willing to go up to Jerusalem and be judged there, Paul said he would be willing to stand before Cæsar's judgment seat. Festus agreed to have Paul go before Cæsar *(vs. 8-12).* A few days later, King Agrippa and Bernice visited Festus. Festus discussed his dilemma regarding Paul with Agrippa: the Jews complaints didn't amount to anything worthy of death, and Paul had appealed to be heard by Augustus. Agrippa said he wanted to hear Paul himself. Festus agreed that on the morrow they would hear Paul. When Festus, King Agrippa, Bernice, and others present were ready, Festus explained that, because he found nothing worthy of death in Paul, he had determined to send him to Augustus. However, he felt he should send a letter detailing the crimes laid against him and hoped that they, after hearing Paul, could help him come up with what to include in the letter *(vs. 13-27).*

Acts 26:30-32. Festus, King Agrippa, Bernice and those who were with them, drew aside and conferred after Paul's presentation. They concluded that Paul had done nothing worthy of death or of bonds. Agrippa told Festus that if Paul had not appealed unto Cæsar, he might have been set free.

PRISCILLA (Prisca)

Acts 18:2, 18, 24-26. **PRISCILLA** was the wife of Aquila who was a tentmaker by occupation. Because Claudius had commanded all Jews to depart from Rome, Priscilla and Aquila left Italy and went to Corinth. Because Paul was of the same craft as Aquila, he stayed with them. When Paul sailed to Syria, he took Priscilla and Aquila with him, leaving them in Ephesus. When a certain Jew by the name of Apollos came to Ephesus, preaching diligently but only knowing the baptism of John, Priscilla and Aquila took him and taught him "the way of God more perfectly."

Rom. 16:3-4. Priscilla and Aquila were Paul's helpers in the work. In Paul's epistles to the Romans, he commended Priscilla and Aquila to the Roman saints, and invited them to greet them. He told the saints that Priscilla and Aquila had put their own necks on the line for him. He and all the churches of the Gentiles were grateful to this couple.

1 Cor. 16:19. Priscila and Aquila sent greetings to the saints in Corinth via Paul's epistle.

2 Tim. 4:19. Paul asked Timothy to salute **Prisca** (Priscilla) and Aquila for him.

PROCHORUS

Acts 6:5. **PROCHORUS** was one of the seven men the apostles chose and set apart to help them with the work.

PUBLICANS

Matt. 9:10-13; Mark 2:15-17. **PUBLICANS** and sinners were invited to have dinner with Jesus. The Pharisees [and scribes] questioned why Jesus ate with such people. Jesus responded that the whole man hath no need of a physician. He said he didn't come to call the righteous to repentance, but the sinner. *(Note: Publicans were men who bought or farmed the taxes under the Roman government. The name also applies to those who actually collected the taxes. They were despised by the Jews, and any Jew who undertook the work was excommunicated (BD).)*

Matt. 10:3. Matthew was a publican, i.e., a tax collector, and was one of Christ's original Twelve Apostles.

Matt. 21:31-32. The publicans and harlots, said Jesus, would go into the kingdom of God before the chief priests and elders because they believed John the Baptist; and the chief priests and elders did not.

Luke 3:12. Publicans asked Jesus what they needed to do to be baptized, and Jesus counseled them to exact no more from the people than what was appointed unto them.

Luke 5:27-29. Levi (known as Matthew after his conversion) was a publican who followed Christ's call to follow him.

Luke 7:29. When Jesus testified that there was no greater prophet than John the Baptist and said that he that is least in the kingdom of God is still greater than he, the publicans and all who heard him justified God, being baptized with the baptism of John.

Luke 15:1. Publicans and sinners drew near unto Jesus and Jesus gave them the parable of the lost sheep. Meanwhile, the Pharisees and scribes murmured because Christ associated with sinners.

Luke 18:13. Jesus gave the parable of the Pharisee and the publican: the Pharisee exalted himself, the publican humbled himself. Jesus taught that he that exalted himself will be abased; and he that humbleth himself shall be exalted.

Luke 19:2, 8. A rich man, chief among the publicans, was Zacchæus, a man short of stature, who desired to see Jesus and climbed up into a tree in order to catch a glimpse of him. *(See the entry for Zacchæus.)*

PUBLIUS

Acts 27:7-8. **PUBLIUS** was the chief man of the island of Melita where Paul and his companions stayed three months after being shipwrecked on the way to Rome. He lodged Paul for three days upon their arrival. Paul healed his father.

PUDENS

2 Tim. 4:21. **PUDENS** joined Paul and all the brethren in sending greetings to Timothy.

NAMES THAT BEGIN WITH "Q"

QUARTUS

Rom. 16:23. **QUARTUS** was "a brother" who joined with Paul and others in saluting the saints in Rome.

NAMES THAT BEGIN WITH "R"

RHODA

Acts 12:3-17. **RHODA** was the damsel who answered Peter's knock at the door of the gate to the house of John Mark's mother, Mary. Because Peter had been arrested by king Herod and put in prison, the people didn't believe Rhoda when she said it was Peter at the door. (However, Peter had been led to freedom by an angel.) When Peter continued knocking, they finally opened the door and were astonished. He told them how the Lord had delivered him and told them to go tell James and the brethren. Then he went into another place.

ROMANS

Rom. 1. **ROMANS**. Paul wrote an epistle to the saints in Rome. He praised them for their faithfulness *(vs. 1-8).* He expressed his desire to come unto them in person. He testified, "For I am not ashamed of the gospel of Christ; for it is the power of God unto salvation to every one that believeth; to the Jew first, and also to the Greek" *(v. 16).* The just shall live by faith. God's wrath is upon all ungodliness. God has revealed "the invisible things of him from the creation of the world . . . and are clearly seen, being understood by the things that are made, even his eternal power and Godhead; so that they are without excuse" *(vs. 17-20).* The people who failed to glorify God and, instead, made him into an image "made like to corruptible man, and to birds, and fourfooted beasts, and creeping things" were condemned *(vs. 21-23).* Because people became wicked, God gave them up unto uncleanness and unrighteousness: homosexuality, fornication, covetousness, envy, murder, deceit, haters of God, etc. Those who commit such sins are worthy of death *(vs. 24-32).*

Rom. 2. God will render unto every man—both Jew and Gentile—according to his deeds. Eternal life to those who live righteously, and tribulation and anguish upon every soul that does evil *(vs. 1-11).* Those who sin without law shall perish without law; those who sin in the law, will be judged by the law. Those who teach others to obey the law and do not obey it themselves, or who judge others according to the law yet break the law themselves, are condemned *(vs. 21-23).* Outward appearance does not justify a person as being a Jew, or of being circumcised. Circumcision must be of the heart, not of the body *(vs. 25-29).*

Rom. 3. God is God of both Jew and Gentile. Jew and Gentile are justified by righteousness and by faith through the redemption of Jesus Christ and his atoning sacrifice.

Rom. 4. Abraham's faith in God was counted unto him for righteousness. The promise given to Abraham that he should be heir of the world was not given according to the law but according to the righteousness of his faith *(vs. 3, 13).* The promise was not for Abraham only, but for all who believe on "him that raised up Jesus our Lord from the dead" *(vs. 23-24).*

Rom. 5. Christ died for us, and we are justified by his blood *(vs. 8-9).* Just as death was brought upon all mankind when one man (Adam) fell, so it is that through the atonement of one man (Jesus Christ), all mankind may be saved *(vs. 12-19).*

Rom. 6. Baptism is a similitude of the death, burial and resurrection of Jesus Christ *(vs. 3-5).* The wages of sin is death, but righteousness brings eternal life through Jesus Christ *(vs. 21-23).*

Rom. 7. Where there is a law, people are bound by the law *(vs. 1-3).* Jesus Christ fulfilled the law of Moses, making that law "dead" *(vs. 4-6).* Paul indicated that the law of Moses governed the physical body; the law of God governs the mind—the inward man *(vs. 21-25).*

Rom. 8. Paul taught that to be carnally minded *(preoccupied with worldly, bodily or sexual pleasures as opposed to spiritually minded)* is death, but that to be spiritually minded is life and peace *(v. 6).* Just as Christ was raised from the dead, so shall our mortal bodies be resurrected *(v. 11).* Those who are led by the spirit of God are the sons of God. We are bonded to God, not by fear, but by adoption. "The spirit itself beareth witness with our spirit, that we are the children of God: and if children, then heirs; heirs of God, and joint-heirs with Christ" *(vs. 14-17, 23).* We are saved by hope, and hope is not seen. The Holy Ghost makes intercession for the saints according to the will of God. All things work together for the good of those who love God *(vs. 24-28).* Christ was the firstborn of the Father. Heavenly Father knew us in a pre-existent state and foreordained those who would become his leaders here on earth *(vs. 29-30).* Christ is at the right hand of God and makes intercession for us *(v. 34).* Christ's love for us is constant. No outside influence can separate us nor cut us off from his love *(vs. 35-39).*

Rom. 9. The Israelites were chosen for adoption by the Lord. Not all that are actually descendants of Abraham are "Israel," for the promise was only given to the seed of Isaac. The promise given to Abraham involved the covenants, and the giving of the law, and the service of God which would fall upon Isaac's seed. The promise was given, not because of the righteousness of the seed (for they had not yet been born), but so that the purpose of God might be accomplished *(vs. 4-14).* Likewise, God raised up Pharaoh that his purposes might be fulfilled. Therefore, God will have mercy on those whom he will have mercy. He also hardens the hearts of those whom he will that his purposes might be brought forth *(vs. 15-23).* The Gentiles, through faith and righteousness, may also attain unto salvation. The law of righteousness must be sought by faith, not by the works of the law *(vs. 24-32).*

Rom. 10. Paul taught the Roman saints that those who testify of Christ with their mouths and believe in their hearts that God had raised him from the dead would be saved. With the heart, man "believeth unto righteousness," and with the mouth he makes confession unto salvation *(vs. 9-10).* The Lord is no respecter of persons: the Jew and the Greek who call upon the Savior are the same unto the Lord, and all those who call upon the Lord shall be saved *(vs. 12-13).* Paul posed the questions: "How can a person call on someone if they have never heard of him? How can they hear of him unless they are taught by someone? How can one preach unless they have been sent by the Lord?" Faith comes from hearing the word of God by the word of God *(vs. 14-17).*

Rom. 11. Paul was of the tribe of Benjamin *(v. 1).* Israel was foreordained to be the chosen people according to the election of grace. Grace is not of works or it is not grace. Works is not grace, or it is not works. Israel was chosen by grace *(vs. 2-7).* Many hardened their hearts against the truth and had eyes that should not see and ears that they should not hear *(vs. 8-10). (Also see Isa. 29:10 and Ps. 69:22.)* When the Jews rejected the gospel, it was taken to the Gentiles. They were grafted into the house of Israel like branches on a tree. Paul cautioned them to not boast against the natural branches which had been cut off. If they turn to unbelief, they will also be cut off. When the natural branches again turn to belief, they will be grafted back into the natural tree *(vs. 11-24).* The Israelites' rejection of God was a blessing for the Gentiles because the gospel was then taken to them. Nevertheless, the Israelites were chosen by election and are beloved for the fathers' sakes. The Gentiles have received mercy because of the Israelites unbelief. The Israelites, in turn, will receive mercy through the mercy of the Gentiles *(vs. 28-31).*

Rom. 12. Paul counseled the saints to serve the Lord, to "present your bodies a living sacrifice, holy, acceptable unto God." Just as there are different offices within the church, so are different gifts given to the members "according to the grace that is given to us." Each one should use the gift(s) he has been given *(vs. 4-8).* He stressed they should abhor evil and cleave unto that which is good; to love one another; to be diligent in business; to serve the Lord; to be patient, prayerful, and hopeful; to care for the needs of others; and to be hospitable *(vs. 9-13).* He reminded them to bless and rejoice with others; to weep with those who weep; to "recompense to no man evil for evil," and to be honest *(vs. 14-17).* He also charged them not to avenge themselves for it was written, "Vengeance is mine . . . saith the Lord." They should overcome evil with good *(vs. 19-21).*

Rom. 13. Paul counseled the saints to be subject unto those who are ordained of God—unto the "higher powers;" to love one another and to owe no man anything *(vs. 1-8).* He stressed the ten commandments: not to commit adultery; not to kill; not to covet nor bear false witness; to love one's neighbor as oneself *(vs. 9-10).* The time of our salvation is nearer than we realize and now is the time to become Christlike *(vs. 11-14).*

Rom. 14. People have varying degrees of faith. Avoid judging others because their degree of faith differs from our own *(vs. 1-9).* We should not judge others: we shall all stand before the judgment seat of Christ and every knee shall bow before him and confess to God. Don't put stumbling blocks before other people *(vs. 10-13).* The kingdom of God is not comprised of material things but of righteousness, peace and joy in the Holy Ghost; therefore, we should follow after those things that lift and edify others *(vs. 17-19).*

Rom. 15. The strong should bear the infirmities of the weak and edify his neighbor just as Christ sought to please *(i.e., help)* others rather than please himself *(vs. 1-3).* All the scriptures have been written for our learning that we might have hope *(v. 4).* We should be united in glorifying God *(vs. 5-6).* Paul observed to the Saints that they were full of goodness, filled with knowledge, and were able to admonish one another. Nevertheless, he desired to come to them but the work kept him away. He recounted his service and indicated that after he went to Jerusalem he hoped to stop by to see the saints in Rome on his way to Spain. He asked them to keep him in their prayers, to pray that he would be delivered from those in Judæa who do not believe and that his service would be accepted by the saints in Jerusalem *(vs. 14-31)*.

Rom. 16. Paul saluted numerous members of the church in Rome *(vs. 1-16, 21, 23)*. He cautioned the saints to be watchful of those who cause division and offenses within the church contrary to the doctrine. Such people deceive others by "good words and fair speeches." He urged them to be wise regarding that which is good, and simple regarding that which is evil *(vs. 17-19)*. Paul refers to himself as Tertius *(v. 22)*. The epistle to the saints in Rome was delivered to them by Phebe, a servant of the church at Cenchrea *(Postscript)*.

RUFUS

Mark 15:21. **RUFUS** was a son of Simon of Cyrene. His brother was Alexander.

Rom. 16:13. Rufus, according to Paul, was "chosen in the Lord." Paul sent greetings to him and his mother in his epistle to the Romans.

RUFUS' MOTHER

Rom. 16:13. **RUFUS' MOTHER**, along with Rufus, was sent greetings by Paul in his epistle to the Romans.

NAMES THAT BEGIN WITH "S"

SADDUCEES

Matt. 3:7. **SADDUCEES** and Pharisees who came to Jesus' baptism were denounced by Jesus who called them a generation of vipers.

Matt. 16; Mark 8; Luke 11, 12. The Sadducees and Pharisees tried to tempt Jesus by asking for a sign from heaven. Jesus pointed out that they could read the signs forecasting the weather—red in the morning equals bad weather, red at night equals fair weather—but they couldn't discern the signs of the times *(Matt. 16:1-3; Luke 12:54-57).* He reprimanded them and said a wicked and adulterous generation seeks for signs. The only sign they would be given was the sign of Jonas *(Jonah was in the belly of the whale three days, signifying Christ would be in the earth three days before his resurrection) (v. 4; Luke 11:16 -29).* Jesus warned his disciples to beware of the leaven (i.e., the doctrine) of the Sadducees and Pharisees *(vs. 6-12; Mark 8:15; Luke 12:1).*

Matt. 22:23-33; Mark 12:18-27; Luke 20:27-38. The Sadducees, who did not believe in the resurrection, queried Jesus about marriage and whose wife a particular woman would be in the resurrection since she had been married to a man who died and then in turn to each of his six brothers—one after another as each died. Christ taught that worldly marriages endure in this life only and that she wouldn't be a wife to any of them in the resurrection.

Acts 4:1-22. The Sadducees, priests and captain of the temple arrested Peter and John as they spoke unto the people about Christ. Peter, filled with the Holy Ghost, spoke boldly, testifying of Christ and that it was through his name that a certain lame man was healed. The rulers, elders, scribes, Annas the high priest, Caiaphas, John and Alexander, and as many kindred of the high priest as there were, met to confer as to what to do about Peter and John. The healed man was with the apostles so they could not deny he had been healed, and they feared the people. They resolved to threaten them and let them go. They commanded Peter and John not to speak or teach in the name of Jesus. They responded with a question: "Was it better to hearken unto them or unto God?"

Acts 5:17-18. The Sadducees supported the high priest in arresting the apostles for preaching about Christ. They cast the apostles into the common prison.

Acts 23:6-9. Because the Sadducees didn't believe in either angels or the resurrection, and because the Pharisees believed in both angels and the resurrection, Paul appealed to the portion of the council in Jerusalem comprised of Pharisees as he pleaded his case. The scribes of the Pharisees' part of the council arose and cried that they found no evil in Paul. A great dissension arose and Claudius Lysias, the chief captain, sent soldiers to rescue Paul and take him to the castle.

SALOME (1)

Matt. 14:6 (3-11); Mark 6:17-28. (See **Daughter of Herodias**.)

SALOME (2) (The mother of Zebedee's children)

Matt. 20:20-21, 23; Mark 10:35-40. **SALOME** is identified in the BD as the wife of Zebedee **[the mother of Zebedee's children]**. She approached the Savior and asked if her sons could sit on his right and left hand in his kingdom. Jesus told her that was not his to give, "but it shall be given to them for whom it is prepared of my Father." *(Note: The account recorded in Mark says James and John petitioned Jesus, not their mother.)*

Matt. 27:56. The mother of Zebedee's children, Mary the mother of James and Joses, and Mary Magdalene were among the women who followed Jesus and ministered unto him who observed from a distance that which occurred when Jesus was crucified.

Mark 15:40. Salome is mentioned by name, rather than "the mother of Zebedee's children," as one of the women who stood afar off and observed what transpired when Jesus was crucified.

Mark 16:1. Salome, Mary Magdalene, and Mary the mother of James went to the sepulchre following the Sabbath, bringing sweet spices with which to anoint Christ's body, but found the stone rolled away from the door to the sepulchre. *(Note: John 20:1 indicates that Mary Magdalene went alone to the sepulchre. See Matt. 28:1-10 and Luke 24:1-4 for varied accounts of this event.)*

SAMARITANS

Matt. 10:5. **SAMARITANS** were the people who inhabited Samaria after the captivity of the northern kingdom of Israel. They were the descendants of foreign colonists placed there by kings of Assyria and Babylonia and also of Israelites who escaped at the time of the captivity *(BD). (Their record is found in the OT.)* Jesus sent his 12 disciples forth to preach and heal the people, but he commanded them that they should not enter any city of the Samaritans nor of the Gentiles.

Luke 9:52. As Jesus set forth to go to Jerusalem because the time had come for him to be delivered up, he sent messengers ahead to a village of the Samaritans to make ready for him. The Samaritans did not receive him because he was headed to Jerusalem so James and John asked Jesus if they should call down fire from heaven to destroy the Samaritans.

Luke 10:33 (29-37). The parable of the Good Samaritan was given by Jesus to teach a lesson about being a good neighbor.

Luke 17:16 (12-19). The only one of ten lepers healed by the Lord to turn back and express thanks was a Samaritan.

John 4:5-26, 39-42. Jesus met a Samaritan woman by Jacob's well and asked her to draw him some water. She was puzzled that a Jew would ask a drink of her since the Jews had no dealings with the Samaritans. Christ spoke of the living waters which he would have given her had she asked. In the interchange that followed, Christ told her things about herself that convinced her he was a prophet. She told the men in the city that Jesus told her ". . . all things that ever I did;" and said, ". . . is not this the Christ?" Many believed because of what she said. The Samaritans went to see Christ. Many more believed because they heard him themselves.

John 8:48. As Jesus taught in the temple and forgave a woman caught in adultery, there were those Jews who contended against him and claimed he was a Samaritan and had a devil.

Acts 1:8. After Christ's resurrection, he told his disciples that they would receive power after the Holy Ghost came upon them. They would be witnesses unto him in Samaria as well as in Jerusalem and Judæa.

Acts 8:4-25. Philip ministered to the people in Samaria and many were converted.

SAPPHIRA

Acts 5:1-10. **SAPPHIRA** was the wife of Ananias. They were followers of Christ following the Lord's death and resurrection at the time the congregation had all things in common. Sapphira and Ananias sold some land but kept part of the profit rather than giving it all to the church. When Peter confronted Ananias, saying, "Thou has not lied unto men, but unto God," Ananias fell down and died. Three hours later, Sapphira came in and Peter asked her how much the land had sold for. She also lied. Peter asked her why they had conspired against the Lord and told her that Ananias was dead and that the young men at the door who had carried him out would carry her out, too. She then fell down and died. They carried her out and buried them together.

SATAN (See Devil)

SAUL(1) (Paul, Tertius) (See Paul)

SAUL'S COMPANIONS (See Paul's Companions)

SCEVA

Acts 19:14. **SCEVA** was a man who had seven sons who were exorcists but who were unsuccessful in casting out devils.

SECUNDUS

Acts 20:4. **SECUNDUS** of the Thessalonians accompanied Paul into Asia, along with Sopater of Berea; Aristarchus (also of the Thessalonians); Gauis of Derbe; Timotheus; and Tychicus and Trophimus of Asia.

SERGIUS PAULUS

Acts 13:7-12. **SERGIUS PAULUS**, a prudent man in Paphos, was deputy of the country. He was associated with Bar-jesus, a Jew who was also a sorcerer and false prophet. When Sergius Paulus heard Barnabas and Paul and witnessed what happened to Bar-jesus when he contended with them, he believed.

SERUG (See Saruch)

SERVANT OF A CENTURION, A

Matt. 8:6-13; Luke 7:2-10. **A SERVANT OF A CENTURION** was sick. The centurion asked Jesus to heal his servant. When Jesus said he would go to the centurion's house, the centurion declined, saying he was not worthy to have Jesus under his roof; but, he said if Jesus would just speak the word, he knew his servant would be healed. Jesus said he had not found so great faith in Israel. He healed the servant of the centurion that same hour.

SERVANT(S) OF THE HIGH PRIEST (See, Malchus)

SEVEN SONS OF SCEVA

Acts 19:13-16. **SEVEN SONS OF SCEVA**, exorcists, tried to exorcise a man in whom there was an evil spirit. The evil spirit acknowledged that it knew Jesus Christ and Paul, but did not know them. The man, in whom the evil spirit was, leaped on them and overcame them. They fled, naked and wounded, out of that house.

SEVENTY WERE CALLED BY JESUS

Luke 10:1-20. **SEVENTY WERE CALLED BY JESUS** and sent two and two into the cities and towns to do missionary work. Jesus told them to go without purse or scrip. They were instructed to bless the houses of those who accepted them and to wipe the dust of their feet off into the streets as a curse against those who rejected them. They were given authority to teach and heal and to have power over the power of the enemy.

SHEPHERDS

Luke 2:8-18. **SHEPHERDS** were abiding in the fields when an angel appeared unto them and declared that Christ the Lord had been born in Bethlehem. Suddenly, a multitude of angels appeared, singing and praising the Lord. The shepherds immediately went to Bethlehem and found the babe lying in a manger. When they left, they spread abroad the word of what had transpired.

SHIPMEN SAILING THE SHIP ON WHICH PAUL WAS SAILING TO ITALY

Acts 27:27-31, 44. The **SHIPMEN SAILING THE SHIP ON WHICH PAUL WAS SAILING TO ITALY** were set to abandon ship during a terrible storm, thinking they were near some country. Paul warned the centurion and the soldiers that if they did, none of them would survive but, if they stayed, none would die. They decided to stay aboard ship. Ultimately, they were all saved as Paul had promised.

SILAS (Silvanus)

Acts 15:22, 32, 34, 40-41. **SILAS** was one of the men the apostles in Jerusalem sent to Antioch with Paul, Barnabas and Judas (surnamed Barsabas) to deliver their epistle to the Gentile converts regarding circumcision. Silas and Judas were also prophets and exhorted the brethren "with many words." After delivering the epistle, Silas chose to remain in Antioch with Paul and Barnabas; however, Judas left to return to the apostles. When Paul and Barnabas decided to visit the church in other areas to see how the members were doing, disputation arose between the two over who should go with them—John whose surname was Mark, or Silas. The dispute was so great that the two men parted ways. Paul took Silas with him and went through Syria and Cilicia, and Barnabas took Mark with him and sailed for Cyprus.

Acts 16. Silas and Paul traveled to Dere and Lystra where they met Timotheus, the son of a Jewess, who believed, and a Greek father. Paul circumcised him and had him go forth with him. They traveled throughout Phrygia and the region of Galatia. The Spirit forbade them preaching in Asia. They traveled to Mysia and contemplated going to Bithynia, but the Spirit again indicated they should not. They passed Mysia and went to Troas where Paul had a vision wherein a man of Macedonia was praying for him to go there. They traveled from Troas to Samothracia and Neapolis; then on to Philippi, the chief city of that part of Macedonia. They went by the riverside where the women resorted and spoke to them. One of the women was Lydia. After her conversion and baptism, she constrained Paul and his brethren to abide in her house *(vs. 1-15).* A certain damsel possessed with a spirit of divination followed Paul. After several days, Paul commanded the spirit in the name of Jesus Christ to come out of her. When her masters could no longer gain anything by her soothsaying, they took Paul and Silas to the rulers and the magistrates and brought charges against them. The magistrates commanded they be beaten and cast them into prison, ordering the jailer to keep them safely. He thrust them into the inner prison and held their feet fast in the stocks *(vs. 16-24).* At midnight, Paul and Silas prayed and sang praises to God; and the prisoners heard them. Suddenly, an earthquake shook the foundation of the prison, the doors were opened and everyone's bands were loosed. When the keeper of the prison went to kill himself because he thought the prisoners had fled, Paul stopped him, saying they were all still there. The jailer fell down before Paul and Silas and had them teach him. He took Paul and Silas and washed their stripes and then he and all who were his were baptized. He took them to his house and fed them *(vs. 25-34).* The magistrates sent sergeants to the jailer the next morning with orders to release Paul and Silas. Paul refused, saying they were Romans and had been beaten openly, uncondemned, and were not going to be thrust out privily. The serjeants reported what Paul said to the magistrates who, when they heard, were fearful because they were Romans. They quickly went to the prison and personally besought them and brought them out and asked them to depart from the city. Paul and Silas went to the home of Lydia, comforted the brethren there, and then left *(vs. 35-40).*

Acts 17. Silas, Paul and Timotheus passed through Amphipolis and Apollonia and went to Thessalonica where Paul preached in the synagogue of the Jews. *(Note: See entry for Paul: Acts 17:1-15.)*

Acts 18:5. Silas and Timotheus went from Macedonia to Corinth where Paul testified to the Jews that Jesus was the Christ.

2 Cor. 1:19. Silvanus, Paul and Timotheus taught the saints in Corinth that the promises of God are positive to those who believe—not negative.

1 Thes. 1:1. **Silvanus,** Paul and Timotheus sent their greetings to the saints in Thessalonica.

1 Thes. 3:2, 6-7. Silas and Paul were in Athens with Timotheus. They decided that it would be better to have Timotheus go to Thessalonica and see how the converts were doing there. Silas and Paul were comforted when Timotheus returned and reported that the saints were being true and faithful.

2 Thes. 1:1. Silvanus, Paul and Timotheus sent their greetings to the saints in Thessalonica again.

1 Pet. 5:12. It would appear Silvanus delivered Peter's epistle from Babylon (i.e. Rome, probably) to the members of the church scattered in Pontus, Galatia, Cappadocia, Asia and Bithynia.

SILVANUS (See Silas)

SIMEON (1)

Luke 2:25-35. **SIMEON** was a just and devout man who had been promised by the Holy Ghost that he would not die before seeing the Lord's Christ. When Joseph and Mary brought the infant Jesus to Jerusalem to present him to the Lord, Simeon was in the temple. He took the child in his arms and acknowledged him to be the Savior, and said that now he was ready to die in peace. He blessed the family and prophesied about Jesus.

SIMEON (2)

Luke 3:30. See **Simeon (2)** in Appendix A.

SIMEON (3) (NIGER)

Acts 13:1. **SIMEON (Niger)** was one of the prophets and teachers preaching in Antioch with Barnabas and Saul.

SIMEON (4) (Peter)

Acts 15:14. See **Peter.**

SIMEON (5)

Rev. 7:7. See **Simeon (5)** in Appendix A.

SIMON (1) PETER (Cephas) (See Peter)

SIMON (2) the Canaanite (Simon Zelotes)

Matt. 10; Mark 3; Luke 6; 9. **SIMON** the Canaanite was one of Jesus' 12 disciples: Simon Peter, Andrew, James, John, Philip, Bartholomew; Thomas, Matthew, James, Lebbæus (Thaddæus), Simon the Canaanite [Simon called Zelotes], and Judas Iscariot *(vs. 2-4; Mark 3:18; Luke 6:15).* Jesus empowered these apostles and sent them forth to teach, but instructed them that they should not go to the Gentiles nor to the Samaritans. They were to go to the lost sheep of the house of Israel. They were to heal the sick and cast out devils. They were to travel without purse or scrip. They were instructed to leave their peace upon those who received them, but to shake the dust off their feet when leaving the houses of those who reject them *(vs. 5-14; Luke 9:1-5).* They were told they would be persecuted for Christ's sake, but that "he that endureth to the end shall be saved." They are of more value than the sparrows for which the Father provides. Even the hairs of their heads are numbered *(vs. 16-32).*

Acts 1:13-14. Following Jesus' ascension into heaven, Jesus' disciples, including Simon Zelotes, met together in an upper room, along with several women (including Mary the mother of Jesus) and his brethren, where they continued in prayer and supplication.

SIMON (3)

Matt. 13:55; Mark 6:3. **SIMON** was the brother of Jesus. He also had other brothers: James, Joses and Judas; and sisters whose names are not given.

SIMON (4) (the leper)

Matt. 26:6-13; Mark 14:3-5. **SIMON the leper** provided respite for Jesus in Bethany. It was in his house that a woman came and anointed Jesus with ointment prior to his crucifixion over the objections of Jesus' disciples. *(This woman is identified as Mary, the sister of Martha and Lazarus in John 11, 12. Also, see Luke 7:36-50 for a similar account of a woman who was a sinner who, when Christ was in the home of Simon the Pharisee, bathed Christ's feet with her tears and wiped them dry with her hair.)*

John 11:2; 12:3. Simon was the father of Judas Iscariot. Jesus and the disciples had supper in his home six days prior to the Passover. It was here that Mary the sister of Martha and Lazarus anointed Jesus' feet with precious ointment, bathed his feet with her tears and dried them with her hair. His son Judas objected to the oil being used in such a fashion and thought it should have been sold and the proceeds given to the poor.

SIMON (5) (Of Cyrene)

Matt. 27:32; Mark 15:21; Luke 23:26. **SIMON (Of Cyrene)**, father of Alexander and Rufus, was compelled to bear Jesus' cross to Golgotha.

SIMON (6), a Pharisee

Luke 7:36-50. **SIMON**, a Pharisee, invited Jesus to have dinner with him. A woman who was a sinner, when she heard that Jesus was having dinner in the home of Simon, brought an alabaster box of ointment and anointed Jesus' feet, washing his feet with her tears, wiping his feet with her hair, and kissing his feet. When Simon disapproved, Jesus gave a parable about two debtors who were forgiven by their master. The one who was most in debt was forgiven the most; and that debtor loved his master the most. Jesus forgave the woman of her sins and reminded Simon that since he had entered Simon's house, Simon had not shown him any of the love the woman had. *(See Matt. 26:6-13 and Mark 14:3-5 for a similar event involving Mary, the sister of Lazarus.)*

SIMON (7)

Acts 8:9-24. **SIMON** was a man with many followers who bewitched the people of Samaria using sorcery. He heard Philip preaching of Jesus Christ and believed and was baptized. When he saw that "through laying on of the apostles' hands the Holy Ghost was given, he offered them money." Peter chastised him for thinking the gift of God could be purchased with money. Simon asked Peter to pray to the Lord for him so that none of the things Peter had said would come upon him.

SIMON (8)

Acts 9:43. **SIMON** was a tanner in whose home Peter stayed during the days he tarried in Joppa following his raising Tabitha from the dead.

Acts 10:6, 9-16, 17, 32. Simon's home was located by the sea side. Peter was staying there when he had a vision that taught him that God is no respecter of persons. Cornelius sent servants and a soldier to Simon's house in quest of Simon Peter, as instructed by an angel of the Lord.

SOLDIERS GUARDING PAUL ON THE SHIP SAILING TO ITALY

Acts 27:27-31, 41-44. The **SOLDIERS GUARDING PAUL ON THE SHIP SAILING TO ITALY** cut the ropes off the boat that the shipmen were lowering (in their plan to abandon ship during a terrible storm) after Paul warned them that if the shipmen left, none of them would survive. Everyone remained on board. When the ship got mired and the hinder part broken by violent waves, the soldiers wanted to kill all prisoners so none could escape but the centurion wouldn't let them. The centurion told those who could swim to cast themselves into the sea and swim toward shore. Others clung to boards or to broken pieces of the ship and made it to shore. All 276 people aboard escaped safely to land.

SON OF A CERTAIN NOBLEMAN, THE

John 4:46-54. **THE SON OF A CERTAIN NOBLEMAN** was ill. The nobleman asked Jesus to heal his son. Jesus told him to go his way, that his son liveth. The man believed. As he journeyed home, his servants met him along the way and told him his son was well. The man wanted to know what hour he had begun to get better. They said it was the seventh hour of the previous day. That was the same hour Jesus had told him that his son liveth. This was Jesus' second miracle when he came out of Judæa into Galilee.

SOPATER

Acts 20:4. **SOPATER** of Berea accompanied Paul into Asia, along with Aristarchus and Secundus of the Thessalonians, Gauis of Derbe, Timotheus, and Tychicus and Trophimus of Asia.

SOSIPATER

Rom. 16:21. **SOSIPATER**, one of Paul's kinsmen, joined Paul and others in sending greetings to the saints in Rome.

SOSTHENES

1 Cor. 1:1-2. **SOSTHENES** was apparently a companion of Paul's. Paul indicated to the saints in Corinth that Sosthenes joined him in sending the epistle to them.

STACHYS

Rom. 16:9. **STACHYS** was one of Paul's beloved. In Paul's epistle to the saints in Rome, he invited them to salute Stachys for him.

STEPHANAS

1 Cor. 1:16. **STEPHANAS**' household was among the small number of people baptized by Paul.

1 Cor. 16, Postscript. Stephanas' household was the firstfruits of Achaia and the members were deeply converted to the ministry of the saints. Paul encouraged the saints in Corinth to submit themselves to them and to all others who labored in the ministry. Stephanas, Fortunatus and Achaicus apparently visited Paul and updated him on the situation in Corinth. Paul welcomed their visit because "that which was lacking on your part they have supplied." Paul said these three also "refreshed my spirit and yours" *(vs. 15, 17-18).* The first epistle from Paul in Philippi to the saints in Corinth was carried to them by Stephanas, Fortunatus, Achaicus and Timotheus *(Postscript).*

STEPHEN

Acts 6:5, 8-15. **STEPHEN** was a man full of faith and of the Holy Ghost. He was one of the seven men the apostles chose and set apart to help them with the work. Stephen performed great works, even miracles, among the people. Some of the people in the synagogue of the Libertines, Cyrenians, Alexandrians, Cilicia and Asia disputed with Stephen and arranged for men to charge that he spoke blasphemous words against God and Moses. They set up two false witnesses against him. Those that sat in council against Stephen saw him transfigured before them. They "saw his face as it had been the face of an angel."

Acts 7. As Stephen was confronted by those who sat in council against him, he reminded them of Israel's history; the promise the Lord made to Abraham; his being led away from his kindred to a new land which the Lord promised him for a possession; his descendants: Isaac, Jacob and Jacob's twelve sons; their sojourn in Egypt; Moses' 40 years in the household of Pharaoh, 40 years in Madian (Midian), and 40 years in the desert *(vs. 1-34).* Stephen named Moses as a prototype of Christ. "This Moses whom they refused, saying, 'Who made thee a ruler and a judge?' The same did God send to be a ruler and a deliverer by the hand of the angel which appeared to him in the bush" *(v. 35).* "This is that Moses, which said unto the children of Israel, 'A prophet shall the Lord your God raise up unto you of your brethren, like unto me; him shall ye hear'" *(v. 37).* The people rejected Stephen's testimony; and as they gnashed on him with their teeth, he looked into heaven and saw the glory of God, and Jesus standing on the right hand of God. They cast him out of the city and stoned him to death *(vs. 54-60).*

Acts 8:1-2. Steven's body was carried away by devout men who buried him, after which Saul made havoc of the church.

Acts 22:20. When Stephen was martyred, Saul stood by, consenting to his death and keeping the raiment of those who slew Stephen. Paul recounted the event to the Jews in Jerusalem as he told of his conversion on the road to Damascus and of his protestations to the Lord as to why he was unworthy to do what the Lord wanted him to do.

SUSANNA

Luke 8:2-3. **SUSANNA** was one of the women, along with Mary Magdalene (out of whom Jesus sent seven devils), and Joanna, the wife of Chuza (Herod's steward), who followed Jesus and ministered unto him as he went throughout the villages and towns preaching.

SYNTYCHE

Philip. 4:2. **SYNTYCHE** was one of the Philippians Paul beseeched to be of the same mind in the Lord as he.

NAMES THAT BEGIN WITH "T"

TABITHA (Dorcas)

Acts 9:36-41. **TABITHA (Dorcas)** was a disciple of Christ living in Joppa. She was full of good works and almsdeeds. She became ill and died. The disciples living in Joppa sent for Peter who was in the nearby city of Lydda. Peter arrived and had the people leave the upper chamber where Dorcas' body lay. He then kneeled down and prayed, saying, "Tabitha, arise." She arose. He took her by the hand and presented her to the saints and widows who had been mourning her death.

TERTULLUS

Acts 24:1-9. **TERTULLUS**, Ananias and the elders arrived five days after Paul was taken to Felix, the governor, and testified against Paul. Tertullus, an orator, was their spokesman. He claimed that Paul had profaned the temple; and said that they were planning to judge him according to their law, but Lysias the chief captain had, with great violence, taken him away from them and had commanded they come and make their accusations to Felix.

TETRARCH

(Note: The BD states that tetrarch originally referred to any ruler who ruled one-fourth part of a country, but that it was also used when a part governed was some other fraction of the whole. For a synopsis of the different Herod's who were tetrarchs, see the entry for Herod.)

THADDÆUS (Lebbæus, Judas (4) "Not Iscariot")

Matt. 10; Luke 9. **LEBBÆUS, i.e., Thaddæus** was one of Jesus' 12 disciples: Simon Peter, Andrew, James, John, Philip, Bartholomew; Thomas, Matthew, James, Lebbæus (Thaddæus), Simon the Canaanite, and Judas Iscariot *(vs. 2-4).* Jesus empowered these apostles and sent them forth to teach, but instructed them that they should not go to the Gentiles nor to the Samaritans. They were to go to the lost sheep of the house of Israel. They were to heal the sick and cast out devils. They were to travel without purse or scrip. They were instructed to leave their peace upon those who received them, but to shake the dust off their feet when leaving the houses of those who reject them *(vs. 5-14; Luke 9:1-5).* They were told they would be persecuted for Christ's sake, but that "he that endureth to the end shall be saved." They are of more value than the sparrows for which the Father provides. Even the hairs of their heads are numbered *(vs. 16-32). (Note: The BD under "Judas" indicates that **Judas "Not Iscariot,"** was also called **Judas, son or brother of James,** and is probably the same as Lebbæus, i.e., Thaddæus.)*

John 14:22-23. **Judas (not Iscariot)** asked how Jesus would manifest himself unto his disciples but not unto the world. Jesus said he who loves him will keep his commandments, and his Father will love him; and "we will come unto him and make our abode with him."

Acts 1:13-14. Following Jesus' ascension into heaven, Jesus' disciples, including **Judas the Brother of James,** met together in an upper room, along with several women (including Mary the mother of Jesus) and his brethren, where they continued in prayer and supplication.

THEOPHILUS

Luke 1:3. **THEOPHILUS** was the person to whom Luke addressed his Gospel.

Luke 3:19. (Note: Theophilus, while not referred to in Luke 3 in the King James version of the Bible, is referred to in Luke 3:19 in Joseph Smith's "New Translation" of the Bible.) Theophilus was apparently a publican and John the Baptist admonished the publicans to exact no more from the people than that which was appointed unto them. He reminded Theophilus that it was well known to him that out of the abundance which was received, every poor man was appointed his portion. *(Luke 3:11-12; Luke 3:17-20 (JST).)*

Acts 1:1. Luke addressed the Acts to Theophilus. *(Theophilus means friend of God (BD).)*

THESSALONIANS

1 Thes. 1:1-10. **THESSALONIANS** were citizens of Thessalonica, the capital of Macedonia. Paul, Silvanus (Silas) and Timotheus sent their greetings to the saints in Thessalonica who had received the gospel by both word and by power and by the Holy Ghost. Their faithfulness had been an example in Macedonia and Achaia and in other places, so much so that Paul indicated "we need not to speak any thing." The Thessalonians had ceased worshipping idols and had turned to God, who raised his Son from the dead, and were waiting for Christ to come from heaven. Through Christ's death, resurrection and atonement, Paul said he delivered us from the wrath to come. *(Note: Paul and Silas preached in Thessalonica. It was the home of Aristarchus. The city was named in honor of Thessalonica, sister of Alexander the Great and wife of the Greek military leader Cassander. See Thessalonica in the BD.)*

1 Thes. 2. Even though Paul and his companions were treated shamefully in Philippi, they preached boldly in a godly way in Thessalonica, and their preaching was not in vain. They used neither flattering words nor sought glory for themselves, but were gentle among the Thessalonians. They were affectionately desirous of them and, because they were dear to them, were willing to impart both the gospel of God and their own souls unto them *(vs. 1-8).* Paul testified that he and his companions had behaved in a godly way and that the Thessalonians could likewise attest to that *(vs. 9-11).* The Thessalonians had also been charged to walk uprightly before God *(v. 12).* Paul acknowledged that the Thessalonians had been faithful and had suffered from their own countrymen just as the apostles in Judæa suffered from their countrymen *(vs. 13-15).* Paul and his companions would soon be taken from the Thessalonians—in body, but not in heart—which caused them an even greater desire to see their faces. However, Paul said Satan hindered their being able to come to them. Nevertheless, the saints were their glory and joy *(vs. 17-20).*

1 Thes. 3. Because of Paul's great need to know how the converts were doing in Thessalonia, he sent Timotheus there to strengthen them in the faith. Paul reminded them that, when he had been with them previously, he had prophesied of the tribulation he would have. Nevertheless, he needed to be reassured that the saints had not been tempted away from the gospel, making his labor vain *(vs. 1-5)*. He and his companion *(probably Silas)* were comforted with the report Timotheus brought back to them *(vs. 6-9)*. They prayed night and day to be able to see their faces and be able to "perfect that which is lacking in your faith" *(v. 10)*. Paul testified that God the Father and the Lord Jesus Christ were in charge and directing his path. The Thessalonians were also being blessed by the Lord so they were increasing and abounding in love one to another to the end that they might be unblameable in holiness before God *(vs. 11-13)*.

1 Thes. 4. Paul beseeched and exhorted the Thessalonians to strive to live even more fully the teachings of the gospel they had received. They should abstain from evil and control their bodily desires. God has called us unto holiness, not unto uncleanness *(vs. 1-7)*. Paul said he didn't need to admonish them regarding brotherly love because "ye yourselves are taught of God to love one another;" and they were already doing that. Still, he encouraged them to increase in love even more *(vs. 9-10)*. They should study to be quiet and work with their own hands so that they could walk honestly toward those who are without, and have lack of nothing *(vs. 11-12)*. Paul testified of the death and resurrection of Christ; that he shall descend from heaven with a shout, with the voice of the archangel, and with the trump of God; and the righteous dead shall rise first. The righteous who are alive at his coming will be caught up together with them in the clouds to meet the Lord in the air *(vs. 13-17)*.

1 Thes. 5. Because faithful members of the church are "children of light," Paul told the Thessalonian saints that he didn't need to write to them regarding the signs indicating when Christ would come. They knew the times and the seasons; they knew that Christ would come as a thief in the night. Therefore, he said, "let us watch and be sober." He said that those who sleep, sleep at night; and those who are drunken are drunken in the night. They are the children of the day, not of the night; and Paul admonished them to put on the breastplate of faith and love and the helmet of hope of salvation *(vs. 1-8)*. Paul encouraged them to edify one another and beseeched them to honor and support the church leaders; to be at peace among themselves; to warn those who are unruly; comfort the feebleminded; support the weak and be patient toward all men. He instructed them not to return evil for evil but to follow that which is good; to rejoice evermore; pray without ceasing, and give thanks in all things; to quench not the Spirit nor despise prophesyings. They should prove all things and hold fast that which is good and abstain from the very appearance of evil *(vs. 11-22)*. Paul attested to his own faithfulness and asked them to pray for him and his companions *(vs. 24-25)*.

2 Thes. 1. Paul, Silvanus (Silas) and Timotheus sent their greetings to the Thessalonians, rejoicing in their exceeding faith, in the charity they all showed one to another, and "for your patience and faith in all your persecutions and tribulations that ye endure." Those persecutions and tribulations were a manifest token of the righteous judgment of God enabling them to be counted worthy of the kingdom of God *(vs. 1-5)*. God will administer retribution to those who afflict the righteous *(v. 6)*. When Jesus returns in honor and glory, vengeance will be taken upon the wicked and they will be punished with everlasting destruction from the presence of the Lord *(vs. 7-9)*. The righteous will be glorified in the name of the Lord Jesus Christ *(vs. 10-12)*.

2 Thes. 2. In 1 Thes. 5, Paul told the Thessalonians that as children of light, they could discern the signs of the second coming of Christ. In this epistle, Paul cautions them not to be deceived regarding Christ's second coming: "for that day shall not come except there come a falling away first, and that man of sin *(Satan)* be revealed, the son of perdition" *(vs. 1-3)*. Paul pointed out some of Satan's traits and the lot of those who choose to follow him rather than the Lord *(vs. 4-12)*. Paul also pointed out that faithful members of the church were foreordained to be saved in the celestial kingdom and inherit glory and power with Christ *(vs. 13-14)*. He admonished them to stand faithful and keep the commandments *(v. 15)*.

2 Thes. 3. The Thessalonian saints were requested by Paul to pray for him and his companions that the gospel might freely go forth and be preached among the people. He expressed his confidence that the Lord would continue to be with the Thessalonian saints. He enjoined them to separate themselves from all who failed to follow Christ *(vs. 1-6)*. He encouraged them to follow the example he and his companions had set for them when they were with them: i.e., to labor with their own hands for their own support and not expect someone else to support them: those who work not should not eat *(vs. 7-12)*. He counseled them not to be weary in doing that which is right, and that even though they should separate themselves from those who do not follow Paul's instructions as given in the epistle, they should not consider that person as an enemy but should admonish him as a brother *(vs. 13-15)*. He asked the Lord's blessings to be upon them all. *(Note: According to the postscripts, both epistles to the Thessalonians were written from Athens.)*

THEUDAS

Acts 5:36, 38-39. **THEUDAS** boasted himself to be somebody but was not. He was used by Gamaliel as an example to illustrate to the council who sat against the apostles that if what the apostles said was false, time would bear that out; but that if what they taught was true, time would also bear that out.

THOMAS (DIDYMUS)

Matt. 10; Mark 3; Luke 9. **THOMAS** was one of Jesus' 12 disciples: Simon Peter, Andrew, James, John, Philip, Bartholomew, Thomas, Matthew, James, Lebbæus (Thaddæus), Simon the Canaanite, and Judas Iscariot *(vs. 2-4)*. Jesus empowered these apostles and sent them forth to teach, but instructed them that they should not go to the Gentiles nor to the Samaritans. They were to go to the lost sheep of the house of Israel. They were to heal the sick and cast out devils. They were to travel without purse or scrip. They were instructed to leave their peace upon those who received them, but to shake the dust off their feet when leaving the houses of those who reject them *(vs. 5-14; Mark 3:18; Luke 9:1-5. The apostles are not named by name in Luke 9:1-5.)*. They were told they would be persecuted for Christ's sake, but that "he that endureth to the end shall be saved." They are of more value than the sparrows for which the Father provides. Even the hairs of their heads are numbered *(vs. 16-32)*.

Luke 6:15. Thomas was among the 12 disciples whom Jesus called to be apostles: Simon Peter, Andrew, James, John, Philip, Bartholomew, Matthew, Thomas, James the son of Alphæus,, Simon Zelotes, Judas the brother of James, and Judas Iscariot.

John 11:16. Thomas was also called **Didymus,** the Greek equivalent of Thomas. When Jesus said he was going to go into Judæa because Lazarus was dead, the disciples tried to discourage Jesus from going because the Jews had sought to stone him when he was there before. When Jesus would not be dissuaded, Thomas told his fellow disciples, "Let us also go, that we may die with him."

John 14:5-6. Thomas asked Jesus how he and his fellow disciples could know the way. Jesus said he was "the way, the truth, and the life, no man cometh unto the Father but by me."

John 20. Following Christ's resurrection and the discovery that his body was not in the sepulchre, Christ's disciples met together in seclusion for fear of the Jews. That evening Jesus appeared to them as they were thus assembled and showed them the wounds in his hands and side and told them to "Receive ye the Holy Ghost." However, Thomas was not with them *(vs. 19-24).* The other disciples told Thomas they had seen the risen Lord, but Thomas refused to believe until he saw for himself. Christ appeared to his disciples again eight days later, at which time Thomas was present. The Lord instructed him to feel the wounds for himself and be believing. Then he admonished Thomas, " . . . because thou hast seen me, thou hast believed: blessed are they that have not seen, and yet have believed" *(vs. 25-29).*

John 21. Thomas, Simon Peter, Nathanael of Cana, James and John and two other disciples were fishing on the sea of Tiberias when Jesus showed himself to his disciples a third time following his resurrection. Jesus stood on the shore and asked if they had any meat. They did not recognize Jesus, but responded that they had none. He told them to cast their nets on the right side of the ship. They did and their nets were so full they were unable to draw them. John declared to Peter, "It is the Lord." Peter quickly put something on and cast himself into the sea. When the disciples were gathered together on shore, Jesus dined with them on bread and fishes *(vs. 1-14).*

Acts 1:13-14. Following Jesus' ascension into heaven, Jesus' disciples, including Thomas, met together in an upper room, along with several women (including Mary the mother of Jesus) and his brethren, where they continued in prayer and supplication.

TIBERIUS CÆSAR (i.e., Cæsar (2))

Luke 3:1. **TIBERIUS CÆSAR** was in the fifteenth year of his reign when John the Baptist came into the country about Jordan, preaching the baptism of repentance for the remission of sins. *(Note: He reigned from A.D. 14 to A.D. 37. His full name was Tiberius Claudius Nero Cæsar Augustus.)*

Luke 23:2. Tiberius was Cæsar when the people brought Jesus before Pilate with the charge that Christ was perverting the nation and forbidding to give tribute to Cæsar, claiming himself to be Christ a King.

Matt. 22:21; Mark 12:17; Luke 20:25. Jesus taught the people that they should render unto Cæsar that which is Cæsar's and unto God, that which is God's.

John 19:12. When Pilate desired to free Jesus, the people cried out claiming that if he did, he was no longer a friend of Cæsar's.

Acts 17:7. When Paul and Silas preached in Thessalonica, the unbelieving Jews complained that they, whom Jason had befriended, did contrary to the decrees of Cæsar.

Acts 25:8-12. When Paul was brought before Festus, procurator over Judæa, he appealed to Cæsar; and Festus agreed to send him before Augustus.

Philip. 4:22. When Paul wrote to the Philippians, he and the saints with him (chiefly those from the house of Cæsar) sent their greetings.

TIMÆUS

Mark 10:46. **TIMÆUS** was the father of Bartimæus, a blind man. *(See **Two Blind Men**.)*

TIMON

Acts 6:5. **TIMON** was one of the seven men the apostles chose and set apart to help them with the work.

TIMOTHEUS (Timothy)

Acts 16:1. **TIMOTHEUS** *(the Greek form of Timothy)* was the son of a Greek father and a Jewish mother living at Lystra, and believed, and was a disciple of Christ. Paul had him circumcised and then took him with him and Silas on their missionary journey.

Acts 17. Timotheus, Paul and Silas passed through Amphipolis and Apollonia and went to Thessalonica where Paul preached in the synagogue of the Jews. *(Note: See entry for Paul: Acts 17.)*

Acts 18:5. Timotheus and Silas went from Macedonia to Corinth where Paul testified to the Jews that Jesus was the Christ.

Acts 19:22. Timotheus and Erastus were sent to Macedonia by Paul, while Paul stayed and preached in Asia.

Acts 20:4. Timotheus accompanied Paul into Asia, along with Sopater of Berea; Aristarchus and Secundus of the Thessalonians; Gauis of Derbe; and Tychicus and Trophimus of Asia.

Rom. 16:21. Timotheus, one of Paul's fellow workers, along with some of Paul's kinsmen, joined Paul in sending salutations to the saints in Rome.

1 Cor. 4:17. Timotheus, who Paul referred to as "my beloved son," was sent by Paul unto the saints in Corinth to bring them back into a knowlege of the things Paul had taught them previously regarding Christ (and as he taught "every where in every church").

1 Cor. 16, Postscript. Timotheus, Paul indicated in his epistle to the Corinthians, was planning to come to them. He asked them to treat him kindly, "that he may be with you without fear." He also looked forward to Timotheus rejoining him (vs. 10-11). The first epistle to the Corinthians was carried to them by Stephanas, Fortunatus, Achaicus and Timotheus *(Postscript).*

2 Cor. 1:19. Timotheus, Paul and Silvanus taught the saints in Corinth that the promises of God are positive to those who believe not negative.

Philip. 1:1. Timotheus was with Paul in Rome when Paul sent the Philippians greetings from both of them.

Philip. 2:19-23. Timotheus, Paul said, had proved himself to the Philippians in the past. Paul hoped to be able to send Timotheus to them soon so that he could learn from Timotheus as to the welfare of the saints in Philippi and be comforted. However, Paul first had to see how his own situation was before sending Timotheus to them.

Col. 1:1. Timotheus and Paul sent their greetings to the saints in Colosse. *(Timotheus might have been one of the first two teachers of Christianity to the Colossians, the other being Epaphras (BD).)*

1 Thes. 1:1. Timotheus, Paul and Silvanus sent their greetings to the saints in Thessalonica.

1 Thes. 3:2, 6-7. Timotheus was in Athens with Paul and Silas. They decided that it would be better to have Timotheus go to Thessalonica and see how the converts were doing there. Paul and Silas were comforted when Timotheus returned and reported that the saints were being true and faithful.

2 Thes. 1:1. Timotheus, Paul and Silvanus sent their greetings to the saints in Thessalonica again.

1 Tim. 1. **Timothy** (Timotheus) is addressed by Paul as "my own son in the faith" *(v. 2)*. Paul reminded Timothy that he had instructed him while in Ephesus to charge certain people to teach only the true doctrine and not to give heed to fables and endless genealogies *(vs. 3-4, 18)*. The essence of the gospel is charity out of a pure heart *(v. 5)*. Unfortunately, certain believers (Hymenæus and Alexander) had apostatized and had been turned over to the buffetings of Satan *(vs. 6-7, 19-20)*. The law is good when used lawfully. The law is not for the righteous but for the unrighteous: the lawless and disobedient, murderers, whoremongers, homosexuals, kidnappers, liars, perjured persons, etc." *(vs. 8-10)*. Christ came to save the repentant, among whom was Paul. Paul said he was forgiven because he sinned ignorantly in unbelief. Paul served as an example of the Lord's longsuffering and as a pattern to others who sinned so they would know that they, too, could repent and be forgiven *(vs. 12-16)*. Paul praised God, giving honor and glory unto him *(v. 17)*.

1 Tim. 2. Paul wrote Timothy that prayers, supplications and thanks should be made for all men, including kings and those in authority "that we may lead a quiet and peaceable life in all godliness and honesty" *(vs. 1-2)*. There is one God and one mediator between God and men: Christ is that mediator *(v. 5)*. Paul testified that he spoke the truth *(v. 7)*. He admonished women to dress modestly, to learn in silence, and not usurp authority over men *(vs. 9-12)*. Adam was not deceived by Satan, Eve was, and they will be saved in childbearing if they remain faithful *(vs. 13-15)*.

1 Tim. 3. Timothy was told what the qualifications were for those who were called as bishops or deacons. Bishops: blameless, the husband of one wife, vigilant, sober, of good behavior, hospitable, apt to teach, not given to wine, no striker, nor greedy of filthy lucre, patient, not a brawler, not covetous; one that rules his own house well, having his children in subjection with all gravity. He was not to be a novice *(i.e., just recently converted),* "lest being lifted up with pride he fall into the condemnation of the devil." He also needed to be worthy of the high regard of those outside the church, "lest he fall into reproach and the snare of the devil" *(vs. 1-7).* Deacons: grave, not doubletongued, not given to much wine, not greedy of filthy lucre; holding the mystery of the faith in a pure conscience. They also needed to have proven themselves worthy of the calling. Married deacons were to have just one wife, and their children were to be well-behaved *(vs. 8-13).* Paul hoped to join Timothy soon. He said that there was great controversy regarding the mystery of godliness; but he testified that God was manifest in the flesh; justified in the Spirit; seen of angels; preached unto the Gentiles; believed on in the world; and was received up into glory *(vs. 15-16).*

1 Tim. 4. Timothy was apparently a fairly young man as Paul told him, "Let no man despise thy youth" *(v. 12).* He counseled him not to neglect the "gift that is in thee *(i.e., the priesthood),* which was given thee by prophecy, with the laying on of the hands of the presbytery" *(v. 14).* Paul told Timothy that in the latter days there would be apostasy; that some would give heed to seducing spirits and to the doctrines of devils. There would be lying, hypocrisy and lack of conscience. There would be those who would forbid marriage; others would forbid the eating of meat, both of which Paul said God had created to be received with thanksgiving by those who believe and know the truth *(vs. 1-4).* Good ministers of Christ need to be well-versed in his teachings *(v. 6).* Timothy was counseled to refuse to be swayed by old wives' tales and fables and to exercise himself in godliness. Christ is the living God and the Savior of all men, especially those who believe *(vs. 7-10).* Timothy was instructed to meditate upon the things Paul wrote to him and to give himself wholly unto them so that both he and those who heard him would be saved *(vs. 15-16).*

1 Tim. 5. Timothy was given instructions regarding caring for widows. Older widows were to be treated as mothers; younger widows as sisters. Widows should turn first to their families for assistance. Worthy widows 60 years of age or older without any living children or grandchildren, were to be cared for by the church. Younger widows were encouraged to marry and raise a family. A "worthy" widow was one who had performed good works, brought up children, lodged strangers, washed the clothes of the saints, relieved the afflicted *(vs. 1-16).* Elderly men were to be treated as fathers *(v. 1).* Leaders of the church who were engaged in full time ministry should receive temporal help from the church: "The labourer is worthy of his reward" *(v. 18).* Complaints against church ministers should only be considered if presented by two or three witnesses. Things should be done in fairness, without partiality. They should not be quick in setting people apart in the church: they need to be sure they are worthy *(vs. 19-22).* Timothy was encouraged to drink wine for his health rather than water *(v. 23).*

1 Tim. 6. Timothy was counseled by Paul to teach servants to honor their masters. Those who have believing masters should not despise them because they are brethren; thus, they should serve them *(vs. 1-2).* Believers should withdraw from those who think gain is godliness. We came into this world without anything and we will carry nothing out of it. People should be content with food and raiment. The rich fall into temptation. The love of money is the root of all evil *(vs. 5-10).* Follow after righteousness; fight the good fight of faith; lay hold onto eternal life *(vs. 11-12).* Charge the rich not to be high minded but to trust in the living God; to do good, willing to distribute, willing to communicate. Paul pleaded with Timothy to keep that which had been committed to his trust and to avoid profane and vain babblings *(vs. 17-20).*

2 Tim. 1. Timothy, in this second epistle from Paul, was reminded of the great love Paul had him, "my dearly beloved son." Paul also reminded him of the great faith of his grandmother Lois and his mother Eunice, and of Timothy's own faith *(vs. 1-5).* Paul admonished him to activate and magnify the gift of God *(i.e., the gift of the Holy Ghost and also the priesthood)* which Paul had confirmed upon him by the laying on of hands. He further admonished him not to be ashamed of his testimony of Jesus Christ, but to be willing to be afflicted for the gospel *(vs. 6-8).* Those who follow Christ are saved by him and are called by him to do his work—not because of our own works, but according to his purposes and grace—and were so foreordained before the world began *(v. 9).* Christ has abolished death *(through the resurrection),* bringing life and immortality to light through the gospel *(v. 10).* Paul testified that he was not ashamed of the gospel of Jesus Christ and urged Timothy to hold fast to the truth, to the gospel, which he had heard from Paul *(vs. 12-14).* Paul acknowledged that there were some who had apostatized from the church: i.e., Phygellus and Hermogenes. Paul prayed the Lord would show mercy unto the house of Onesiphorus because he previously had befriended Paul and had not been ashamed of Paul's bondage *(vs. 15-18).*

2 Tim. 2. Timothy was counseled by Paul to be strong in the gospel and in the teachings he had received from Paul. He should commit those same teaching unto other faithful men so they could teach them to others *(vs. 1-2).* Paul reminded him to remain focused on the ministry, on the war against sin, and not entangle himself in the affairs of this life. Those who are faithful and teach others are saved first and the convert second *(vs. 3-6).* Paul testified that Jesus Christ was of the seed of David and was raised from the dead. Even though those who preach of Christ may be imprisoned, the gospel which they preach cannot be bound. Paul was willing to endure all things so that others could obtain salvation and eternal glory *(vs. 8-10).* If we die for Christ, we shall live with Christ. If we suffer for him, we will reign with him. If we deny him, he will deny us *(vs. 11-13).* Paul counseled Timothy to study the scriptures, discern that which is true and of eternal value, and shun profane and vain babblings. Those who engage in contention, debate and disputations can lose their faith: "And their word will eat as doth a canker: of whom is Hymenæus and Philetus" who had erred and had apostatized. The Lord knows those who are his. Paul instructed those who bear the name of Christ to depart from iniquity *(vs. 15-19).* We should seek righteousness and shun contention. Teach in meekness *(vs. 22-25).*

2 Tim. 3. Paul prophesied to Timothy of the apostasy and of the evil condition of the world in the last days *(vs. 1-5).* "Silly women" who listen to those who are "lovers of pleasures more than lovers of God" will be led away "captive . . . laden with sins . . . with divers lusts, ever learning, and never able to come to the knowledge of the truth" *(vs. 6-7).* Just as people resisted Moses in ancient days, the wicked will resist truth in the last days *(v. 8-9).* Timothy was reminded that the scriptures "are able to make thee wise unto salvation through faith which is in Christ Jesus." All scripture comes by inspiration of God—profitable for doctrine, for reproof, for correction, for instruction in righteousness: that the man of God may be perfect, throughly furnished unto all good works" *(vs. 15-17).*

2 Tim. 4; Postscript. Timothy was charged by Paul to preach the word of Christ. Christ shall judge the quick and the dead. There will come a time of apostasy, "when they will not endure sound doctrine . . . And they shall turn away their ears from the truth, and shall be turned unto fables" *(vs. 1-4).* Paul admonished him to be watchful, to endure afflictions, to do the work of an evangelist and to make full proof of his ministry *(v. 5).* Paul said he was ready to die for Christ: he had fought a good fight, had kept the faith, and had finished his course. A crown of righteousness awaited him in heaven, as was true for all who loved the Lord *(vs. 6-8).* Paul urged Timothy to try to come to him, before winter, if possible *(vs. 9, 21).* He named several who had left him: Demas, Crescens, Titus. He asked Timothy to bring Mark with him when he came to see him as well as to bring certain items: a cloak and some books, especially the parchments. Alexander the coppersmith had done Paul much evil. He warned Timothy to be especially wary of Alexander. Nevertheless, the Lord had been with Paul and would continue to be with him *(vs. 10- 18).* He asked Timothy to give his greetings to certain saints and told him that Erastus stayed in Corinth and Trophimus was at Miletum, ill. He sent Timothy greetings from some of the saints in Rome *(vs. 19-21).* Timotheus was the first ordained bishop of the church at Ephesus. Paul's second epistle was written to him from Rome when Paul was brought before Nero the second time *(Postscript).*

Philem. 1:1-2, 23. Timothy joined Paul in sending a letter to Philemon from Rome regarding Onesimus. They also sent greetings to Apphia and Archippus.

Heb. 13:23. Timothy had been set at liberty. Paul hoped that, if Timothy came soon, he (Paul) would be able to come to the Hebrews shortly.

Heb. Postscript. Timothy carried Paul's epistle from Italy to the Hebrews.

TIMOTHEUS' (Timothy's) FATHER

Acts 16:1. **TIMOTHEUS' FATHER** was a Greek.

TIMOTHEUS' (Timothy's) MOTHER (Eunice)

Acts 16:1. **TIMOTHEUS' MOTHER** was a Jewess. Her husband was a Greek.

2 Tim. 1:5. Timothy's mother's name was **Eunice.** Her mother was Lois. Paul indicated that he knew both women had unfeigned faith in the Lord.

TITUS

2 Cor. 2:13. **TITUS** was referred to by Paul as "my brother." Paul could not find him in Troas and he traveled on to Macedonia.

2 Cor. 7:6, 13-14. Titus visited Paul in Macedonia and carried a positive report regarding the Corinthians to him, which lifted Paul's spirits. Titus' spirit had been refreshed by the saints in Corinth and his affection for them had been greatly increased.

2 Cor. 8:6, 16, 23-24. Titus was sent back to Corinth after visiting Paul in Macedonia. His love for the saints there was the same as Paul's. Paul assured the saints that if anyone inquired regarding Titus and his companions, that Titus was "my partner and fellow-helper concerning you," and the other brethren "are the messengers of the churches, and the glory of Christ."

2 Cor. 12:18, Postscript. Titus and another brother had been sent to the Corinthians by Paul. Paul reminded the saints that Titus and his companion had not made any gain from them; that he and Titus walked after the same spirit; and that everything they did was for the edification of the saints. Paul's second epistle to the Corinthians was written from Philippi and carried to the saints in Corinth by Titus and Lucas.

Gal. 2:1, 3. Titus, a Greek, went with Paul and Barnabus to Jerusalem to meet with the apostles and elders regarding circumcision. Paul did not allow him to be compelled to be circumcised. *(See Acts 15:1-2.)*

2 Tim. 4:10. Titus was in Dalmatia when Paul wrote his second epistle to Timothy.

Titus 1. Titus was in Crete when Paul wrote his epistle to him. Paul testified that the hope of eternal life was promised by God before the world began *(v. 2).* Paul referred to Titus as "mine own son after the common faith," and said he had left him in Crete so he could set things in order in the church there. He outlined the qualities of one who would be worthy to be ordained a bishop: blameless, the husband of one wife, having faithful children not accused of riot or unruly, not self-willed, not soon to anger nor given to wine, no striker, not given to filthy lucre, a lover of hospitality, a lover of good men, sober, just, holy, temperate, and holding fast the faithful word as he had been taught so that he could explain the doctrine to others *(vs. 4-9).* The Cretians, one of their own prophets declared, were liars, evil beasts, slow bellies. Paul said that witness was true and that Titus needed to rebuke them sharply, "that they may be sound in the faith" and not give credence to Jewish traditions *(vs. 12-14).* All things are pure to the pure in heart. To those who are defiled and unbelieving, nothing is pure *(v. 15).*

Titus 2. Titus was admonished to speak things which become sound doctrine. The aged men should be taught to be sober, grave, temperate, etc. The aged women should also be taught to behave in a manner that "becometh holiness," not to be false accusers, not given to much wine, to be teachers of good things. The older women should teach the younger women to be sober, to love their husbands and their children, to be discreet, chaste, keepers at home, obedient to their own husbands, etc. Young men were also to be instructed in doctrine and proper behavior (vs. 1-8). Titus was to exhort servants to be obedient unto their own masters, "that they adorn the doctrine of God our Saviour in all things" *(vs. 9-10).* Titus was told to speak, exhort and rebuke with all authority *(v. 15).*

Titus 3. Titus was told to encourage the saints to be careful to maintain good works. Those who apostatize and don't repent after being admonished twice are to be rejected *(vs. 8-10).* Paul asked Titus to come to him at Nicopolis, where he planned to stay for the winter, as soon as either Artemas or Tychicus, whom Paul had sent to Titus, arrived. He also asked Titus to bring Zenas and Apollos with him *(vs. 12- 13).* Titus was ordained the first bishop of the church of the Cretians *(Postscript).*

TOWNCLERK AT EPHESUS

Acts 19:35-41. The **TOWNCLERK AT EPHESUS** calmed the people down after they caught Gaius and Aristarchus, two of Paul's traveling companions, and rushed them into the theatre. He talked to them about the proper legal recourse they had if there was a problem; and then he dismissed the assembly.

TROPHIMUS

Acts 20:4. **TROPHIMUS** of Asia accompanied Paul into Asia, along with Sopater of Berea; Aristarchus and Secundus of the Thessalonians; Gauis of Derbe; Timotheus; and Tychicus, who was also of Asia.

Acts 21:29. Trophimus was an Ephesian. The Jews in Jerusalem said Paul had polluted the temple because they had seen him with Trophimus in the city and assumed he had taken him into the temple.

2 Tim. 4:20. Trophimus was ill and Paul left him at Miletum to recover.

TRYPHENA

Rom. 16:12. **TRYPHENA** and Tryphosa were two of the saints who labored in the Lord in Rome. Paul sent greetings to them in his epistle to the Romans.

TRYPHOSA

Rom. 16:12. **TRYPHOSA** and Tryphena were two of the saints who labored in the Lord in Rome. Paul sent greetings to them in his epistle to the Romans.

TWO BLIND MEN (1)

Matt. 9:27-31. **TWO BLIND MEN** asked Jesus to have mercy on them and heal them. Jesus asked them if they believed that he could do that. When they said yes, he touched their eyes and healed them according to their faith. Then they spread his fame abroad in the country.

TWO BLIND MEN (2)

Matt. 20:30-34; Mark 10:46-52. **TWO BLIND MEN**, as they heard that Jesus passed by, petitioned him to heal their eyes. The Lord had compassion on them, touched their eyes, and they could see. They then followed him. *(Note: The account recorded in Mark indicates there was just one blind man, and his name is given as Bartimæus, the son of Timæus.)*

TWO FALSE WITNESSES

Matt. 26:60-61. **TWO FALSE WITNESSES** were eventually found to testify against Jesus as he was tried before Caiaphas (the high priest) and the scribes and elders. Jesus was found guilty of blasphemy and sentenced to die. *(Note: Mark 14:56, 59, states that the witnesses' testimonies didn't agree with each other.)*

TWO MEN DRESSED IN WHITE

Acts 3:10-11. **TWO MEN DRESSED IN WHITE** stood by Jesus' apostles and asked them why they stood gazing into heaven after Jesus ascended there. They told the apostles that Jesus' return would be in like manner.

TWO POSSESSED WITH DEVILS

Matt. 8:28. **TWO POSSESSED WITH DEVILS** met Jesus in the country of the Gergesenes. The devils acknowledged Jesus as the Son of God. He cast the devils out. The devils then went into a herd of swine which ran into the sea and were drowned.

TWO THIEVES

Matt. 27:38, 44; Mark 15:27-32; Luke 23:32-33, 39-43; John 19:18. **TWO THIEVES** were crucified with Jesus: one on his left hand side and one on his right hand. They also insulted the Savior. *(Note: The account in Luke states that just one malefactor railed on Christ. The other rebuked his fellow thief, and asked Jesus to remember him when he came into his kingdom. Christ told him, "Today shalt thou be with me in paradise." The account in John merely states that two others were crucified with Christ, one on one side of him and one on the other side.)* The soldiers received permission from Pilate to break their legs so they would die more quickly because the Sabbath was about upon them *(John 19:31- 32).*

TYCHICUS

Acts 20:4. **TYCHICUS** of Asia accompanied Paul into Asia, along with Sopater of Berea; Aristarchus and Secundus of the Thessalonians; Gauis of Derbe; Timotheus; and Trophimus (also of Asia).

Eph. 6: Postscript. The epistle Paul wrote to the Ephesians was delivered to them by Tychicus.

Col. 4:7-9, Postscript. Paul sent his epistle to the Colossians via Tychicus, "a beloved brother, and a faithful minister and fellowservant in the Lord," and Onesimus. Tychicus would bring them up to date on Paul's state, and would also learn of their state and comfort their hearts.

2 Tim. 4:12. Tychicus was sent to Ephesus by Paul.

Titus 3:12. Paul indicated in his epistle to Titus that he was sending Tychicus or Artemas to him, and asked Titus to come to him in Nicopolis as soon as either of them arrived.

TYRANNUS

Acts 19:9-10. **TYRANNUS** had a school in Ephesus where Paul "disputed" daily with the people for two years so that all the people who dwelled in Asia, both Jews and Greeks, heard the word of the Lord Jesus Christ.

NAMES THAT BEGIN WITH "U"

URBANE

Rom. 16:9. **URBANE** was referred to by Paul in his epistle to the Romans as "our helper in Christ." In Paul's letter to the saints, he invited them to salute Urbane for him.

NAMES THAT BEGIN WITH "W"

WISE MEN (Magi)

Matt. 2:1-12. **WISE MEN** from the east came to Bethlehem to find the Savior when Jesus was born. They asked where he could be found—where was born the King of the Jews—saying they had seen his star in the east and were come to worship him. Herod questioned the wise men as to when the star had appeared and asked that, when they found the child, they bring him word so he could come worship him, too. When they found the child, they fell down and worshiped him. They were warned by God in a dream not to return to Herod, so they departed into their own country another way.

WOMAN, A (1)

Matt. 9:20-22. **A WOMAN** who had had an issue of blood for 12 years had faith that if she could just touch Jesus' garment she would be healed. Jesus sensed when she touched his garment and told her that her faith had made her whole.

WOMAN, A (2)

Matt. 26:7-13; Mark 14:3-9. (See ***Mary (2),*** *the sister of Martha.)*

WOMAN OF CANAAN, A

Matt. 15:22-28; Mark 7:25-30. **A WOMAN OF CANAAN** [A certain woman who was a Greek, a Syurophenician by nation] went to Jesus when he was in the coasts of Tyre and Sidon and asked him to heal her daughter who was vexed with a devil. Jesus responded that the children of the kingdom should first be cared for: "for it is not meet to take the children's bread, and to cast it unto the dogs" *(i.e., give that which belongs to the children of the kingdom of God to those who are unworthy).* Her response was that the dogs under the table eat of the children's crumbs. Because of her response, Jesus told her to go her way and that the devil was gone from out of her daughter, and it was so.

WOMAN OF SAMARIA, A

John 4. **A WOMAN OF SAMARIA** went to Jacob's well to draw water. Jesus asked the woman to draw some water for him. She was surprised that he would speak to her since the Jews would have nothing to do with the Samaritans. In the interchange that ensued, Jesus taught her that whosoever drank of the water he gave them would never thirst again. When the woman said she had no husband, Jesus agreed, saying she had had five husbands but that the man she now lived with was not her husband. When she said she knew that the Messias, called Christ, cometh, Jesus said, "I that speak unto thee am he" *(vs. 3-26).* The woman went into the city and told the men of the city, and said, "Is not this the Christ?" *(vs. 28-29).* Many Samaritans believed because of the woman. Others believed because they heard Jesus speak *(vs. 39-42).*

WOMAN WHO WAS A SINNER, A

Luke 7:37-50. **A WOMAN WHO WAS A SINNER**, when she heard that Jesus was having dinner in the home of Simon, a Pharisee, brought an alabaster box of ointment and anointed Jesus' feet, washing his feet with her tears, wiping his feet with her hair, and kissing his feet. When Simon disapproved, Jesus gave a parable about two debtors who were forgiven by their master. The one who was most in debt was forgiven the most, and that debtor loved his master the most. Jesus forgave the woman of her sins and reminded Simon that since he had entered Simon's house, Simon had not shown him any of the love the woman had. *(Note: See Mary (2) the sister of Martha for a similar account of a woman anointing the Savior with oil, washing his feet with her tears and wiping them dry with her hair.)*

WOMEN IN PHILIPPI

Acts 16:13. The **WOMEN IN PHILIPPI** were wont to make prayer by the riverside. Paul and Silas and their brethren sat down by the riverside and spoke unto them.

NAMES THAT BEGIN WITH "Z"

ZACCHÆUS

Luke 19:1-10. **ZACCHÆUS** was a rich man, a chief among the publicans. He was short in stature and could not see over the crowd so when Jesus passed through Jericho he ran and climbed a tree. Jesus saw him in the tree and invited him to come down, saying he needed to abide at Zacchæus' house that day. Zacchæus informed Jesus that he always gave half of his goods to the poor, and returned everything fourfold if he ever took anything from any man by false accusation. He was told that salvation had come to his house that day, for he also was a son of Abraham.

ZACHARIAS (1)

Matt. 23:35; Luke 11:51 (45-52). **ZACHARIAS** was the son of Barachias. He was slain by the scribes and Pharisees between the temple and the altar. Jesus told the scribes and Pharisees that the blood of the righteous which had been shed from Abel to Zacharias would be upon their heads.

ZACHARIAS (2)

Luke 1:5-23; 59-62. **ZACHARIAS** was of the lineage of Abia (Abijah) and a descendant of Aaron. He was the father of John the Baptist. His wife was Elisabeth. She also was of the lineage of Aaron. An angel appeared to him and informed him that his wife Elisabeth, who was "well stricken in years" would bear a son. They were to call his name John. Zacharias asked how he would know this was really true; and the angel said that, because of his lack of faith, he would be dumb until it came to pass. He was in the temple a long time, causing the people to wonder. When he emerged from the temple, he could not speak; and the people perceived that he had seen a vision. After the baby was born, when it was time to circumcise him, the people wanted to name him Zacharias after his father. Elisabeth said, "Not so, but he shall be called John." The people objected because that was not a family name. They asked Zacharias what they should name the baby. He wrote down, "John." His mouth was immediately opened and he was able to talk. He praised God. He was filled with the Holy Ghost and began to prophesy.

ZEBEDEE

Matt. 4:21-22; Mark 1:19-20; Luke 5:10. **ZEBEDEE** was the father of James and John, two of Jesus' disciples. He and his sons were fishermen and were mending their nets when Jesus called James and John to follow him.

Matt. 20:20-21; Mark 10:35. Zebedee's wife petitioned Jesus to grant her sons to sit on his left and right hands in his kingdom. *(Note: In the account recorded in Mark, James and John made the request of Jesus, not their mother.)*

ZENAS

Titus 3:13. **ZENAS** was a lawyer. Paul instructed Titus to hasten Zenas and Apollos on their journey diligently so that nothing would be wanting unto them.

APPENDIX A

OLD TESTAMENT PEOPLE AND ANCESTORS OF JESUS

—ADAM TO JOSEPH—

REFERRED TO IN THE NEW TESTAMENT
(In Alphabetical Order)

AARON

Acts 7:40. **AARON** was the brother of Moses, Stephen testified before the Libertines, Cyrennians, Alexandrians and others of the synagogue who disputed with him, charging that he spoke blasphemously against Moses and against God. He recounted Israel's history and reminded them that Aaron gave in to the demands of the children of Israel to build a golden calf for them to worship while they sojourned in the desert when Moses went up the mountain and was gone for such a long time.

ABEL

Matt. 23:35; Luke 11:45-52. **ABEL** was the son of Adam. He was slain by his brother, Cain. Jesus told the scribes and Pharisees that the blood of the righteous which had been shed from Abel to Zacharias would be upon their heads.

Heb. 11:4. Abel, by faith, offered a more perfect sacrifice unto God than Cain did.

Heb. 12:24. The promises Christ offers through the new covenant are greater than those offered to Abel under the old covenant.

ABIA (Abijam)

Matt. 1:7. **ABIA** (Abijam) was the son of Roboam (Rehoboam) and the father of Asa. He was an ancestor of Jesus Christ through the lineage of David's son Solomon.

ABIATHAR

Mark 2:26. **ABIATHAR** was the high priest when David was king. When the scribes and Pharisees criticized Jesus' disciples for plucking corn on the Sabbath, Jesus reminded them of what David did in the days of Abiathar when he was hungry. And stressed that he, the Son of Man, is Lord also of the Sabbath.

ABIUD

Matt. 1:13. **ABIUD** was the son of Zorobabel and the father of Eliakim. He was an ancestor of Jesus Christ through the lineage of David's son Solomon. *(He is not listed in the Old Testament, but apparently lived during the intervening years between the end of the record of the Old Testament and the beginning of the record of the New Testament.)*

ABRAHAM

Matt. 1:1-2, 17; Luke 3:34. **ABRAHAM** was the father of Isaac and an ancestor of Jesus Christ. *(His genealogy through the line of Solomon is given in Matthew 1:1-16. His genealogy through the line of Nathan is given in Luke 3:23-38).*

Matt. 3:9. Jesus warned the Pharisees and Sadducees that they couldn't count on their being descendants of Abraham to save them—they needed to bring fruits meet for repentance—because God could raise up children unto Abraham from the stones before them.

Matt. 8:11-12; Luke 13:28-29. "Many," Jesus said, "shall come from the east and west, and shall sit down with Abraham, and Isaac, and Jacob, in the kingdom of heaven. But the children of the kingdom shall be cast out into outer darkness: there shall be weeping and gnashing of teeth."

Luke 3:34. Abraham's descendants are listed again. This line extends to Christ through David's son, Nathan, whereas the listing in Matt. 1:1-16 extends to Christ through David's son, Solomon.

Luke 13:28-29. (See entry for Matt. 8:11-12.)

Luke 16:19-31. Jesus gave a parable of the rich man and a beggar named Lazarus, which Lazarus, when he died, he was caught up into the bosom of Abraham whereas the rich man was buried in hell. Moral of the parable, "If they hear not Moses and the prophets, neither will they be persuaded, though one rose from the dead."

John 8:56-58. Abraham rejoiced to see Christ's day. "Before Abraham was," Christ said, "I am."

Acts. 7:2-17. Abraham's history is briefly recounted by Stephen to those who sat in council against him.

Acts 13:26-28. Abraham's posterity and all who feareth God, were sent the word of salvation. Nevertheless, they condemned Christ to death, fulfilling the words of the prophets.

Rom. 4:3, 13. Abraham's faith was reckoned unto him for righteousness. The promise of being heir of the world was not based upon the law, but through the righteousness of faith. The same promise extends to his posterity.

Rom. 9:4-12. Not all of Abraham's children are "Israel." Just being of the seed does not make them "Israel." In Isaac "shall thy seed be called." The children of the promise are counted for the seed (i.e., the promise given to Sarah that she would have a son, and the promise given to Rebecca, Isaac's wife that the older son would serve the younger son).

Heb. 11:8, 17. Because of faith, Abraham traveled to a new land, not knowing where he was going. By faith, he sojourned in a land of promise with Isaac and Jacob. Also, by faith, Abraham offered Isaac as a sacrifice to the Lord as God commanded.

James 2:21-23. Abraham was justified by his works. He didn't just have faith in the Lord, he offered Isaac upon the altar. His faith was made perfect by his works.

ACHAZ (Ahaz)

Matt. 1:9. **ACHAZ (Ahaz)** was a son of Joatham (Jotham) and the father of Ezekias (Hezekiah). He was an ancestor of Jesus Christ through the lineage of David's son Solomon.

ACHIM

Matt. 1:14. **ACHIM** was the son of Sadoc and the father of Eliud. He was an ancestor of Jesus Christ through the lineage of David's son Solomon. *(He is not mentioned in the Old Testament and, apparently, lived in the intervening years between the end of the Old Testament record and the beginning of the New Testament record.)*

ADAM (Michael the archangel)

Luke 3:38. **ADAM** was the son of God, the first man God created. He was the father of Seth, and the first mortal ancestor of Jesus Christ.

Rom. 5:12-15. When Adam partook of the forbidden fruit, sin entered the world, as did death. "Sin is not imputed *(attributed to anyone)* when there is no law." Nevertheless, death reigned from Adam to Moses, even over those who never sinned. Just as by the offense of one man, all men die, also by the gift of one man, Jesus Christ, shall all be made alive *(through the atonement and resurrection of Christ).*

1 Cor. 11:9-12. God created both male and female *(i.e., in the beginning, Adam and Eve)* and Paul stressed that, while man was not created for the woman, but the woman for the man, "Nevertheless, neither is the man without the woman, neither the woman without the man, in the Lord." *(They are equal.)* "For as the woman is of the man, even so is the man also by the woman; but all things of God."

1 Cor. 15:22, 45. Adam was the first man God created. When Adam partook of the forbidden fruit in the Garden of Eden, mortality was ushered in and with it death. Christ's resurrection overcame mortal death. "For as in Adam all die, even so in Christ shall all be made alive."

1 Tim. 2:13-15. Adam was not deceived by Satan, Eve was. Thus, Paul, in his epistle to Timothy, indicated that women should not usurp authority over men. If Adam and Eve continued in faith, charity and holiness with sobriety, Paul said they would be saved in childbearing.

Jude 1:9. **Michael the archangel** and Satan disputed over the body of Moses. *(Jude apparently had scriptures that referred to this disputation, which scriptures are among other lost scriptures. There is no other record of it in the Bible. Modern-day revelation states that Adam and Michael are one and the same.)*

> *Three years previous to the death of Adam, he called Seth, Enos, Cainan, Mahalaleel, Jared, Enoch, and Methuselah, who were all high priests, with the residue of his posterity who were righteous, into the valley of Adam-ondi-Ahman, and there bestowed upon them his last blessing.*
>
> *And the Lord appeared unto them, and they rose up and blessed Adam, and called him Michael, the prince, the archangel (D&C 107:53-54).*

Rev. 12:7. There was a war in heaven, and Michael and his angels prevailed against Satan.

ADDI

Luke 3:28. **ADDI** was the son of Cosam and the father of Melchi. He was an ancestor of Christ through the lineage of David's son Nathan.

AMAZIAH

*(**AMAZIAH**, 2 Kgs. 12:21, is not listed in Matt. 1:8-9. However, the OT record indicates he was a son of Joash (Jehoash) and the father of Azariah. Thus, he was an ancestor of Jesus Christ through David's son Solomon.)*

AMINADAB (Amminadab)

Matt. 1:4; Luke 3:33. **AMINADAB (Amminadab)** was a son of Aram (Ram) and the father of Nasion (Nahshon). He was the father-in-law of Aaron and was an ancestor of Jesus Christ.

AMON

Matt. 1:10. **AMON** was a son of Manasses (Manasseh) and the father of Josias (Josiah). He was an ancestor of Jesus Christ through David's son Solomon.

AMOS

Luke 3:25. **AMOS** was a son of Naum and the father of Mattathias. He was an ancestor of Jesus Christ through David's son Nathan. *(Amos is not mentioned in the Old Testament and probably lived during the intervening years between the end of the Old Testament record and the beginning of the New Testament record.)*

ARAM (Ram)

Matt. 1:3-4; Luke 3:33. **ARAM (Ram)** was a son of Esrom (Hezron) and the father of Aminadab (Amminadab). He was an ancestor of Jesus Christ through the lineage of David's son Solomon.

ARPHAXAD

Luke 3:36. **ARPHAXAD** was the son of Shem, grandson of Noah, and the father of Cainan. He was an ancestor of Jesus Christ.

ASA

Matt. 1:7-8. **ASA** was the son of Abia (Abijam) and the father of Josaphat (Jehoshaphat). He was an ancestor of Jesus Christ through David's son Solomon.

ASER (Asher)

Luke 2:36. **ASER (Asher)**. Anna the prophetess was of the tribe of Asher. *(Note: Asher was a son of Jacob and Zilpah, Leah's handmaid.)*

ASSIR

*(Note: **ASSIR** is not listed in Matt. 1:12. He was a son of Jehoiachin (Jeconias, Coniah) and the father of Salathiel. He was an ancestor of Jesus Christ through David's son Solomon.)*

AZARIAH (Uzziah)

*(Note: **AZARIAH** (Uzziah), 2 Kgs. 14:21, is not listed in Matt. 1:8-9. He was a son of Amaziah and the father of Joatham/Jotham. He was an ancestor of Jesus Christ through David's son Solomon.)*

AZOR

Matt. 1:13-14. **AZOR** was the son of Eliakim and the father of Sadoc. He was an ancestor of Jesus Christ through David's son Solomon. *(Note: He is not mentioned in the Old Testament and probably lived during the intervening years between the end of the Old Testament record and the beginning of the New Testament record.)*

BALAAM

2 Pet. 2:15. **BALAAM**, son of Bosor (Beor), was on Old Testament prophet who was petitioned by Balak, king of Moab, to curse the children of Israel.

Jude 1:11. Jude condemned the "filthy dreamers" who defile the flesh and engage in other evil works, and said they follow in the paths of Cain (who killed Abel), Balaam (who divined for money), and Core (i.e., Korah, who rebelled against Moses and Aaron in the desert).

Rev. 2:14. In this revelation to John, the Lord chastised the leader of the church in Pergamos for his tolerance of those in his midst who followed the doctrine of Balaam. Balaam taught Balac (Balak) "to cast a stumblingblock before the children of Israel, to eat things sacrificed unto idols, and to commit fornication."

BALAC (Balak)

Rev. 2:14. **BALAC** (Balak) sought a blessing from Balaam so he would be successful against the children of Israel. The Lord chastised the servant of the church in Pergamos for allowing followers of the teachings of Balaam (who had taught Balac to cast a stumblingblock before the children of Israel) to be a part of the church.

BARAK

Heb. 11:32-35. **BARAK** was one of the Old Testament people Paul said accomplished great things through faith *(i.e., under the command of Deborah, he led the army of Israel).*

BATHSHEBA

Matt. 1:6. **BATHSHEBA** was the woman who had been the wife of Urias (Uriah), who King David took. She was the mother of Solomon.

BOOZ (Boaz)

Matt. 1:5; Luke 3:32. **BOOZ (Boaz)** was a son of Salmon and Rachab and the father of Obed. He was an ancestor of Jesus Christ.

BOSOR (Beor)

2 Pet. 2:15. **BOSOR (Beor)** was the father of Balaam. Peter condemned the saints who had gone astray and were following the ways of Balaam, "who loved the ways of unrighteousness."

CAIN

Heb. 11:4. **CAIN**, a son of Adam and Eve, slew his brother Abel, who through faith, offered unto God a more perfect sacrifice than Cain did.

1 Jn. 3:12. Cain followed the devil and killed his brother because his own works were evil and his brother's were righteous.

Jude 1:11 (10-13). Jude condemned the "filthy dreamers" who defile the flesh and engage in other evil works, and said they follow in the paths of Cain *(who killed Abel),* Balaam *(who divined for money),* and Core *(i.e., Korah, who rebelled against Moses and Aaron in the desert).*

CAINAN (1)

Luke 3:36. **CAINAN** was a son of Arphaxad and the father of Sala (Salah). He was an ancestor of Christ.

CAINAN (2)

Luke 3:37. **CAINAN**, Adam and Eve's great-grandson, was a son of Enos and the father of Maleleel (Mahalaleel). He was an ancestor of Christ.

CIS (Kish)

Acts 13:21. **CIS (Kish)**, of the tribe of Benjamin, was the father of Saul, the first king of Israel.

CORE (Korah)

Jude 1:11. **CORE (Korah)**. Jude condemned the "filthy dreamers" who defile the flesh and engage in other evil works, and said they follow in the paths of Cain *(who killed Abel),* Balaam *(who divined for money),* and Core *(i.e., Korah, who rebelled against Moses and Aaron in the desert).*

COSAM

Luke 3:28. **COSAM** was the son of Elmodam and the father of Addi. He was an ancestor of Jesus Christ through the lineage of David's son Nathan. *(Note: He apparently lived during the intervening years between the end of the Old Testament record and the beginning of the New Testament record.)*

DANIEL

Matt. 24:15. **DANIEL**, Jesus reminded the people, spoke anciently of the desolation that would occur before the Second Coming of the Son of Man.

DAVID

Matt.1:6; Luke 3:31. **DAVID** was a son of Jesse, the father of Solomon and Nathan, and an ancestor of Jesus Christ. His genealogy to Jesus through Solomon is listed in Matt. 1:6-16 and through Nathan in Luke 3:23-35.

Matt. 22:41-46; Mark 12:35-37; Luke 20:41-44. The Pharisees said Jesus was the Son of David. Jesus countered that David in spirit [in the book of Psalms] called him Lord. If David called him Lord, how could he be his son.

Mark 2:25-26. When the Pharisees complained that Jesus' disciples plucked ears of corn on the Sabbath, Jesus reminded them of what David had done when he was hungry. In the days of Abiathar the high priest, David went into the house of God and ate the shewbread.

Acts 2:29-35. David, Peter testified, had also spoken of the resurrection of Christ.

Acts 13:22-23. David, son of Jesse, was made king over Israel when God removed Saul. He was "a man after mine own heart, which shall fulfill all my will," said the Lord. Jesus was of David's seed.

Heb. 11:32. David was one of the Old Testament leaders who Paul said accomplished great things through faith.

EBER (Heber)

Luke 3:35. **EBER (Heber)** was the son of Sala (Salah) and the father of Phalec (Peleg). He was an ancestor of Jesus Christ. *("The word Hebrew is a patronymic name derived from Eber" (BD).)*

EGYPTIANS

Heb. 11:29. **EGYPTIANS** who followed after Moses and the children of Israel when they left Egypt and tried to pass through the Red Sea as Moses and his group did were drowned.

ELEAZAR

Matt. 1:15. **ELEAZAR**, the son of Eliud and the father of Matthan, was an ancestor of Jesus Christ. He was Joseph's great-grandfather through the lineage of David's son Solomon.

ELIAKIM (1)

Matt. 1:13. **ELIAKIM** was the son of Abiud and the father of Azor. He was an ancestor of Jesus Christ through the lineage of David's son Solomon.

ELIAKIM (2)

Luke 3:30. **ELIAKIM** was the son of Melea and the father of Jonan. He was an ancestor of Jesus Christ through the lineage of David's son Nathan.

ELIAS

(Note: According to the BD, the name ***ELIAS*** *is used in several different ways in the scriptures. It may refer to John the Baptist. It is also the Greek form of Elijah (which is the Hebrew form) and may refer to the prophet Elijah. It is also the title given to someone who is a forerunner and to others who have been given specific missions or restorative functions that they are to fulfill, i.e., John the Revelator; Noah, i.e., Gabriel. There was also a man named Elias who lived in the days of Abraham.)*

ELIAS (Elijah)

Matt. 16:13-14; Mark 8:27-28. **ELIAS**, as mentioned in these verses, refers to the prophet Elijah. When Jesus asked his disciples who people said he was, they responded that some said he was John the Baptist and others said he was Elias or Jeremias . . ."

Matt.17:3-4, 10-11, 11-14 (JST); Mark 9:4-5, 11-13; Luke 9:30, 33. On the mount of Transfiguration, Peter, James and John not only saw Christ transfigured, but they also saw Elias (the prophet Elijah) and Moses *(vs. 3-4)*. Elias (the restorer) will yet come, as the prophets have written *(vs. 10-11)*. When Jesus, Peter, James and John came down from the mount of Transfiguration, Jesus spoke of another Elias (John the Baptist), the messenger, who would come before him and prepare the way *(vs. 11- 14 JST)*.

Mark 6:15-16; Luke 9:7-9. When Herod heard of Jesus' works, he thought the person he heard of was John the Baptist, who he had beheaded, come back from the dead. Others said it was Elias. *(Also see Matt. 14:1-2.)*

Luke 1:17. Zacharias was told that his son John would go before the Lord preaching in the spirit and power of Elias (Elijah).

Luke 4:25-26; James 5:17-18. Elias prayed that the heavens be sealed, and there was no rain for three-and-a-half years. He prayed for the heavens to be unsealed, and there was rain again. James cited Elias as an example of one whose prayers were effectual. *(See 1 Kgs. 17:1; 18:44-45.)*

John 1:19-28 (JST). Elias in verses 22 and 26 refers to Elijah who will restore all things. Elias in vs. 21-22 refers to John the Baptist as one who will come before and prepare the way of Christ. Elias in v. 28 refers to Christ as the prophet whose shoe's latchets John said he was not worthy to unloose.

ELIAS (during Abraham's day)

Rev. 7:2. **ELIAS**. In answer to Joseph Smith's inquiry regarding the Revelation of John, he was told that "the angel ascending from the east is he to whom is given the seal of the living God over the twelve tribes of Israel; wherefore, he crieth unto the four angels having the everlasting gospel, saying: Hurt not the earth, neither the sea, nor the trees, till we have sealed the servants of our God in their foreheads. And, if you will receive it, this is Elias which was to come to gather together the tribes of Israel and restore all things." Elias appeared and committed the dispensation of the gospel of Abraham unto Joseph Smith and Oliver Cowdery. *(Note: this Elias is found in D&C 77:9; 110:12.)*

ELIEZER

Luke 3:29. **ELIEZER** was the son of Jorim and the father of Jose. He was an ancestor of Jesus Christ through the lineage of King David's son Nathan.

ELIUD

Matt. 1:14-15. **ELIUD**, great-great-grandfather of Joseph, was the son of Achim and the father of Eleazar, through the lineage of David's son Solomon. He was an ancestor of Jesus Christ.

ELMODAM

Luke 3:28. **ELMODAM** was the son of Er and the father of Cosam. He was an ancestor of Jesus Christ through David's son Nathan.

EMMOR (Hamor)

Acts 7:16. **EMMOR (Hamor)** was the father of Sychem (Shechem). Stephen, one of the seven men the apostles chose to assist in the work, stated that Abraham bought a sepulchre from the son of Emmor the father of Sychem. *(Note: Gen. 33:19 indicates that Jacob, not Abraham, bought the land from the children of Hamor, Shechem's father.)*

ENOCH

Luke 3:37. **ENOCH** was the son of Jared and the father of Methuselah *(Mathusala in the NT).* He was an ancestor of Jesus Christ.

Heb. 11:5. Enoch, an Old Testament prophet, did not taste of death but was translated because of his faith *(as was his entire city).*

Jude 1:14-15. Enoch, Jude reminded the people, had prophesied of the latter days and said that Christ would come with ten thousand saints to execute judgment upon the whole earth.

ENOS

Luke 3:38. **ENOS** was the son of Seth, grandson of Adam, and the father of Cainan. He was an ancestor of Jesus Christ.

ER

Luke 3:28. **ER** was the son of Jose and the father of Elmodam. He was an ancestor of Jesus Christ through King David's son Nathan.

ESAIAS (Isaiah)

Matt. 3:3; John 1:23. **ESAIAS (Isaiah)** was a prophet. He prophesied of John the Baptist when he prophesied regarding "The voice of one crying in the wilderness, Prepare ye the way of the Lord, make his paths straight." *(Isaiah 40:3.) (This prophecy was fulfilled in John. 1:23.)*

Matt. 4:14-16. Christ quoted another of Isaiah's prophecies regarding the land of Zebulon and Nephthalim whose people which sat in darkness saw great light. *(This prophecy is found in Isa. 9:1-2.)*

Matt. 8:17. Esaias' prophecy that the Savior would take our infirmities and bare our sicknesses is fulfilled.

Matt. 15:7. Jesus said that Esaias was right when he prophesied that the people "draweth nigh unto me *(the Lord)* with their mouth and honoureth me with their lips; but their heart is far from me." *(See Isa. 29:13.)*

Luke 4:17-21. When Jesus was in the synagogue in Nazareth, someone gave him the book of Esaias. Christ opened it to the place where Isaiah had written, "The spirit of the Lord is upon me, because he hath anointed me to preach the gospel to the poor . . . ;" and Christ said to them, "This day is this scripture fulfilled in your ears."

John 12:38-41. In spite of Jesus' miracles, many did not believe him that the prophecies given by Esaias *(Isa. 53:1 and 6:9-10)* might be fulfilled.

Acts 8:27-35. A eunuch of great authority under Candace queen of Ethiopia was reading from Isaiah when he was approached by Philip. Philip taught the eunuch and subsequently baptized him.

1 Cor. 2:9. Isaiah is quoted in Paul's letter to the Corinthians: "Eye hath not seen, nor ear heard, neither have entered into the heart of man, the things which God hath prepared for them that love him." *(See Isa. 64:4.)*

1 Cor. 15:54. Isaiah is again quoted by Paul in his letter to the Corinthians: "Death is swallowed up in victory *(Isa. 25:8)*.

Rom. 9:27. Paul taught the Roman saints that the day would come when those not originally called to be the "chosen people" would, through their faith and righteousness, be called the Lord's people and he would call them beloved. He reminded them that Esaias had prophesied that even though the children of Israel would be as numerous as the sand of the sea, just a remnant would be saved. *(See Isa. 10:22.)*

ESAU

Heb. 11:20. **ESAU** was a son of Isaac. He and his brother Jacob, Paul wrote to the Hebrews, were blessed by their father Isaac, by faith, concerning things to come.

Heb. 12:16-17. Esau sold his birthright for a morsel of meat *(Gen. 25:33)*. Later, he wanted the birthright blessing back but it was not to be so. Paul cautioned the Hebrews to be cautious and diligent lest any of them become profane like Esau and lose their birthright.

ESLI

Luke 3:25. **ESLI** was a son of Nagge and the father of Naum. He was an ancestor of Jesus Christ through David's son Nathan.

ESROM (Hezron)

Matt. 1:3; Luke 3:33. **ESROM (Hezron)** was a son of Phares (Pharez) and the father of Aram (Ram). He was an ancestor of Jesus Christ.

EVE

1 Tim. 2:13-15. **EVE**, not Adam, was deceived by Satan. Thus, Paul, in his epistle to Timothy, indicated that women should not usurp authority over men. If Adam and Eve continued in faith, charity and holiness with sobriety, Paul said they would be saved in childbearing.

EZEKIAS (Hezekiah)

Matt. 1:9-10. **EZEKIAS (Hezekiah)** was a son of Achaz (Ahaz) and the father of Manasses (Manasseh). He was an ancestor of Jesus Christ through David's son Solomon.

GEDEON (Gideon)

Heb. 11:32. **GEDEON (Gideon)** was one of the Old Testament prophets who Paul said accomplished great things through faith.

HEBER (See Eber)

ISAAC

Matt. 1:2; Luke 3:34. **ISAAC** was a son of Abraham and the father of Jacob. He was an ancestor of Jesus Christ.

Matt. 8:11-12. When Jesus healed the centurion's servant, he was impressed with the faith of the centurion and said, "Many shall come from the east and west, and shall sit down with Abraham, and Isaac, and Jacob, in the kingdom of heaven. But the children of the kingdom shall be cast out into outer darkness: there shall be weeping and gnashing of teeth."

Luke 13:28. Christ taught that if people did not repent, they would be cast out and there would be weeping and gnashing of teeth when they see Abraham, Isaac, and Jacob and all the prophets in the kingdom of God, while they themselves are excluded.

Acts 7:8. Isaac was the son of Abraham and the father of Jacob. Stephen reminded the high priest and the men and brethren as he recounted the history of Israel that Isaac was circumcised when he was eight days old.

Gal. 4:28. Isaac was a child of the promise and, Paul reminded the Galatians, they were children of the promise just like Isaac was.

Heb. 11:18-20. Isaac, son of Abraham, was offered as a sacrifice unto God by Abraham because of Abraham's great faith. By faith, Isaac was able to give Jacob and Esau patriarchal blessings concerning things to come.

ISAIAH (See Esaias)

JACOB (1)

Matt. 1:2; Luke 3:34. **JACOB** was a son of Isaac and the father of Judas (Judah). He was an ancestor of Jesus Christ.

Matt. 8:11-12. "Many," Jesus said, "shall come from the east and west, and shall sit down with Abraham, and Isaac, and Jacob, in the kingdom of heaven. But the children of the kingdom shall be cast out into outer darkness: there shall be weeping and gnashing of teeth."

Matt. 22:32. Christ reminded the people that God said he was the God of Abraham, and the God of Isaac, and the God of Jacob.

Luke 13:28. Christ taught that if people did not repent, they would be cast out and there would be weeping and gnashing of teeth when they see Abraham, Isaac, Jacob and all the prophets in the kingdom of God, while they themselves are excluded.

Acts 7:8-16. Jacob's history is briefly recounted by Stephen to those who sat in council against him.

Rom. 9:11-13. Paul explained to the Romans how the law of election *(foreordination)* operates. As part of that explanation, he quoted Malachi 1:2 wherein

Malachi quoted the Lord saying, "As it is written, Jacob have I loved, but Esau have I hated.

Heb. 11:20. Jacob and his brother Esau were given blessings concerning things to come by their father Isaac. By faith, Jacob, in turn, gave his grandsons, Ephraim and Manasseh (sons of Joseph), patriarchal blessings.

JAMBRES

2 Tim. 3:8. **JAMBRES**, Paul wrote to Timothy, was one of the people in Moses' day who withstood Moses; and just like Jambres and Jannes, who also withstood Moses, people will resist the truth in the last days. *(Note: Neither Jannes nor Jambres is mentioned by name in the Old Testament.)*

JANNA

Luke 3:24. **JANNA** was the son of Joseph and the father of Melchi. He was the great-great-great- grandfather of Joseph the husband of Mary, mother of Jesus. He was an ancestor of Christ though the lineage of David's son Nathan.

JANNES

2 Tim. 3:8. **JANNES**, Paul wrote to Timothy, was one of the people in Moses' day who withstood Moses, and just like Jannes and Jambres, who also withstood Moses, people will resist the truth in the last days. *(Note: Neither Jannes nor Jambres is mentioned by name in the Old Testament.)*

JARED

Luke 3:37. **JARED** was the father of Enoch and the son of Mahalaleel. He was an ancestor of Jesus Christ.

JECHONIAS (Eliakim, Jehoiakim)

Matt. 1:11. **JECHONIAS (Eliakim, Jehoiakim)** was a son of Josias (Josiah) and the father of Jehoiachin (Jeconiah, Coniah) and grandfather of Assir. *(Note: Neither Jehoiachin nor Assir are listed in Matt. 1:12. However, they are found in the OT.)* Jecohonias was an ancestor of Jesus Christ through David's son Solomon. *(His record is found under the name of Eliakim/Jehoiakim.)* Jechonias and his brethren were begotten by Josias about the time they were carried away to Babylon.

JEHOIACHIN (Jeconiah, Coniah)

*(Note: **JEHOIACHIN** is not listed in Matt. 1:11-12, but he is found in the OT. He was a son of Jechonias Eliakim (Jehoiakim, the father of Assir and the grandfather of Salathiel. He was an ancestor of Jesus Christ.)*

JEPHTHAE (Jephthah)

Heb. 11:32. **JEPHTHAE (Jephthah)** was one of the Old Testament people who Paul said accomplished great things through faith.

JEREMIAS

Matt. 16:14. **JEREMIAS**, an Old Testament prophet, was one of the people the men in Cæsarea Philippi thought Christ might be, according to Christ's disciples.

JEREMY (Jeremiah)

Matt. 2:17. **JEREMY (Jeremiah)** was an Old Testament prophet who prophesied over 40 years—between the years 626-586 B.C. He prophesied that Rachel would weep" for her children, and would not be comforted, because they are not." *(Jer. 31:17-18.)* This prophecy was fulfilled when Herod slew the children.

Matt. 27:9-10. Jeremy, in ancient times, had prophesied, "And they took the thirty pieces of silver, the price of him that was valued, whom they of the children of Israel did value; And gave them for the potter's field, as the Lord appointed me." Thus, prophecy was fulfilled when Judah returned the thirty pieces of silver he received for betraying Jesus and the chief priests bought the potter's field with the money. *(Note: Jeremias and Jeremy/Jeremiah are probably one and the same. The BD indicates that there was another Jeremy who lived about the time of Abraham who held the Melchizedek Priesthood, but that he is a different Jeremy and nothing more is known about him.)*

JESSE

Matt. 1:5-6; Luke 3:32. **JESSE** was a son of Obed and was the father of David. He was an ancestor of Jesus Christ.

Acts 13:22-23. Jesse was the father of David. Jesus was of David's seed.

JEZEBEL

Rev. 2:20-23. **JEZEBEL**, a Phoenician princess whose life is recorded in the Old Testament, introduced into Israel the worst forms of Phoenician worship, contributing to the downfall of the northern kingdom. The BD indicates that her name is applied figuratively to a woman or sect in these verses where John writes that Jezebel, a false prophetess in Thyatira, was condemned by the Lord for calling herself a prophetess, for teaching and seducing the Lord's servants to commit fornication and to eat things sacrificed unto idols. The Lord gave her "space" to repent and she refused. The Lord said he would destroy her, kill her children, and cause her followers to suffer great tribulations.

JOANNA (1)

Luke 3:27. **JOANNA** was the son of Rhesa and the father of Juda. He was an ancestor of Jesus Christ through the lineage of David's son Nathan.

JOASH (Jehoash)

*(Note: **JOASH**, 2 Kgs. 11:2, is not listed in Matt. 1:8-9. He was a son of Ozias/Ahaziah and the father of Amaziah, who is also not listed in Matt. 1:8-9. He was an ancestor of Jesus Christ through the lineage of David's son Solomon.)*

JOATHAM (Jotham)

Matt. 1:9. **JOATHAM (Jotham)** was a son of Ozias (Ahaziah) *(probably great-great-grandson)* and the father of Achaz (Ahaz). He was an ancestor of Jesus Christ though the lineage of David's son Solomon.

JOB

James 5:11. **JOB** was faithful through many trials. James cited Job as an example of the ancient prophets whose examples of patience we should follow.

JOEL

Acts 2:16-21. **JOEL** prophesied that the Lord would pour out his spirit upon all flesh, "and your sons and your daughters shall prophesy, your old men shall dream dreams, your young men shall see visions: And also upon the servants and upon the handmaids in those days will I pour out my spirit" *(Joel 2:28-29).* When the people thought the apostles were drunk with wine when they spoke in tongues on the day of Pentecost, Peter assured them that they were not drunk, but they were seeing the fulfillment of Joel's prophecy.

JONAN

Luke 3:30. **JONAN** was the son of Eliakim and the father of Joseph (5). He was an ancestor of Jesus through the lineage of David's son Nathan.

JONAS (1) (Jonah)

Matt. 12:39-41; Luke 11:16, 29-32. **JONAS (Jonah)** was a prophet. When the scribes and Pharisees asked Jesus for a sign, he gave them the sign of Jonas who was three days and three nights in the belly of the whale. This foreshadowed the Savior's being three days and three nights "in the heart of the earth." The people in Jonas' day listened to him, but the Pharisees and scribes refused to listen to Jesus who was greater than Jonas.

JORAM (Jehoram)

Matt. 1:8. **JORAM (Jehoram)** was the son of Josaphat (Jehoshaphat) and the father of Ozias (Ahaziah). He was an ancestor of Jesus Christ through the lineage of David's son Solomon.

JORIM

Luke 3:29. **JORIM** was the son of Matthat and the father of Eliezer. He was an ancestor of Jesus through the lineage of David's son Nathan.

JOSAPHAT (Jehoshaphat)

Matt. 1:8. **JOSAPHAT (Jehoshaphat)** was the son of Asa and the father of Joram (Jehoram). He was an ancestor of Jesus Christ through the lineage of David's son Solomon.

JOSE

Luke 3:29. **JOSE** was the son of Eliezer and the father of Er. He was an ancestor of Jesus Christ through the lineage of David's son Nathan.

JOSEPH (3)

Luke 3:24. **JOSEPH** was the son of Mattathias and the father of Janna. He was an ancestor of Jesus Christ through the lineage of David's son Nathan.

JOSEPH (4)

Luke 3:26. **JOSEPH** was the son of Juda (1) and the father of Semei. He was an ancestor of Jesus Christ through the lineage of David's son Nathan.

JOSEPH (5)

Luke 3:30. **JOSEPH** was the son of Jonan and the father of Juda (2). He was an ancestor of Jesus Christ through the lineage of David's son Nathan.

JOSEPH (7) (son of Jacob)

Acts 7:9-18. **JOSEPH** was the son of Jacob and was sold into slavery by his brothers. His story is briefly referred to by Stephen as he faced the council who sat in judgment against him.

Heb. 11:21-22. Joseph's sons *(Ephraim and Manasseh)* were blessed by Jacob. Prior to Joseph's death, because of his faith, he was able to prophesy of the departing of the children of Israel from Egypt; and he instructed them to carry his bones with them when they departed.

JOSIAS (Josiah)

Matt. 1:10-11. **JOSIAS** was a son of Amon and the father of Jechonias (Jehoiakim). He was an ancestor of Jesus Christ through the lineage of David's son Solomon.

JUDA (1)

Luke 3:26. **JUDA** was the son of Joanna and the father of Joseph (4). He was an ancestor of Jesus Christ through the lineage of David's son Nathan.

JUDA (2)

Luke 3:30. **JUDA** was the son of Joseph (5) and the father of Simeon. He was an ancestor of Jesus Christ through the lineage of David's son Nathan.

JUDAS (1) (Judah) and his brethren

Matt. 1:2-3; Luke 3:33. **JUDAS (Judah)** was a son of Jacob. He was an ancestor of Jesus Christ.

LAMECH

Luke 3:36. **LAMECH** was the son of Methuselah and the father of Noah. He was an ancestor of Jesus Christ.

LEVI (2)

Luke 3:24. **LEVI** was the son of Melchi and the father of Matthat. He was the great-grandfather of Joseph, the husband of Mary, mother of Jesus. He was of the lineage of David through David's son Nathan.

LEVI (3)

Levi 3:29. **LEVI** was the son of Simeon and the father of Matthat. He was an ancestor of Jesus Christ through the lineage of David's son Nathan. *(Note: Jacob's, i.e., Israel's, third son was also named Levi.)*

LOT

Luke 17:28-30. **LOT**, the son of Nahor and nephew of Abraham, lived in the wicked city of Sodom. The day he left Sodom, it rained fire and brimstone from heaven and destroyed the rest of the people, just as the Lord destroyed the wicked in Noah's day. So it will be at the Second Coming.

2 Pet. 2:7. Lot was saved because of his righteousness but the cities of Sodom and Gomorrha were destroyed because the people were so wicked. Peter used Lot to illustrate that the Lord can deliver the godly out of temptations and allow the unjust to reap the rewards of sin.

LOT'S WIFE

Luke 17:32. **LOT'S WIFE** was destroyed when she turned back *(Gen. 19:26).* He who seeks the things of this world will lose his life. He who loses his life for the Lord's sake, will preserve it.

MAATH

Luke 3:26. **MAATH** was the son of Mattathias and the father of Nagge. He was an ancestor of Jesus Christ through the lineage of David's son Nathan.

MALELEEL (Mahalaleel)

Luke 3:37. **MALALEEL**, a great-great-grandson of Adam, was the son of Cainan and the father of Jared. He was an ancestor of Jesus Christ.

MANASSES (Manasseh)

Matt. 1:10. **MANASSES** was a son of Ezekias (Hezekiah) and the father of Amon. He was an ancestor of Jesus Christ through the lineage of David's son Solomon. *(Note: Joseph, who was sold into Egypt, also had a son named Manasseh.)*

MATHUSALA (See Methuselah)

MATTATHA

Luke 3:31. **MATTATHA** was the son of Nathan and grandson of king David. He was the father of Menan. He was an ancestor of Jesus Christ through the lineage of David's son Nathan.

MATTATHIAS (1)

Luke 3:25. **MATTATHIAS** was the son of Amos and the father of Joseph. He was an ancestor of Jesus Christ through the lineage of David's son Nathan.

MATTATHIAS (2)

Luke 3:26. **MATTATHIAS** was the son of Semei and the father of Maath. He was an ancestor of Jesus Christ through the lineage of David's son Nathan.

MATTHAN

Matt. 1:15. **MATTHAN** was the son of Eleazar and the father of Jacob the father of Mary's husband Joseph. He was an ancestor of Jesus Christ through the lineage of David's son Solomon. *(Note: Matt. 1:15 lists Joseph's father as Jacob through the lineage of Solomon while Luke 3:24 lists Joseph's father as Heli through the lineage of Nathan. The BD lists Heli as Joseph's father.)*

MATTHAT (1)

Luke 3:24. **MATTHAT** was the son of Levi and the father of Heli the father of Mary's husband Joseph. He was an ancestor of Jesus Christ through the lineage of David's son Nathan. *(Note: Matt. 1:15 lists Joseph's father as Jacob through the lineage of Solomon while Luke 3:24 lists Joseph's father as Heli through the lineage of Nathan. The BD lists Heli as Joseph's father.)*

MATTHAT (2)

Luke 3:29. **MATTHAT** was the son of Levi (3) and the father of Jorim. He was an ancestor of Jesus Christ through the lineage of David's son Nathan.

MELCHI (1)

Luke 3:24. **MELCHI** was the father of Levi (2) and the son of Janna. He was an ancestor of Jesus Christ through the lineage of David's son Nathan.

MELCHI (2)

Luke 3:28. **MELCHI** was the father of Neri and the son of Addi. He was an ancestor of Jesus Christ through the lineage of David's son Nathan.

MELCHIZEDEK (Melchisedec)

Heb. 5:6. **MELCHIZEDEK** was a high priest. Jesus Christ was a high priest forever after the order of Melchizedek.

Heb. 7:1-25. Melchizedek was the king of Salem and a priest of the most high God. Melchizedek blessed Abraham. Abraham paid tithes (one tenth of all he had) to Melchizedek. Melchizedek was known as the King of righteousness, King of Salem, and King of peace *(vs. 2-3).* Paul explained the importance of the Melchizedek Priesthood to the Hebrew saints *(vs. 4-25).*

MELEA

Luke 3:31. **MELEA** was the father of Eliakim and the son of Menan. He was an ancestor of Jesus Christ through the lineage of David's son Nathan.

MENAN

Luke 3:31. **MENAN** was the father of Melea, the son of Mattath and the great-grandson of David. He was an ancestor of Jesus Christ through the lineage of David's son Nathan.

METHUSELAH (Mathusala)

Luke 3:37. **METHUSELAH**, the son of Enoch, was the father of Lamech and the grandfather of Noah. He was an ancestor of Jesus Christ.

MICHAEL, THE ARCHANGEL (See Adam)

MOSES

Matt. 17:3; Mark 9:4; Luke 9:30. **MOSES** appeared as a transfigured being, along with Elias, to Jesus, Peter, James and John on the mount of transfiguration.

Matt. 19:7-8 (4-8). Moses had commanded that if a person wanted to divorce his wife, he had "to give a writing of divorcement." The Pharisees queried Jesus about that since Jesus had said, "What . . . God hath joined together, let no man put asunder." Jesus said the only reason Moses had commanded that a letter of divorcement be written was because of the hardness of the hearts of the people, but that "from the beginning it was not so."

Matt. 23:2-3. Moses pointed out that the scribes and Pharisees sat in Moses' seat. He told the multitude and his disciples to do what they said to do, but not to follow what the scribes and Pharisees actually did because they said one thing and did another.

Luke 16:31. If the people would not accept Moses and the prophets, neither would they respond to someone even if he were risen from the dead.

John 1:17, 44-45. Moses gave the law, but grace and truth came by Jesus Christ. Philip found Nathanael and told him they had found him of whom Moses in the law and the prophets wrote: Jesus of Nazareth.

John 5:46. If they had believed Moses, Jesus told the people, they would have believed him, because Moses wrote of him.

Acts 3:22. Moses testified that the Lord would raise up a prophet like unto himself; and he counseled the people to follow whatsoever this prophet would say unto them.

Acts 6:11-14. The Libertines and others in the synagogue hired people to testify that Stephen blasphemed against Moses.

Acts 7:20-40. Moses' story was recounted by Stephen to those who sat in council against him. Stephen pointed out that Moses was a prototype of Christ; and said that Moses killed an Egyptian in defense of an Israelite who was being oppressed by an Egyptian. *(Ex. 2:11-12.)*

Acts 26:22-23. Moses and the other prophets, Paul declared to King Agrippa, Bernice and Festus, all testified of that which was to come: Christ would suffer and die and be the first to rise from the dead. He would show a light unto the world, both to the people (i.e., Jews) and to the Gentiles.

1 Cor. 10:2-4. Paul told the Corinthians that ancient Israel was "baptized unto Moses in the cloud and in the sea; and did all eat the same spiritual meat; and did all drink the same spiritual drink: for they drank of that spiritual Rock that followed them: and that Rock was Christ."

2 Cor. 3:6-16. The law of Moses was fulfilled in Jesus Christ and the gospel of Jesus Christ surpasses the law of Moses.

2 Tim. 3:8. Moses was withstood by Jannes and Jambres. *(Note: Paul told Timothy that just as these two men resisted Moses in ancient days, men in the last days would also resist the truth. Neither men is mentioned by name in the Old Testament.)*

Heb. 11:23-24. Because of the faith of his parents, Moses, when he was born, was hidden three months by his parents. By faith, Moses, when he became of age, refused to be called the son of Pharaoh's daughter. Through faith, he was able to forsake Egypt, keep the Passover, the sprinkling of blood lest he that destroyed the firstborn should destroy the children of Israel, and pass through the Red Sea.

Jude 1:9. Michael the archangel and Satan disputed over the body of Moses. *(Note: Jude apparently had scriptures that referred to this disputation, which scriptures are among other lost scriptures. There is no other record of it in the Bible.)*

Rev. 15:3. John saw the exalted saints praising God and singing the song of Moses.

MOSES' BRETHREN IN EGYPT

Acts 7:26-28. **MOSES' BRETHREN IN EGYPT** were in a dispute. When Moses attempted to intervene, the one in the wrong asked Moses if he planned to kill him like he had killed the Egyptian the day before, which caused Moses to flee from Egypt. *(Ex. 2:13-14.)*

MOSES' PARENTS

Heb. 11:23. **MOSES' PARENTS**, because of their faith, hid Moses for three months after he was born.

NAAMAN

Luke 4:26-27. **NAAMAN**. Jesus taught in the synagogue in Nazareth on a Sabbath day and said that no prophet is accepted in his own country and, as a result, many people who could be blessed were not. He testified that he had been sent by his Father to preach the gospel to the poor, the broken-hearted, the captives and to set at liberty all who were bruised; and he reminded the people that Naaman was the only one of many lepers in ancient Israel who was cleansed in the time of Eliseus (Elisha) the prophet, and a widow woman was the only person Elias (Elijah) was sent to help when the heavens were shut up for three and a half years.

NAASSON (Nahshon)

Matt. 1:4; Luke 3:32. **NAASSON (Nahshon)** was a son of Aminadab (Amminadab) and the father of Salmon. He was an ancestor of Jesus Christ.

NACHOR (Nahor)

Luke 3:34. **NACHOR** was the son of Saruch (Serug) and the father of Thara (Terah) the father of Abraham. He was an ancestor of Jesus Christ.

NAGGE

Luke 3:25. **NAGGE** was the son of Maath and the father of Esli. He was an ancestor of Jesus Christ through the lineage of David's son Nathan.

NAPHTALI (Nephthalim)

Matt. 4:13-15. **NAPHTALI** was the second son of Jacob and Bilhah, Rachel's handmaid. Isaiah had prophesied that the people in the land of Zebulun and the land of Naphtali that walked in darkness would see a great light *(Isa. 9:1-2).* When Jesus heard that John the Baptist was in prison, he went there via Zabulon and Nephthalim, that Isaiah's prophecy might be fulfilled.

Rev. 7:6. John saw in the revelation given to him that there were 12,000 servants of the Lord from the tribe of Nephthalim who were sealed.

NATHAN

Luke 3:31. **NATHAN** was the son of king David and the father of Mattatha. He was an ancestor of Jesus Christ. *(His genealogical line to Jesus is given in verses 23-31.)*

NAUM

Luke 3:25. **NAUM** was the son of Esli and the father of Amos. He was an ancestor of Jesus Christ through the lineage of David's son Nathan.

NERI

Luke 3:27. **NERI** was the son of Melchi and the father of Salathiel. He was an ancestor of Jesus Christ through the lineage of David's son Nathan.

NOE (Noah)

Matt. 24:36-38; Luke 17:26-27. **NOE (Noah)** built an ark as directed by the Lord, and he and his family were saved from the great flood that covered the earth. Jesus told his disciples that just as the people in Noe's day did not know the day nor the hour when the flood would occur, but had to be watchful and prepared, so it would be with his Second Coming—no one knew the day nor the hour when it would be, not even the angels of heaven, only his Father in Heaven.

Luke 3:36. Noah was the son of Lamech and the father of Shem. He was an ancestor of Jesus Christ.

Heb. 11:7. Noah, because of his faith, built an ark as instructed by God, and his house, i.e., his family, was saved.

1 Pet. 3:20. After Christ died, he preached to the spirits in prison, some who had been disobedient in the days of Noah.

2 Pet. 2:5. Noah, a preacher of righteousness, and seven other family members were all who escaped being destroyed by the flood. The others were destroyed because of their wickedness.

OBED

Matt. 1:5; Luke 3:32. **OBED** was a son of Booz (Boaz) and Ruth and was the father of Jesse. He was an ancestor of Jesus Christ.

OSEE (Hosea)

Rom. 9:25. **OSEE (Hosea)** prophesied that the time would come when those who were not the "chosen" people would be called his *(the Lord's)* people and would be called the children of the living God *(Hosea 2:23)*. *(Note: OSEE (Hosea) probably died before 736 B.C. (BD).)*

OZIAS (Ahaziah)

Matt. 1:8-9. **OZIAS (Ahaziah)** was the son of Joram (Jehoram) and the father of Joash (Jehoash). *(Note: Joash is not listed in Matt. 1:8-9.)* Ozias was an ancestor of Jesus Christ through David's son Solomon. *(See 2 Kgs. 8:24.)*

PELEG (See Phalec)

PHALEC (Peleg)

Luke 3:35. **PHALEC (Peleg)** was the son of Heber (Eber) and the father of Ragau (Reu). He was an ancestor of Jesus Christ. *(Note: It was in his day that the earth was divided.)*

PHARAOH

Rom. 9:17-18. **PHARAOH** is the title given to Egyptian kings. This Pharaoh ruled at the time the Lord sent Moses to Egypt to free the children of Israel from bondage. *(Note: Pharaoh refused to let the children of Israel leave Egypt with Moses.)* Paul explained to the Roman saints that God raised up Pharaoh so that his *(God's)* power could be made known to the people.

PHARAOH'S DAUGHTER

Acts 7:21. **PHARAOH'S DAUGHTER** retrieved the infant Moses from the river where he was floating in his ark and raised him as her own son. *(Ex. 2:5-10.)*

Heb. 11:24. When Moses came of age, through faith, he refused to be called the son of Pharaoh's daughter.

PHARES (Pharez)

Matt. 1:3; Luke 3:33. **PHARES (Pharez)** was the firstborn twin son of Judas (Judah) and Thamar (Tamar). He was the father of Esrom (Hezrom) and was an ancestor of Jesus Christ.

QUEEN OF THE SOUTH (Queen of Sheba)

Matt. 12:42; Luke 11:31. **QUEEN OF THE SOUTH** undoubtedly refers to the queen of Sheba who went to Solomon to evaluate his wisdom for herself. The Savior berated the scribes and Pharisees for asking for a sign and indicated that the queen of the south, who traveled to meet Solomon and was impressed with his wisdom, would rise up in judgment against that generation because they rejected one who is even greater than Solomon.

RACHAB

Matt. 1:5. **RACHAB** was the mother of Booz (Boaz) the son of Salmon.

RAGAU (Reu)

Luke 3:35. **RAGAU (Reu)** was the son of Phalec (Peleg) and the father of Saruch (Serug). He was an ancestor of Jesus Christ.

RAHAB

Heb. 11:31. **RAHAB** was a harlot who protected the spies sent to scout out Jericho. Because of her faith, she was saved from destruction when the walls of Jericho were brought down by Joshua and the children of Israel.

James 2:25. Rahab was not saved from destruction simply by her faith. She hid the spies sent to scout out Jericho. Rahab's faith was justified by her works.

RAM (See Aram)

REU (See Ragau)

RHESA

Luke 3:27. **RHESA** was the son of Zorobabel and the father of Joanna (1). He was an ancestor of Jesus Christ through the lineage of David's son Nathan.

ROBOAM (Rehoboam)

Matt. 1:7. **ROBOAM (Rehoboam)** was the son of Solomon and the father of Abia (Abijam). He was an ancestor of Jesus Christ.

RUTH

Matt. 1:5. **RUTH** was the mother of Obed and the wife of Booz (Boaz). She was king David's great-grandmother and an ancestor of Jesus Christ. *(She was Naomi's widowed daughter-in-law.)*

SADOC

Matt. 1:14. **SADOC** was the son of Azor and the father of Achim. He was an ancestor of Jesus Christ through the lineage of David's son Solomon.

SALA (Salah)

Luke 3:35. **SALA (Salah)** was the son of Cainan (the son of Arphaxad) and the father of Heber (Eber) He was an ancestor of Jesus Christ. *(In the OT, it states that Salah was the son of Arphaxad. This Cainan, son of Arphaxad, is not listed in the OT.)*

SALATHIEL (1)

Matt. 1:12. **SALATHIEL**, the son of Assir *(not listed in Matt. 1:12 but listed in the OT, 1 Chr. 3:17),* was the father of Zorobabel. He was an ancestor of Jesus Christ through the lineage of David's son Solomon.

SALATHIEL (2)

Luke 3:27. **SALATHIEL** was the son of Neri and the father of Zorobabel. He was an ancestor of Jesus Christ through the lineage of David's son Nathan. *(Note: The scriptures indicate that both Salathiel (1) and Salathiel (2) had sons named Zorobabel. It is either coincidental or an error has possibly crept into the record.)*

SALMON

Matt. 1:4-5. **SALMON** was a son of Naasson (Nahshon) and the father of Booz (Boaz). He was an ancestor of Jesus Christ.

SAMSON

Heb. 11:32. **SAMSON** was one of the Old Testament people who Paul said accomplished great things through faith.

SAMUEL

Acts 3:24. **SAMUEL** was an ancient prophet. Peter said that all the prophets from Samuel on had foretold of the days and events surrounding the time of Jesus.

Acts 13:20-21. Samuel the prophet served Israel after 450 years of judges. When the people demanded a king, God had Samuel anoint Saul, the son of Cis (Kish).

Heb. 11:32. Samuel was one of the people who Paul said accomplished great things through faith.

SARA (Sarah)

Rom. 4:19-21. **SARA**, Abraham's wife, was barren. Even though both Abraham and Sara were old, still Abraham did not doubt the Lord's ability to fulfill the promise that Sara would have a baby.

Heb. 11:11. Sara, through faith, also received strength to conceive and have a child when she was well-beyond child-bearing age.

1 Pet. 3:1, 5-6. Just as Sara obeyed Abraham, Peter counseled the women of the church who had been scattered throughout Pontus, Galatia, Cappadocia, Asia, and Bithynia to obey their husbands. (He also counseled the husbands to honor their wives.)

SARUCH (Serug)

Luke 3:35. **SARUCH (Serug)** was the son of Ragau (Reu) and the father of Nachor (Nahor), Abraham's grandfather. He was an ancestor of Jesus Christ.

SAUL (2)

Acts 13:21. **SAUL** was the first king of Israel. He was the son of Cis (Kish). Paul recounted part of Israel's history to the men of Israel as he pointed out that Jesus was raised unto Israel to be a Savior. Following Saul's removal as king, David was made king.

SEM (See Shem)

SEMEI

Luke 3:26. **SEMEI** was the son of Joseph and the father of Mattathias. He was an ancestor of Jesus Christ through the lineage of David's son Nathan.

SETH

Luke 3:38. **SETH** was the son of Adam and the father of Enos. He was an ancestor of Jesus Christ.

SHEM (Sem)

Luke 3:38. **SHEM (Sem)** was the son of Noe (Noah) and the father of Arphaxad. He was an ancestor of Jesus Christ.

SIMEON (2)

Luke 3:30. **SIMEON** was the son of Juda (2) and the father of Levi (3). He was an ancestor of Jesus Christ through the lineage of David's son Nathan.

SIMEON (5)

Rev. 7:7. **SIMEON** was the son of Jacob, head of one of the tribes of Israel. John saw in a revelation that there were 12,000 servants of the Lord who were sealed from each tribe. Simeon's tribe, along with the others, is mentioned by name.

SOLOMON

Matt. 1:6-7. **SOLOMON** was a son of David and Bathsheba, the widow of Urias (Uriah). He was the father of Roboam (Rehoboam) and was an ancestor of Jesus Christ.

Matt. 6:24; Luke 12:27. Jesus counseled his apostles not to worry about their temporal affairs as they ministered in his behalf and reminded them that Heavenly Father provides for the plants and the fowls of the air, and that Solomon, even in all his glory was not arrayed like one of these. If Heavenly Father provides for the plants and animals, which are here today and gone tomorrow, how much more will he provide for his servants.

Matt. 12:42. People, including the queen of Sheba, recognized the wisdom of Solomon. Unfortunately, the scribes and Pharisees refused to recognize the wisdom of Jesus who was greater than Solomon.

Luke 11:31. Solomon's wisdom was sought by the queen of the south *(the queen of Sheba);* and she will rise up in judgement against the men of Christ's generation who reject the wisdom of one who is greater than Solomon, *(i.e., the wisdom of Jesus).*

Luke 12:27. See entry for Matt. 6.

Acts 7:47-48. Solomon built a house for the Lord, but Jesus reminded the people that "the Most High dwelleth not in temples made with hands."

SYCHEM (Shechem)

Acts 7:16. **SYCHEM (Shechem)** was the son of Emmor (Hamor). *(Note: The New Testament records that Stephen, one of the seven men the apostles chose to assist in the work, stated that Abraham bought a sepulchre from the son of Emmor the father of Sychem. The Old Testament, Gen. 33:19, indicates that Jacob, not Abraham, bought the land from the children of Hamor, Shechem's father.)*

THAMAR (Tamar)

Matt. 1:3. **THAMAR (Tamar)** was the widow of Judah's sons Er and Onan. She was the mother of Pharez and Zarah, twin sons begotten by Judah, her father-in-law and was an ancestor of Jesus Christ.

THARA (Terah)

Luke 3:34. **THARA** was the son of Nachor and the father of Abraham. He was an ancestor of Jesus Christ.

URIAS (Uriah)

Matt. 1:6. **URIAS (Uriah)** was Bathsheba's husband and was placed at the forefront of battle so he would be slain; thus, David could marry Bathsheba who was with child—David's child.

URIAS' WIFE (See Bathsheba)

TERAH (See Thara)

WIDOW WOMAN, A

Luke 4:26-27. **A WIDOW WOMAN**. Jesus preached the gospel to the poor, the broken-hearted, the captives and to set at liberty all who were bruised, he said, and he reminded the people that a widow woman was the only person Elias (Elijah) was sent to help when the heavens were shut up for three and a half years and that Naaman was the only one of many lepers in Israel who was cleansed in the time of Eliseus (Elisha) the prophet.

ZARA (Zarah, Zerah)

Matt. 1:3. **ZARA (Zarah)** was the second-born twin son of Judas (Judah) and Thamar (Tamar).

ZOROBABEL (1)

Matt. 1:12-13. **ZOROBABEL** was the son of Salathiel and the father of Abiud. He was an ancestor of Jesus Christ through the lineage of David's son Solomon.

ZOROBABEL (2)

Luke 3:27. **ZOROBABEL** was the son of Salathiel and the father of Rhesa. He was an ancestor of Jesus Christ through the lineage of David's son Nathan. *(Note: Both Zorobabels were sons of fathers named Salathiel. However, one is through the lineage of Solomon and the other through the lineage of Nathan. This could be coincidental, or possibly an error has crept into the record.)*

APPENDIX B

The Generations of Joseph (Ancestral Chart)

The Generations of Joseph

According to Matt. 1:1-16 ***According to Luke 3:23-38.***

1. God
2. Adam
3. Seth
4. Enos
5. Cainan
6. Maleleel (Mahalaleel)
7. Jared
8. Enoch
9. Mathusala (Methuselah
10. Lamech
11. Noe (Noah)
12. Sem (Shem)
13. Arphaxad
14. Cainan (This name does not appear in this order in other listings.)
15. Sala (Salah)
16. Heber (Eber)
17. Phalec (Peleg)
18. Ragau (Reu)
19. Saruch (Serug)
20. Nachor (Nahor)
21. Thara (Terah)

Matt. 1:1-16. There were 42 generations from Abraham to Jesus.

a. 14 generations from Abraham to David

Matt. 1:1-16	Luke 3:23-38
1. Abraham	22. Abraham
2. Isaac	23. Isaac
3. Jacob	24. Jacob
4. Judas (Judah) and his brethren	25. Juda (Judah)
5. Phares (Pharez)	26. Phares (Pharez)
6. Esrom (Hezron)	27. Esrom (Hezron)
7. Aram (Ram)	28. Aram (Ram)
8. Aminadab (Amminadab)	29. Aminadab (Amminadab)
9. Naasson (Nahshon)	30. Naasson (Nahshon)
10. Salmon	31. Salmon
11. Booz (Boaz)	32. Booz (Boaz)
12. Obed	33. Obed
13. Jesse	34. Jesse
14. David	35. David

b. 14 generations from David to Josias.

(Note: Only 13 are listed in Matthew 1:8-11. However, three additional generations are given in the Old Testament.)

1. Solomon
2. Roboam (Rehoboam)
3. Abia (Abijam)
4. Asa
5. Josaphat (Jehoshaphat)
6. Joram (Jehoram)
7. Ozias (Ahaziah)
8. Joash (Jehoash) *(not listed in Matt. 1:9)*
9. Amaziah *(not listed in Matt. 1:9)*
10. Azariah (Uzziah) *(not listed in Matt. 1:9)*
11. Joatham (Jotham)
12. Achaz (Ahaz)
13. Ezekias (Hezekiah)
14. Manasses (Manasseh)
15. Amon
16. Josias (Josiah)

c. 14 generations from Josias to Jesus *(carried away to Babylon) (Note: 14 are listed in Matthew 1:11-16. However, two additional generations are given in the Old Testament.)*

1. Jechonias (Jehoiakim, Eliakim)
2. Jehoiachin (Jechoniah, Coniah) *(not listed in Matt. 1:12)*
3. Assir *(not listed in Matt. 1:12)*
4. Salathiel
5. Zorobabel
6. Abiud
7. Eliakim
8. Azor
9. Sadoc
10. Achim
11. Eliud
12. Eleazar
13. Matthan
14. Jacob
15. Joseph (husband of Mary)
16. Jesus (considered to be of Joseph)

36. Nathan
37. Mattatha
38. Menan
39. Melea
40. Eliakim
41. Jonan
42. Joseph
43. Juda
44. Simeon
45. Levi
46. Matthat
47. Jorim
48. Eliezer
49. Jose
50. Er
51. Elmodam
52. Cosam
53. Addi
54. Melchi
55. Neri
56. Salathiel
57. Zorobabel
58. Rhesa
59. Joanna
60. Juda
61. Joseph
62. Semei
63. Mattathias
64. Maath
65. Nagge
66. Esli
67. Naum
68. Amos
69. Mattathias
70. Joseph
71. Janna
72. Melchi
73. Levi
74. Matthat
75. Heli
76. Joseph (husband of Mary)
77. Jesus (considered to be of Joseph)

About the Author

Lynn Price is a native of Utah with an extensive background in church service, volunteer work and politics. A cum laude graduate of the University of Utah in music theory, she has served on a stake and ward level in all the Church auxiliaries. Her volunteer work has ranged from chair of the Salt Lake County Republican Party to public school presenter on substance and child abuse.

The author has written three other books with this same research theme: *Every Person in the Book of Mormon, Every Person in the Doctrine and Covenants,* and *Every Person in the Old Testament.* Lynn created these books out of a life-long study and deep love for the scriptures. She also is the author of two other books published by Horizon Publishers: *Find a Silver Lining,* and *Bless Mom . . . in Whatever She Does—Making the Most of Motherhood.*

Her hobbies include writing poetry and creating ward music programs. She is married to Richard R. Price, a general surgeon. They have five grown sons and numerous grandchildren.

Identifying every person in the scriptures is a valuable research tool in bringing a greater understanding of these sacred books, and a great aid in helping you find a given person for whom you may be looking.